THE GITA FOR ALL

THE GITA FOR ALL

Dr. Bhagwati Sharan Mishra

SERIALS PUBLICATIONS
New Delhi

First Published : 2004

ISBN : 81-86771-44-1

Published by

Head Office : **SERIALS PUBLICATIONS**
4, B.S.S. Hall, Khyber Pass Market,
Civil Lines, Delhi-110054 (India)
Phone: 0091-11-23811659
Fax: 91-11-23812678
E-mail: serials@satyam.net.in

Branch Office : 4830/24, Prahlad Street, Ansari Road,
Darya Ganj, New Delhi-110002 (India)
Phone: 2324225

Printed at : R.K. Offset Process, Naveen Shahdara, Delhi-110032

FROM THE AUTHOR

Shri Krishna willed that this book should come out despite the market having been flooded with such works.

Reasons, I conceive are the following:

I) Almost all commentaries on the Gita are tilted this way or that. Mostly written by the 'Saampradaayik'— writers, its real meaning has not been allowed to emerge. Some of them called it to be a book of 'Sanayas', some of 'Bhakti' and some of 'yoga'. The common reader is confused with the divergent interpretations subscribed to the 'shlokas' which have more often than not been explained to mean which they never meant.

In such situation a book was needed which told only that which Krishna meant to tell.

Meaning of 'shlokas' and commentary there on; in the book are not distorted in any way as it is not a 'saampradaayik' book, so the readers come face to face with only the facts, the Lord wants to disclose.

II) Secondly most of the commentaries in volumes available in the market are so intricate and loaded with unnecessary references that ordinary readers are unable to go through them and they abandon their perusal after going through some initial pages.

This is not the case with this book. This is a *Book For All.* This does not speak more about other scriptures and less about the Gita. Its language has knowingly been kept down to earth, simple and sweet.

Commentaries are just sufficient to reveal the real meaning of the 'Shlokas' thus rendering the volume to a really handy size. Most voluminous books available in the market scare the readers away. I hope the Lord did not like it; so the book 'For All.'

You may be a scholar, you may not be but this book will decidedly make you well-versed in the 'Gita'—a scholar of the most important work in the whole world.

So believe it; this book is for you, you who are really desirous to know what is after all the real message of the Gita.

Go through it and you will come to know that the book called the 'Gita' is more a philosophy of life, a way to a peaceful and contented existence than a discourse on religion or spiritualism.

Yes, the 'Gita' is a way of life. It is why it is produced in this volume in an understandable way so that you follow its valuable guidelines and live a life breft of anxieties, fears and failures.

The Lord in no uncertain words has promised to take care of you, so where are the reasons of being disturbed by the day to day ups and downs? All paths showed by Shri Krishna lead to peace, fulfilment and success.

One who fails to read the 'Gita' and does not understand its correct and untilted meaning, should not blame others for his unhappiness and failure.

Though the 'Shlokas' are printed in Roman we have avoided the phonetic signs to make it easy for every one to go through.

The book is thus meant to cater to the needs of even those who do not know the 'devanagari' script; it is thus useful for all. It will certainly benefit them also who know 'Sanskrit' but do not know the real meaning of this wonderful book; having been bombarded with scholarly volumes confusing and bewildering them to no extent.

The full text of the Gita in Sanskrit is provided at the end for the sake of those who know 'devanagari' and thus can have a better understanding of 'Roman'—shlokas.

So *The Gita For All* is for you also. *Go through it and change your life* because it will go straight to your heart and mind without subjecting you to wed through confusing and contradicting scholarly observations and unwanted explanations.

At some times it may appear that things are being repeated unnecessarily. As for example, the words 'lack of attachment' etc. will come often. This is the fault of none. The Lord in a bid to drive down His thesis repeats the main points from time to time. This is certainly the way to establish something new and the Lord is undoubtedly intent on very that.

Thanks go to Him for enabling an unworthy man like me to complete this book.

I am very much thankful to Mr. S.K. Jha of Serial Publications who brought out this book in a record time.

Bhagawati Sharan Mishra
GH-13/805
Paschim Vihar
New Delhi-87

Vijaya Dashami
6-10-2003

CHAPTER-I

At the very outset some thing must be told about the almost abrupt beginning of the Book.

The real reason being that the Gita though regarded as one of the top most works of Hinduism is not a complete work in itself like the Vedas, Bible, Quran or even Unpunishads of different hues. It is just an episode of the largest ever produced epic in human history known most popularly as the Mahabharat though even this nomenclature has undergone different versions through the passage of time.

Any way, the Mahabharat now a book of not less than one lakh shlokas (Sanskrit couplets) tells the story of one of the biggest battles fought on this earth notwithstanding the 1st and 2nd world-wars which are of very recent origin compared to that oldest mass scale involvement of human beings in mutual killings, slaughters and sanguinity. There is no dearth of people who opine that the most devastating means of destruction taken recourse to in the recent wars; including the nuclear ones were not unknown to and were used by the skillest of the warriors of those times.

This theory is not so untenable as to be brushed aside just casually. There is no wonder that a great civilization which had excelled in every thing including the evolution and use of devastating lethal weapons and warheads, might have been wiped out of the earth-surface in the wake of that urprecedented war and as a consequence of which all that had been achieved in different spheres of development including those of weaponries perished if not for ever at least for a long time to come.

This observation is rooted in the study of the Mahabharat

where heart-rendering, unimaginingly widely and spontaneously killing devices are described to have been used by the said skillest warriors including Arjuna, Karna, Bhishma, Drona and even Ghatotkach, son of mighty Bhim and born of a mother belonging to a race exceedingly aweprovoking as well as unparalleled in strength and vigour, known as Rakshasas dwelling in the dense forests of those days.

That war, thrust unwittingly upon almost all the rulers of India of those days by Duryodhana the eldest son of Dhritarashtra who was in the throne of Hastinapur (near Delhi, of these days) was fought freely between the sons and followers of Dharitarashtra known as Kauravas and the sons and followers of Pandu the deceased brother of Dhritarashtra, known as Pandavas. The fight was necessarily for the occupation of the great kingdom which Pandu the father of five sons namely Yudhisthir, Bhim, Arjun, Nakul and Sahadeo, had founded and nurtured with great care before his premature demise. Dhritarashtra now fully entrenched in the gorgeous throne of Hastinapur and his ambition constantly fanned by his highly crafty eldest son Duryodhan with his eyes fixed on the throne, was in no mood to relent despite the advice of many well-meaning friends, associates and wellwishers including even Lord Krishna who was considered to be the very incarnation of the all-pervading supreme.

As the luck would have it Dhritrashtra had no eyes but he was very much willing to know whatever was going on in the battle-field where the armies of both sides were arrayed in aggressive postures. Vyas great seer and mystic of his time came to his rescue and endowed Sanjay the charioteer and confidant of Dhritrashtra with the power to see and hear, sitting beside the throne in the palace of Hastinapur, whatever was taking place on the battle-field and to narrate the same to the sovereign.

It is in this back ground that the 1st shloka of the Gita is composed in which the blind king asks his aide to describe what is taking place on the war-field.

Thus the opening lines of the Gita-**Dhritrashtra uvaach** :
Dharm kshetre Kurukshetre Samvetaa yuyutsavah,
Maamkaah Paandavaaschaiva Kimakurvat sanjay [1].

Meaning—Dhritarashtra enquired "O Sanjaya, assembled on the Dharma-field known also as the filed of Kuru, what did my men and those of Paandavas do, eager to engage one other in the battle.

Commentary—The field where the battle line was by now clearly drawn has been given two names by the blind despot—'Dharma kshetra' and 'Kurukshetra' Kuru was the founder of kaurava dynasty of which Dhritrashtra was one of the descendants. The vast barren field apparently belonged to Kuru, thus the appropriateness of the name 'Kurukshetra'.

Many sacrificial rituals called 'yagya' had been performed here from time immemorial, the vastness as well as aloofness of the field providing the necessary surroundings and facilities for such pious performances; it is why the name Dharmakshetra. 'Kshetra' stands for field in Sanskrit. Dharm stands for faith, religion.

There is one hidden purpose too in calling it Dharmkshetra by Dhritrashtra. Himself not very religious owing to his partisan and selfish attitude, the king desperately believes that a battle fought on a Dharmkshetra (religious place) may bless him with a victory, other wise hard to have. There is a saying in Sanskrit that religion protects him who protects it—'Dharmo rakshati Rakshitah.' No irreligious person is in a position to find approval of his anti religious deeds and whatever he does finds religious approval for the same by dubious arguments of his won creation. The 'Ygyas' etc. which he performs ostensibly with a religious purpose are only to befool them over whom he rules and to kindle the fire of envy in the hearts of the friends and foes. The blind king thus, fooishly hopes that the so-called religious deeds performed in charity, piety etc. by him will stand in good stead in a battle fought at Dharmkshetra (religious field).

Sanjay uvaach :

Dhrishtvaa thu paandvaanikam vyudham Duryodhanastada
Achaarymupsamgamya Raja vachanamabravit [2].

Meaning—**Sanjay replied :** Then Duryodhan, having witnessed the army of Pandavas drawn up in battle-array approached the reverend teacher of both 'Karuavas' and 'Pandvas' and spoke thus.

Commentary—'pandavaanikam' is composed of two words Pandav and anikam. Anikam in Sanskrit denotes an army. 'Pandavaanikam' thus stands for the army of Pandavas.

'Vyudham' is derived from Sanskrit 'vyuh' which is a way to arrange the army in a way to render it unvulnerable. The 'vyuh' can be of any kind. It can be in the shape of a crocodile, serpent or 'chakra'—of a round about shape almost empregnable by the enemy-assault. In the eighteen days for which the fierce battle raged the 'vuhas' of both parties were to be changed almost daily.

Reverened teacher here has been used for Aacharya. An Aacharya is a teacher most respected, he may teach not only the holy scriptures but also the art and skill of handling different weapons. Aacharya here stands for Dronhacharya who was the teacher of both Kauravas and Pandavas.

This couplet explicitly shows the nervousness and lack of confidence on the part of Duryodhan as it is he and not any warrior of the opposing army who feels the need of ventilating his concern about the well arrayed enemy's army to any of his elders.

This second couplet of the very first chapter thus implicitly outlines the certain outcome of the ensuing battle.

Pashyitam panduputranhamacharya mahatim chamum
vyudham Drupaduptren tavashishyen Dheemataam [3]

Meaning—O master behold this mighty army of the sons of Pandu arrayed by your talented disciple, the son of Drupad.

Commemtary—By the son of Durpad is here denoted Dhrishtdumna who is the commander-in-chief of the Pandvas and on whose shoulders naturally rests the responsibility of arraying the army in the most suitable manner.

The shrewdness of Duryodhan is clearly evident in indicating to the master that the army facing him has been arrayed by non else than his own disciple. This is certainly aimed at hurting the ego of the master and to excite him to be as aggressive as possible by bringing home to him the fact that one who once learned the art of warfare sitting before his feet, to-day has the audacity of challenging him face to face.

By declaring him (Dhrishtdumna) talented, one obvious hint has been dropped for the master; not to take the disciple to be as naive or unskilled as he might have appeared during his apprenticeship—as it is more often than not that the student exceeds the teacher in the very discipline in which he is tutored.

Atra shoora maheshvaasa Bhimaarajunsmayudhi,
yuyudhaano viraatashch Drupadashch mahaarathah [4]

Meaning—Here (in this army of Pandavas) are war-heroes capable of wielding powerful bows, who are not less than Bhima and Arjuna in military prowess. They are the men like yuydhaan, Viraat and Mahaarathi Drupada.

Commentary—Yuyudhaan is actually the name of the charioteer of Lord Krishna. He is popularly known as Saatyaki. Though Krishna had taken a vow not to participate in the battle and his army was on the side of Duryodhan, Saatyaki a great archer had associated himself with Paandavas in the Mahabharat-war.

Mahaarathee is a mighty warrior ascended of course on a chariot of his befitting, who can engage single handed ten thousand combatants.

In the following two coupletes Duryodhan proceeds to name some more men of valour who constitute potential danger to the fulfilment of his selfish and unjust desire i.e. to secure the throne of Hastinapur for him and his progenies.

Question which naturally crops up in every thinking mind is as to why Duryodhan is indulging in an unnecessary exercise of enumerating the names of the valiant men of the opposite side. Does he want to awe-strike his master? No he can not take this suicidal step, certainly not. Then the reason in obvious. He does not want his master to be complacent only because of the fact that he is the teacher of most of them and can easily take over them as a lion takes over a lamb. No, this is certainly not going to be just a walkover. Duryodhan crafty and wily as he is, he wants to drive down this to his master's mind.

Dhrishtaketushchekitaanah kaashiraajashch viryavaan

Purujitkuntibhojashch shaibyashch narpungavah [5]

Meaning—All are names except narpungavah and viryavan which stand for the best among men and a man of valiance respectively.

Commentary—Dhrishtaketu was the son of the king of chedi kingdom, named Shishupaal an avowed enemy of Lord Krishana and was killed earlier by Krishna during a yagya being performed by paandvas. Dhrishtketu nevertheless chose to side with the righteous Paandavas.

Chekitan was a famous warrior from yaadava clan. Kashiraaja was the king of Kashi now renamed as varanasi. Purujit and Kuntibhoj both were the brother of Kunti the mother of Yudhishthir, Bhim and Ajrun and also of Karna a fact not widely known. Nakul and Sahadeva were the sons of Maadri another wife of Paandu.

Shaivya was the father-in-law of Yudhishthir as he married his daughter Devaki (not to be confused with the mother of Krishna) with him.

Yudhaamanushch Vikraant Uttamaujaashch viryavaan
Saubhadro Draupdeyaashch sarva eva mahaarathaah [6]

Meaning—(And) ferocious Yudhaamnu, brave Uttamauja, Saubhadra and Draupdeyaah who are all 'mahaarathees.'

Commentary—Yudhaamanu and Uttamauja were full brothers of appreciable valour. Saubhadra means the son of Subhadra another wife of Arjuna and was best known as Abhimanu and was slaughtered at a very young age having been ambushed by a host of skilled archers of kaurava-side, when the battle advanced. Draupdeyaah denotes the sons of Draupadi the common wife of five paandavas-brothers. These sons were also five in number. Mahaarathi has been explained earlier.

The enumeration of the important warriors of the Paandava side by Duryodhan ends here. Now he proceeds to give a brief account of the brave and important personaliteis of his own side.

Asmaakam tu vishishta ye taannibodh dvijotttam
Nayaka mam sainyasya Samngyaartham tan brabimi te [7]

Meaning—O most important among the twice born (Dvijottam) know also them well who are the distinguished ones on our side—leaders of my army who I mention for your knowledge.

Dvijottam is composed of two words dvij and uttam dvij is a twice born, uttam stands for the best. Twice born usually stands for a brahmin because he is supposed to be born twice, once from his mother-womb and once more when at a later stage at the age of eight or nine he is invested with the sacred thread (yagyopavit) and is thus entitled to perform all those religious acts and rituals which give him entry in to the field of spirit and supreme knowledge. Without this apparent act of purification a man of ordinary flesh is not supposed to be really born because having been denied entry in to the realm of knowledge he remains engulfed in the darkness of ingnorance. The first birth is thus while in an ordinary world full of all kinds of impurities and with lack of real knowledge, the second birth is a birth in a world of enlightenment, full of potentialities to explore the supreme and try to achieve Him.

Dronhacharya is a Brahmin, a twice born. Duryodhan's addressing him as the best among Brahmins is the evidence of his dexterity as he is indirectly indicating him to be true to the cause which he has undertaken not-with-standing some of his own disciples being on the other side including Arjuna the most favourite of his pupils.

Bhavaanbhishmashcha karnashcha kripashch samitinjayah
Asvathaama Vikarnashceha Saumdattistathaiva cha [8]

Meaning—Thyself and Bhishma and karna and kripa ever victorious in battle, vikarna and also the son of Somadatta;

Commentary—Though the commander-in-chief Bhishma is the oldest and mightiest of all and held in high esteem by everyone owing to his austere and pious life with a promise of life-long celibacy to allow his father to culminate a love-marriage with a girl whose father was all out to forestall it by adding a precondition to it that only the son born of his doughter and his progeny will be entitled to the throne;

yet is placed by Duryodhan at second position in the list of names just to placate the mighty master. Duryodhan apparently had more hope from Dronhacharya, though in command was Bhishm who was supposed to be inclined towards Pandavaas.

Bhishma was in fact the grandsire of both the Kauravas and Pandavas but had chosen to remain with Duryodhan perhaps just to exercise a sobering effect on an otherwise unreasonably ambitious and ruthless prince.

Karna in fact is the son of kunti conceived and delivered while she was still a virgin and was abandoned on a river-water and reared by a charioteer, thus leaving no scope for him to be recognised as one of the Paandavas. As the mythology goes Karna was the son of the sun-god whose presence Kunti had unwittingly evoked just to test a 'mantra' given by some, on the recital of which she could allure any god for copulation. Later when she was married to Pandu and the latter was discovered to be impotent she was compelled to take recourse to this device in full knowledge of Pandu and produced Yudhishthir by the grace of Dharmraj, Bhim by the wind god and Arjun by Indra the god of gods. Nakul and Sahadeva the rest two brothers were the sons of Ashvinikumars and were born by Madri the second wife of Pandu.

Kripa is the brother-in-law of Dronhaacharya, his wife being the sister of the latter.

Asthaama is the son of Dronhacharya himself. Vikarana was the third son of Dhritrashtra and a mighty hero.

The name of the son of Somadatta is Bhurishrava, the former king of Bahalika.

It is to be noted that amongst all including Bhishma only Kripa is added with an objective samitinjaya (ever victorious). The design is hardly disguised, it is again to please the brother-in-law of the master, the mighty Dronha.

Anye cha bhavah shooraah madarthe tyaktjivitaah
Naana shastrapraharanhaah sarve yudhvishaardah [9]

Meaning—And there are other warriors armed with various weapons skilled in warfare and ready to stake their lives for me.

Commentary—In this couplet Duryodhan does not name any other hero. He just concludes by calling the rest "the others" though the much bigger army of his compared to that of the opposite side comprises of many valiant archers like Jayadrath, Shalya, Kritverma etc. This shows nothing but the highly inflated ego of the spoilt prince who cares two hoots for other heroes and thinks below his dignity to name them, much superior in power and prowess as he considers himself in comparison to them.

Aparyaaptam tadasmaakam balam Bhishmaabhirakshitam
Paryaptam Tvidmeteshaam balam Bhimaabhirakshitam [10]

Meaning—Inadequate is our army protected by Bhishma while adequate is their army under the protection of Bhima.

Commentary—this couplet has often been interpreted in divergent ways.

Some maintain that by declaring his army as 'aparyaapt' and that of Paandavas as 'paryaapt' he wants to convey to the master that his army is 'unlimited' and hardly to be conquered and the army of his enemy is limited and thus to be vanquished without much effort. This opinion has been held by many a commentators.

But my understanding is quite different. The translation of 'aparyaapt' in to English is inadequate and that of 'paryaapt' is adequate.

The meaning is therefore quite clear. Duryodhan simply maintains that his army is inadequate and that of the enemy is adequate and thus hardly to be conquered. Duryodhan clever as he is, does not want Acharya to be coplacent so he cautions him about the strength of the enemy which may be quantitavely inferior but is no doubt qualitatively superior to his own army. It will be more evident from the following couplet as to how serious he is to see that his warriors don't fall an easy prey to the army of the opposite side.

Ayaneshu cha Sarveshu Yathaabhaagamavashthaah
Bhishmevaabhirakashantu bhavantah sarv eva hi [11]

Meaning—Therefore all ye stationed in your respective divisions on all fronts of the battle, guard Bhishma in particular.

Commentary—The underlined meaning of the instruction by the worried prince has been explained in III Part of the commentary of the preceding couplet.

Tasya Samajanayan harsham kuruvridhah Pitaamah,
Singhnadam vinodyachchaih sanhkham dadhmau prataapvaan [12]

Meaning—The mighty grandsire Bhishma, the ancient of the Kaurvas roared terribly like a lion and blew his conch thus cheering the heart of Duryodhan.

Commentary—Bhishma is vividly moved by the honour bestowed on him by prince and thus tries to cheer him up.

In a way he also declares the commencement of the callous combat by blowing his conch.

Tatah Shankhaashcha bheryashcha panvaanakgomukhah,
Sahsaivaabhyahanyant sa shbdastumulo'hbhavat [13]

Meaning—Then conches, Kettledrums, tabors, drums and horns suddenly blared forth and this clamour proved to be tumultuous.

Commentary—After the green signal provided by the conch-blowing by Bhishma, different instruments of war were blared forth on both sides.

Tatah Shvetairhayairyukte mahati syandane shitau,
Madhavah Paandvashchaiva divyau shankham pradadmatuh [14]

Meaning—Then seated in a big chariot yoked to white horses Madhava (Shri Krishna) and the Paandava (son of Pandu, here Arjuna) blew their celestial conches.

Commentary—Shri Krishna had killed a ferocious monster Madhu, it is why he is called Madhava.

This special address used for Shri krishna is intended to show his unearthly strength. He might be piloting the chariot of Arjuna but he is not a charioteer. He is an unparalleled hero as well.

Paandava may stand for any of the five sons of Pandu but here it is unmistakably used for Arjuna because it is his chariot on which Shri Krishna was seated as a charioteer.

The mention of white horses here is of special importance. White colour symbolizes purity and righteousness. This implies that Arjuna and Lord Krishna are going to adhere to the values which are so much cherished by the righteous in battles. But every thing considered to be fair in love and war, the adherence to values by Arjun and Krishna were hardly continous and consistent. The ways in which Jayadratha and Karna were killed especially at the instances of Lord Krishna tell volumes about the value-oriented approach of the twin associates. Jayadratha was killed in a treacherous way and Karna was slained unarmed while engaged in extricating a wheel of his chariot from the earth which had engulfed it owing to a curse by some enlightened austere for an unseemly behaviour on his part.

Paanchajanyam Hrishiksho Devadattam Dhananjayah
***Paundram Dadhmau mahaashankham bhimkarma virkodarah* [15]**

Meaning—Hrishikesh (Shri Krishna) and Dhananjay (Arjuna) blew conches named paanchajanayah and Devadattah respectively. Vrikoder Bhim capable of performing terrible deeds blew a big conch named Paundrah.

Commentary—Hrisikesh is one who has absolute control over the senses. Dhananjay is one who has won enough wealth.

The conch of Lord Krishna, Panchajanyaha takes its name from the demon Panchajanyaha from whose bones the conch was made.

The conch of Arjuna was called Devadatta as it was given by a god (Indra)—his own father.

Brik stands for a wolf, Brikodar is therefore one whose belly is like that of a wolf. Bhima was called Brikodar because he ate a lot like a wolf.

The conch of Bhima is aught to be big keeping with his own enormous body.

Anantvijayam raja kuntiputra Yudhishthtirah
Nakulah Sahadevashch Sughoshmanipushpakau [16]

Meaning—The king Yudhishthira son of kunti blew the conch named Anantvijay; Nakul and Sahdeva blew Saughoshah and Manipusspakah respectively.

Commentary—Calling Yudhishthira a king carries some significance. Yudhishthir was certainly not a king, not even a king in making like Duryodhana. If there was only king of Hastinapur at that time, it was the blind ruler Dhritarashtra. Is it not the providence itself speaking through, perhaps, an absent-minded Sanjaya the ultimate result of a war yet to be fought? True it was Yudhisththir himself and none-else who became the legitimate heir to the throne after the decisive battle of Kurukshetra.

Kaashyashcha parameshvaasah Shikhandi cha maharathah
Dhristdumno Viraatashch Saatyakishaparaajith [17]

Meaning—The noted archer the king of Kashi, Sikahandi the Maharathee, Dhrishtadumna and Viraat as well as the unsubdued Saatayaki did like wise.

Commentary—Shikhandi deserves special mention because it he is who ultimately became the cause of the demise of great Bhishhma who was endowed with the blessing not to die till he wanted, was never to be vanquished but for Shikhandi whom he would in no case engage in a combat knowing him fully well to be a female who later underwent a gradual sex-transformation and became a male. Arjuna could conquer Bhishma only when the latter threw his arch seeing Shikhandi standing like a shield before the former. The death of Bhishhma shattered all hopes of victory of Duryodhana to pieces and the outcome of the battle of Kurukshetra was decided the very day, the mightiest among men, Bhishma was rendered unable to fight and fell off his magnificent chariot pierced all along his body with the shafts shorted off from Arjuna's great bow. Bhishm however did not immediately succumbed to his injuries and remained lying on what was called a 'sharsaiya' (the bed of arrows) till he decided to depart from this earth when the sun become 'uttaraayan' (moved towards north from south)

Drupado Draupadeyaashch Sarvashah Prithivipate
Saubhadrashcha mahabhahuh shankhandadhmuh prithakprithak. [18]

Meaning—O king of the earth (Sanjaya addressing Dhritrasahtra) Drupada as well as the five sons of Draupadi along with mighty-armed Saubhadra all blew their respective conches.

Commentary—Saubhadra stands for the son of Subhadra who was the sister of Shri Krishna and the wife of Arjuna. He was named as Abhimanyu. This has been stated earlier. Amongst of five sons of Draupadi one each was believed to be from one of his five husbands.

Saghosho Dhartraashtraanaam hridyaani Vyadaarayat
Nabhashch prthivim chaiva tumulo vyanunaadayan [19]

Meaning—This tumultuous uproar echoing through sky and earth rent the hearts of Dhritarashtra's sons.

Commentary—Mark the irony of the situation-Sanjaya is appointed to narrate the happenings on the battlefield to Dhrithrashtra and he is compelled to confess that the sounds emitting from the different conches of the warriors of the opposite side nothing less than tore the hearts of the blind emperor's sons. Why not the hearts of those in the opposite camp was torn apart by the lion like thunder of Bhishma and sounds of various war-instruments? Does not Sanjaya appear to throw a hint at every possible opportunity to Dhritrashtra as to what was to come of this unnecessary bloodshed? Was Sanjaya endowed with divine vision not only to witness what was happening on the battle-field but also to look in to the veiled future?

Ath Vyavashthitaandrishtva Dhaartraasstraankapidhvajaha
Pravrite shashtrasampaate dhanurudyamya paandavah [20]
Hrishkesham Tadaa vaakyamidmaah mahipate
Arjun uvaach :
Senayoruubhayormadhye ratham sthaapaya me'chuta. [21]

Meaning—Then beholding your sons arrayed before and the flight of missiles about to commence, Arjuna whose banner bore the image of Hamuman, took up his bow and thus spoke to Lord Krishna: Achuta! place my army between the opposing armies.

Commentary—Arjuna is called Kapidhvaj here. 'Kapi' in English means monkey and dhvaj is banner. Arjuna's chariot is fluttering a banner, marked with a monkey but this monkey is none else than Hamuman who though has a body of monkey is regarded as a god very devoted to Rama a symbol of victory as well as righteousness. In fact it is said that; Hamuman himself remained seated throughout at the banner-staff of Arjuna at the behest of Bhima who happened to be the brother of Hanuman both having a common father in the wind god (Pavan).

This again foretells the victory of the Paandavas. When Hanuman himself was on the side of Arjuna who was going to forestall his victory?

Yavadetaannirikshe'ham Yodhukaamaanavasthitaan
Kairmayaa sahyodhabyam'sminran samudyame [22]

Meaning—(And make it stand there) till I may observe those myriads longing for battle, with whom I have to engage myself in this fight.

Commentary—It is for the 1st time in the Gita that Arjuna as the archer gives orders to his charioteer who is not less than the Almighty Himself in human form. The order will continue till next couplet then we shall she what reaction it brings to the charioteer turned Super being of His time (if not Supreme himself in some persons' eyes).

Yotsyamaanaanvekhe'hm yaete'tra samaagataah
Dhaaratraashtrasya durbuddheryuddhe priyachikirshavah [23]

Meaning—I shall look at those willing to do good to the evil- minded Duryodhana in this war and have assembled here to fight on his behalf.

Commentary—The purpose of the orders is explained further. Arjun naturally wants to know about warriors who are ready to help an evil minded prince. Till now Arjun has no mind to desist from fighting. He desires to see the people assembled on the other side just to apprise himself with the fact as to who are they who have openly sided with his enemy.

Sanjay uvaach :
Evamukto Hrisikessho Gudaakeshen Bharat,
Senyorubhayormadhyesthapayitavu rulhottamam [24]
Bhishmdronhpramukhatah sarvesham cha mahikshitaam,
Uvaacha Parth pahyaitaansamvetaankuruniti [25].

Meaning—Sanjaya said "O King", thus invoked by Arjuna, Krishna having drawn up that significant chariot between the opposing armies placing it specially in front of Bhishma, Dronha and all other rulers spoke thus; Arjun! behold these Kauravaas assembled together.

Commentary—The orders are complied with; the chariot

is stationed between the two armies by the charioteer not less than the Almighty Himself in human form. This abundantly shows his humility as well as readiness and willingness to discharge promptly whatever responsibilities he is entrusted with. This is also to put an example before the lesser mortals—not to desert from the works assigned—because from the study of following chapters of the Gita it is more than clear that the Lord is always conscious of the fact that whatever will he do will set an example for the other—"Mamvartmaanuvartante manusyaahapartha sarvaharshsh—O Arjun my path are followed by men every where'.

The meaning of Hrishikesh has been explained earlier.

Gudakesh is one who has mastery over sleep. It stands for Arjuna.

Two things need to be marked here. It is only for the 1st and last time in the Gita that Arjuna appears to be in command. From here onward it is the charioteer the Lord Himself that holds the command. Most of the talking is to be done by Him and Arjuna has had to perform His command ultimately.

Secondly it is for the first time that Shri Krishna speaks to Arjuna in the Gita in the well measured few words. "Behold these Kauravaas assembled together".

This opening speech is of immense significance. After beholding the warriors arrayed before his eyes, he shows the necessary reaction which gives birth to the Gita—the world's finest work.

Tatraapashyatsthitan paarthah Pitreenathpitaamahaan
Achaaryaanmaatulanatbraatreenpautraanpautraansakhinstatha
Shvashuraansuhridashchaiva senayorubhayorapi [26]

Taansamikshya sa Konteyah Sarvanbandhoonavasthitaan

Kripaya parayaavishto vishidannidambravit [27]
Arjun Uvaach
Drishtvemam svajanam Krishna yuzutsum samupashthitam [28]
Seedanti mam gaatranhimukham cha parishushyati
vepthushch shareere me romharshashch jaayate [29]

Meaning—Arjuna beheld in both the armies; uncles and grandsires, teachers, maternal-uncles, brothers, sons and grandsons, friends father-in-laws as well as well-wishers and having seen all these Kinsmen and overpowered by great pity and full of grief and dejection he spoke thus, O Krishna having seen my own men arrayed for battle my limbs are failing, my mouth is parched, my frame quivers and my hair stands on end.

Commentary :

After the following couplet.

Gaandeevam sransrate hastattvaakchaiva paridahayate,
Na cha Shaknomyavasthaatum bhramteeva cha me manah [30]

Meaning—Gandeeva (the bow of Arjun) slips from my hands and my skins burn all over. I am unable to be steady on my feet and my mind goes on whirling.

Commentary—Here comes the real catalystical force which produces the profoundest philosophy of life and death ever produced before. Arjun having been hopelessly caught by the love for his kins-men young and old, have a mind full of illusion as well as attachment towards this world and this illusion and attachment are in the root of suffering which can otherwise be avoided with actual knowledge of the scheme of things and events.

Illussion is important for it sets at naught the very belief of real seers and philosophical theorizers especially of the propounders of the philosophy that life in itself is indestructible as it is spirit not the body. The body may die, may be killed, mutilated and destroyed but the spirit which dwells inside never dies. It is never killed or destroyed by any means. In other words the weapons or means which can kill the spirit-'atma' is yet to be discovered and it is unlikely to be discovered in ages to follow. The spirit or life is thus immortal and there is no point in lamenting for the destruction of body which is nothing more than the cage of a bird. Then what is of importance? The cage or the bird? Even if you destroy the cage, the bird remains, it becomes free and more powerful; independent to fly high and to make the sky its limit if it so chooses.

Arjun is lametnting the impending destruction of the cage and has forgotten all about the bird. In other words he is repenting for an otherwise commendable work of liberating the immortal soul from the mortal cage it has chosen or forced to dwell in.

It is nothing but attachment as explained above which creates this illusion and attachment is complete in this case as it is not limited to his mind but has affected his body too. Body is bound to react to the condition of mind and not only his mouth is parched, his body is trembling, his bow is failing; but even standing in a warrior-like posture has become impossible for him and his poor mind is whirling like any thing—indecisive and unsteady.

The ground has started to be gradually prepared for explaining the real meaning of life and death to Arjuna and thus to the whole world by the creator of all kinds of life Himself, the very incarnate of the Spirit Supreme.

Some more times will be allowed to the mighty archer to ventilate his fear and doubts fully and then the Supreme in human form will start to pooh-pooh all his fears as well as doubts and misgivings.

Nimittaani cha pashyaami viparitaani Keshava
Na cha shreyo'nupashyaami hatvaa svajan maahave [31]

Meaning—And O Krishna, I see the omens which are quite opposite to victory i.e. they are hardly auspicious. I see no virtue in slaying my own Kith and Kin in the battle.

Commentary—A fear-riddled mind becomes superstitious as well. Though there is hardly any good or bad omen but Arjun full of illusion as he is; is perceiving bad omens all around. He is at the same time seeing no good in killing them whom he terms as his own men—men who are hardly his own men, who tried to roost him with his brothers and mothers alive in Lakshaagrih and men who took away every thing in a deceitful gamble and but for Krishna timely help his wife Draupadi stood naked amidst the large assembly of kauravaas-men who compelled him and his brothers to wander in wild forest bereft of all comforts to which they were entitled and men who were now not ready to part even with a piece of earth as small as a point of needle.

What is this if not illusion and foolish attachment to those who are never attached to you?

Na Kaankshe Vijayam Krishna na cha raajyam Sukhani cha
Kim no raajyen govind Kim Bhogairjeeviten vaa. [32]

Meaning—O Krishna I covert no victory (in the battle) nor a kingdom nor pleasures. Of what avail O ! Govinda will a kingdom be to us or to that effect even luxuries of life itself?

Commentary—The height of dejection and depression precludes Arjuna in seeing any advantage in a victory—a victory which is bound to turn paandavas from beggar to rulers. But this mortified man has no use of even a kingdom and ultimately the life itself seems meaningless to him. Any pshycologist will diagnose this as the ultimate in mental imbalance caused by imaginary fears as well as unwanted attachments. This is in no way indicator of any sense of relinquishment on his part but is a clear symptom of a sick and weakened mind which is trying to seek solace in its own fairy world of foregoing everything for sake of others, even life.

Yeshaamarthe kankshitam no raajyam bhogah sukhaani cha,
Ta eme'vasthita yudhe pranhanstyaktvaadhanani cha [33]
Acharyaah pitarah putraastathaiva cha pitaamahaah
Maatulah shvashuraah pautraah shyalaah sambadhinastatha [34]

Meaning—Those for whom we covet a kingdom, luxuries and pleasures—masters, uncles, sons, as well as grandsires, maternal uncles, fathers-in-law grandsons, and brothers-in-law and other kith and kin—are arrayed on the battle field staking their lives and riches.

Commentary—Here Arjuna tries to justify his cowardice by backing his lack of will to act by what appears to him a profound logic. 'Why should he desire a kingdom or the associated benefits when for whom he wants them are here staking nothing less than their lives and possessions?

Etaanna hantumichhaami ghanto'pi Madhusoodan,
Api trailokyaraajyasya hetoh kim nu mahikrite [35]

Meaning—O Krishna these I do not want to slay though slain myself, even for the sake of the three worlds, how then for this earth?

Commentary—This is the height of cowardice and inaction. One does not want to kill even when he stands the chance of being killed. It is this inaction which will be subjected to severe criticism and condemnation by the Lord in the ensuing chapters. Three worlds here mean—Aakaas (Sky), Patal (World below the earth) and this globe inhabited by humans.

Nihatya Dhaartraashtraasannah Kaa preeteeh syaajjanaardan,
Paapmevaasahrayedasmaan hatvaitaanaatataayinah. [36]

Meaning—O Janardan (Krishna) what happiness can we derive from slaying the sons of Dhritarashtra? Sin alone will take hold of us by slaying these perpetrators of iniquity.

Commentary—Arjuna, desperate as he is, endeavours to win a point by equating his act of fighting with sin; knows as he well that Krishna being a virtuous man will easily fall prey to his this argument. He will further bolster this argument in following verses taking recourse to words like Dharm (religion), adharm, (opposite to religion) and of course sin.

He undoubtedly wants to touch the weakest chord in Krishna's heart knowing full well that one of the reasons for the Supreme to incarnate Himself in human form is to uphold the religion and eradicate its opposite.

Tasmannarha vayam hantum Dhaartrashtransva bandhavan,
Svajanam hi katham hatvaa sukhinah syaam Maadhava [37]

Meaning—Therefore, O Madhav (Krishna) it does not behove us to slay the sons of Dhritraashtra, who are our brothers. Indeed how should we be happy after killing our own Kinsmen.

Commentary—Again Arjuna, full of illusion and lacking in real knowledge takes the destruction of body as the destruction of the whole being even of the spirit, it is why he thinks as to what he will earn in killing his kinsmen is nothing else than unhappiness. It is on this point that Lord will dwell at length in the second canto.

Yadyapyete na pashyanti lobhopahatchetasah,
Kulkshyakritam dosahm miltradrohe cha paatakam [38]
Katham na gyeamasmaabhih paapaadasmannivaratitum
Kulakshyakritam dosham prapasyadbhirjanaardan [39]

Meaning—Although they with a consciousness griped with greed perceive no evil in bringing destruction to the family and no sin in treachery to friends, Janardan! why should not we who see clearly the wrong in bringing destruction to the family desist from this crime?

Commentary—As indicated earlier the whole act of bravery and chivalery which is ready to be staged shortly appears nothing more than sin to an illusioned Arjun. He is even ready to flee away from the battle-field to escape this unwarranted sin.

Kulakshye pranhashyanti kuldharmaah sanaantanaah,
Dharme nashte kulam kritsanmdharmo' bhibbhavatyuta [40]

Meaning—The age-long religion of the family is destroyed in the annihilation of the family and in the collapse of religion, sin overcomes the whole family.

Commentary—As maintained earlier the over doze of religion and sin are being administered by Arjuna just to retrieve himself by hook or by crook from the situation he is facing—to fight, to act, to win a battle against his so called own kinsmen. The religion has been made more pointed by limiting it to family's-religious-traditions. How can religion stand if there is no family to uphold it? The crafty archer thinks that he is able to elbo krishna in to a blind alley from which he will find no way out.

Adharmaabhibhavaatkrishna pradushyanti kulstriyah,
Strishu dushtaashu vaarshneheya jaayaate varnshanakarah [41]

Meaning—O Krishna, when vice prevails, the women of the family become corrupt and with women corrupted O Vaarshnheya there arises the intermixture of castes.

Commentary—Casteism was very much prevalent during the Mahabharata-age. Again Arjuna tries to touch the most sensitive chord in Krishna's heart. He the Almighty Himself cannot bear the corruption of women due to disappearance of religion and thus allow the intermixture of castes to go aglore.

Sankaro narakaayaiva kulaghnaanaam kulasya cha
Patanti pitaro hyeshaam luptpindodakkiryaah [42]

Meaning—Hell is the only place reserved for the destroyers of the family as well as the family itself and this nemesis is caused by the intermixture of castes. Their ancestors fall (are deprived of the comforts of the unseen worlds they dwell in) due to the non-offering of 'Pinda' (lump of rice) and libations.

Commentary—'Pindodok kriya'—offering of lumps of rice and water on different occasions to the departed souls of the family is supposed to be an essential act in Hindu religion. Arjuna wants to horrify the lord by pointing out to the certain possibility of such offerings being stopped leading to the fall of the deceased ancestors.

Doshairetaih Kulaghnaanaam varnshanakarkaarkaih
utsaadyante jaatidharmaah kuldharmaashcha shaashvataah [43]

Meaning—Through the evils brought by the destroyers of the family in causing the intermixing of castes, the age-long religions of castes and families become extinct.

Commentary—Again the emphasis is on dharm, rather dharmaas—dharmaas of castes as well as of families—hoping against the hope that the upholder of religion (Lord Krishna) will allow Arjuna to desist from the act he is supposed to perform shortly.

Utsannakuldharmaanhaam manusyhaanhaanm Janaardan
Narke'ninyatam vaaso bhavateetyanushushrum [44]

Meaning—O Krishna it has been heard by us that the men who have relinquished their family-religions dwell for ever in hell.

Commentary—The same emphasis on religions continues. But the point to be marked here is that the Arjun's conception of religion is limited only to the family trituals. He is either knowingly relegating the real religion—world-religion or 'vishva Vandhutva' as they call in Sanskrit—to the back ground or is really ignorant of it. The first appears to be more probable. The threat of hell has been introduced for the first time to augment the arguments of Arjuna in the vain hope that at least this if nothing else will compel Krishna to allow Arjuna to have his way.

Aho but muhatpaapam kartum vyavasthitaa vayam
yadraajyasukhlobhen hantum svajanamudyataah [45]

Meaning—Alas! We are resolved to commit a great sin as we are ready to slay our kinsmen for the lust of the pleasure associated with kingdom.

Commentary—A mortal trying to highlight to the Supreme Immortal the consequences of an ensuing important event which in his thinking is just for the lust of throne and is thus nothing but sin.

Yadi maamapratikaaramashashtram shastrapaanayah
Dhaartrashtra ranhe hanyustanme kshemataram bhavet [46]

Meaning—It would be better for me if the sons of Dhritarashtra armed as they are should slay me unarmed and unresisting as I am.

Commentary—Arjun is no doubt suffering from a high degree of depression as he is ready to commit suicide by offering him to be slain unarmed and unresisting. In this desparate way he wants to find a solution of the situation he is not ready to face. Arjuna has thus led himself to the lowest ebb and now it will be the arduous task of his Saviour to retrieve him from it.

Sanjay Uvaach :

Sanjaya said :

Evamuktvaarjunah sankhye rathopasth upaavishat,
visrjiya Sasharam chaapam shoksamvignamaanasah [47]

Meaning—Having thus spoken Arjun his mind overwhelmed with sorrow sank in to the hinder part of his chariot having laid down his bow and arrows.

Commentary—The climax of inaction illusion and apprehension of the outcome of a great event has been reached. Arjun's decision appears to be final and irrevokable with his laying down the weapons and taking the back seat. But is anything final in this world? Subsequent cantos will show how futile is a human-design before the will of the Supreme.

Om tatsaditi Shrimadbhagawadgeetasoopasishatsu Brahmvidyayaam yogshashtre shrir-rishnarjunsam

vaade'rjunvishadyogo nam prathamo'dhyaayah. [1]

Thus in the upanishad of the Bhagavat Gita, the science of Bhrama, the scripture on Yoga, the dialogue between Shri Krishna and Arjuna ends the first canto named as dejection of Aryuna. [1]

CHAPTER II

Sanjay uvaacha :

Tam tathaa kripayaavishtamashrupuranhaakulekshnham Vishidantamidam waakyamuvaach Madhusoodanh [1].

Meaning—Sanjaya said : to him who was thus overcome by compassion and full of sorrow and whose eyes were filled with tears and were agitated; Madhusoodan thus spake:

Commentary—The over all effect on Arjuna facing the army composed of his own kinsmen, of the love and attachment towards them is depicted in this couplet. The eyes distressed and full of tears show that the grief is not superficial but real and his concern for the welfare of his kith and kin is genuine and beyond doubt. He is really full of sorrow and distress and whatever he has told has come from the depth of his heart.

Shri Bhagavaanuvaach :

Kutastva Kashmalmidam vishame samupasthitam, Anaaryajushtamasvargyamakirteekararjun [2].

Meaning—The blessed Lord said—Arjuna, whence has this blemish come upon you at this odd hour? It is shunned by honourable men and will bring neither heaven nor fame to you.

Commentary—It is here for the first time that the charioteer takes in his hands not only the reins of horses but also that of the man occupying the chariot. It is here for the first time that Arjuna receives the shock he deserves at the hand of the Supreme Who has chosen to be his charioteer. His action has been denounced as not suitable to Aryas (the noble souls) and harbinger of digrace. But the harsher admonition is yet to follow.

Klaivyam ma asm gamah Paarth naitattvayupapadyate,
Kshudram hridaydaurbalaym tyaktvotishth prantap [3].

Meaning—O Parth! (Arjuna, son of Pritha) do not yield to unmanliness. It is not worthy of you. Shake of this paltry faintheartedness and arise O ! Parantap (scorcher of enemies)

Commentary—The Lord intends to administer maximum shock to Arjuna in order to bring him in to a frame of mind which can receive and appreciate fully what He desires to divulge. Unmanliness is no ordinary word. Had it come from the mouth of any other man than Krishna Himself, Arjuna would have slain his neck with a single stroke of his sword.

But Lord is not that unkind as well. He admonishes him to eschew the meaningless weakness to accept the challenge thrown to him. He also calls him the scorcher of enemies and thus tries to enthuse courage and confidence in his heart which has fallen prey to cowardice and uncalled for compassion.

Arjun Uvaach :

Katham Bhishmaham Sankhye Dronham cha madhusoodan,
Ishubhih pratiyotsyaami pujaarhaavarisoodan [4].

Meaning—Arjun said :-O Madhusudan (krishna) how shall I engage in fight Bhishma and Dronha with arrows on the battle-filed. They are both worth of reverence O! Slayer of enemies.

Commentary—Arjuna like a good lawyer is making his arguments pin-pointed and focuses his attention on the very sensitive issue that may bewilder even Shri Karishna. Even if the slaughter of his relations may not matter much, how can he pierce with arrows the bodies of Bhishma and Dronha? The former being the grand sire of the family and the latter the very teacher who has taught the art of warfare to him including the kauravas. Both of them are revered by all.

Arjun vainly thinks that this logic of revering the elders and not to challenge them on battle-field will find favour with Krishna as the latter Himself is the upholder of higher values of life.

Gurunahatvaa hi mahaanubhaawaan
shhreyo bhoktum bhaikshyamapih loke,

hatwaarthkaananstu gurunihaiva
***Bhunijya bhogaan rudhirpadigdhaan** [5].*

Meaning—It is better to sustain oneself on alms in this world than to slay these high souled masters though they are full of desires, having slain them we shall enjoy only blood-stained pleasures.

Commentary—this couplet has often been subjected to wrong interpretation. This is especially due to the 'hatwaarthkaamaanstu,' The word 'hatwaathrkaamaan' is surely the adjective of 'guru' and thus denotes the 'gurus' who have been lured by the gains of the palace but some interpreters object to see these masters as slaves of wrong desires, therefore they distort the meaning of 'hatwaarthkaamaan', suggesting it to stand for desires of wealth or comfort on the part of slayers. This interpretation is erroneous and vitiates the rules of grammar, it is why I have chosen the meaning not taken recourse to by many.

By talking of living on alms Arjun appears to be ready to follow the path of renunciation (Sanyaas), a practice which was rampant in those days—people leaving their home and hearth and sporting saffron grobes to live on the earning of others. They were real parasites of the society, shunning every action and bathing in the self propounded glory of sanyaas. It is one and perhaps the most important reason which compelled Krishna to put forward a novel theory of action without attachment (karmyoga). This is certainly a via media, a compromise between 'sanyaas' and 'karm' (action). We shall return to it later in subsequent 'shlokas' (couplets).

By emphasizing the importance of 'gurus'—masters—and declaring them so reverened as not to be touched by the point of arrow, Arjuna again intends at touching one of the most vital points in Krishna's heart. He knows how He Himself was the most respectful towards gurus being Himself the guru of the whole world :- Krishnam vande 'jagadgurum'.

Arjun undoubtedly occupies for himself the position of a knowledgeable preacher by firstly denouncing the combat, with kinsmen and putting forward the logic of religion and sin and now trying to uphold the significance of 'gurus'—even when full of lust and greed they have forfeited the right of being revered and held in high esteem.

Lured by lust these gurus certainty are. Otherwise they would not have chosen the side of Dhritrirashtra as Paandvas had equal right over them but the passion for pleasure of the palace made these gurus forget all norms as well as scruples. Bhishm was though not a guru in the real sense of the term but being the oldest as well as the austerest among the kauravaas, he has deservedly been addressed as one of the gurus by Arjuna.

Na chaitadvidmah kataranno gareeyo-
yadva jayem yodi vaa no jayeyuh.
Yaaneva hatvaa na jijivishaama-
steav'sthitaah pramukhe dhaartraashtraah [6].

Meaning—We do not know which is better for us (to fight or not to fight) nor do we know whether they will come out victorious or we. Before us arrayed are the sons of Dhritrashtra whom having slain we should not even will to live.

Commentary—Another, but disastrous trait of the character of Arjuna is revealed in these lines i.e. indecisiveness and suspicion. To be suspicious is to follow the path of destruction. This the Gita will itself up hold in one of the insuing lines—'sanshayaatmaa vinashyati.'

This suspicion and indecisiveness have been denounced in other religions also. The Bible says "But let him ask in faith with no doubting, for he who doubts is like a wave of the sea that is driven and tossed by the wind. For the person must not suppose that a double minded man, unstable in all his ways will receive any thing from the Lord" (James—I-6 to 8)

kaarpanhyadoshopahatsvabhaavah
prichhaami twaam dharmsammudh chettaah.
yacchreyah syaannischitam bruhi tanme
Shishyaste'ham shaadhi maam twaam prapannam [7].

Meaning—My nature having been smitten by the taint of helplessness and my consciousness bewildered in regard to right and wrong, I am asking Thee which may be the better for me. I am Thy disciple and have taken refuge in Thee so, enlighten me.

Commentary—Here the ground is ultimately prepared to sow the seed Krishna would like to sow. Arjuna is being most humble here and he openly admits the fact of his being at the end of his wits and in a confused state of mind. He perhaps realizes at last that whatever he was arguing was not all correct and it is beyond him to take any decision about the course to be followed.

The most subtle and at the same time most significant point to be marked here is his acceptability of discipleship without which he would not have been able to learn what he learns from Krishna and the world would have been deprived of the knowledge called the Gita. It is a time-honoured practice in India that only a disciple is entitled to have the sacred knowledge from the 'guru.' Thus by declaring himself as His disciple and surrendering himself to Him casting off his ego aside he has made himself most suitable to know what he aught to know at this juncture of his career. In fact Krishna Himself in a subsequent statement demands whole hearted and unconditional surrender to Him in order to bestow His benedictions : 'Sarva Dharmaan parityajaya mamekam sharanam vraj'—kicking aside all religions come to Me and Me only.

In fact demand is made in every religion to recognize only one supreme and omniscient power. In Islam also it is only Allah or Khuda who is to command the devotion of all. In the old testament in the Bible it is Jahoda who is the only god. In new testament also it in only one God who has sent his son Christ to this world to enlighten the path of those gone way-ward, and He is to be respected by all.

In Buddhism also none else than Buddha himself is considered to be supreme. Even Buddha used to keep mum when asked about the existence of any God.

Na hi prapashyaami mamaapanudyaa
dyachhokamuchhoshanhamindriyaanhaam
Avaapya Bhoomaavasapatnamridham
Raajayam suraanhaamapi chaadipathyam [8].

Meaning—For even on securing undisputed sovereignty and a prosperous kingdom on earth and also the subjugation of gods, I do not see what could dispel the dejection which is drying up my senses.

Commentary—Here the state of dejection, Arjun is encountering, has been explained in the profoundest manner possible.

His hopelessness is such and he even admits it that what to talk of kingdom on earth even the lordship over gods will not satisfy him. His suffering is intense and unbearable. This is testified by the fact that his very senses (eyes, ears, nose, skin etc.)., appear to go array. He has no control over them and he is not finding any way out of this impasse.

This shows man's utter helplessness before the adversity of circumstances. Only god can come to his rescue if he is wise enough to surrender himself whole heartedly to Him. That Arjun has done in the preceding verse. Now the result, the solution is awaited. This verse, takes to the dazzling height to which Arjun's griefs have risen. This is the climax. He will have to be rescued now. Only the following last act and the Master will take over the situation.

Sanjay Uvaach :

Evamuktvaa Hrishikesh Gudaakeshah, parantap
Na yotsya iti Govindamuktvaa tushnhim babhoova ha [9].

Meaning—**Sanjaya said**:—

Arjuna (Gudakesh—oppressor of the foes) having thus spoken to Shri Krishna, told him I will not fight and fell silent.

Commentary—The last act is over. The surrender is complete. Arjuna has ventilated his feeling as vividly and strongly as possible and has even declared himself a disciple of the Lord before he becomes speechless. Now it is for the Lord to do whatever He wants to do with him. He may make or mar him. He is just like a lifeless tool in His hands dumb and grief-stricken. But once in His care none is to fear any thing. It is told in the Bible itself "When Christ be with us who can be against us" or "I can do all things in Him Who strengthens me" (Philippines 2, 4.19) The Lord Krishna himself in a subsequent verse declares"—My devotee is never vanquished—'Na me bhaktaah pranhashayati.'

Sir Bhagavaanuvaach—

Ashochyananvashochastvam pragyavadunshcha bhashase,
Gataasoonagataasoonshch naanushochanti panditaah [11].

Meaning—The blessed Lord said, "thou grieves for those who should not be grieved for, yet speak like the learned. The enlightened men never grieve neither for the dead nor for the living.

Commentary—Lord taunts on Arjuna in His own ways. He points out the contradiction in his statements. On the one hand he is sorry for which he must not by soory, on the other hand he talks of Dharm, Ardharm etc. He is at the same time thus an ignorant fool and a wise preacher. This dichotomy is a source of enjoyment for Krishna. Any way without making much fun of it, he declares—it is not worthy of a wise man to grieve either for the living or for the dead.

This assertion of the Lord will be elaborated in much detail in the following verses. What he wants to drive down is the fact that in reality there is nothing to dread in death. The body is just the outer cover of the spirit (Atmaa). What is important is the spirit and the death of body never means the death of the spirit as well, because latter is deathless and indestructible in all cases.

As told above he will elaborate it further by taking recourse to several examples and illustrations.

Tamuvaach Hrishikesh prahasanniva Bhaarat,
Senyorubhayormadhye visidantamidam vacham [10].

Meaning—O Bharat, Shri Krishna smilingly thus spake to sorrowing Arjuna in the midst of the opposing armies.

Commentary—Smiling by Krishna must not here be taken as ridiculing the pitiable condition of Arjuna. The Lord in no case can think of humiliating His devotee. Smiling by Lord here is the silver lining of hope and expectation on the gloomy horizon of Arjuna's mind, yes it is an assuring gesture on the part of the Lord who wanted to instill instant belief in the heart of Arjuna that his desperation and the benumbled condition of his senses (remember the pathetic condition of the mighty archer when he said that his senses were is if drying up) are nothing and Arjuna can immediately be released from the bondage he himself has created for himself and also that the problems which he thinks to be insurmountable are not really so.

The irony of the situation is well evident here. There is on one side a warrior dejected and depressed and with eyes full of tears and on the other side the incarnate of the Supreme Itself smiling merrily as if on the childish behaviour of the former.

In any way by His smiling countenance He hands down an assurance to Arjuna and wants to convey that his problem is no problem however gigantic it might appear to him. He is not talking of the loss of family-religion, intermixture of castes, fall of forefathers as a result of the lack of offer of 'pind' etc. He dwels only on the important issues which are relevant in this context.

It may be emphasized that the Gita is not mere a gospel of vice and vitrue. It is a philosophy of life itself. A practical guide for a fearless and peaceful earthly existence.

What a man cherishes most? Peace. There can not be any doubt about it. And what are the impediments on the path of achieving this peace? Fears and doubts. Fears of all kinds and doubts of every shed. If a man is allowed to live a life bereft of fears and doubts, nothing else he will want. The Lord in the Gita has tried to enable man to be free from all kinds of fears and doubts and to lead a contented life free from anxieties and apprehensions.

It need not be exaggerated that the most fierce enemy of man kind is anxiety of all sorts. A number of pages have been devoted since time immemorial as how to avoid worries but with no tangible results. Anxieties continue to haunt human-minds, unabated. The Gita in a single short volume shows the way to get rid of this deadliest enemy of the mankind. And here lies the success of the Gita as a sure guide to a successful living. It makes the man free from anxieties and cares.

The Gita bit by bit removes firstly the fear of death

making it meaningless. Then it proceeds towards the removal of doubts and uncertainties by advancing the theory of detachment i.e. indulging in activities without caring for the outcome. Leave the outcome in the hands of God. Do your bit and the rest will be taken care of by God Himself. Why to worry about a thing over which you have no control? You have of course the control over the activities, you are free to indulge in them. The trouble starts when you start to wonder about their results—success or failure. Here steps in the Gita; do your work, results are not in your hands.

It is why it was said in the very beginning that the Gita teaches the most effective way of living—living a life free of fears and anxieties. The Gita thus teaches the very philosophy of a perfect living. It is hardly a gospel or a high fie spiritual discourse. It teaches the simple and down to earth techniques of life and living. Long before the best seller of Dale Caranedgie—'How to stop worrying and start living'—appeared, the Gita had taught this technique in a no uncertain but more convincing and concise manner. It fell upon its interpreters to spread its message far and wide; a duty in which they miserably failed.

Thus, the Lord will first advance to demolish the edifice of death which is the first and the foremost fear plaguing the human-mind. And here he will be not niggardly. He will use profusely all metaphors, similes and parallels to root this fear out of human-mind for ever. And here is the 1st step in this direction :

Natvevaaham jaatu naasam na tvam neme janaadhipaah,
na chaiva na bhavishyaamah, sarve vayamatah param [12].

Meaning—In fact there never was a time when I was not and when you or these rulers of men were nor will, there ever be a time when we shall all cease to be.

Commentary—This is the most revealing statement. By implication it means that there was never a time when we yes we who formed or did not form a part of the opposing armies of Kurukshetra not existed; similarly it is not that in future we will not exist.

It is simply pointing out that the life is an eternal and

unending flow. We pass from birth to birth only changing our outer forms. Then where is the death? Who kills whom and who is killed by whom?

Dehe'smin yathaa dehe kaumaaram yauvanam jara
Tathaa dehaantarpraaptirdhirastatra na muhyati [13].

Meaning—Just as childhood, youth and old age are attributed to the dweller in this body (the soul) even so it attains another body. The enlightened one is not bewildered by this.

Commentary—The so called death is not the destruction of any human or non human identity. The soul just passes from one body to another and that is all.

Mataraasparshaastu kaunteya shitoshnhsukhdhukhdah,
Aagamaapaayino anityaastaantitikshsva Bharat [14].

Meaning—Contacts between the senses and their objects, O! son of Kunti, give rise to the experience of cold and heat, pleasure and pain. They are transient and fleeting so bear them pataiently O Arjuna!

Commentary—The senses (i.e. eyes, ears, nose etc.) and their objects e.g., objects of eyes are beauty and ugliness, of ears melodious and unwelcome sounds, of nose sweet and repulsive scetns; are the cause of cold and heat as well as of pain and pleasure. This is as simple as any thing. If the skin (one of the senses) touches a hot or cold piece of stone it well feel heat and cold respectively. Similarly in the summer it is the skin which comes in to contact with the outwardly atmosphere and one feels hot. In the winter the skin comes in touch with a cold atmosphere and it feels cold.

Similarly the eyes give you a pleasant feeling when they locate a beautiful sight and the same eyes give you a different feeling when they fall on a repulsive thing. Similar is the case with other senses. It is thus established that our senses which include even the mind are the cause of pain and pleasure. When we control them we are free from both. Moreover they are transient. So the advice of the Lord, bear them patiently, as none of them has come to exist for ever.

Yam hi na vyathayantyete purusham purusharashabh,
Samaduhkhsukham dhiram so'mritatvaay kalpate [15].

Meaning—O! Best of men, the man to whom pain and

pleasure are alike and who is not disturbed by these (contacts) and who is steadfast is fit for immortality.

Commentary—Though man is mortal but he has long been longing for immortality. If not through body he wants to live through his deeds. It is said in Sanskrit that who has earned respectability never dies—'Kirtir yasya sa jivati'

Thus here is one way of earning immortality. Do not hanker after the objects of senses, be steadfast in all your deeds and treat pain and pleasure alike.

Another interpretation of gaining immortality (amarttva) is what is called salvation or 'Moksha'. A person eschewing the pleasure of senses and putting on equal footing both the pain and pleasure, is on way to achieve salvation and become immortal, having mingled with absolute spirit (Parmaatmaa) by virtue of his possessing the above qualities.

The another interpretation is more acceptable.

Naasato vidyate bhaavo naabhaavo vidyate satah,
Ubhayorapi drishto'antastvanayostattvadarshibhih [16].

Meaning—That which is non existent or unreal has no existence; that which really is cannot go out of existence. The final truth about these both has been pereceived by the seers of truth.

Commentary—The body is unreal so it can not exist for ever but the spirit (Atma) being real can not cease to be. It may change the form through which it manifests. Soul is thus an imperishable self and therefore none should lament on its perishable abode which goes on changing.

Avinaashi tu tadvidhi yen sarvamidam tatam
Vinaashamavyasyaasaya na kashchitkartumarhati [17].

Meaning—Know That to be indeed imperishable by Which all this (the entire universe) is pervaded. None can bring about the destruction of This immutable substance.

Commentary—The indestructibility of the inner reality or spirit (Atma) has been underlined here. This spirit is said to pervade every thing because this is part and parcel of the Super Spirit (Parmaatama) which is omnipresent. The superiority of spirit (Atma) over the body is again tried to be established in a different way.

This assertion is further substantiated in the Gita when the Lord says later that God has made abode of His in the heart of every body—'Ishwarah sarvbhutaanaam hriddeshe Arjun Tishthati.' Again, it is My own part which is in every being—'Mamaivaansho jeevaloke jeebhootosanaatanah.

Antvanat eme deha nityasyoktaah, shareerinhah.
Anaashino'prameyasya tasmaadudhyasva Bharat [18].

Meaning—All these forms (bodies) belonging to the imperishable unparalleled and eternal soul are said to be perishable therefore fight Arjun.

Commentary—Where is the question of shirking from fighting when it is established that the body in any case is perishable and that dwelling in it is imperishable and eternal and haivng no parallel (in its capacity to exist and pervade every thing)

ya enam vetti hantaaram yaschainam manyate hatam.
Ubhau tau na vijaneetto naayam hanti na hanyate [19].

Meaning—Both who takes the soul to be the slayer and he who takes it to be slain are ignorant, for verily it neither slays nor is slain.

Commentary—In fact the self or spirit is free from any attributes. All attributes belong to the body. The spirit in its real nature stands only the witness of every thing. It is thus beyond it to kill or even to be killed.

The Lord gradually preparing Arjuna for the battle by emphasizing in different ways the perishable nature of body and the enternal character of the soul.

Na jaayate mriyate va kadaachi-
nnaayam bhootvaa bhavitaa vaa na bhooyah,
Ajo nityaah shaashvto'yam puraanho
Na hanyate hanyamaane shareere [20].

Meaning—It (the soul) is never born nor does it ever die nor once having been it ceases to be. It is unborn, eternal, everlasting and primeval and even though the body is slain it is never subjected to slaying.

Commentary—The eternal imperishable nature of the self remains unaffected by the going on in the body it is inhabiting, thus the immutable, eternal life continues to be the same through the ever changing phases of the frames which it takes.

Thus the body is subject to death by killing or otherwise but the soul dwelling in it remains ever the same.

Vedaavinaashinam nityam ya enamajamavayam,
Katham sa purushah, Parth kam ghaatayati hanti kam [21].

Meaning—O! Arjun how does the man who knows it to be indestructible, eternal, unborn and undying, slay any body or cause any one to be slain?

Commentary—It is by repetition of the same truth in divergent ways that the Lord wants to establish in Arjuna's consciousness the futility of death or killing. Soul is immortal, so how Aryuna who is knowledgeable can attribute anything of perishable nature to an everlasting thing?

Vaasaansi jirnhaani yatha vihaay
Navaani grihnhaati naro' paraanhi
tathaa shareeraanhi vihaay jeernha
Nyanyaani sanyaati navaani dehee [22].

Meaning—As a man discards worn out clothes and takes new ones, So the dweller in this body (the soul) discards worn out bodies and takes others which are new.

Commentary—It is for the first time that the Lord takes a very simple and commonplace example to illustrate the actual relation between body and soul and at the same time the real meaning of a natural happening which is dreaded as death. The relationship between that of a dress and the body which wears it. The body is nothing more than the garment of the soul and as the body often discards the worn out dresses for new ones, so the soul discards the old or uninhabitable bodies for new and fresh ones. This is an oft-quoted verse for its down to earth approach and simplicity of putting the things in a language discernible even by an ordinary person.

The death has completely been made a regular, natural but at the same time a fearless phenomenon as simple as changing of clothes.

Nainam chhindanti shastraanhi nainam dahati paavakah.
Na chainam kledyantyaapo na shoshayati maarutah [23].

Meaning—Weapons are incapable of cleaving him, fire of burning him, water of wetting him and wind of drying him off.

Commentary—Here the example of fire, water and wind is worth noting. The body is supposed to be composed of 'panch tattwaas' (five elements). They are earth, water, fire, sky and wind. Sky and earth have little but the rest three can have devastating effect on the body. But as the soul is made of none of them so it is beyond them to touch it what to talk of causing any damage to it. The self is transcendental and is thus uninfluenced by anything of this world.

The mention of weapons is also not out of context though they appear some what incongruous as they are not among the elements of nature.

Their occupying the first position in narrating the probable factors of destructions owes to the apprehension of Arjuna that his weapons may mutilate the bodies of his kinsmen as well as of his revered masters thus earning for them an untimely and useless death.

Acchedyo'ayamdaahyo'yamakledyao'shoshya eva cha
Nityah sarvgatah shthaanheurachalo'yam sanatanah [24].

Meaning—It is incleavable it is fire proof, it is impervious of water and undriable as well. It is eternal, all pervading, immovable, constant and everlasting.

Commentary—The imperishable as well as eternal nature of soul has been dwelt upon in this verse. It is almost elaboration of the points made in the preceding verse.

Avyakto'yamachintyo'yamavikaryoay'muchyate,
Tasmaadevam viditvainam naanushochitumarhasi [25].

Meaning—It is unmanifest, unthinkable, unchangeable. Thus knowing this as such you need not grieve (for the death for your dear ones).

Commentary—The soul may not be manifest like the body it inhabits but is certainly greater than all manifestations, thoughts may not analyse them but it is greater than all minds. It is no doubt unchanging but it is the supreme reality worth striving to know in its different dimensions, a task which is indeed impossible for a human to perform.

Ath chainam nityajaatam nityam va manyase mritam
Tathaapi twam mahaabaaho naivam shochitumarhasi [26].

Meaning—And o Arjuna even if thou regard it as constantly taking birth and constantly dying, you need not grieve as you do.

Commentary—The Lord is coming to a common-place approach which will be evident in the following verse.

Jaatasya hi dhruvo mrityurdhruvam janm mritasya cha
Tasmaadaparihaarye'rthe na tvam shochitumarhasi [27].

Meaning—The death of him who is born is certain and the birth of him who is dead is certain as well. It does not therefore, proper for you to grieve over the inevitable.

Commentary—The futility as well as bankruptcy of Arjun's thinking has been brought out in these lines. When you see yourself, people dying and coming to existence every day, nay, the every hour, every moment where is the scope of lamenting for them who are likely to be slain.

Avyaaktaadeeni bhootaani vyaktamadhyaani Bharat
Avyaktnidhanaanyeva tatra kaa parivedana [28].

Meaning—O Bharat! All being are unmanifest in the beginning (before they are born) they are manifest in the middle-state (i.e. during there physical existence) and are unmanifest again at end (i.e. after their death). What cause is there for lamentation.

Commentary—An ordinary man does not know where does a creature come from and where does it go or what happens to it after death though it is very much there in unmanifest form as the self never cease to exist; he knows only about the manifest form, about the physical existence of it during its life-span on this planet. So when the two third part is unmanifest and only one third is manifest, why to bother about the last one third? If it has gone unmanifest it will certainty manifest again.

Aashcharyavatpashyati kashiciden—
maashcharyavadvadati tathaiva chaanyah.
Ashcharvachchainamanyah, shrinhoti
Shrutvaapyenam ved na chaiva kashchit [29].

Meaning—Some perceives it as wonder, some likewise

speaks of it as wonder, another hears of it as a wonder but even on hearing of it some do not understand it.

Commentary—Here the Lord describes the special trait of the self. Its nature has been explained as far as possible by Lord Krishna in the preceding verse. By that itself the wonderful nature of the self is evident. It is wonderful no doubt for many. But the real trouble is that even after getting full explanation of it many fail to understand it. Is Lord apprehensive of the fact that even Arjuna having heard so much about it has not been able to fully comprehend it.' No wonder if it is so. There is a line in Kathopanishad which means that discourse is no way to know it—'Naayamaatma pravachanenn labhyah (kath. 1.2.22)

This is in no way a digression from the path Krishna has set in to convince the mighty archer of the futility of body and the significance of the soul. He just further emphasizes its importance by maintaining that its full comprehension is not that easy. It will require a direct experience of the Supreme to fully understand it. And this is, what happens ultimately. The Lord is compelled to show his 'Viraat' swarup (the mighty form) to his disciple by first endowing him with divine sight. The ordinary eyes could not stand it. This happens in the eleventh canto. This is nothing but the manifestation of the Supreme soul—the soul of souls.

Deheenityamvadhyo'yam dehe sarvasya Bhaarat,
Tasmaatsarvaanhi bhootaani na tvam shochitumarhasi [30].

Meaning—The dweller in the bodies of all can never be slain therefore it does not behove you to grieve for any creature whatsoever.

Commentary—Lord till this verse has in so many words tried to convince Arjuna about the mortality of body and the immortality of soul. Here he concedes finally by declaring that souls residing in all creatures is indestructible so he must not grieve for the destruction of any one human or non human.

The Lord has by now succeeded in driving out the fear of death from Arjuna's heart. Now with the following verse he starts to convince about the importance of duty he is called upon to perform.

The Gita is after all a gospel of duty. It believes in action as explained before. It is thus in fitness of things that the Lord switches over to the importance of duty.

Svadharmapi chaavekchya na vikampitumarhasi
Dharmyaaddhi yudhhaacchreyo'nyatkshatriyasya na vidyate [31].

Meaning—Besides, if you consider your own dharma (duty) you should not waver because there is nothing better for a kshatriya (a man of the warrior class) than a righteous war.

Commentary—'Dharm' does not always mean religion. It means duty as well. It is why it is said that the 'Dharm' of the fire is to burn, the 'Dharm' of a student is to study—'Kshatraanhaam svaadhyaay dharmah'. Thus while talking of the 'Dharm' of Arjun, Krishna does not mean the religion but the duty. He thus declares that the foremost duty of 'Kshatriya' is to indulge in a righteous war to restore the balance between the evil and the good forces.

From this very verse it is clear than Lord Krishna is not an advocate of war but he is at the same time not averse to a battle which is to restore jutice and equity. To allow the perpetrator of injustice and inequity is never welcome and the negative forces must not over power the positive ones. In this sense war is justified and even unavoiddalle. It is why the warrior caste Kshatriya has been entrusted with the special task of war—war against all that is undesirable, corrupt and unjust. Such kind of war is always beneficial not only for those for whom it is fought but also for those who fight. This point is elaborated in the following verse.

Ydrichyaachopapannam svargdwaaramapaavritam
sukhinah kshatriyaah Parth labhante yuddhmidrisham [32].

Meaning—Fortunate are the kshatriyaas O ! Arjuna who get such an unsought opportunity for war—an open door to heaven.

Commentary—It is believed that one who fights for a righteous cause is a hero of cosmic life and gets immediately an entry in to heaven if he is killed in the encounter. War, a righteous war is thus always beneficial for a warrior as victorious he is adorned with glory and vanquished and dead he enjoys happiness in heaven.

Athchchetvamiman dharmyam samgraamam na karishyasi,
Tatah svadharmam kirtim cha hitvaa paapmavaapsyasi. [33]

Meaning—Now if you desist from waging such a righteous war, them casting away your own duty and losing your reputation you will be liable for sin.

Commentary—Sin has different dimensions. In Krishna's eyes desisting from one's duty is also a sin.

Arjuna in the beginning was talking a lot regarding vice and vitue. Now he is made to realise that he himself was exposing himself to sin by neglecting to do his own duty i.e. to fight against injustice and oppression.

Arjuna at this time is running the risk of losing his fame by abstaining from fight. This point has been further emphasized in the following verse.

Akirtimchaapi bhootaani kathayeshyanti te'vyayam
Sambhaavitasya cha kritirmaranhaadatirichyate [34].

Meaning—Besides men will tell of your undying disgrace and for the one enjoying a noble station in life disgrace is worse than death.

Commentary—Shri Krishna with his uncanny approach towards the problem he is facing, is taking recourse to all possible ways open to him to persuade Arjuna not to desist from figting. It has been said in one of the sacred scriptures of Hinduism that the wise must take recourse to all possible means to get his mission achieved. These means may include peace, allurement and if need be punishment or threat 'Sam, dam aur dand vibhedaa'.

Shri Krishna has already taken recourse to peaceful methods, he has employed allurement even as a means when he talked of entering heaven by indulging in righteous wars. Now he is taking recourse to threat by making clear that in case he bows out of the battle people will start pouring infamy on him and this will amount to his virtual death.

The last line has become a famous quote for Sanskrit-scholars—'Sambhaavitasya cha kirtim marnhaadatrichyate.'

Bhayadaranhaaduparatam mansyante twam mahaarathaah. yesham cha twam bahumato bhootva yasyasi laghawam [35].

Meaning—The mighty warrior will deem that you have fled from the battle-field out of fear and those who held you in esteem will belittle you.

Commentary—The threat continues. Lord says that do not be a fool to think that the great archers assembled here will think that you have left the field out of compassion for the kinsmen. They will deem you a coward.

Avaachyavaadaanshcha bahoon vadishyanti tavaahitaah Nindantstav saamarthyam tato duhkhataram na kim [36].

Meaning—Your enemies will speak many unseemly words of you and will deride your strength. What can be more disgraceful than this?

Commentary—Speaking in the same vein Krishna goes proclaiming that it will be very disgracing of him when his enemies will start uttering unseemly words once he flees away from the battle-field.

Hato vaa praapsyasi svaragam jitvaa vaa bhokshyase mahim Tasmaaduttishth kaunteya yudhay kritnishchayah [37].

Meaning—If slain you will attain heaven, if victorious the soverignty of the earth, therefore arise O ! son of Kunti, resolved to fight.

Commentary—Again the allurement-part. He is a gainer in both ways. If killed in battle the gates of heaven are opened to him, if coming out victorious the kingdom is there to share with his rest brothers.

Sukhe dukhe same kritvaa laabhaalaabhau jayaajayau Tato yuddhaay yujyasva naivam paapmavaapsyasi [38].

Meaning—Having acquired equanimity take pleasure and pain, gain and loss, victory and defeat alike and get ready to fight, thus you will not incur sin.

Commentary—Mark the sudden departure. The real message of the Gita starts to unfold—the principle of equanimity and equality—equality in every respect, considering not only the human beings but all beings equal, considering pleasure and pain, gain and loss, friend and foes equal. This most important theory has been elaborated from time to time and extensively dwelt upon by Krishna in verses and chapters to follow. This is the real yoga of the Gita—equality. In this very chapter he will define yoga in this fashion—'Samatvam yog uchyate'—equality itself is yoga.

In fact as stated earlier the sole objective of the Gita is to make man's existence full of peace which is the only worth achieving mission in this life. It you become indifferent to friend and foe, victory and defeat, high and low; in other words if you consider all of them of similar nature—equal—then where is to scope to grieve and to nourish jealousy and envy or even uncalled for compassion, sympathy or love for any body? It is to be worth noting that it is total detachment which the Gita emphasises to practise. As told earlier the Gita teaches a practical way of life and living. It is the philosophy and at the same time a sacred doctrine of conducting oneself in this world of utter confusion, chaos, greed and selfcetredness.

But achieving this state is not that easy. It will necessitate a particular type of discipline which a man will have to develop. The mind will have to be trained in a way to respond to the above kinds of phenomena and persons in the way defined above. The help of mind is as essential as anything in gaining equanimity, to perceive equality every where.

One thing more is worth noting. Krishna declares that acting in this way you will incur no sin. To avoid sinning is no doubt essential. But how is it possible? The answer is straight and unambiguous; by practising indifference and equality you see through the real aspects of life with a broadened vision, the mundane and routine business of life any man's coming and going, circumstances being favourable or unfavourable lose meaning to you. Yes a man must not sin and you are not a sinner when you take a detached view of life doing nothing but doing every thing at the same time. This aspect will be further explained as the message of the Lord, is slowly but surely disclosed by Him to His discipline. The role of mind in however foremost as indicated earlier. Shri Krishna is coming to the same in the proceeding verse.

Esha te'bhihitaa saankhye budhiryoge tvimam shrinhu, budhya yukto yaya Paarth karmbandham prahaasyasi [39].

Meaning—Up till now what has been propounded is in terms of 'sankhya' (a branch of philosophy emphasizing the importance of knowledge—knowledge of body, soul and the super soul and their interactions) now hear in terms of mind-yoga (budhi-yoga) by joining yourself with the mind you will shake of completely the shackles of action.

Commentary—The last thing first. It is a firm belief in almost every faith that what you sow your reap. Action is bound to have a re-action. The cause and affect relationship has been recognized by almost every branch of philosophy and learning.

Hinduism believes that this is the theory which explains the man's coming in and going out of the world. In other words the acts he indulges in drags him again after he departs from the world to taste the fruits of them sweet or sour.

The Gita Tries to axe the very root of it. It says that actions can be so performed that they will not have a binding influence and the man doing his act in this way will have eternal liberation.

The hint was dropped in the commentary of the preceding verse itself. Now it is crystal clear that the yoga of the Gita is mind-yoga (mind the world 'budhiyog' in the previous verse). It is your rattaching yourself with mind in such a way that your actions fail to have a binding effect.

Yoga is certainly in simple words adding something to something or something with some thing. Here you are to add or attach yourself to an intelligent mind, indifferent and unattached to any thing or any body.

This point, the importance of particularly trained mind will be explained in details in the coming verses.

Nehaabhikramnashoa'ti pratyavaayo na vidyate,
Svalpamasya dharmasya traayate mahto bhayaat [40].

Meaning—There is no loss of efforts (put in the beginning and then eschewing them midway for some reasons) nor it has any adverse effect. Even a little practice of this Dharm protects from great fear.

Commentary—There is always every possibility that you start on certain practice or proceeds on certain path and abandon it abruptly. The Lord says that even if this happens; in this type of yoga-practice it does not render it useless. Whatever initial efforts are made in this connection are stored and at the same time there is no adverse effect of this discontinuances on the practising individual. This is a great guarantee as well as the most tempting bait put forward by the Lord for those who are inclined to follow the path he is advocating. He also adds that even a small practice of this yoga (dharm) protects one from great fear or danger.

Vyavasaayaatmika budhirekeh kurunandan
bahushakha hyanantaashcha budhyo'vyavasaayinaam [41].

Meaning—O Arjun here the resolute mind or intellect is only one (or in other words one pointed) but multibranched and endlessly diverse are the minds or intellects of them who lack resolution.

Commentary—The importance of mind or intellect is to be properly emphasized upon by the Lord for let no one forget that so diversely and differently interpreted yoga of Lord Krishna is essentially and basically mind-yoga.

The mind which is to achieve something is to be resolute and single pointed. It cannot be allowed to run in different directions like unfeigned horses of a chariot. It is exactly this what happens with the irresolute and indecisive persons. Their minds branch out in different directions and these branches are endless. They cannot concentrate on one point.

Thus the first requirement is a resolute and decisive mind. A real 'yoga' is possible only with such a mind.

Yaamimaam pushpitaam vaacham provadyantyavipashchitah
vedvaadrataah, Paarth naanyadasteeti vaadinah [42].
Kamaatmanah svargaparaa janmkarmphalpradaam
kriyaavisheshbahulaam bhogaishwaryagatim prati [43].
Bhogaishvaryaprasaktaanaam tayaapahritchetsaam
Vyavasaayaatmika budhih shamaadhau na vidheeyate [44].

Meaning—O Parth! Those filled with desires and devoted to (only) vedaas and who look upon heaven as their goal and insist that their is nothing (worth attaining) except heaven are undiscerning. They speak flowery words (to fool others) and recommend many acts of different kinds to attain enjoyment and prosperity, the certain result of such acts is rebirth. Those who are thus deeply attached to worldly enjoyment and prosperity and whose minds are captivated by such flowery words cannot attain the determinate mind fully concentrated on the supreme (i.e. they can not attain the state of 'samaadhi').

Commentary—Here the Lord denounces and ridicules them who take recourse to attractive speeches to attract people to perform the rituals and rites of the Vedaas to gain certain advantage here or here after. They convincingly declare that there is nothing more important than clinging to these rituals and rites. Lord maintains that these actions thus indulged in to attain prosperity during the life and heaven after death are the sure sourse of birth. Thus the cycle of birth and death never ceases for such people.

Not only this, their mind hankering after the enjoyment here and attainment of heaven after their departure from this world becomes indicisive and indeterminate and is unable to concentrate on one point or be at rest. It is always wandering; lacks in purpose and meandering in different and some times opposite directions fails to achieve 'Samaadhi' i.e. one pointedness and concentration on the Supreme.

The Lord appears to advise against the 'Vedas', yes it is true but in fact He is not against everything contained in the Vedas.

There are mainly two aspects of the Vedas—one is the 'karmakaand' part another concerns the 'mantraas' or hymns.

The 'karmakaand' concentrates on rituals as sacrifice ('yagya') etc. The main purpose is to gain prosperity here and heaven after the death.

The Lord, as he is against the desire-oriented action is clearly against this part of the Vedas. He will return again to this subject in a subsequent chapter where he will speak high of the 'yagyaas' whose basis is in the 'vedas'. This discourse will of course address those interested in the instant fulfilment of wishes but it will surely establish that He is not entirely against the 'Vedas'. But in these and following verses he does appear to denounce them. This however makes clear that he is not out and out against them but he is surely not to give much weight to the 'vedas,' eager as he is to create a new thesis of life and living, he is to discard much of the old and obsolete.

The fact is that the Gita appears at the third stage of Hindus' religious or spiritual evolution. The first being the Vedas and the second 'Upanishadas' itself. It is thus more akin, to 'upnishadas' than 'vedas'. In fact some of its verses are to be found in some of the 'upanishadas' especially in the 'Chhandogyopanishad'.

One, to be very honest, can not hold this brief for Krishna that He in not anti 'vedaas' as some commentators declare. As the aim of this commentary is not to back any school of thought (Sampradaaya) which distorted the Gita; this commentator does not hesitate to declare that at places His advices are quite at variance with those contained in the 'Vedas' and in his heart of hearts he is certainly against the 'Vedas'. It is His compulsion as well. He can not find favour with the people till they are engrossed in what is described in their most sacred and oldest doctrine, the 'vedas'.

Traigunhyavishayaa vedaa naishtraigunhya bhavaarjun.
Nirdvandvo nityasattvastho niryogkshem aatmvan [45].

Meaning—O Arjun ! The 'Vedas' concern themselves with the there 'gunhaas' but you do become free of these triple 'gunhaas'. You cast off dualities. Be ever firm in the eternal existence, be not concerned with 'Yog and Kshema' (or what has been attained and what is to be attainded) and be possessed of the self (Aatmvaan).

Commentary—There gunhaas are the three modes of nature—sat, Raj and tam. The Vedas are not free from them rather advocating the several rituals concerning wish-fulfilment they deeply indulge in 'Raja' and 'Tama' both being opposite to 'sat' the purest mode. Raj is a bit superior to 'tam' which is the worst of the three. 'Sat' stands for purification, holiness and sublimity, 'Raj' for arrogance, pride etc., and 'tam' for the undesirable qualities.

Here the denouncement of the 'Vedas' is explicit. Shri Krishna without mincing words declares that the man's mission is to rise even above the vedaas.

Yavaanarth udpaane sarvatah samplutodake,
***Taavan sarveshu vedeshu brahmanasya vijaanatah* [46]**

Meaning—An enlightened Brahmin has the same use for all the 'Vedas' as one standing at the side of a vast sheet of water spreading all over, has for a small well.

Commentary—The 'Vedas' here have been rendered useless for a Brahm-knowing enlightened person. When there is flood all over, what is the use of a well (of water)? Thus knowing the Brahma through intellect is getting a flood of water instead of a petty well.

Will now any one claim that the Lord is not against the 'Vedas'? He is. He is not. The 'Vedas' are at least useful for unenlightened Brahmins. Brahmin here does not denote a caste. One who knows Brahma is a Brahmin.

Karmanhyevaadhikaaraste maa phaleshu kadaachan
***ma karmphalhetrubhuramaa te sango'stvakarmanhi* [47].**

Meaning—Thou hast control over action but never over its fruits. Let not the fruit of action be the object, nor there be in thee any attachment to inaction.

Commentary—This is the oft' quoted shloka of the Gita. It aims at annihilating almost all anxieties. Men are always bothered about the result of their efforts and activities whether they are going to get good results or bad ones, whether their efforts are going to bear fruits or not. But the final outcome or result, as we know, is in unseen hands. So the Gita says why to worry about results, go on making your efforts sincerely, never bother about the outcome. If it goes to be good, it is all right, if it turns to be the opposite, where is your fault?

The Gita at the same time warns not to be inactive. Never, cease for a moment in doing your duties. It is why the advice to Arjuna, not to detach himself from the fight.

The Gita lays much emphasis on action, on efforts, on endeavour. In so many verses, from time to time, the Lord reminds, Arjuna of the importance of action.

Yogasth kuru karmaanhi sangam tyaktva Dhanajaya,
***sidhyasidhyoh samo bhootva samatvam yog uchyate* [48].**

Meaning—O winner of wealth (Dhananjaya) perform your actions dwelling in yoga, abandon attachment and be indifferent to success and failure for yoga is nothing but equality.

Commentary—The same vein available in the preceding verse is continuing i.e. you are to be equally receptive to success and failure. But here the path is shown to accomplice this impossibility. How can one react similarly to success and failure? By establishing one self in yoga, answers the Lord. Though yoga will be further defined and explained in courses of his discourse but here he clearly says that the very meaning of yoga is equality. Success and failure are the two sides of the same coin and both sides do not differ in any way.

Durenha hyavaram karm bhudhiyogaaddhananjaya,
Budhau sharanhamanvichcha, kripanhaah phalhetavah [49].

Meaning—Action is far inferior to yoga of the intellect Dhananjay. Thus seek refuge in the intellect; wretched are they who run after fruits.

Commentary—The mention of intellect is here of added significance. The yoga according to Krishna is actually a discipline of intellect owing to which it enables the man to view with equanimity both success and failure. The importance of such kind of intellect is vital to yoga. This will be further elaborated by the Lord.

Bhudhiyukto jahaateeh ubhe sukritdushkrite
Tasmaadyogaay yujyasva yogah karmsu kaushalan [50].

Meaning—one who is united with the intellect (i.e. one who use his intellect not to be bothered by success of failure) sheds both good and evil. Thus exert thyself for this yoga. Yoga is nothing but skill in action.

Commentary—As indicated earlier Lord again lays emphasis on the importance of a trained intellect which views success and failure not as good and evil.

As the intellect is unattached to action, caring little for the outcome; the one who is endowed with such intellect or trains one's intellect in such a way is free from the bondage of Karma (action) and thus sheds both good and evil in this life itself and enters the life after death free from all bondages.

Thus till now there is little doubt that yoga of Krishna is quite different from the traditional yoga. It is a simple training of intellect on the strength of which it detaches itself from to action and is indifferent to its outcome.

Yoga, in its crude form is of course addition of someone or something with someone or something. Here yoga is addition of an individual with his own (trained) intellect.

Karmajam budhiyuktaa hi phalam tyaktvaa maneeshinhah,
Janmbandhvinirmuktaah padam gachantyanaamayam [51].

Meaning—The wise men who are aided with the (right) intellect renounce the fruits of work without doubt and having achieved this they are liberated from the shackles of birth and attain a state devoid of misery.

Commentary—There is nothing new in this verse. The importance of developing a right intellect which is indifferent towards the outcome of human endeavours has been emphasized upon. A person with such intellect is freed from the cycle of birth and death and attains a place-divine where there is no pain, no suffering, no misery, but only bliss and blessings.

Yadaa te mokhalilam budhirvyatitarishyati
Tada gantaasi nirvedam shrotabyasya shrutasya cha. [52].

Meaning—When thy intellect crosses beyond the mire of delusion, then shalt thou gain indifference to what has been heard and what is to be heard.

Commentary—One is often bewildered and sometimes offended by what he hears about himself. The trained mind which transcends the dualty becomes endifferent to what has been said and what may be said in the future. This is real yoga, to become unattached to every thing seen, heard and unheard. This is possible when the intellect is disciplined in a particular way. This point is being emphasized upon time and again which underlines its undisputed importance.

Shrutivipratipannaa te yada sthaasyati nishchala,
Samaadhaavachala budhistada, yogamavaapsyasi [53].

Meaning—When thy intellect bewildered by conflicting statements shall stand unshaken and firm in meditation (on supreme) then shalt though attain the yoga.

Commentary—These conflicting statements often flow from the 'Vedas' or the 'upanishadas'. The Lord's message naturally transcends all the previous instructions. At many a place he never misses an opportunity to criticize Vedic knowledge. He has done so previously in this very chapter and will do so again in no uncertain terms.

Thus one of the important conditions to attain yoga (or to have a disciplined intellect) is to forget what the Vedas or the 'upanishadas' have propounded. The yoga as conceived by Krishna is to start on a clean slate. One at last reaches this conclusion—welcome or not.

Arjun Uvaach :

Sthitapragyasya kaa bhasha samaadhisthasya keshava,
Sthithdheeh, kim prabhaashet kimaaseet vrajet kim [54].

Meaning—Arjuna asked : What is the sign of a man of stable mind and established in samaadhi. How does the man of steady intellect speak, how he sits and how he moves.

Commentary—Arjuna by now appears to be fully aware of a self established and trained intellect, of a mind steadfast. It is why he wants to know the signs of such a person who has all these qualifications—his speech, his movement and most important of all, the posture of his sitting. The Lord may not answer the question point by point but will certainly dwell upon the important issues.

This may be noted at the very outset, that the Lord has coined a new word—'Sthitapragya'—for them whose intellect is steadfast and hardly to be influenced by the going in the inner self and the outer world. 'Sthitapragya' is in a sense the real yogi. The Lord will return to it again and again in the ensuing verses so the importance of this word must not be missed.

Shri Bhagwan Uvaach :

Prajahaati yadaa kaamasarvan Parth manogataan,
Atamnyevaatmana tushtah sthitpragyastadochyate [55].

Meaning—The Lord said, O Arjuna when a man completely abandons all cravings of the mind and when he is satisfied in the self through the self alone then he is said to possess a steady intellect (i.e. then he is 'sthitpragya').

Commentary—As hinted earlier Lord is hardly interested in meeting the queries of Arjun point by pint. He is to hammer the real point i.e. to be free from all desires and to seek peace and happiness not outside but with in one self through a trained intellect. The self itself is sufficient to provide all satisfaction if it has the co-operation of rightly tuned intellect. This is the real message of being satisfied in the self through the self.

Dukheshvanudvignmanaah sukheshu vigatsprih,
Vitraagbhayakradhah sthitdheermunruchyate [56].

Meaning—He who is unshaken in the midst of suffering and has no lust for pleasures and is free from passion, fear and anger is stable in mind ('sthitpragya').

Commentary—Remember 'equality is yoga' ('samatvam yog uchyate'). From whom pain and pleasure are equal is a 'sthitpragya', a yogi at the same time he is free form three most disastrous human weaknesses—passion or lust or attachment, fear and anger.

Yah sarvatraanabhisnehstattpraapya shubhashubham,
Naabhinandati na dveshti tasya pragyaa pratisthita [57].

Meaning—Who in every thing good or bad is without affection and neither rejoices nor recoils, his intellect is established.

Commentary—The main crux of this verse is the consistency of the out look and behaviour towards fellow men. The sense of equanimity in pain and pleasure is emphasised upon again. The consistency in behaviour with other persons implies that for him there is neither a friend nor a fow. He attaches undue importance to no body nor he is jealous of any body.

Yada sanharate chaayam kurmo'gaanieeva sarvashah,
Indriyanheendriyarthebhyastasya pragyaa pratishtita [58].

Meaning—When he draws away the senses from all their objects as a tortoise draws in his limbs from all directions in to his shell, then his intellect is established.

Commentary—The senses are uncontrolled because they are attracted automatically towards their objects i.e. eyes are drawn towards beautiful beings and scenes, ears towards melodious sounds be of men or women or the nature, similarly the nose is mad after fragrance, the tongue towards delicious dishes and what to talk of objects of sex towards which is drawn all senses.

A man of established intellect (a 'Sthitapragya') does not allow his senses to be thus drawn away toward their objects of enjoyment. Like a tortoise who at the hour of imaginary or real danger draws in all his limbs in to his shell.

Vishayaa vinivartante niraahaarasya dehinah,
Rasvarjam raso'pyasya param drishtvaanivartate [59].

Meaning—Even the abstention from food does not help in controlling the senses. The objects of sense of course cease to have any effect but the lust remains, eve the lust disappears when the supreme is seen.

Commentary—Now the focus switches over completely to the senses.

Different people take recourse to different means of controlling the senses, the most popular being the method of starving the body in order to weaken the senses. The Lord wants to draw home the point that this approach is simply ludicrous. The senses devoid of nourishment may weaken but the lust to enjoy persists. The Lord maintains that to drive away this lust one will have to be face to face with the supreme i.e. to establish in the self by meditation as the interview with the supreme is not that easy.

Yatato hyapi kaunuteya purushasya Vipashchitah,
Indriyanhi pramaatheeni haranti prasabham manah [60].

Meaning—Even the mind of the wise man who is trying hard to control their senses is carried away by these turbulent senses.

Commentary—The emphasis continues to be over the control of senses. The wise man endeavoring to have his control over them must not be over confident, the powerful senses are capable of carrying away his mind and force him to adulate in the enjoyment of sense-objects.

Taani sarvaanhi samyamya yukt aaseet matparah.
Vashe hi yasyendriyaanhi tasya pragyaa partishthita [61].

Meaning—having controlled them all, one must be firm in yoga (the connection with right intellect) and should wholly give up to Me for whose senses are subdued, his intellect is established.

Commentary—The emphasis upon the control of senses continues. But the warning is clear and sharp. Even yoga cannot help here. The dedication to the Lord is also essential. It is only with His help that one can subdue the unbraided senses and to repeat the same fact again only he is established in intellect (is 'sthitpragya') whose senses are under control.

Dhyaayato vishayaanpunshah samgasteshupajaayate
Sangaat samjaayato kaamah kamaatkrodho'bhijaayate [62].

Meaning—The man pondering the objects of the senses develops attachment to them, attachment gives birth to desire and from desire ensues anger.

Commentary—The dissidence from the sense-objects is not sufficient. Even pondering on them, thinking about them, is disastrous because such pondering necessarily results in a desire to enjoy them, the 'kam' (sex) and any hindrance in the fulfilment of such desire naturally results in anger. One who proves to be an obstacle in the fulfilment of desire or enjoyment of sex is to bear the burnt of anger. But this anger not necessarily harms only him towards whom it is directed. It certainly harms him also who nourishes it. This point is made clear in the following verse.

Krodhaadbhavai sammoh sammohatsmritivibhramah,
Smritibhransaadbhudhinaasho budhinaashatpranhasyati [63].

Meaning—Anger results in delusion, delusion gives birth to confusion of memory, from the confusion of memory, the intellect is destroyed and the destruction of the intellect causes the complete ruin.

Commentary—With the over excitement of mind owing to anger the mind loses its balance as a result of which reasoning-power is adversely affected. The anger thus gets the upper hand and a man with excited mind and disturbed reason can commit any such act which is suicidal to himself.

Raagdveshviyuktaistu vishayaanindriaishcharan,
Atmavashyairvidheyaatma prasadamadhigachchati [64].

Meaning—Whose senses are freed from attachment and aversion and who is self disciplined and enjoys the sense-objects remaining under complete control, attains delight.

Commentary—The attainment of peace and delight is craved by every one, rather delight includes the peace of mind. Real delight is actually the blessings of God.

The Lord here outlines the method to achieve this delight. The ways are similar—detachment and the control of senses in a way that they do not hanker after their objects.

The enjoyment of sense-objects is here however not totally forbidden, the only condition is that one must not associate with it. The senses which are fully indifferent towards their objects can very well enjoy them without being soiled in any way. For example if the eyes perceive a beautiful human frame but they do not become lustful, or indulgent, commit no sin and they are really non-indulgent.

Prasade sarvadukhaanaam hanirasyopajaayate,
Prasannchetso hyashu budhih paryavatisthate [65].

Meaning—With this delight all the sorrows of the person concerned vanish and the intellect of this delightful person becomes firmly established.

Commentary—The modern psychology also holds that in delight one achieves health. Most of the diseases are supposed to originate in a depressed mind. Many of a disease are psychosomatic i.e. the psyche (Mind) and soma (Body) both are involved in it.

Thanks must go to the writer of the Gita, who about five thousand years ago apperceived this truth. A happy mind not only pushes off most of the body-ills but is itself completely contented and thus fully established (in yoga). This state of being established in yoga is of paramount importance. Lord dwells at length on it in the ensuing verse.

Nastibudhirayuktsya na chaayuktsya bhaavana
Na chaabhaavayatah shantirashaantasya kutah sukham [66]

Meaning—One who is not established, lacks in intellect; he also does not possess a steady thought-pattern. One without a steady thought-pattern has no peace and man without peace cannot dream of happiness.

Commentary—As maintained in the preface itself, the Gita is a philosopy of a successful living. Peace is the first requirement of every human self and the Gita all though promises peace. All talks of detached action and behaviour, control of senses etc. aim at guaranteeing peace. And the peace is rightly the source of happiness in this verse. If one is devoid of peace where from he can hope of happiness?

Indriyanhaam hi charataam yanmanno'nuvidhiyate
Tadasya harati pragyaam vaayurnaavamivaambhasi [67].

Meaning—When one's mind is driven towards any of the wandering senses, his discriminatory power is carried away by it as a barge upon the water.

Commentary—on a turbulent sea a ship or barge is hardly steady. It is on the mercy of raging waves and is carried away by wind in different directions.

Similarly if the mind associates itself with any of the wandering senses, his discrimination fails and he is bound to fail prey of that particular sense and do the deeds which will result in miseries as well as shackles.

Tasmaadyasya mahaabaho nigriheetaani sarvashah
Indriyaanheeindriyaarthebhyastasya pragya pratisthitaa [68].

Meaning—Thus whose senses are completely withdrawn from their objects his intellect is established.

Commentary—The association of senses with their objects is continued to be decried upon. In former verse the enjoyment by senses in a detached manner has been advocated. But the ideal state is the withdrawal of senses from all sense-objects. This is described as the highway to an established intellect.

Ya nisha sarvbhootanuum tasyam jaagarti sanyamee
yasyaam jaagrati bhootani sa nisha pasyhyato muneh. [69].

Meaning—That which is night to all creatures there in the self-controlled keeps awake. In which all creatures keep awake, is night for the seer.

Commentary—Different and divergent meanings have been credited to this simple verse. Many say that the night really means the darkness of ignorance. Thus darkness does not affect the self-controlled and according to them the transient worldly happiness which is like a day-light for the ignorant and in which he awakes or relishes, is actual night or darkness for the selfrealized man.

But this is a farfetched meaning. Every one knows that the quiet hours of night are conducive for meditation and other mental activities. Those who have nothing worth to pursue sleep the night out, but the seers and knowledgeable do not. It is just natural that who will have a night-keeping will rest during the day when the lesser selves will be madly pursuing their material ends.

This is no secret that yoga is better practised during nights so it is pointless to provide a farfetched meaning of this verse.

Aapoormaanhamachalapratishtam—
Samudramaapah pravishanti yadvat,
Tadvatkaama yam pravishanti sarve,
Sa shaantimaapnoti na kaamkaamee [70].

Meaning—He attains peace whose all desires enter in to him as the waters (of all rivers) inter the ever full and unmoved sea, not he who hankers after sense-enjoyments.

Commentary—Again the importance of taking the services of senses without attachment. He sees but he does not see. He eats but he does not know the taste of the morsels he is fed upon.

He enjoys the sense-objects without in any way being disturbed by them. Actually he is desireless but as he is to dwell in this material world he enjoys whatever he gets without allowing it to affect him in any way. The real peace lies there. As he is not disturbed by the senses or desires, his peace is also not disturbed.

The simile of the sea is very appropriate. The level of seawater hardly changes even though thousand of rivers continuously pour their water in it.

Vihaay kamaanyah sarvaanpumaanshcharati nisprih,
Nirmamo nirhankaarah sa shantimadhigachhati [71].

Meaning—He who relinquishes all desires and moves devoid of attachment and ego, attains peace.

Commentary—Peace is important as maintained earlier.

The first and foremost objective of the Gita is to provide the man with peace. Here is given another recipe but not very different from the original ones. One is to give up all desires. The state of desirelessness is the state of peace. He must not have the sense of 'I' and mine.

Then what is to disturb his peace?

The state of disirelessness however does not maan that one allows one self to be starved and keeps himself devoid of all enjoyment. The message is straight and simple. He does not hanker after the desires but he satisfies them all and this satisfaction comes without any attachment.

He is certainly not full of ego nor he himself is to be friendly or passionately attached to any body.

Eshabraahmi sthtitih Paarth nainam praapya vimuhyate Sthitvaasyaamantkaale'pi Brahmnirvaanhamrichhati [72].

Meaning—O Parth this is the state of the God-realized one. Having attained it one is not deluded. Established in this state, even at the time of departure from this world, he attains divine bliss.

Commentary—The state described in the preceding verse is the state of God-realization.

The Indian thinking believes in the life after death. The verse therefore maintains that if one continues to remain in this state at the time of leaving this world he will be free from the chain of birth and death and will live with the supreme Himself as a liberated soul.

The Gita thus advocates a life with long vigil to see that one does not indulge in sense-enjoyment, does not develop attachments, is free from ego and refrains from hankering after desires.

Om Tatsaditi Shrimadbhagawadgitasoopanishatsu Brahmvidyaayaam yogshashtre shrikrishnarjunsamvade saankhyayogo naam dvitiyo'dhyaayah. [2]

Thus in the Upanishad sung by the Lord in the glorious Bhagavad Gita in the science of the supreme, the scripture in yoga, the dialogue between Shri Krishna and Arjuna ends the second chapter entitled the yoga-knowledge (sankyayoga).

CHAPTER III

Arjun Uvaach :

Jyaayasi chetkarmanhaste mata budhirjanaardan
Tatkim karmanhi ghore maam niojayasi Keshava [1].

Meaning—**Arjun Said :** O Janaradan if thou holdest he intelligence superior to action, why then dost thou spur me to this dreadful deed, Keshava?

Commentary—The query of Arjun is quite natural. Krishna in a bid to stir Arjuna to action—to fight the 'Kauravas' in battle field—has preached the importance of action in the beginning of the second canto. He deprecates inaction in no uncertain terms especially in shloka 47 where he maintains that thou must not be associated with no-work. He even admonishes him for his unmanliness in refusing to participate in the war. But all of a sudden he switches his emphasis over to the application of intelligence. In 'shlokas' 49, 50, 51 and 52, he especially dwells upon the significance of intelligence. It is why Arjuna wonders that if intelligence stands superior to action then why he is pestered and pressurized to plunge in to action, even that of killing his kith and kin, superiors and seniors in age, knowledge and relation.

But Arjun fails to grasp the message which is very clearly conveyed in the concluding shlokas that this intelligence is just required to perform the action without any attachment. This is actually what is termed as real yoga i.e. adding different things together. Here the things to be added together are only deed and intelligence. Deed must be backed by a sharp intelligence which enables the doer to be so detached from the deed he performs that he does not become responsible for the fruits that are expected to follow. Yoga, is certainly defined in the Gita in different forms depending on the circumstances under which the lesson is imparted by the Master, but yoga of the Gita is certainly 'Budhi-yoga' (combination of action and intelligence). Krishna himself especially mentions the 'Budhi-yog' in shloka 49 where He says—'Durenhahyavarm karm Budhiyogaat Dhananjaya' (The action is far inferior to this 'Budhi-yoga'—the combination of intelligence and action).

Let us understand for ever that real yoga propounded in the Gita is this significant addition of intelligence to our action because the aim of the Gita is to free the man from the unwelcome fruits of attachment with one's action and this is only possible when he performs his works without attachment. And here it is that his intelligence comes to his rescue. It helps in reaching this stage of detachment.

This is why the Lord bestows laurels on intelligence which baffles Arjuna and prompts him to ask this question.

Vyaamishrenheva vaekyen budhim mohayaseeva me,
Tadekam vad nishchitya yen shreyo'hmaapnuyaam [2].

Meaning—Thou bewilder my mind by this confused speech, so tell me then decisively the only one discipline by which I may obtain the highest good.

Commentary—Mark the discipl laying the same charge of indecisiveness which his Master had laid on him. He tells him in no uncertain words to tell him decisively which is beneficial to him—action or intelligence—and not to confuse him by His mingled statement.

Shree Bhagawaan Uvaach :

Loke'smindvividhaa nishtha pura prokta Mayaanagh,
Gyaanyogen saankhyaanaam karmyogen yoginaam [3].

Meaning—**The Lord said :** O sinless one, in this world two fold of spiritual discipline was enunciated by Me in the past. In the case of the saankhya—yogis, this discipline proceeds along the path of knowledge. In the case of the karmyogi, it proceeds along the path of action.

Commentary—The word saankhya has been introduced for the first time in the Gita. It requires a bit of explanation, 'Saankhya' has been in India a path of knowledge-seekers. They contemplate on the nature of the universe—its origin and its importance as well as the forces or force which created it. They have little to do with action or 'karma'. They are in other words philosophers trying to acquire more and more knowledge about not only the world and universe but also about the soul (Atma) and the super soul (Parmatma).

They are of course in a sense recluse with little relation with the day-to-day struggle of a house-holder who works not only for him and his family but also maintains these knowledge-seekers by the fruits of his labour and endeavours.

The Lord accepts here the importance of both. There must be a body of persons investigating the secrets of life and nature, man and God, but at the same time there must be a body of doers. But ultimately he will establish the superiority of the latter over the former and for doing it he is after enunciating a new form of yoga—karm-yoga where the intelligence is so applied to the day-to-day work that the work does not become be all and end all of life; it is done because it is essential for existence and it is done with ulter detachment, so that the doer is free from the effects of karma (work) which are bound to follow in an ordinary course. It is a common knowledge that there exists a cause and effect relationship in this world. If there is a cause the effect is bound to follow. If you commit some sin you are bound to suffer. But if the commitment of sin (like the killing of people in the ensuing Mahabharat-battle) becomes essential and is committed in the most detached way, the suffering fails to follow.

Na karmnhamanarambhanniashkarmyam purushosnute,
Na cha sanyasanadeva sidhim samadhigacchati [4].

Meaning—The mere abstaining from action one does not achieve non-action, nor by mere renunciation one attains the state of perfection (sidhi).

Commentary—It is generally believed that by doing nothing and sitting idly one really does not do any thing.

Similarly it is maintained that renunciation-'Sanyas'-is the only gateway to perfection-state i.e. sidhi.

The Lord denounces both. In fact his theory is that one is never idle. He is always doing something of this sort or that.

Similarly converting himself in to a recluse or embracing 'sanyas' is no guarantee of perfection or 'sidhi'. Even a recluse can be a way-ward. 'Sanyas' may result in perfection or 'sidhi' but that is not the only regal road to it. He wants to underline the fact that the only way to have the best of both the worlds is 'karmyog' i.e. doing every thing with detachment. In this way his earthly existence also becomes comfortable and ultimately having nothing accumulated as a result of non indulging in action he enters the stage of perfection free from all bondages.

Na hi kashchitkshanhampi jaatu tishatyakarmkrit,
Kaaryate hyabashah karm sarvah prakritijairgunhaih [5].

Meaning—None remains inactive even for a moment. All are helplessly driven to action by the characteristics of nature.

Commentary—The theory propounded in the preceeding 'shloka' is expanded in no uncertain terms here. The nature is so designed that it does not allow any body to remain inactive. Even by doing nothing we are doing something. Are we breathing or not? Do we attend to natural calls or not? Does even a recluse eat or drink or not and for that does he move from house to house to collect arms or not? Do we a trample upon or not on ants and other insects while moving? Do we scratch or body or not while we feel like it? And finally is or mind free even for a moment? Is it always doing something or not? Is it ever thought—free? The world has been designed in such a way with a driving force called nature that none right from a tiny being to a huge elephant or monstrous-like creatures of sea are not free even for a moment from acting or doing this or that. Even in our sleep we are not free from action. The dreams are always driving our mind from this thought to that, from this scene to that. And more often than not these dreams compel the body to react according to their nature. After all what happens in case of nightmares? Do we arise perspiring and perplexed or not?

Karmendriyanhi sanyamaya ya aaste mansa smaran,
Indriyarthanvimudhatma mithyacharah sa uchyate [6].

Meaning—He is a hypocrite and of deluded intellect who outwardly restrains the organs of action but dwells mentally on the objects of senses.

Commentary—As stated earlier mind is never free. One may not be outwardly doing anything doning the garb of a 'sanyasi' but his senses may be dwelling on their objects of pleasure e.g. he might he contemplating the beauty of a woman he has just seen or he may be day-dreaming to enjoy a delicious food to-day or tomorrow and thus watering his mouth.

Such a person's intellect is certainly deluded and he is indulging in hyporcisy.

Yastwindriyaanhi manasa niyamyaarabhathe'ryun,
Karmendriyaih karmyogamasaktah sa vishishyate [7].

Meaning—O Arjun one who controlling the senses through the mind and remaining unattached engages oneself with the organs of action in 'karm-yoga', excels.

Commentary—Here two things have been emphasised upon. The fist is the control of senses i.e. eyes, ears, nose etc. and the second is the performance of karmyoga with the help of sense organs (karm indriyaih) in an unattached way.

The senses are supposed to be controlled by mind but how this feat is achieved has not been explained. But later at some stage the method to control the senses have been fully elaborated. We shall have to wait till we come to that part of the sacred book. For the time being it is sufficient to suggest that mind is to a great extent capable of controlling the senses. It is a common-knowledge that senses in themselves are hardly effective unless backed by mind. If the mind is engaged otherwise or dwelling upon some pleasant or disturbing thought, we fail to see something which passes before our very eyes, fail to listen a sound that may be directed towards us. Thus, mind has much to do with senses and if mind is controlled through proper training, the senses can be tamed to a great extent.

The second aspect is very clear. The organs of actions like hands, feet tongue etc. are to be engaged in action, may not in simple action but 'karmyog' in a detached way. The mention of both karmyog and detachment is simply to emphasise the point, the Lord is making out. In fact the very fact of detachment makes an actin (karm), karmyoga i.e. yoga of actin. One should not fail to notice that the word detachment is emphasised upon repeatedly. One must have understood by now that the detachment is the real essence of Gita's karmyog. By actin in a detached manner one does not allow the senses to register deep expression of actions and this makes one perfect, free (or 'mukt'). In other words by engaging oneself in this way in day-to-day actions, one is not designed to reap the consequences of what he sows. He is doing nothing even by doing everything.

Niyatam kuru karm twam karm jyaayo hyakarmanhah,
shareeryaatraapi cha te na prasidhyedakarmnhah [8].

Meaning—Perform your allotted duty. Action is certainly superior to inaction. Neglecting action you cannot even ensure the survival of your body.

Commentary—The Lord Krishna almost for the first time sets at rest all controversies surrounding 'sanyas' (renunciation) and action.

The Gita as maintained in the preface has been subjected to interpretations as suited to the different cult-leaders. More often than not it has been called a gospel of sanyas (inaction) especially by those believing in and following this cult. It has certainly been a bone of contention whether the Gita preaches renunciation (sanyas) or action (karm).

The Lord will certainly dwell upon it in some more verses to follow in ensuing chapters but here he very categorically underlines the supremacy of action over inaction. He tells in no uncertain terms that action is superior to inaction. He goes as for as to tell the vital truth that even your survival is at stake if you take recourse to inaction. An actionless man can at most lead a vegetable-existence. Indispensability of action is established beyond an iota of doubt in this verse.

The Lord does not leave one to grope in to dark about the work one is supposed to perform.

He directs to do whatever work is attached to you. Most of the dissatisfaction and even depression arise due to one's attaching least importance to his or her work. The pasture on the other side of the fence is always greener. As told earlier, the Gita preaches a way of peaceful life and it is why the Lord advises to do whatever duty is allotted to you (certainly till one finds a more important one because no body and at least the Lord can deny one's evolution or a better chance in life and career).

This allocation of duty can be in any way. If we take in to consideration the time when the Gita came in to being one naturally thinks of the 'varnhaashram' which is nothing more or less than division of work. A Brahmin is to perform ygyaas etc., a 'kshatriya' (the warrior) is to fight the enemies, a 'vaishya' (the business-man) is to transact business and there are others to till the land and help the others in performing their duties. Here, there is no question of caste. There have been examples when 'kshatriyaas' and 'shudraas' became Brahmins and Brahmins become warriors. The writer of the great epic Ramayana, Valmiki is remembered more as a Brahmin than a 'shundra' which he was before having been inunciated in to the art of learning and devotion by some 'risis' (wise men).

In the modern context also it is equally true. A doctor is to act as a doctor and an engineer as an engineer. Both should consider their duties no less important than other's. A farmer should be as content as an industrialist and a clerk should feel as dignified as an officer (certainly no body bars him from becoming an officer if he can).

The infailable message of these lines is to be active and active in the field of one's domain of work. Action far surpasses inaction and no action is inferior to another. What a peaceful way to live!

Yagyaarthaatkarmanho'nyatra Loko'yam karmbandhnah,
Tadartham karm kaunteya muktsangah samaachara [9].

Meaning—Excepting works performed for 'yagya', this world of men is in bondage to action. For the sake of 'yagya' perform your duty, O son of Kunti (Arjun) in a detached way.

Commentary—Here the discourse takes a sudden 'u' turn. Till now the lord had been talking of duties etc. and of acting in a detached way. The religious rite of any kind had not come in to focus. But here it comes in a big way.

He clearly states that all duties not performed for 'yagya' leads to bondage. It also in other way indicates that whatever you earn or get from your work, keep in mind that you are going to perform yagya with it (or with a part of it certainly).

He therefore advises to act only with a view to perform yagya and of course even this action is also to be free from attachment. This radar of detachment is to be taken for granted in any action as the main objective of the Gita is to free the man from the bondage of action (action which is mandatory for every body as maintained earlier by the Lord) and this can be achieved by acting in a detached way only.

But what is this 'yagya'? The origin of 'yagya' is traced to the Vedas. The Vedas attach much significance to yagya. It usually means offerings in the fire to be consumed by it and then transferred by the same fire to the different gods whom these offerings are meant for. Usually grains of different kinds mingled with processed butter ('ghee') are thrown in to a pool of fire but during the vedic periods even animals especially horses were also offered to the fire for onward transport. These animals were usually cut in to pieces before being thrown in to fire. These offerings were done with the chanting of 'mantraas'. Later on this practice of burning animals was abandoned and offerings consisted of only grains mingled with different kinds of roots and also small pieces of sandle-woods mingled with 'ghee'.

'Yagyaas' were supposed to fulfil the wishes of those who perform them. Yagyas are performed even these days. They can be either at large scale—mass yagyaas—in which tons and tons of offerings are consumed in a number of pools of fire or individual in nature where only one man performs it by offering in to fire, quantities of different ingredients mixed together.

The reference to 'yagya' in the Gita has been termed by me as a 'U' turn owing to the fact the Gita has decried the Vedas in no uncertain terms (refer to verses 42, 45 and 46 of canto II). The Gita is thus supposed to be anti—'Vedas' and this is but natural because it came close on the wheels of 'Upanishads' which have sprung after the Vedas and were called 'Vedaantaas' (end of the 'Vedas').

It is nothing less than surprising that the Gita dwells at length on 'yagyas' in this canto as well as in the following one and describe them as a means of wish-fulfilment.

It is a different thing that it does not limit itself to conventional form of 'yagya' i.e. offering in to fire but also talks of unconventional ones in the next canto. But here, it unmistakably dwells on the conventional form only.

Sahyagyaah prajaah shrishtwaa purovaach prajaapati,
Anen prasvishyadhwamesh wo'stwishtkaamdhuk [10].

Meaning—Having created men along with 'yagya' at the beginning of the creation, the Lord of creation (Brahma) said: "By this (Yagya) you shall prosper and this may bring the fulfilment of desires".

Commentary—The significance of yagya has been further underlined. The Lord maintains that men and 'yagya' were created together and the latter was the source of former's prosperity and fulfilment of all kinds of wishes.

Devaanbhaawayataanen Te deva bhaawayantu wah,
Parasparam bhaawayntah, shreyah paramwaapsyatha [11].

Meaning—Through this (yagya) foster the gods and let the gods foster you. Thus fostering one another attain the supreme good.

Commentary—The verse takes for granted the existence of gods. This does not talk of one God but of gods. These gods are supposed to get sustenance from 'yagya' performed by men and in return they are capable of granting them prosperity and fulfill their wishes.

Gods are certainly more evolved beings of creation and their existence is beyound doubt for those who have experienced it. Sure, they are not seen but to be not seen is not to be not in existence. There are many things in this world we do not see but they do exist. Who can see the wind but who will deny its existence? Who sees the electricity?

Certainly they are experienced and this is a sure proof of their existence. Similarly presence of gods is also experienced and has been experienced by many.

There are lesser beings and higher beings than men in this universe but they are often formless but they can even take forms if they so desire. This is based on personal experience of the writer of these lines.

Ishtaanbhogaanhi wo devaa daasyante yagyabhaavitaah,
Tairdattaanapradaayaibhyo yo bhunkte sten ewa sah, [12].

Meaning—Fostered by 'yagya', the gods will grant desired enjoyment. He who enjoys the enjoyment granted by them by not giving a part of them in return is nothing less than a thief.

Commentary—Performance of 'yagya' is thus made mandatory by the Lord, whatever riches and other blessings we enjoy is granted by gods and if we do not part with some of them for their sake, we are bound to be charged with the offence of theft.

Yagyashishtaashinah santo muchyante sarvkilbishaih,
Bhunjatete twagham papa ye pachantyaatmkarnhaat [13].

Meaning—The righteous who partake of what is left of the yagya are absolved of all sins. But the evil eat sin who cook for themselves alone.

Commentary—Whatever left after performing 'yagya', after rightful offerings made to gods are blessed by them and after partaking these remains man is naturally freed from all sins. But who eat food (or get it prepared) only with the purpose of satisfying their own appetite are sinful and eat nothing but sin.

Needless to add that the quality of the mind depends on the qualities of food we partake. The remains of 'yagya' having been blessed with the gods are stuff of superior qualities and they make our minds far superior than those of others.

Annaadbhawanti bhoottaani parjnyaadannsambhawah,
yagyaadbhawati parjanyo yagyah karmsamudbhawah [14].

Meaning—It is food through which creatures come into being. Rain is responsible for production of food and rain is caused by 'yagya'. The 'yagya' is dependent on action.

Commentary—'Yagyas' performed at large scale or even by a number of different individuals form clouds due to smokes emitted by them and these clouds offer rains. These rains are certainly a significant source of production of foods and foods bring forth life or at least sustain it. But this yagya cannot be performed without action because where will you find the materials of yagya if you don't act and earn?

The significance of 'yagya' is once more emphasised but in a more subtle way.

Karm Brambhodbhawam vidhi Bramaksharsamudbhavam,
Tasmaatsarvagatam Bramh nityam yagye pratishthitam [15].

Meaning—Work know to be born of Brahma the creator. Brahma springs from the indestructible. Hence the all pervading Brahma is established in 'yagya'.

Commentary—The real thrust of these liners is upon showing the presence of 'Brahma' in all 'yagyas'.

The divine is no doubt omnipresent and it is thus supposed to be present in latent form in everything, every action. But the Lord does not say that the divine consciousness is in all actions, it is in actions connected with 'yagya' only. One may be reminded of the 'shloka' 9 of this canto where the Lord clearly states that man is bound by shackles of 'karma' in all actions other than those performed for 'yagya'.

This in no way diminishes the importance of action. Permeated by Divine or not, the action is all supreme. Its importance has been underlined time and again, so far. The only thing about the 'yagya' is that the Lord or the creator is always there in.

Evam prawartitam chakram naanuwarteeh yah,
Aghaayurindriyaaraamo mogham Parrth sa jeewati [16].

Meaning—O Parth, he who does not follow the wheel thus set in motion, in this world, sinful is his life and his contentment lies in the senses. He lives in vein.

Commentary—What is this cycle? Commentaries have often confused it with the cycle of creation i.e. life, death and then life. But the real explanation lies in shlokaas 14 and 15 of this canto. The cycle is evolution of beings from grains, production of grains by rains and ensuing of rains from yagya and thus performance of yagya through action. This cycle is indeed necessary for existence and maintenance of life in this world and those who do not add in revolving this cycle commit sin, they are indulged in sensual pleasures and their life carries no meaning; they are better dead than alive.

Yastwaatmaratirewa syaadaatmtriptshch maanawah,
Atamannyewa cha santushtstasya karyam na vidyate[17].

Meaning—There is no duty for him who however, takes delight in the self alone and is gratified with the self and who is content in the self.

Commentary—Mark the difference in emphasis and approach. So long action has been made mandatory for man. Even the survival of body has been declared impossible in absence of work, but here comes an exception. Those who are contented in the self i.e. those who are contented inwardly and need nothing and are pleased with in themselves have nothing to do with any duty.

Naiwa Tasya kritenaartho naakriteneh kashchan,
Na chaasya sarvabhooteshu kashchidarthvyapashrayah [18].

Meaning—He has no use whatsoever for works done or not done nor there is any being on whom he need depend for any object to be gained.

Commentary—If he does anything, it hardly matters, if he does not do anything, it also does not matter. This self-contented man has nothing to gain from any living creature of the world. He is indeed set free and dependent upon none. What can be a more blissful existence?

Tasmaadasaktah satatam kaaryam karm samaachar,
Asakto hyaacharankarm parmaapnoti purushah [19].

Meaning—Do, therefore, without attachment, perform always the work that is to be done because performing work without attachment man attains the Supreme.

Commentary—Again emphasis on action and action with detachment. The preceding two verses are certainly exceptions in the sense that they absolved those persons of the necessity of indulging in action, who have reached a stage where they are happy and contented with in. But this verse comes as a conclusion. After considering every thing the Lord maintains that there is only one way and that is to perform your duty incessantly and without any attachment.

The second line is for them who have got spiritual ambitions too and for that sake they abandon every thing and try to be one with God. The Lord feels that this is not necessary. In His opinion action without attachment can fulfill this ambition also. Doing one' duty in a detached way, one will not only ensure his survival but will also reach his spiritual goal. One day he will be one with the Supreme. Here one is reminded of the saying 'work is worship'.

Karmnhaiva hi sansidhimaasthita Janakaadayah,
Loksangrahamevaapi sampashyankartumarhasi [20].

Meaning—It is by action alone that Janak and other attained perfection. Even for the sake of maintaining the world-order you should perform action.

Commentary—It is through concrete examples that the abstract principle of 'karm yoga' (action without attachment) has been illustrated here. The Lord extols action not for its own sake but also as a means of achieving eternal liberation from bondage.

Two things need to be explained. The first is the expression 'Janak' and others.

Janak, the father of legendary Sita was supposed to be a great thinker and seer though he was not a recluse. He ruled over a large state but power and perks never corrupted him. In fact, he was a real 'karmyogi' who performed such responsible actions without any attachment. He was bestowed upon the Title of 'Rajarshi' (King of risis the seer or a king who was a risi). Thus by performing his demanding duties in the most detached way, he would attain perfection. By the term 'and others' the Lord wants to point out to similar detached persons who also attained perfection by merely performing their duties in a detached way.

The other term is "Lok sangrahmevaapi sampashyankartumarhasi" i.e. even for the sake of the maintenance of the world-order you are to indulge in action. The action is, therefore, necessary not only for one's own sake but also for the sake of people at large. If one abstains from duties others will follow suit. Nothing will stir in the world of men and every thing will come to a stand still. No farming, no business, no navigation, nothing to eat and drink, then what will happen to this world? It will simply perish so, the need of action and action alone and action without attachment because in that case one will have best of both the worlds.

Ydyadaacharati shreshthastattdevetaro janah,
Sa yatpramaanham kurute lokastadanuvartate [21].

Meaning—In whatever way the great man acts, is followed by the Lower kind of man. Whatever the standard he sets, the rest of the people follow it.

Commentary—The Lord, here throws great responsibility over a leader of the society or a great man. He is supposed to set an example for others by performing his allotted duties in a detached manner as the masses are supposed to emulate him.

In an indirect way the Lord wats to convey to Arjun that he is not an ordinary mortal. He is venerated in society and people are bound to follow the example set by him, so he must act and bid a good-bye to his cowardice.

Na me Parthaasti kartbyaam trishu lokeshu kinchan,
Naanawaaptamawaaptabyam wart ewa cha karmanhi [22].

Meaning—O Son of Pritha (Arjun whose mother was called Pritha, kunti etc.) There is nothing in the three worlds which I need to do not there is anything worth attaining which I have not attained, yet I engage myself in work.

Commentary—Again underlining the importance of action but through his own example. The Lord Krishna is supposed to be the very incarnation of Bhagwan (God). Bhagwan in Indian mythology is supposed to lack nothing rather having everything in abundance. He is capable of granting any wish of those who love Him, out of His endless treasure. He is like an ocean of valuables of which one utmost asks of a drop even if he asks to his heart-content.

Such Bhagawan (Krishna) certainly is not required to do any thing in all the three worlds. Indians imagine firstly this earthly world (Prithbi lok) itself, secondly the world above it (Swarg lok) abided by the gods and thirdly the world beneath it (Paataal lok) which is supposed to be populated by demons. God is supposed to preside over all of these three. He is also not to attain any thing because he possesses everything. The very fact that He is capable or granting anything to His devotee proves this that He lacks nothing but possesses everything in immeasurable quantity. Even then the Lord, says He is never idle. He is always engaged in work.

Thus work is supreme. The message is very clear. Even if you are so affluent that you need do nothing you are to work. Work for work shake. No? Thus there is no scope from action if you are to dwell on this planet.

These line should work as an eye-openers for those who go on advocating that the Gita is a book of 'sanyas' (rennuciation) and leads one to eschew the world and do nothing but concentrate on God and survive on alms.

Yadi hyaham na warteyam jaatu karmnhyatandritah,
Mam vartmaanuwartante maṇushyaah Parth sarvashah [23].

·*Meaning*—If I do not engage in action untiredly at any time, (men will also do so) for they follow my path in all matters.

Commentary—Lord says that He goes on working incessantly without showing any sign of tiredness or laziness or negligence because if he does not do so people will simply follow Him and also do nothing. This is why at this very moment He is working as a charioteer of Arjun who is no where in comparison to Him. This is the simple example of indulging one self in the work in hand—great or small. One is reminded of the Gita's clear injunction to do the allotted duty in a verse of this canto (niyatam kuru karm twam).

Utsideyurime lokaa na kuryaam karm chedaham,
Sankarasya cha kartaasyaamupaahanyaamimaah prajaah [24].

Meaning—In case I do not engage in action, this world would perish. I should be the author of confusing of caste and of the destruction of all beings.

Commentary—This is in continuation of what has been told in the previous verse. The Lord had posed a question in that verse as to what would happen if He did not act ceaselessly. The answer was not fully provided in the outgoing lines. It was simply said that people would follow His example.

Here, in this verse the question is fully answered. He says that in case He does not act all the worlds would perish. By all the worlds he surely means the three worlds he has talked before—this earth, the world above (swarg) and the world below (paataal).

The one thing is remarkable. Though the Lord has not openly declared till now that He is not an ordinary mortal but God himself yet He is hinting at the same. He says the worlds would perish if He does not engage is action. Certainly they would do, because as the presiding Lord of these words He is responsible for their maintenance and if He sits idle these worlds are bound to perish for non-maintenance.

Not only that He says that He would be responsible for creating confusion of castes i.e. cross breeds (sankars) will abound and this will also lead to the destruction of the people. Cross-breeds leading to death and destruction is no secret any more. It has been scientifically proved that various fatal diseases appear in case of close-marriages. If such marriages or unguarded and unchecked and illicit sexual relations take place due to lack of discipline in people, they are bound to be destroyed. Now, it is time to think seriously about 'Aids'.

Saktaah karmanhyavidwaanso yatha kurvanti Bharat,
Kuryadvidwaanstathasaktshchikirshurloksangrahm [25].

Meaning—O Bharat! (Arjun) as the unwise act with attachment, so should the wise man act without attachment for the sake of the maintenance of the world-order.

Commentary—The command word is act. Action is important. This point is emphasised time and again.

One point is clear. The unwise generally desists from

works. They are to benefit from them, they are to maintain themselves, to take care of their bread and butter so they must act. The only thing is that they act with attachment. They equate themselves with their acts as a result of which they are subjected to bondage.

The wise people are doubting Thomases. They are ever pondering over to do or not to do. It was more common during the days of Mahabharata or when the Gita was pronounced. Due to fear of bondage many wise people were eschewing works and weie tempted to live the life of a recluse.

The injunction in these lines for these wise people is : they also must act as others are acting but act with detachment to escape the bondage they are so much afraid of.

Na budhibhedam janayedagyaanaam karmasamginaam,
Josayetsarvakaramaanhi vidwaanyuktah samaacharan [26].

Meaning—Let not the wise man create a confusion in the minds of the ignorant who are acting with attachment but he having achieved yoga (yuktah) get the ignorant perform their actions, duly performing all his duties.

Commentary—Lord is not prepared to witness inaction any where. He is prepared to see some ignorant being bonded due to attached actions on their part but not to let them confused by the wise by trying to teach them the results of attached and unattached works. Let the ignorant act as they are acting but act they must. Let the wise not interfere with their actions and they should go on performing their duties in a detached way. So the whole world must act. Action and action of any nature—detached or unattached is the very root of the existence of this creation.

Prakriteh kriyamaanhaani gunhai karmaanhi sarvashah,
Ahankaarvimoodhaatma karthaahmiti manyate [27].

Meaning—Actions are entirely done by the modes of nature. The fool whose self is bewildered by egoism, considers himself to be the doer.

Commentary—Here the Lord wants to make it clear that action is the very essence of nature. It is rooted in it. In any case your are to act whether you want or not. It is only a fool full of ego who thinks that he is the doer.

Circumstances as well as the characteristics of nature compel you to act. So better to act willingly or otherwise the nature is bound to force you to act. Let us take an example. The metabolic processes of the body make you feel hungry and thirsty. You have nothing to do with it, you have not invited hunger and thirst. But once they are felt you are to do something to fulfill them. You are to act to feed your body, to quench the thirst. It is why most of the people are said to work for bread and butter, for the sake of stomach.

This is one and a very rudimentary example of how people are forced to act. Let us understand it in another way. The Gita talks in these lines of modes of nature. These modes compel you to act in the way you are acting. As for example why one is forced to earn one's bread through service—govt. or private—and doing a business or running a factory? This is because of difference in modes of nature they possess. Some possess higher modes. Other lower ones. In Sanskrit there are three different modes of nature—'Sat', 'Raj' and 'Tam', 'Sat' stands for the very best and purest of modes, 'Raj' is bit inferior to the former and 'tam' is the very worst. One who likes to indulge in his own business certainly possesses the 'Sat'—mode, one who seves others is guided by Raj mode and who earns his or her bread through questionable means by burglary and begging etc. are the victims of 'Rajmode'.

Ever if you earn your food through some means or do some other acts—good or bad—you are simply guided by one of the nodes of nature. For example, I had no need to do this translation of the Gita for the sake of bread and butter, yet I am doing it. I must have been motivated by some mode of nature. Imagine which one. Similarly a man who earns sufficient to keep the body and soul together and even then he indulges in gambling etc., he is certainly guided by the 'tam' mode of nature.

Tattwittu mahaabaaho gunhakarmvibhaagayoh,
Gunha Gunheshu vartant itimatvaa na sajjate [28].

Meaning—O mighty of men! He who knows the truth about the divisions of the modes (of nature) and actions, knowing that it is modes that move among the modes, remains unattached.

Commentary—This is about the enlightened who know the truth that every thing is happening here through the interaction of different divisions of modes of nature—'satva', 'Rarja' and 'Tama'. Actions are the direct results of this interaction. This has been extensively dwelt upon in the commentary of the preceding verse. The only thing to be underlined here is that such an enlightened one aware of various actions, remains free of bondage without any extra effort on his part.

Prakritergunhasamudhaa sajjante gunhakarmasu,
Taankritsavido mandaankritsnavinn vichaalayet [29].

Meaning—Who are deviled by the modes let not the man perfect in his knowledge disturb the mind of these fools who possess only insufficient knowledge.

Commentary—This is another warning to the enlightened one (See verse 26 of this very chapter) not to thrust their knowledge over the ignorant—let them do their work as they are doing even in attached ways. They need not be enlightened on the interplay of the modes of nature, resulting in action, it will simply confuse them and they may take recourse to unnecessary reflections ignoring action. What will suffer is the latter.

The 'go' word is action. Activities must continue. No body should shun it—wise or fool.

Mayi sarvaanhi karmaanhi sannyaasyaadhyaatm cheatasaa,
niraashirnirmamo bhootvaa yudhyaswa vigatjwarah [30].

Meaning—surrendering all actions to Me with your mind fixed in the self, freed from longings and the feeling of meum and delivered from the (mental) fever, fight.

Commentary—The main issue before the Lord here is to motivate Arjuna to fight, who has firmly refused to do so on the very plea that he would be committing sins of slaying his own kins-men as well as the elders and respectable and also of corrupting the society in this process.

The Lord here provides a way out in clear terms by which he can fight without committing in reality any sin or irregularity. The crux is on the detachment as usual and this is best possible by asking no credit for what he is performing. He therefor, asks Arjun to surrender all his actions to the Lord (mentally of course) thinking that whatever he has done has been done to fulfill the wishes of the Lord. He is not the doer. He is just an instrument, God does instead. He will return to this subject again in ensuing chapters.

The next recipe is to be spiritually inclined. That is to be of spiritual minded thinking Spirit or God to be every thing—the only driving force of this creation, worth pondering over, worth getting nearer by any means. Then you can surrender your all activities to God (Krishna here of course claims directly on indirectly to be God Himself).

The third requirement to fulfill the very first one is to be freed from all hopes and feelings towards any thing or any body. This is the best way to lead a peaceful existence. The hope is regarding the outcome of any activity and the Lord has decried it many a time. Its repetition is only to drive home the point fully. Go on performing your allotted duties without expecting any thing, without caring two hoots for failure or success. Nourish no hope. Similarly become attached to none-nothing, no body, no action, not to the fruit of action. Love no body, hate none. Become indifferent and unattached to every situation, every being.

The fourth and important instruction is to be free from the fever. The fever in general parallel is the disorder of body, its getting high temperature. Fever is never welcome as it cripples the whole body. Here the fever stands for the fear Arjun is facing in fighting. It is generally supposed that in case of fear, body develops unhealthy symptoms including fever. The Lord therefore admonishes Arjun to get rid of this fear and fight. As told earlier Arjun is being exhorted to fight and all apprehensions of his regarding the commitment of sins have been tried to be removed by adding one more dimension to his discourse i.e. to surrender all his activities to God not taking any responsibility of his deeds. So if any one is responsible of sin or commitment of any unworthy activity it is Krishna Himself and not Arjun.

Ye me matmidam nityamanutishthanti maanavaah,

Shradhaawanto'nysuyanto muchyante te'pi karmbhih [31].

Meaning—Those who are possessed of faith and who do not find fault (with My above teaching) and always follow the above instruction, they are also liberated from action.

Commentary—The main fear is the bondage of action. What is needed is the freedom from this bondage. The Lord asserts that this freedom is realised by even them who faithfully practise the advice rendered in the preceding verse. Faith is the most important thing. Even the Bible says if ^you have faith as a mustard seed then if you ask this mountain to move, it will move.' So faith is the first requisite. If you have faith in God and His teaching whatever you say will certainly materialise.

The second thing is not to find fault with what the Lord is saying. Krishna is very much conscious of critics of spiritual techniques. The different cults use to criticize each other and reach no where. This situation must also be prevailing during the time of Krishna. So this **injunction** not to find fault with what He is teaching. By now having seen so much of ups and downs of life and having practised yoga and having learnt His spiritual lessons at the feet of Guru Sandipani during the adolescence and later on having practised it in real life, He was very much capable of cultivating of a cult of His and He was naturally apprehensive of the critics of the same. He thus warns Arjun to be aware of these critics and follow His advice in spirit and letters.

He concludes with the observation that who practises His preaching faithfully and without doubting he will also be liberated from action whether he understands it or not. Understanding is not significant, what matters is an unfaltering faith.

Ye Twetadbhyasooyanto naanutishthanti me matam,
sarwagyaanvimoodhanstamwidhi nashtanachetashah [32].

Meaning—But, however, who find fault and do not follow My teaching, know them to be deluded about all knowledge, doomed and devoid of a thinking mind.

Commentary—This is a warning for those who find fault with the teachings of Lord and do not follow it, they are fools, no nothing worth knowing and they are bound to be doomed as their mind has failed to act in the manner it should.

Sadhrisham cheshtate swasyaah prakritergyaanwaanapi
Prakritim Yanti bhootaani nigraham kim karishyati]33].

Meaning—All creatures follow their nature : even the enlightened one acts according to their nature. What the restrain will result in to?

Commentary—The importance of nature has again been emphasised upon. But this time it is not the outer nature, but it is the nature of the being. The Lord says that not only the human being but all beings behave according to their own nature. Thus the serpents will bite and the lions will devour at the simplest pretext. This is their nature. Similarly human beings act according to their nature. If some one is selfish, he will not become generous to his brethren. If one is righteous, he will hardly engage in questionable acts. The Lord says that what to talk of ignorant even learned people act according to their nature. Learning may increase one's knowledge but it cannot change one's nature. If he is greedy he will continue to be greedy despite his high learning. There is no dearth of people in temples and other places of worship who are highly learned but whose greed knows no limits.

The Lord opines that so far as nature is concerned, even restraints cannot work. You can hardly restrain yourself and even others in acting according to your or their nature.

The Lord simply wants to change the subject here and focuses light on some of the human-characteristics. This will be more evident form the following line.

Indriyasyeindrriya syaarthe raagdwesh vyawasthitau,
Tayorn vashamaagachhettou hyasya paripanthinau [34].

Meaning—Attachment and aversion are rooted in all sense-objects, let no one come under their control, for both indeed are his enemies.

Commentary—Again a diversion but a very useful one. Senses are denounced time and again by the Gita as they are capable of leading one, away to undesirable acts. The eyes, ears and nose and reproductive organs are powerful evils if not properly controlled. Eyes are meant to see not to be attracted away by the beauty and thus subject the possessor to bondage here and as a result of it, there (in life after death) also.

Here the Lord explains the mechanism as to how one is subjected to bondage though this word is not directly used here.

He explains that the senses alone are of no harm. When combined with their objects they become your potential enemy.

They have got either attachment or aversion to their objects. So take an example, the object of eyes is whatever they see. If they see a beautiful thing or person they are inclined to be attached but if they see an ugly thing or being say a leper they feel repulsion. According to the Lord both are bad. Your are neither to love nor to loathe any body. In both cases your balance is unnecessarily disturbed. You are to remain indifferent. A detached spectator. Let the things be as they are. Why to be attached to or repulsed by them?

God, therefore, warns us to be aware of both the sense and its object. According to Him both are our enemies. One in isolation is not enough to harm you. Eyes., if they have not got an attractive object to fall upon they cannot compel you to be attached to it. Thus there is need to be cautious of both the eyes and the beautiful woman. Let not the eyes continue to feed upon her beauty and let us not care for the beauty of her that is bound to bind us. Similar examples can be given of other senses say ears. Praise or say even buttering inflates your ego but criticism hurts you. So, be aware of both—the ears and the words you hear.

The Lord will return to this subject again after a while.

Shreyaanswadharmo vigurhah pardharmaatswanuusthitat,
Swadharme nidhanan shreyah pardharmo bhayaawah [35].

Meaning—One's own duty even if devoid of any merits is preferable to another's duty (capable of being well performed due to its certain merits). Even if one dies in course of performing one's duty it is welcome but other's duty is fraught with fear.

Commentary—'Dharma' is here often confused with

religion. And many commentaries thus hold Gita to be non-secular or at least against other religions. But that is hardly so. In the whole of the Gita the Lord has hardly talked about religion as such. The Gita is a spiritual work not a religious one.

It is almost a philosophical work or as maintained earlier it advocates a way of life—life full of peace and contentment—but it is in no case a religious treatise.

'Dharm' in fact, in Sanskrit, means not only religion but also one's duty, some times one's nature as well. The 'dharm' of fire is thus to burn and that of ice to make one cool. It is in this sense that Dharm has been spoken of here. The emphasis is again on action. One reason due to which action suffers is that the grass on the other side of the fence appears to be greener as told before. One leaves one's own work and tries his hands on some body else's work. In this process be loses his peace also. He remains dissatisfied. And the Gita is very much against this dissatisfaction and loss of peace. It therefore advocates for concentration on one's own work even if it appears to be inferior to another's. Even if one embraces death in course of performing one's work, it is better than hankering after one work to another. There are of course some dangerous works where death is not ruled out. Take for example the warfare itself. Death can visit you any time but if due to fear every soldier leaves his work and takes to farming what will happen to the boundaries of a nation?

The Lord in this verse, also indirectly indicates that Arjun may die in performing his duties, after all it is a battle-field. But this apprehension is not a pretext to drive him away form his allotted duty to non-action or any other kind of action, say even 'begging' as Arjun himself indicated in the beginning.

Another point which has been indirectly indicated by the Lord is that one by one's nature is suited for one kind of work and another is suited for another kind of work. The whole **'varnhaashram'** of Hinduism is based on this truth. **Varnhashram** which later on detoriorated in to casteism is nothing but division of labour based on the natures and inclinations of people. It is why it is maintained here that the work of some body else which is not suited to you may be raught with fear. If one used to teaching takes to fighting what will happen? He is almost sure to be killed or if some one used to farming, turns to navigation, rowing the boats, he is sure to be drowned. Thus though business may be superior to cultivation, a farmer is better advised to stick to his own than to try his hands on a work for which he has neither aptitude nor training.

Arjun Uvaach :

Ath ken prayukto'yam paapam charati purushah,
Anichchanapi Vaarshnheya balaadiva niyojitah [36].

Meaning—**Arjun said**—Now, what is that impels this man to commit sin, even involuntarily as if driven by force, O ! Vaarshnheya?

Commentary—Again a diversion. As said the Gita is a philosophy, a way of life, a solution of besetting problems one faces in the day-to-day life.

The one question, the answer to which illudes every body is that why a man (or a woman) commits sin even if he or she does not want. There appears to be some force compelling him or her to do so. What is that force?

It often happens. One knows that what he is doing is not right but even then he fails to refrain from doing it. Does a theif not know that committing theft is a sin, then why does he commit it?

Arjun desires this tangle to be solved and therefore this poser.

Shri Bhagawan Uvaach :

Kaam esh krodh esh rajogurha samudbhawah,
Mahashano mahaapaapmaa widhyenmih barinham [37].

God said—It is sex, it is wrath born of the element of 'rajas' all consuming and most evil. Know this to be the enemy here in this world.

Commentary—'Kaam' has been described by many commentators as desire. But this is not the case. This will be evident from the following verse. Lord is really talking of sex which in his words is like fire which burns up everything that comes in its path. It is a great evil and this is the first enemy to be attacked by man. It is not born of 'satva' (the best of all modes of nature) but of rajas (the not very desirable mode). It is thus bound to be harmful and destructive. But sex alone is not that powerful. It is associated with anger and anger is like a whirlpool in a stream. The Lord in condoning sex equates it with anger. Both are same or latter is the by-product of the former. Thus the Lord will explain at a later stage as to how the sex gives birth to anger and how anger destroyes the person who is thus trapped in this cycle.

The words all consuming and most evil are certainly for sex. It is said and rightly so that it is never satisfied. In a Sanskrit couplet, it has been observed that satisfying sex is not stopping it form reemerging or sub-doing it. As the fire burns more fiercly after being sprinkled with 'ghee' (the processed butter) similarly the desire for sex goes on increasing as it is tried to be satisfied. It is the most evil because it keeps the mind hankering after the sensul experience and keeps the man's life in perpetual bondgage and draws him down to the level of the life of an animal.

Dhumenaabriyate vahniryathaadarsho malen cha,
yatholbenaabrito garbhastathaa tencdamaavritam [38].

Meaning—As fire is enveloped by the smoke, as mirror by dust the embryo is covered by the amnion so this (self or soul) is enveloped by it.

Commentary—The Lord is very critical of sex or sensual desire in these lines. In His word the very nature of self is disfigured and harmed by it. To emphasise His point, He takes recourse to three metaphors.

What doe restrict the flame of fire? It is the ugly smoke. It will not allow the fire to manifest in its full strength.

And what does mar the efficiency of a mirror? It is dust. If it is covered by dust, it can hardly reflect your face.

And what does amnion do to the embryo? It covers its true form.

Thus, the all powerful sex makes the self way-ward, hinders its development and keeps it engulfed in what it is not supposed to remain engulfed in.

Aabritam gyaanameten gyaanino nityavairnhaa
Kaamrupenh konteya dushpoorenhanalen cha [39].

Meaning—O, Son of kunti, wisdom is veiled by this eternal enemy of the wise, the insatiable flame in the form of sex.

Commentary—Two things are remarkable. One is repeted only to underline its importance. This is the insatiable nature of sex. He has already stressed in a previous verse that it is all consuming like fire. Here He emphasises that it never satisfied. It goes on increasing with every attempt to satisfy it.

The second and not less significant is that it does not allow the wisdom or knowledge to function. Sex makes one blind. There is no question of discerning between right or wrong when one is caught by the flame of sex. The Lord rightly says that it is the eternal ememy of the wise. The scriptures are full of stories how sex has been the cause of fall of many a seer and saint. The Lord undauntedly is bent upon to make it evident that if there is any real enemy even of the wise, it is the unquenchable fire of sex. The fate of the unwise can better be imagined than said.

Endriyaanhi Mano budhirasyaadhisthaanamuchyate,
Etairvimohayatyesh mano gyaanvigyaannaashanam [40].

Meaning—Its abode is the senses, the mind and the intellect. It envelopes the knowledge through these and thus deludes the dweller in the body (i.e. the soul).

Commentary—The desire for sex or sex has already been declared to be the enemy of man. This enemy will have to be destroyed. But unless you know the abode of your ememy how can you vanquish it? So, the Lord here enumerates the places from which the desire of sex emanates. They are three—

i. Senses.
ii. Mind
iii. Intellect

By influencing these three the desire for sex envelopes wisdom—the discerning power—and man is thus subjected to the full control of this desire or becomes a victim of sex.

In other words the desire for sex functions through these three instruments.

The order in which these abodes have been described is important. The first is, senses. Then comes the mind them lastly the intellect.

The desire of sex naturally originates in mind at the signal of senses. The intellect may try feebly to check it but in most cases it succumbs to the pressure of mind and senses. It is why the Lord says that these all three are its abodes.

The role of senses is however most important. As told earlier they provide the signals. The eyes see a beautiful being, it directly informs the mind and the mind being unstable starts finding out ways and means to enjoy this beauty. Intellect some times feebly tries to dissuade the mind but usually it fails an easy prey to the machinations of senses and mind an it also shows ways to the senses to fulfill their desire.

But the real culprits are senses. If the eyes are not attracted by beauty, if the ears do not fall easy prey to melodious voices, the desire of sex cannot originate.

Now as the abodes of this desire for sex have been identified the Lord will proceed to control or destroy it.

Tasmaatvamindrayanhyaadau niyamya Bhartarshabh,
Paamaanam prajahi hyenam gyanvigyananaashanam [41].

Meaning—Therefore, having first controlled the senses O, Bhartarshabh! (Best of Bharatas) kill this evil, the destroyer of knowledge and super knowledge.

Commentary—As the villain of piece is senses so the Lord advises Arjuna, first to control them and kill the desire of sex. This desire is again described as enemy of all kinds of knowledge—ordinary and super.

Indriyaaanhi paraanhiyahurindriobhyoh param manah,
manasastu paraabudhirya budheh paratastu sah [42].

Meaning—Senses are stronger (than the body). Stronger than senses is the mind and stronger than mind is the intellect. What is stronger than the intellect is he (this 'he' stands for soul).

Commentary—The sequence is remarkable. The main

purpose is to control senses. The senses are certainly stronger than body in the sense that body becomes helpless under the sway of senses. It acts as the senses direct it and it is why it indulges in gratification of desire—sexual and other. So to control the body, the control of senses is necessary. The preceeding verse has therefore emphasised the importance of controlling these senses.

But is this control very easy? No. It is why the description of these sequences. Mind is superior to senses—stronger than them. Thus if mind is controlled, senses are controlled. But mind is also not that easy to be controlled. At one place Arjun tells in this very Gita that mind is very uncontrolled, strong and obstinate; to control is as difficult as to control a tempest. Then how to control this mind? By intellect which is superior to it. Train the intellect properly. Apply it and the mind is controlled. But this intellect is also not always reliable. In Sanskrit is it said that at times even the intellect of great intellectuals is deluded. Then how to control the intellect? The hint is obvious—by the soul. This is dealt in the next verse.

Evam buddheh param budhvaa sanstabhyaatmaanamaatmna,
jahi shatrum mahaabaho kaamrupam duraasadam [43].

Meaning—Thus O Mighty armed (Arjun) having known that (soul) which is beyoond the intellect; having stilled the self by self, kill the enemy in the form of sex which is hard to overcome.

Commentary—The cycle is complete. The ultimate said in context of killing the desire for sex, the greatest enemy of the mankind.

In the preceding verse, reference has been made to him that is the soul. Mind has been said to be controlled by intellect. This intellect is now to be controlled by one superior to it and that is soul. This soul embodied in the body is nothing less than a part of God—the Super Soul. The Lord has made it clear in an ensuing chapter that His very part is residing in every being.

The Lord therefore advises Arjun to regard the soul to be superior to intellect and with its assistance let the self exert and control itself by controlling all the disturbing factors enumerated above and thus kill the sexual desire which is repeatedly described to be hard to be subdued.

The soul is thus the master key. Constant contact must be established with it and being the representative of the Super Soul it will never let you down . It will help you in subduing the sexual desire, your greatest enemy, the destroyer of all kinds of knowledge and even discretion.

Om Tatsaditi Shrimadhbhagavadgitaasoopanisahtsu bgrahma vidayaayaam
yogshaashtre Shrikrishnaarjun sambaade karmyogo naam tritiyo'dhyaayah.

Thus in the Upanishad sung by the Lord in the science of the absolute, the scripture of yoga, in the dialogue between Shri Krishna and Arjun ends the third canto entitled, the yoga of action.

CHAPTER IV

Shri Bhagawanuvaach—

EmamVivaswate Yogam proktvaanahamabyayam,
Vivaswaanmanavae praah manurikshwaakave'brabit [1].

Meaning—**The lord said**—I proclaimed this immortal yoga to Vivaswaan; vivaswan conveyed it to Manu and Manu told it to Ikshvaaku.

Commentary—Vivaswaan is the sungod. Manu is told to be his son and the first man of the present creation. Ikshvaaku was his son and the first ruler of Ayodhya.

This yoga is termed by the Lord as immortal or imperishable. It has remained forever. This will be made more clear in the coming verse.

Evam poramparaapraaptamimam rajarshayoh viduh
Sa kaaleneh mahataayogo nashtah Parantap[2].

Meaning—Thus having got it one from another, the great sages knew it. By great **efflux** of time, it got disappeared.

Commentary—For some time it continued to be known from father to son when ultimately the great sages came to know about it. Great sages may also mean the royal sages. King Janak was one of them about whom we have talked earlier. It was not known to the people of Arjuna-time because with a great lapse of time it had disappeared. The conclusion is quite evident. The Lord is just reviving a lost knowledge.

Sa evaayam mayaa te'dya yogah proktah puraatanah,
Bhakto'si me sakhaa cheti rahasyam hyetaduttamam [3].

Meaning—The same ancient yoga which is full of great secrecy has been narrated to you to-day by Me as you are My devotee and friend.

Commentary—This 'yoga' is deemed to be a secret

knowledge not supposed to fall in undeserving hands. But is has been made known by the Lord to Arjuna because he is not only His friend but also a devotee of Him. Nothing can be kept secret from a friend and follower.

Arjun uvaach—

Aparam Bhavato janm param janm vivaswatah,
Kathametdvijaaneeyaam twamaadau proktwaaniti [4].

Meaning—Arjun said—You were born a few years back while the birth of sun-god dates back to antiquity. How am I to believe that you are the first proclaimer of it?

Commentary—This reservation of Arjun is natural. Sun is supposed to have been created in the beginning of this creation. Arjun was the contemporary of Krishna.

Shri Bhagawaanuvaach—

Bahooni me vyateetaani janmaani tava chaarjun,
Taanyaham ved sarvaanhi na tvam weth Parantap [5].

Meaning—The Lord said—O Schorcher of enemies (Arjun), you and I have passed through many births, I know them all, you know them not.

Commentary—This refers to verses 12 and 22 of the second chapter where it has been enunciated that soul is immortal and it just goes an changing the body like one changes clothes. It is thus correct that both Krishna and Arjuna might have gone though several births and lives. Krishna being the almighty Himself is omniscient and thus knows all these lives of both. Arjuna being an ordinary mortal does not remember any thing about them.

Ajo'pi sannavyayaatmaa bhootaanaameehwar'pi san,
prakritim swaamadhisthaay sambhavaamyaatmamaayayaa [6].

Meaning—Though unborn and of imperishable nature and Lord of all beings yet remaining in My own nature I take birth through my own divine potency.

Commentary—Though the lord is unborn and not supposed to take birth, but He does so. Whatever the procedure of manifesting Himself explained in the verse is not important, what is important is as to why He is to take birth at all. This is explained in the following verse.

Yadaa yadaa he dharmasya glaanirbhawati Bharat,
Abhuthaanamadharmsya tadaatmaanam srijamyaham [7].

Meaning—Whenever religion is in decay and religionlessness is in the ascendant, O Bharat (Arjun) then I create Myself.

Commentary—The purpose of manifesting Himself has been made clear in this verse. The Lord is really interested in upholding religion or rigteousness. This religion or faith has not been provided with any nomenclature. For there is no difference among different religions. What He is interested in is that righteousness must prevail on the earth and whenever it declines and unrighteousness starts flourishing He is compelled to take a form of flesh and blood.

Paritraanhaay saadhoonaam vinaashay cha dushkritaam
Dharm sansthaapanaarthaay sambhavaami yuge yuge [8].

Meaning—To protect the virtuous and to destroy the evildoers and to establish religion firmly I take birth from age to age.

Commentary—The purpose of taking birth is further explained or underlined. It is the duty of the Lord to provide protection to virtuous and at the same time to destroy them who practise evil. In case the virtuous are tortured and not allowed to practise righteousness and evildoers have their field-days, religion is certainly to suffer and the Lord is to incarnate Himself to establish faith on a firm footing.

Janm karm cha me divyan yo vetti tattwatah,
Tyaktvaa deham punarjanm naiti maameti so'rjun [9].

Meaning—O Arjun divine are My birth and activities. Who knows them in very essence does not take birth again on leaving this body. He attains Me.

Commentary—The coming in to the world of the Lord is not like the coming of other mortals. It is divine in the sense that the Lord chooses on His own to incarnate Himself for the purposes He has enumerated in the preceding verses. Similarly His indulgence in wordly activities is not like the indulgence of ordinary people. His activities are divine in nature because He performs them for the welfare of virtuous and performs them without actually being indulged in them.

He does every thing indifferently, without caring for the outcome, as He advises others to do in the similar fashion, with the same detachment. Those who care to understand the divine nature of His birth as well is His activities (during His life-span and after that) they are freed from the cycle of death and birth and they become one with Him.

Vitraagbhayakrodha Manmaya Mamupaashritaah
Bahavogyaan Tapasa poota Madbhaamaagataah [10].

Meaning—Freed from passion, fear and anger absolved in Me; taking refuge ·in Me and purified by the penance of wisdom, many became one with Me.

Commentary—It is not for the sake of saying that the Lord is telling that people can become one with Him and thus freed from tentacles of birth and death. Many in the past merged with Him. But here the conditions have been elatborated. Those who merged with Him were free from the evils like passion (or attachment), fear and anger. He was be all and end all for them. They also took recourse to penance especially that connected with attainment of wisdom (through the learning of the holy scriptures).

Ye yatha mam prapadyante tamstathaiva bhajamyaham,
Mam vartmanuvartante manusyhah Parth sarvashah. [11].

Meaning—O Parth (Arjun) as men approach Me so do I seek them; for in all ways men follow My path.

Commentary—Here the Lord wants to convey that all ways lead to God. Some people worship one god, some another but ultimately all such worships go to Him. He can manifest before them in the form they worship Him in or they can get whatever they desire (from Him) by simply worshiping in the way they do. All kinds of devotion, worship or prayer ultimately reach Him because He is the supreme God of all gods.

This truth will be made more clear later.

Kaankshantah karmanhaam sidhim yojant eh devatah,
Kshipram hi manushe loke sidhirbhavati karmja [12].

Meaning—Here men seeking the fruition of their activities, make offerings to the gods, the success due to action follows quickly.

Commentary—The Lord emphasises the importance of the worship of gods. By pleasing the higher powers men can receive their favour and succeed in their efforts in a comparatively shorter time. Action is, however, necessary. The worship of gods only expedite the results. The Lord thus admits the existence of unseen powers and their ability to fulfill the wishes of men provided they worship them and at the same time do not cease to act.

Chaaturvarnhyam maya shrishtam gunhkarmvibhaagashah,
Tasya kartaaramapi maam vidyakartaaramavyayam [13].

Meaning—The four fold order of society (viz., the Brahmian, the Kshatriya, the vaishya, and the shudra) were created by Me classifying them according to their prenatal qualities and action. Though I am the author of this order, know Me yet to be a non-doer and immortal.

Commentary—Much is told about the caste-system and its evils in India. The Lord clarifies it. He says that these four castes were created by Him but not according to their birth but depending on their natural inclinations and the duties they can perform. Thus if one was performing worships, devoting his time in reading and teaching scriptures and it was in his very nature he was called Brahmin similarly if one showed the inclination to fight and participate in battle he was called kshatriya and so on and so forth.

It was with the passage of time that the caste-system became an established way of life. It was originally nothing but a division of labour. The Lord, However, makes it clear that He is the author of this order yet He should not be considered a doer (as he did all this with non-attachment which He has been teaching to others).

Na maam karmaanhi limpanti na me karmphale spirhaa
Eti maam yobhijaanaati karmbhhirn sa badhyate [14].

Meaning—Actions do not contimate Me, nor I have craving for the fruits of action. He who really knows Me thus escapes the bonds of actions.

Commentary—The Lord cites His own example. He says He is not contimated by action. This is only because He does not aspire for the results. They may be bad. They may be good, they may be favourable or unfavourable. He is of the opinion that even that person who truly knows this nature of Lord is not bound by Actions. Why? Because, knowing this, he will try to emulate Him and thus himself escape the bonds. The Lord has already maintained in an earlier verse that people do follow His path.

Evam gyaatvaa Kritam Karm poorvairapi mumukshubhih
Kuru karmaiva tasmattwam poorbaih poorbataram Kritam [15].

Meaning—Even the ancient seekers of salvation performed action having known this. You therefore, also perform action as the ancients did in older times.

Commentary—This verse follows as a conclusion of the previous verses. The Lord wants to give authority to this statement and endeavours to arouse Arjun's faith in it. If the ancient seekers having known the fact that those who know the real nature of Him escape the bondage of action, performed action and achieved salvation, why should Arjun shun action? He can also do his allotted duty and achieve salvation provided he also understands the true nature of the Lord. What is this true nature? The true nature as depicted in the preceding verse is that He is not interested in the results of action, He is not contaminated by action. If a devotee will understand this nature of Lord he will certainly follow His foot-prints and thus himself will not he contaminated by action and achieve salvation due to this non-attachment.

By ancient seekers Lord naturally means king janak and others like him.

Kimkarm kimakarmeti kavayo'pyatra Mohitaah,
Tattekarm prabakshyaami yazgyatva mokshyase 'shubhaat [16].

Meaning—What is action and what is inaction, as to this even the wise are deluded. I shall expound that action to you, knowing this you will be freed from the evil i.e. its binding nature.

Commentary—Man is provided with a brain and two hands. He is therefore to indulge in action but even the wisest of them do not know what is really worth doing and what is not worth doing. The Lord proposes to tell the worth-doing and this will free the doers from the bondage of action.

'Kavayah' is really the plural form of 'kavi' (poet). A poet in general parlance is meant one who composes poems. But in the Sanskrit a poet also means a scholar as will be evident from the following lines of 'Kathopanishad'—

Chhurasya dhaara nisita duratyaya,
Durgampathastat kavayo vadanti.

The path of knowledge is rager—sharp and difficult to traverse, thus is said by the scholars (Kavayah).

Karmanho hyapi bodhavyam bodhavyam vikmanhah,
Akarmanhashch bodhavyam gahana karmnho gatih [17].

Meaning—Action must be understood and also the wrong action. Inaction is also to be understood as mysterious are the ways of action.

Commentary—The Lord promised in the preceding verse that He will let Arjun know what is action, here He proceeds to elaborate. The real nature of action can be comprehended only when one knows simultaneously about action, inaction and wrong action. A comparative study of these three will certainly reveal the real nature of work worth doing i.e. action.

These three words are however important and need elaboration.

'Action' indeed is really the right action which is necessary for one's existence and also evolution and in the process it provides him with much cherished salvation. Action benefits not only the doer but also them who surround him and come in his contact. Inaction is absence of action.

'Wrong action' is certainly that which is beneficial neither to the doer nor to the men around him. It of course leads to bondage and can not provide salvation. Theft, cruelty, sensuality, untruthfulness, violence, anger, jealousy, greed etc. are certainly 'wrong action'.

The nature of action is said to be mysterions as it is not very easy for an ordinary mortal to know all these three. It has already been maintained in the preceding verse that even the wise are deluded about the true nature of action.

Karmanhyakam yah pashyedakarmanhi cha karm yah
Sa budlimaan manushyeshu sa yuktah kritasnakarmkrit [18].

Meaning—One who sees inaction in action and action

in inaction is wise among people. He is 'yogi' and has accomplished actions.

Commentary Here Lord goes to define who is a real yogi and who is really wise. This is again the same theme of action and inaction, what seems to be action is really not different from inaction if it is done with complete detachment. Similarly the Lord has already stated in a previous verse that inaction is not inaction in the real sense. According to Him none is inactive even for a moment. Thus even in inaction there is action.

One who realises this truth is a real 'yogi' and he is wise among the men. Not only this, the lord testifies to the fact that He has performed all actions. This implies that in only one cycle He has done all His works and He is no more going to be born again. He has in other words achieved salvation which is the ultimate goal of all human beings.

Yasya sarve samaarambhaa kam samkalpvarjitaah,
Gyanaagnidagdhkarmanham tamahuh panditam budhah. [19].

Meaning—Whose all undertakings are free from the will or desire and whose actions are burnt up by the fire of knowledge, they are called wise by the most knowledgeable one.

Commentary—No action should be started with a desire to achieve something, with a determination to accomplish something, with a will to reach some goal. The reason is clear and repeated many times. The fruit of any action is not in your hands. Reaching the goal is not with in your power. You may reach it, you may not reach it. It is for the circumstances or Lord to decide what is going to be the outcome of the action you have embarked upon. But it does not mean that you will not undertake any work. You will, but without having in mind any desire for fruits. If you act in such a way even the wisest of the wise will call you the real wise. This is the truth of existence in this world and if you know this you are certainly wise and at the same time powerful which the Gita wants you to be—to lead a life free from all kinds of fears, doubts and dualities.

Tyaktvaa karmphalaasamgam nityatripto niraashrayah,
Karmanhyabhipravritto'pi naiv kimchitkaroti sah [20].

Meaning—He who has cast off attachment to the fruit of action, is very satisfied; depends on nothing and no body; he does nothing though fully engaged in actions.

Commentary—Nothing to comment on casting off the attachment which has always been underlined in the Gita and which is its essential teaching. To be ever satisfied is also a way to seek peace. One should learn to be satisfied with whatever he has got. So to be dependent on nothing or no body of the world is the way to develop confidence. As told earlier the Gita is a way of life. It teachers everything which is essential for a peaceful existence.

The Lord is emphasising that a person of such nature performs nothing even performing everthing. In other words he is free from the bondage that follows from indulgence in action.

Niraashiryatchittaatma tyktsarvaparigrah,
Shaareeram kevelam karm kurvannaapnoti kilbisham [21].

Meaning—He who expects nothing, has got his mind and soul disciplined and has relinquished all possessions and performs only bodily actions, he does not incur any sin.

Commentary—If one expects nothing one will be free from anxiety. The action of a yogi is supposed to be free from the expectation of tis results so he acts expecting nothing.

Disciplining mind and soul means killing the desire as desires are the impulses of the mind. If the mind is subdued, desires will not arise. A disciplined soul will automatically discipline the mind, so the need of disciplining the soul.

One must not think that soul is naturally disciplined. One's activities more often than not spoils its true nature. It is why in the Gita and also in Upnishads it has been cautioned that soul must not be tarnished.

Relinquishing all possessions is to shun the materialistic attitude towards life. One should try to live with the bare minimum of life. If one hankers after material possessions, he cannot act without expectation.

Doing only bodily actions or performing action by the body alone means the mind remains unattached while the body performs at the level of senses. This the clue of performing without attachment.

Yudrichchaalaabhasntushto dvandvaateeto vimatsarah,
Samah sidhaavasidhau cha kritvaapi na nibadhyate [22].

Meaning—Content with whatever comes without seeking, beyound the pairs of all opposites, free from jealously, not differentiating between failure and success; though fully engaged in action yet he does not do even a bit.

Commentary—Main purpose it to free the doer from the bondage of action. The recipes are here. Some oft repeated, only to drive them home successfully.

One should not hanker after things, should be satisfied with whatever comes without asking. He thus gets rid of greed, one of the evils which the Gita calls later to be one of the three doors to hell.

To be beyond the pairs of all opposites is a big achievement. One is usually caught between opposites—happiness and sadness, success and failure, bliss and grief, name-fame and bad name etc. The Gita teachers us to transcend these opposites. Happiness is as good as sadness. Both are welcome. This is the high way to a peaceful existence.

Jealousy, has of course been introduced by the Lord for the first time. To be jealous is to burn ones own blood. Let every one prosper. You also do your best, why to be jealous of any ones' achievement. His success should be rather an inspiration for you to achieve more.

To be indifferent to success and failure is one of the main teachings of the Gita. It has been repeated time and again because it is the root of anxiety and some times the cause of inaction. One is often plagued with the idea whether he will succeed or not, while doing something. Some times he refuses to act due to sheer fear of failure.

A man of above disposition is certainly not bound by action as there is nothing to bind him. He goes on acting without bothering for either his failure or others' success.

Gatsamgasya muktasya gyaanaavasthitchetasah,
yagyaayaacharatah karm samagram pravileeyate [23].

Meaning—He who is detached, liberated, whose mind is established in wisdom, who works for the sake of 'yagya', all action of his is melted away.

Commentary—Much has been talked about detachment. Such a detached man is certainly liberated. Liberation is the natural outcome of acting without attachment. The importance of knowledge or wisdom has been emphasised earlier also. What is this knowledge? Certainly to see the real nature of things and happenings, their transitory nature, the futility of success and failure, the knowledge the has been taught in several verses so far, even in he preceding one.

So to act for the sake of 'yagya' only is not to act for one's self. One is to act for charity, for the welfare of others. 'Yagaya' is not just only a sacrificial act. It has been talked upon earlier also, now it will be elaborated in its all forms in the following verses :

If one acts only for the sake of 'yagya' one's actions are just dissolved. They fail to bind him.

Brahmaarpanhambrahmhavirbarahmaagnou brahmnhna hutam
Brahmaiva ten gantavyam brahmkarmsamaadhina [24].

Meaning—The act of offering is Brahma, the oblation itself is Brahma and the fire is Bhrama, in Brahma is which the oblation is poured and the pourer is Brahma as well. Thus one who is fixed in Brahma through action goes to Brahma Himself.

Commentary—This is to see Brahma in everything Upanishads have been telling that whatever there is in this world is the manifestation of Brahma. 'Sarvam Khalvamidam Bramh' (All things manifested are Brahm) and 'Aham Brahmaasmi' (myself is Brahm) are the known sayings of the Upanishads.

This verse is especially connected with the offerings made in the fire the most popular form of yagya. To underline the significance of this yagya, every thing connected with this has been declared Brahma. Not only that; the one who performs this 'yagya' ultimately mingles with the absolute.

The Gita despite being antivedic has not been able to dissociate itself with yagya. But it tries to improve upon the vedic concept of yagya, a fact which will be evident from the following verses.

Daiviamevaapare ygyam yoginah paryupaasate,
***Brahmaagnaavapare yagyam yagyenaivopajuhvati* [25].**

Meaning—Some yogis perform yagya simply by worshiping the gods, other offer the yagya itself though ygaya in to the fire which represents Brahma Himself.

Commentary—The first part is quite clear. There are people who worship the various gods. According to the Gita they also perform yagya and they are as good as yogis because after all they perform some kind of sacrifice in worshipping the gods.

The second part is a bit difficult and has been interpreted in different forms. We shall not enter in to controversies and try to present the message, this part intends to convey.

This is the simple act of offering sacrifice or oblation in to the fire. It is in a way repetition of the some part of the preceding verse. The act of performing yagya through oblatian in to the fire has been elaborately explained in that verse. Fire has been described as Brahma there also. Here the difference is represented by the very act of performing 'yagya' which is also termed as 'yagya'. While performing 'yagya', the person concerned becomes all permeated with the sense of sacrifice, it is why offering 'yagya' through 'yagya' itself.

Shrotraadeeneendriyanhyanye samyamaaghnishujuhvati,
***Shabadaeenvishayaananya indiriyaagnishu juhvati* [26].**

Meaning—Some offer as sacrifice their sense of hearing etc. in to the fires of self-control. Some offer sound and other objects of the senses in to fires of the senses.

Commentary—It has been maintained earlier that the Lord will describe different kinds of yagya in this chapter.

To control senses like ears, eyes etc. is also a 'yagya'. Some do this and perform a kind of yagya. They do not allow their senses to be way-ward. Ears, eyes and other sense-organs are controlled and not allowed to indulge in enjoyment for enjoyment sake. They perform only that is necessary for man's existence and continuance of this creation.

But there is another form of yagya also so far as senses

are concerned. Thus objects of senses are of course enjoyed by them but in a different way. The objects of senses are in way burnt. For example a thing of beauty is of course preceived by the eye but when there is no attachment that object of beauty is as good as non-existent (burnt) for eyes.

Sarvanheeindriya karmaanhi praanhkarmaanhi chaapare,
Atmosamyamyogaagnau juhvati gyaandeepite [27].

Meaning—Other sacrifice all the activities of the senses and of the life-breath in to the fire of yoga, in the shape of self control kindled by **enlightenment**.

Commentary—Nothing to comment upon the activities of senses to be controlled. It has been commented upon more than once.

The question of controlling the activities of life-breath is significant. It is a known fact that the breath performs a lot of important body-functions and influences our system including the digestive process. At the same time it provides impulses to the various senses. In fact this emphasis on the control of life-breath comes from 'yogsutra' of Patnajali. There hc describes in detail different kinds of wind existing in the system and their importance. These winds must also be controlled but to control both the activities of senses and the 'life-breath' influencing the human-system in different ways, an enlightened mind is essential. Thus the importance of knowledge or wisdom in our day-to-day activities.

Dravyaygyaastapyagyaa yogyagyastathaapare,
svadhyayayagyanayagyashch yatayah samshitvrataah [28].

Meaning—Some perform yagya with material things, some in the form of penances, others through 'yoga', other of rigid vows and enlightened perform yagya through the study of scriptures.

Commentary—Performing 'yagya' through material means pertains to the acts of monetary and other donations. Penance and 'yaga' have also been characterised as yagya. Even the reading of scriptures is a yagya and this is supposed to be one of the best types as it is performed by enlightened people who have almost taken a vow to go through the sacred books.

Apaane juhvati praanham praanhe'paanam Tathaapare,
Praanhaapan gatee rudhvaa praanhaayaamaparayaanhah [29].

Meaning—Other who are expert in praanhaayaam pour the inward into the outward breath the outward in to the inward, having stopped the course of inhalation and exhalation.

Commentary—'Pranhaayaam' is the breathing-exercise. This has been awarded much importance in many scriptures including 'Patanjal yog' and Upanishadas. The breath is taken in through the nostrils turn by turn and then it is taken out. After that for sometimes they are totally stopped. This process cultures the nervous system.

Apare niyataahaaraah praanhaanpraanheshu juhvati,
Sarve'pyete yagyavido yagyachhapit kalmashah [30].

Meaning—Other having regulated their diets, pour their life-breaths in to life-breaths. All these have their sins cast away by 'yagya' as they are the knowers of 'yagya'.

Commentary—Here the emphasis is laid upon restricted diet besides the practice of breathing exercise (pranhaayaama). Pouring the life-breaths in to life-breaths is the yogic process of inhalation and exhalation. The importance of restricted diet has been realised by the modern science also. Practising 'pranhaayam' with regulated diet is certainly more effective.

The practice of pranhayaam is also described as a form of yagya and the destroyer of sins, most probably to underline the importance of breath-exercise (pranhayaam). This is but natural. As indicated from time to time, the Gita is a way of life, a life peaceful and healthy. The breathing-exercise no doubt is a promoter of good health.

Yagyashishtaamritbhujo yaanti Brahm sanaatanam,
Naayam loko'styayagyasya kuto'nyah Kurusattam [31].

Meaning—Partaking the remains of the yagya, which is (like) nectar, people reach the eternal 'Brahma'. O Arjun (the best of kurus) even this world is not for him who is the non-performer of yagya what to talk of the other world.

Commentary—The emphasis is on sharing one's earnings and possession with the gods and needy men (think of 'drabya-yagya', donations etc.). If one enjoys after sharing his material things with others what one enjoys is just like nectar. The Lord rightly says that the selfish person who abstains from this sharing can be happy neither here nor there (i.e. in the other world). In life after death also his soul remains disturbed and repenting for his selfish deeds here.

Evam bahubidhaa yagyaa vitataa Brahmanho mukhe,
karmjaanvidhi taansarvaanevam gyaatvaa vimokshyase [32].

Meaning—Thus many forms of yagya are set forth through the month of Brahma. Know them to be born of action. Thus knowing you will be liberated.

Commentary—These forms of 'yagya' are not for the first time described by Krishna himself; they were prescribed by Brahma Himself. Some take Brahma for the Vedas and say that they have been set forth by the Vedas themselves. In a way it is true because yagyas are of course elaborated in the Vedas and the Vedaas are said to be 'Apourususheya' (not written by any human being but given by the Almighty Himself).

The emphasis is once more on action by describing 'yagyas' to be the product of action. If you do not act, you do not earn and if don't earn you cannot perform yagyas. The Lord says you are liberated by knowing the truth that the action is super most.

Shreyaan dravyamayaadyayagyaajgyaanayagyah parantap,
Sarvam karmakhilam Parth gyane parisamaapyate [33].

Meaning—O Scorcher of enemies (Arjun) the yagya of knowledge is better than the yagya through the material means. All actions without exception, O son of Pritha, culminate in knowledge.

Commentary—The yagya through knowledge is the yagya through learning the scriptures or writing about them. This is certainly better than yagya through material means because it enhances your knowledge.

All actions culminate in knowledge is certainly true because through actions we acquire experience and experience is nothing else but knowledge.

Tadvidhi pranhipaaten pariprashnen sevaya,
Upadekshyanti te gyaanam gyaanisastattvadarshinah [34].

Meaning—Attain this (knowledge) by prostrating yourself (at the feet of the wise) by repeated questions, by service. The men of knowledge experienced in reality will unfold that knowledge to you.

Commentary—Having established the importance of knowledge, the Lord enumerates the ways to attain it.

It is certainly to be achieved from them who are the repository of it—the enlightened seers knowing the reality of the world and its contents.

In olden days the importance of oral teaching was of much significance compared to the present time as there was dearth of reading materials. For a long time the scriptures were passed on from generation to generation though mouth.

The best way to extract the knowledge from the knowledgeable is to express one's whole hearted reverence towards him and make queries after queries till one is satisfied.

The total surrender of the disciple to the seeker of knowledge, to the master, the seer is the main point made in this 'shloka'. This point will be again emphasised in this very chapter in the verse thirty nine.

Yazgyatva na punarmohmevam yaasyasi Pandav,
Yenbhootanyasheshenh drakshyasyatàamnyatho mayi [35].

Meaning—O son of Pandu (Arjun) knowing this you will no more fall in to such delusion and through this you will see all beings in yourself and them in Me.

Commentary—This is the real enlightenment—to know that all souls are really same in nature and they have sprurg up from the same source, the Super Soul.

The delusion to which the Lord refers is that which compelled Arjun to declare not to fight his so called kinsmen.

Once the knowledge dawns upon some one that all souls are in him, not different than him, and above all the fact that they ultimately rest in the Super Soul the Almighty, he will never bother to kill or not to kill the bodies.

Api chedasi paapebhyah sarvebhyah paapkrittamah,
Sarvam gyaanplvenaiva vrijinam samtarishyasi [26].

Meaning—Even in case you are the most sinful of all sinners you will cross (the river of all) sins through the raft of knowledge only.

Commentary—Again the emphasis on knowledge. Action is undoubtedly the focus point of the Gita, but ignorance is a curse while the knowledge is a bliss. It is to be acquired at any cost. It is why this temptation thrown out to those afraid of sins that they can be liberated through knowledge.

This knowledge is not necessarily to be taken as the super knowledge. It may be just knowledge—absence of ignorance.

To-day world-over, we are giving so much importance to literacy (in a sense knowledge). The Gita realised its importance five thousand years back.

Yathaidhaansi samiddho'gnirbhasmasaat kurute Arjun,
Gyaanaagnih sarvkarmaanhi bhasmsaatkurute tatha [37].

Meaning—O Arjun as the blazing fire consumes the fuel so does the fire of knowledge consumes all actions.

Commentary—One is afraid of action because it is the cause of bondage. Both good and bad actions bind you to the world and keep the cycles of birth and death moving. But the Lord says that knowledge is like fire which burns all actions into ashes. The knowledge that actions done without attachment and without an eye on results is bound to burn them. Refer to verse 18 of this chapter itself, where one is asked to see inaction in action and action in inaction. In fact, with even by doing every thing you do nothing if you have got this technique (knowledge) known to you.

Na hi gyaanen sadrisham pavitramih vidyate,
Tatsvayam yogsamsidhah kaalenaatmani vindati [38].

Meaning—There is nothing in this world as purifier as knowledge; he who is perfected in yoga, in time, finds it automatically with in himself.

Commentary—Man has apparently got two personalities external and internal. The external one, the body can easily be purified by bath etc. but it is knowledge alone which purifies the inner self.

This knowledge, Lord maintains comes automatically to one having perfected one self in yoga. It comes not immediately but in the course of time i.e. it unfolds itself to him gradually.

The yoga is here presented in a different sense. Here it is the 'yoga' of self with the 'superself,'. No knowledge is unknown to the superself rather all knowledge flows from it. One attached to it is bound to acquire this knowledge in due time.

Shradhaavaanlabhate gyaanam tatparah sanjatendriyah,
gyaanam labdhva paraam shaantimachiraanhaadhigachhati [39].

Meaning—He who is possessed of faith, is attentive and has subdued his senses, attains knowledge. Having attained knowledge he attains perfect peace in no time.

Commentary—There are two conditions of attaining any knowledge :

(*i*) **Faith**—Faith or reverence in the master or the repository of knowledge. Unless you have regard for him you cannot believe in what he says. He also may not like to impart knowledge to you if he does not find you full of respect for him.

(*ii*) **Attention**—This is but natural. Unless you are fully attentive you cannot grasp what is being given to you in form of knowledge.

(*iii*) **The Control of senses**—This is an important condition. If one indulges in sexual pleasure, one can not be attentive and thus can not fulfill the second condition. This is why in olden days there were 'Tapovans' (schools in forests in the very abode of the seers (the knowledgeable) where the disciples attained knowledge controlling their all senses and practising celibacy.

By fulfilling all the above three conditions he acquires knowledge and this knowledge gives him perfect peace.

Peace is what the mankind has been striving for. The peace is what the Gita intends to guaarantee. With the real knowledge of this and event, one naturally attains peace. The knowledge that there is nothing like death and the fruits of actions are not in our control, is certainly to lead you to a peaceful state.

Agyashchashraddhanashch sanshayatma vinashyati
Naayam loko'sti na paro na sukham sanshayatmanah [40].

Meaning—One who is without knowledge, without faith and possessed by doubt perishes. For the doubiting soul there is neither this world nor that nor happiness.

Commentary—An ignorant man of douting nature and without reverence towards scriptures and the knowledgeable people is bound to perish. He may not rise in life, rather full of doubts he will not believe in anything beneficial and thus may harm his body, mind and even soul.

He cannot thus enjoy this world, what to talk of the world beyond. The Lord firmly believes in life after death. Till one is reborn one lives in different world meant for souls. In this world also the foolish, faithless doubting Thomases are not welcome.

Yogsannyastkarmaanham gyaansanchhinnasanshayam,
Atmvantam na karmaanhi nibadhnanti, Dhananjayah [41].

Meaning—O Arjun! Who has renounced action through yoga, whose doubts have disappeared by knowledge and who is self-possessed, actions do not bind him.

Commentary—Renouncing actions through yoga does not mean shunning actions altogether. It is simply 'karmyog'—indulging in action without any expectation, without caring for success or failure.

The very fact that 'actions' do not bind him, suggests that there is no hints in this shloka to shun action.

Disappearance of doubts and being self-possessed also help in freeing one from the bondage of action in the sense that one who is full of the knowledge that indulging in action does not necessarily mean being bounded by it. He guided by his self (self is the part of the superself) effortlessly escapes the bondage of action.

Tasmaadagyaansambhotam hritsthan gyaanaasinaatmanah,
Chhitvainam sanshayam yogamaatishthottishth Bharat [42].

Meaning—Therefore, O Bharat (Arjun) having cut asunder with the sword of wisdom this doubt of yours rooted in your heart, establish yourself in yoga and stand up.

Commentary—Emphasis is on getting free of doubt. If

one is prone to doubting he will doubt even the words of the Lord regarding 'karmyoga' i.e. doing works without attachment and thus leading a peaceful and contented life.

This doubt can be removed by knowledge alone. The knowledge that action performed without attachment does not lead to bondage dispels all doubts.

Free of doubt one can thus establish oneself in yoga (Karmyoga, of course). The Lord says that by thus establishing in yoga Arjun should stand up and (fight) as he has discarded his weapons and promised not to fight.

For the common man the message is that embrace 'karmyoga' and march. The line from the 'Upnanishad' 'utishtha, yaagrat praapya varaannivodhat' (rise, arise and by learning from the wise be wise) seems to be the source of the last words of this 'shloka'.

Om Tatsaditi Shrimadbhagawadgeetaashu upanishadsu Brahmvidyaayaam yogshaashtre Shrikirisnaarjun samvaade gyankarm sannyaas yogo naam chaturtho'dhyaayah.

Thus in the upanishad of the Bhagavad Gita, the scripture on yoga, the dialogue between Lord Krishna and Arjun ends the fourth chapter entitled "The yoga of knowledge as well as the Renunciation of Action."

CHAPTER V

Arjun uvaach—

Sannyasam Karmnham krishna punaryogam cha shansasi,
yachchreya etayorekam tanme bruhi sunishchitam [1]

Meaning—O Krishna you praise renunciation of Action (Sankhyayoga) and then the yoga (of action-karmyoga). Tell me which of the two is decisively the better.

Commentary—Now the discourse is to take a new turn, it is why this poser. This question is going to be responsible for a flow of great wisdom which will not only present the essence of His teachings so long but will also settle the quarrel between 'sanyaasis' (believers in sanyaas) and 'karmyogis' (Doers).

Arjun finds apparent contradiction in Lord's teaching. He by the end of the last chapter some times praises 'sannyaas' and sone times 'karmyog'. This is intentional. To stir his worthy disciple to pose this question which will allow Him to settle the dispute between 'sannyaas' and 'yoga' for ever.

Shri Bhagvanuvaach—

Sannyasah karmyogashch nihshreyasakarauubhau,
Tayostu karmsanyaasaatakarmayogo vishishyate [2].

Meaning—**The Lord said**—Both the renunciation of action and the yoga of action lead to one's welfare but the yoga of action is superior to the renunciation of action.

Commentary—The dispute between the 'sannyaas' and 'karm' (action) is settled for ever. Many of the 'sanyasis' had been claiming in those days the renunciation of all actions to be superior to the act of indulgence in action. The Lord in no uncertain terms tells that both are good but the 'karmyog' is certainly superior.

It will not be out of place to mention that it is one of the aims of the Gita to denounce renunciation and establish the supremacy of action. Act, and act is the watch word of the Lord.

This is why he has propounded this novel theory of 'karmyoga' i.e. act without attachment. Men are afraid of bondage born out of action, so he says acting without expecting any thing is the high way to liberation. So why to renounce action? Absence of action implies destruction. The Lord told earlier 'without action you cannot even preserve your body'.

Gyeyah sa nityasannyaasee yo na devshti na kanchhati,
Nirdvandvo hi mahabhaho sukham bandhatpramuchyate [3].

Meaning—O mighty—armed (Arjun), consider him ever a 'sanyasi' who neither hates nor desires. One who has freed himself from the pairs of opposites is easily released from bondage.

Commentary—If 'sanyas' is worth seeking (as it was considered those days), he is also a sanyasi who takes life as it comes. He desires nothing, he rejects nothing. He acts without attachment. He is free from the opposites i.e. success and failure, pleasure and sorrow etc. He is indifferent to both. He thus very easily frees himself from bondage. 'Sanyasis' have to suffer a lot to achieve this goal but the 'karmyogi' does it easily. So, he is in no way not a 'sanyasi.' He is inferior to no body.

Saankhyaogau prithagbalah pravadanti na panditaah,
Ekamapyaasthitah samyagubhayorvindate phalam [4].

Meaning—It is those of childish disposition and not wise who speak of 'sanyas' (knowledge) and 'yoga' (action) as different. One who is properly established even in one gets the fruit of both.

Commentary—As stated earlier the Gita is a very practical work. It aims at not only providing the human beings with a peaceful and contented earthly abode but also at removing a number of dichotomies and contradictions; at settling dispute between different approaches towards a liberated life especially between the path of knowledge ('saankya' or sanyas-tradition) and yoga (action oriented way).

Followers of the both of them were at logger heads during and before the Mahabharata-period—eager to establish the superiority of one over the other.

This verse is unique in the sense that it very crudely admonishes both the followers of 'sanyas' and those of 'action.'

It calls them nothing more than children (having very little knowledge) who call them different. There can not be a stronger stricture. This verse as told earlier is not only unique in itself rather it is one of the rarest of gems embedded in the holy book so skillfully. This is certainly a memorable verse. No body would have rebuked them quarrelling over their obstinacy in the way the Lord has done in this verse.

He thus reconciles both approaches for ever. He clearly states that both yield the same fruits. Enough is to establish in any one of them—but establish properly. This is important. There is no halfway house. Whole hearted approach to any one of them is essential to get desired result i.e. liberation. One cannot be half 'sanyasi' and half 'yogi'. Be one in the perfect sense of the term and get what another gets being similarly perfect in his own field. (But one must remember that despite this equality advocated with an eye on reconciliation the Lord has clearly stated in the verse 2 that 'yog' is superior to 'sanyas').

Yatsankhyaih prapyate sthanam tadyogyairapi gamyate,
Ekam sankyam cha yogam cha yah pashyati sa pashyati [5].

Meaning—The place where goes the follower of 'saankhya', the 'yogi' also goes to the same. One who sees 'saankhya' and 'yoga' to be the same, really sees.

Commentary—It is widely believed that 'sanyasis' go to a more exalted place after death than do the 'yogis'. The Lord calls off the bluff by stating that both go to the same place (exalted of course).

He once more referees to the both. He clearly says that one who sees both to be one i.e. not different, really sees. Every body does not see despite having eyes. These outer eyes are not of importance. The inner eyes are not opened till one sees both to be the same. Needless to add that this is another attempt at reconciliation.

Sannyaasastu mahaabaaho duhkhamaptamayogatah,
yogyukto munirbrahm naachirenhaadhigacchati [6].

Meaning—O mighty armed, 'sanyas' is indeed hard to attain without 'yoga' where as the 'yogi' reaches 'Brahma' in no time.

Commentary—After placating the both, the Lord again returns to his real purpose i.e. to prefer 'yog' to 'sanyas'.

'Sanyas' is really difficult to attain without 'karmyoga' i.e. acting without attachment. The detachment makes the path of 'sanyas' easy. But 'yogi' does not require the help of 'sanyas'. He reaches Brahm earlier than does the 'sanyasi'.

The supremacy of 'karmyoga' is thus once more established over 'sanyas'.

The Gita is no doubt a book of action as told repeatedly. Do, and do whatever is the result; is the catch word of this book handed over to the mankind by the Lord Himself (or some real seer of the ancient times).

Yogyukto bishudhaatmaa vijitaatmaa jitendriyah,
sarvhootaatmbhootatmaa kurvannapi na lipyate [7].

Meaning—The yogi, pure in self, with complete control on it and his senses, who has made his self the self of all beings, is not bound even while he is performing actions.

Commentary—The aim is again to emphasise that action does not necessarily lead to bondage. Some conditions have been laid down to escape this bondage. They are four :

(*i*) One must be a yogi, necessarily a 'karmyogi'—performing actions with detachment.

(*ii*) One must have conquered his self. It implies that he is his own master. He is not swayed away by the desires.

(*iii*) The control of senses has been advocated time and again. The preceding chapter has almost fully been devoted to it. Senses are the most potent enemies and they must be conquered.

(*iv*) One must not differentiate between his self and self of others. He must think that his self and that of all beings are parts of the super self so they are one and the same. In that case one will not do harm to others. There is a very good line of the scripture which says he who see the other beings as he sees himself is the only person who really sees. ('Atmaupamen bhuteshu yah pashyati sa pashyati').

Naiva kinchitkaromiti yukto manyet tattvavt,
pashynshrinvanspirshanjighrannshnangacchansvapan shvasan [8].

Pralapanvisirijangrihnhannunmishanimisannapi
Indryiaayanheeindriyaartheshu vartant iti dhaarayan [9].

Meaning—The yogi, who knows the truth even though seeing, hearing, touching, smelling, eating, going, sleeping, breathing, speaking, letting go, seizing, and in opening and closing the eyes must believe that he does nothing, thinking that it is the senses that are acting on sense-objects.

Commentary—It has been stated previously as well that really one does not do any thing but simply senses act on sense-objects. (See verse 28. Chapter 3).

Here almost all acts are performed automatically like breathing and passing urine and stool (letting go) or intentionally like going, seeing and learning etc. They are categorised to make the point that one well-versed in yoga sees these actions not as performed by him but as the simple interaction of senses with sense-objects.

Brahmnhyaadhay karmaanhi sangam tyaktva karoti yah,
Lipyate na sa paapen padmpatramivaambhasa [10].

Meaning—He who performs actions by surrendering them to 'Brahma' and abandoning attachment is not touched by sin as lotus-leaf remains untouched by water.

Commentary—Here one more method is hinted at to get rid of sin accruing from actions. This is surrendering one's actions to the Almighty Himself. Do not think that any act has been performed for yourself. Think that all actions have been performed for Him. Another condition is the old one—absence of attachment.

Such person is left untouched with sin as a lotus-leaf remains untouched by water. Every body knows that if you place some drops on the leaf of a lotus, they do not remain on it but roll out.

The contention of this verse must not be misconstrued. It does not give one a blanket permission to indulge is sinful acts like theft, murder etc. You kill some one unnecessarily and surrender this act to the Almighty, then do not think that you have got rid of the sin. This is about sin accruing from normal acts. Even while performing our normal or allotted duties we may earn sin e.g. while walking and breathing we destroy thousands of small beings. In many cases we hurt the feelings of others in course of performing actions we must perform. Such sins are here meant not the sins emerging out of willing sinful acts.

This surrendering one's all actions to the Almighty will again be emphasised upon in some of the verses of other chapters.

Kaayen mansaa budhyaa Kevalairindriyairapi,
Yoginah karm kurvanti samgam tyaktvaatmshudaye [11].

Meaning—'Yogis' perform action by the body, by the mind, by the intellect even by the senses alone, with detachment for the sake of self-purification.

Commentary—The actions related to 'karmyog' certainly lead to self-purification because they are performed without attachment. In this process the soul learns how to remain detached to the activities of body, mind, intellect and even senses-senses which are usually prone to sinful activities. Any way, the aim of a 'yogi' ('karmayogi') is self-purification and he indulges in it through actions e.g. if he takes bath or performs 'pranhaayaams,' he aims at exterior and interior purifications.

Zuktah karmphalam tyaktva shantimapnoti naishthikam,
Ayuktah kaamkaarenha phale sakto nibadhyate [12].

Meaning—The 'yogi' having abandoned the fruit of action, attains the lasting peace. He who is not a 'yogi' spurred by desire and attached to the fruit (of actions) is tied down.

Commentary—As maintained earlier one of the major aims of the Gita is to provide peace to the turbulent soul of the man.

The ways are oft-repeated. One who is a yogi i.e. a

'karmyogi' attains this peace by abandoning the desire of the fruit or actions.

One who is yet to be a yogi is motivated to act by the desire of fruit as a result of which he is bound and peace and bondage never go side by side. If you are in bondage with anything you can not dream of peace.

Sarvkarmaanhi manasaa sannyasyaste sukham vashee,
***Navadvaare pure dehee naiv kuruvann kaarayan* [13].**

Meaning—The self-controlled man having renounced all actions through the help of mind rests happily in the city of nine gates, neither acting nor causing others to act,

Commentary—This is the description of an absolutely peaceful existence. Who has got control over himself renounces all actions through the help of mind. Mind is really a link between the action and the actor. If we feel in mind that though doing every thing we are doing nothing then we are really in a state of happiness.

The emphasis is here on the happiness of soul and not of the body. The soul is a dweller in the body which is supposed to be a city with nine exits. These nine exists are nine holes in the body i.e. two eyes, two ears, two nose-holes the mouth and the two doors discharging urine and stool respectively.

The point is that all these doors are open and if the dweller is not peaceful and contented and is disturbed and restless, it can at any moment escape out from any of these nine doors causing what we call in common parlour death. So, there is the apparent need to provide a peaceful, restful abode to this soul and this can be done only by controlling the mind in such a way that even it causes one and even others to act it actually does not do so, by taking recourse to the technique of detachment.

Na kartitvam na karmaanhi lokasya srijati Prabhuh
***Na Karmphalsanyogam svabhaavastu pravartate* [14].**

Meaning—The Almighty creates neither the authorship of actions nor the link between the action and its fruits. It is nature that carries all this out.

Commentary—It is been repeatedly told by the Lord

that all actions are really interaction between senses and sense-objects. One who considers himself doer is one who is bound.

The Creator has nothing to do with the creating of actions, not with the process of actions, neither the linkage between actions, nor with the process of actions, neither the linkage between actions and fruit of actions. It is all the mischief of nature i.e. the interaction of senses with sense-objects.

If this is taken in this way i.e. if the things are taken in real persepective one remains unattached and peaceful. It is foolish to think that actions, the desire to act and to even get fruits out of these actions are the creations of God, embodied in man from very birth. God, or Almighty is just an indifferent spectator. The forces of nature are creating all this. Control the nature and you are at peace with everything and every body. In other words control senses and you are contented as senses are the only tools of the nature to cause you to act (act with attachment).

Naadatte kasyachitpaapam nachaiva sukritam Vibhuh,
Agyaanenaavritam gyaanam ten muhyanti jantavah [15].

Meaning—The Almighty never partakes of the vice or virtue of any one. Knowledge is veiled by ignorance. It is why creatures are deluded.

Commentary—Why this 'U' Turn? What was the necessity of telling that God does not share any one's vice or virtue?

There is. People often think that by performing some virtuous acts they can get rid of the vices they have incurred. The Gita says this is a fallacy. Lord is not going to write your vices off for your virtues.

Similarly some people are of the view that by doing some virtuous act i.e. by performing worship or playing out alms they will please the Lord.

This is not so. Vice is yours and so the virtue is. Vice must harm you. God is not going to condone them for the virtues of yours. So the virtues are also yours and Lord is not going to take any part of it. They will certainly benefit you in different ways but they are cent-per-cent yours. Lord is not going to be a partner in them. He is very indifferent.

People think in the way they do because they are

ignorant. The knowledge is enveloped by ignorance.

The conclusion, certainly is while going on earning virtues, refrain from vice. Don't expect virtues to wipe away your vices.

Gyaanen tu Tadagyaanam yesham nashitamaatmanah,
teshamaadityajgyanam prakashayati tatparam [16].

Meaning—In the case of those whose said ignorance has been destroyed by knowledge, that knowledge, like the sun, illumines the supreme.

Commentary—This ignorance is no doubt harmful. It creates several fallacies. But once it is destroyed by knowledge, that knowledge it self reveals the supreme as the sun dispels darkness and reveals real nature of many an object.

Tadbudhyastadaatmaanastannishthaastatparayanhaah,
Gacchntyapunraraavritim gyaannirdhootkalmashaah [17].

Meaning—Their mind rooted in Him, their being established in Him, they exclusively devoted to Him, are cleansed of all impurities by knowledge and go to whence there is no coming back.

Commentary—Not returning back is to attain salvation. Knowledge is here imparted an exalted importance and also the all out devotion to the supreme.

Thus devotion and knowledge combined are capable of making one free from the cycle of birth and death. One must always think of Him, be of Him and Him only. In that case he will automatically acquire knowledge and that knowledge will cleanse him of all impurities so that he will reach His abode from where there is no return.

Vidya vinay sampanne braambhanhe gavi hastini,
shuni chaiva shvapaake cha panditaah samdarshinah [18].

Meanings—The wise perceive similarity in a Brahmin, endowed with learning and humility, in a cow, in an elephant, in a dog and in an outcast.

Commentary—A really enlightened man has evenness of vision everywhere. The mind of the enlightened man perceives the oneness of the life in every being be it a learned and humble man (a Braahmin who has realised Brahm) or a cow or an elephant or a dog or even an outcast.

This verse teaches real socialism or the sense of equality. The Gita says, 'samatvam yog uchyate'—equality itself is yoga and here it is elaborated.

The verse reminds of a line of 'lshaavaasyopanishad' where it is maintained that whatever is here, in this world is inhabited by Him—'Isha vaasymidam sarvam yatkinchit yagatyaam jagat'.

Ehaiva Tarjitah sargo yesham saamye sthitam manah,
Nirdosham hi samam Brahm tasmad brahmanhi te sthitaah [19].

Meaning—Here itself is conquered this mortal plane by those whose mind is established in quality. Flawless indeed and equal (towards every thing) is Brahma, therefore they are established in Brahma.

Commentary—The emphasis on equality or evenness of vision continues. As stated in the commentary of the preceding verse 'samatvam yog uchyate' (canto II verse 48) is one of the profoundest messages of this sacred book.

Here the Lord tries to lure us towards this equality by stating that one with evenness of vision conquers this world (the cycle of birth and death) in this life itself. He says what to talk of us or a yogi, Brahm itself recognises equality so one with sense of equality towards every being is always established in Brahma i.e. he is always one with Him. There cannot be a better way to teach this principle of equality which is so dear to the Lord (Krishna) as it is the best way to lead an equanimous life in this world full of useless ego.

Na prahrishyetpriyam praapya no dvijetpraapya chaapriyam
Sthirbudhirasamooddho brahmvid brahmanhi sthitah [20].

Meaning—One who does not rejoice on obtaining what is agreeable not grieves on obtaining what is unpleasant, whose reason is firm and free from delusion is a knower of Brahma and established in Him.

Commentary—Again the importance of having a detached approach towards life's dispensations. One whose intellect is steady and who is not deluded looks equally at pleasant and unpleasant aspects of life. The Lord describes that He is the real knower of Brahma and is therefore not different from Him.

Vaahyasparshesvasaktaatmaa vindyaatmani yatsukham,
sa brahmayogayuktaatmaa sukhamakshyamashnute [21].

Meaning—One whose self remains unattached to external contact derives that happiness which is inherent in the soul. His soul completely identified with Brahma, he enjoys eternal bliss.

Commentary—These lines are a bit confusing. In fact many commentators have taken advantage of this confusion and interpreted these lines in a way that suits them.

They say that the same bliss which is enjoyed by one whose self is unaffected by the external contacts is enjoyed by one who has identified himself with Brahma.

It could have been true had there been 'tat' in place of 'sa' in the beginning of the second line. That not being, their interpretation is grammatically wrong. In fact there aught to have been 'tat' (that) in place of 'sa' in the second line then it could have matched with 'yat' of the first line. 'Tat' is neutral as 'yat' but 'sa' is masculine so 'sa' cannot match with 'yat'.

As the case is we have no option but to interpret the line in the way we hare done. Had there been 'tat' in place of 'sa' their interpretation would have certainly been correct.

Thus we have to remain content with the meaning that one with the soul unattached to external contacts may not enjoy the happiness enjoyed by those indulgent in sensual pleasures but he enjoys much more than that—a bliss which is particular to the self or soul. Similarly a person whose self a is in complete union with Brahma enjoys not only bliss but eternal bliss. The first kind of bliss may fade away but the second kind will not.

Ye hi samsporshajaa bhoga duhkyonaya eva te,
Aadyantavantah kaunteya na teshu ramate budhah [22].

Meaning—O son of Kunti (Arjun), the pleasures which are born of contact are verily the sources of pain. They appear and they vanish. A wise man does not indulge in them.

Commentary—By pleasures born of contact the Lord means sensual pleasure as it is derived from the contact of senses with sense-objects.

They are bound to be a source of sorrow because they do not last. They have a beginning so they have to have an end, a separation. A separation causes griefs. Besides, the medical science has discovered that the sensual pleasures especially the sexual ones if indulged indiscreetly give rise to many ailments. They are the cause of physical and mental degeneration also.

It is therefore, wise to refrain from them.

Skaknoteehaiva yah soddhum praaksharirvimokshnhaat
Kaamkrodhodbhavam vegam sa yaktah sa sukhi narah [23].

Meaning—One who is capable of even here, before casting off his body, to resist the urges of lust and anger is a 'yogi'; he is a happy person.

Commentary—The emphasis is here on happiness. The Lord is rightly of the opinion that those who control the excitement born out of lust (especially sex) and anger achieve happiness.

Much has been told earlier about the unhappiness brought about by sexual and sensual pleaures. Even in the preceding verse sense-contacts have been decried.

Another potent factor responsible for unhappiness-anger—has been added in this verse. This will be taken up again by the Lord in this and some other subsequent chapters.

Anger of course is a cause of unhappiness and injurious and sometimes even fatal to human-health.

But the important point is that Lord insists upon controlling these urges here itself before one leaves his earthly abode. This is important because if one does not control these urges here itself, they will persist hereafter also, rendering his soul restless.

The person who succeeds in his or her endeavour of controlling sex and anger is termed as 'yogi' by the Lord. This is a great tribute.

Yo'ntah sukho'ntaraaraamastathaantaroyotireva yah,
sa yogi brahmnirvanham brahm bhooto'dhigachahati [24].

Meaning—One whose happiness is within, whose enjoyment is within who is illuminated from within, that 'yogi' identified with Brahma, attains eternal freedom (brahnirvaanham).

Commentary—Every thing is with in—happiness, contentment, even elightment—one who feels as such becomes not an ordinary yogi but one attached with the Almighty Himself.

Naturally after relinquishing this mortal cover he or she attains an eternal liberation—from which there is no coming back.

Labhante Brahmnirvaanhamrishyah chhinhakalmashah,
Chhinnadviadha yatatmaanah sarvbhootthite rataah [25].

Meaning—Those seers whose sins are washed away, whose doubts are dispelled, whose mind is firmly established in God, who are engaged in promoting the welfare of all creatures, they attain eternal liberation.

Commentary—The eternal liberation is again in focus. In the preceding verse some conditions were laid down but they are not all.

Here the Lord enumerates some others.

(*i*) Destruction of sins (through penances etc.)

(*ii*) Doubts having been dispelled. This is certainly by virtue of gainging knowledge.

(*iii*) Having been firmly established in God, certainly through constant yoga-practice.

(*iv*) Engagement in the welfares of all beings. This is very important as it has been maintained in the scriptures that there is no virtue greater than taking interest in the welfare of others.

The following saying is very famous :"Ashtadash puraanheshu Vyaasasya vachanam dvayam, paropkarah punyay paapaaya parpinhanam".

Meaning there by that from all the eighteen purahnas, only two conclusions of Vyaas emerge. They are : welfare of others is virtue and doing wrong to others is vice.

People having all these distinctions are termed as seers (rishis) by the Lord.

Kaamkrodhviyuktaanaam yateenaam yatchetasaam,
abhito brahmnirvaanaham vortate vidtaatmnaam [26].

Meaning—To those disciplined men who are free from lust and anger, who have subdued their mind and have realised the self, the eternal liberation is all round.

Commentary—Emphasis on eternal liberation continues. The absence of sensual pleasure and anger has again been underlined. The only point added is the realisation of the true nature of self and control over mind.

To realise the true nature of self means the knowledge that it is just a part of the bigger self i.e. Lord Almighty Himself. In such case eternal liberation is bound to be every where.

Control over mind is also a great feat. An uncontrolled mind makes one the slave of senses

Sparshaan kritva bahirbahyaanschakkchuschaivaantare bhroovhoh,
Pranaapanau samau kritvaa nasaa bhyantarchaarinhau [27].

Meaning—Having ousted external contacts outside, with the eyes fixed between the eye-brows, having balanced the ingoing and out-going breaths through the nostrils.

Commentary—The Lord is now in a mood to explain some aspects of 'Paatanjal yog' which is coming just as a passing reference as the yoga of the Gita is quite different from the traditional yoga-practices. This short elaboration continued through the next verse has taken quite a part of the coming chapter.

Here the preliminary preparations have been outlined. One is first to get rid of the thoughts of external sense-enjoyments and then to fix the eyes on the space between the two eye-brows. The next requirement is to equalise ingoing and outgoing breaths—this is the first step towards 'praanhaayaam', balancing the breaths.

This is of course more or less a mechanical process but it gives one relaxation and has a softening effect on the entire system which is the aim of 'Patanjal yog.'

Yatendriyamanobhoodhirmunirmokkshparaayanhah,
vigatechchaa bhaykrodho yah sada mukt eva sah [28].

Meaning—His senses, mind and intellect under control, such a sage intent on liberation and free from desire, fear and anger is indeed for ever liberated.

Commentary—As stated earlier this verse is in continuation of the preceding one. The physical technique described in the out-going verse provides automatic control over the senses, mind and reason. Having achieved this control, the person becomes more or less a sage and is free from desire, fear and anger. This man is liberated for ever.

Liberation is no doubt the ultimate aim of a mortal, it is why the Lord returns to it again and again.

One must mark that fear has been added almost for the first time as a bottleneck to liberation. Fear is certainly one of genuine enemies of mankind. It is not only an obstacle on the path of 'saadhanaa' (efforts to achieve one's spiritual aim) but is bad to one's physical welbeing also. Some times even fatal.

Bhaktaaram yagyatapasaam sarvlokmaheshvaram,
Suhridam sarvabhotaanaam gyaatva mam shantimrichhate [29].

Meaning—Having known Me as the partaker of 'yagyas' and austerities, as the supreme Lord of all the worlds and as the friend of all beings, one attains to peace.

Commentary—It was stated in the very beginning that attainment of peace is one of the important aims of the Gita. Here again another way is identified which leads to peace. This is the realisation of the real nature of the Lord—Krishna here, He Himself states that he is the enjoyer of all 'yagyas' and austerities men perform. He declares Himself to be the real friend of not only man but of all beings. He also in no uncertain words declares Himself to be the Master of all the worlds i.e. the Almighty Himself.

It is almost for the first time that Krishna proclaims Himself to be the Almighty.

Om Tatsaditi shrimadbhagvageetashoopanishadsu brahmvidyaayaam yogshasthre, Shri Krishnarjun samvaade karmsanyays yoganaam panchamo'dhyayah.

Thus in the upanishad sung by the Lord, the science of Brahma, the scripture of yoga, the dialogue between Shri Krishna and Arjun, ends the fifth chapter entitled "The yoga of Action and Knowledge"

CHAPTER VI

Shri Bhagawanuvaach

Anaashritatahkarmphalam, Kaaryam karm Karoti yah,
Sa sanyasee cha yogee cha na nirgrin chaakriyah [1].

Meaning—One who performs action that aught to be performed without expecting any fruits, is a sanyaasee and is a yogi, not one who has renounced fire and given up all activities.

Commentary—Once more the supremacy of action over 'sanyas' has been tried to be established.

'Sanyayees' generally renounce fire i.e. they do not even cook their food, beg it. In a way they do not indulge in any action. The Lord says this is no 'sanyas'.

One who performs actions without depending on fruits is both 'sanyasee' and 'yogi.' Thus there is no difference between 'sanyassee' and 'yogi' & 'sanyasee' is also a yogi and a yogi is also a 'sanyaasee.' The only condition is that he must perform worth doing actions without expectation of fruits.

Moreover action which aught to be done is important. It means that any action performed with detachment does not make one sanyaasee or yogi. In that case even theft and murder can be justified on the ground that they have been performed with detachment.

Yam sannyaasmiti praahuryogam tam vidhi Pandava,
Na hyasannyastsamkalpo yogi bhawati kashchan [2].

Meaning—O Arjun, which they call sanyaas know it to be the same as yoga because never who has not renounced the desire can become yogi.

Commentary—Again an attempt at reconciliation between sanyas and yoga.

The Lord very specifically states that what is sanyas is also yoga because if the sanyasee renounces action, yogi also renounces something very significant and that is the intensity of desire itself. So if renouncement is sanyas, yogi is also a sanyasee. It implies that once one becomes a yogi he becomes sanyasee automatically. As stated earlier those were the days of predominance of sanyas, so the Lord is to emphasise time and again that it is unseless to renounce the world, renounce the desire, the expectation of fruit and you also are a sanyaasee.

Aarurukshomuneryogam karm kaarnamuchyate,
Yogaarudhasya tasaiva shamah kaaranhamuchyate [3].

Meaning—So the man of thought (muni) who wishes to ascend to yoga, action is said to be the means; for one who has ascended to yoga, for him only, tranquillity is said to be the means.

Commentary—The importance of action again being emphasised. According to the Lord one who wants to be a yogi must take recourse to action—action without the desire of fruits of course. To who has become a yogi tranquility is the means, through which he will rise further. That implies that once you have become established in yoga you attain tranquillity of mind—absence of all desires and this will certainly serve as a ladder to the higher goals.

Yada hi nendriyaartheshu na karmsvanushajjate,
Sarvasmkalpsannyaasee yogaarrudhastadochyate [4].

Meaning—When one ceases to have any attachment either for the objects of senses or for action and has relinquished all incentives of desire, one is said to have attained yoga

Commentary—The first there conditions laid down to attain yoga in the two preceding verses are not new. They have been oft repeated with a view to drive them deep in our heart. The fourth has also been hinted upon in the verse two of this chapter where it has been stated that one who has not relinquished the incentive of desire can not think of becoming a yogi.

At best all these four conditions have been summed up

here.

Udhharedatmanaa'tmaanam naatmaanamavasaadyet,
Atmaiva hyatmno bandhuratmaiva ripuraatmah, [5],

Meaning—One should upgrade one's self by his self and should not degrade one's self for one's self is indeed one's friend and one's self itself is one's enemy.

Commentary—This is an important verse. It aims at refining and raising the status of one's self that is soul. The same is refined or upgraded by the hints provided by it self. These hints are regarding performing good deeds and harbouring noble thoughts. An upgraded self is one's real friend. It can lead one to great spiritual and other heights. But if the soul is not upgraded there cannot be a greater enemy than it.

The light which we term as hunches and intuitions comes from with in and upgrade one's self or soul. Often these intuitions will come to an upgraded soul and they will be correct.

Even Upahishads insist on upgrading the soul and on not degarding it. 'Esaavaasypaishad' clearly says : 'Andhah Tamh pravishanti ye ke aatm hano janaah'—those who degenerate their soul enter pitch darkness (of ignorance and suffering).

The message of this verse is clear and loud. The real guide is sitting with in. If it is not degraded and degenerated by misdeeds and evil thoughts it will provide never failing guidance. The Lord will state in one of the verses in a subsequent chapter (canto XV shloka 17) that a part of his own Self resides in every being—'Mamaviaansho Jeevaloke jeevabhooto sanatanah.'

This is not only a spiritual dictum of belief. It is believed by many enlightened men of different fields. Even Kalidas the renowned Sanskrit poet says in his universally acclaimed work "Abhigyaan Shakuntalm" that when one is in doubt the best guide comes from with in-'Sataam hi sandeh padeshu vastushu pramaanh antahkaran pravritayah.'

Bandhuraatmaatmanastasya yenaatmaivaatmanajitah,
Anaatmanstu shatrutve vartetaatmaiva shatruvat.[6].

Meaning—One's own self is the friend of one who has conquered his self, but the very self which has not been conquered behaves inimically like one's own foe.

Commentary—The idea contained in this verse is just the extension of that contained in the previous one. A conquered or disciplined self is one's best friend while an undisciplined one is one's worst enemy. It can lead one to any disaster by giving wrong signals and subjecting one to different allurements.

Jitaatmanah, prashaantasya parmaatma samaahitah,
Shitoshnhasukhduhkeshu tathaa manaapamaanyoh [7].

Meaning—For one who has controlled his self, who is peaceful, established in the supreme self, there is no difference between cold and heat, pleasure and pain, honour and ignominy.

Commentary—There is nothing especially new in this verse. The emphasis is as usual on conquering the self and to establish it in the supreme self which will make one indifferent to the pairs of opposites like cold and heat, joy and sorrow etc. as enumerated above. The importance of equanimity has once more been underlined.

Gyaanvigyaan triptaatmaa kootastho vijitendriyah,
Yukt ityuchyate yogi samloshtaashmakaanchanah, [8]

Meaning—That yogi is said to be united (with the supreme self and to be satiated with 'gyaan' (knowledge) and vigyaan (special knowledge of manifest Divinity), and unshakable in every circumstance and whose senses are subdued and to whom clay, a piece of stone and gold make no difference.

Commentary—The emphasis is on knowledge and knowledge of the supreme.

To maintain one' equanimity in all circumstances is also important. This unchanging nature speaks of one's control over the mental faculty.

The control of sense is not new. The new concept introduced for the fist time is to regard material possessions useless. Gold symbolizes prosperity and precious possessions. A yogi who possesses the qualities enumerated in the beginning of this verse considers gold nothing more than a piece of stone or clay.

To decry gold has been part of the Indian enlightened thinking. This will be evident from the following lines also :

"Matrivat pardaareshu pardrayeshu loshtwat,
aatmvat sarvabhooteshu yah pashyati sa pashyati."
—He who sees as mothers, others 'women, as pieces of dust others' precious metals (gold, silver etc.) and one's own self in all beings does really see.

Suhrinmitraayurdaasenmadhyasthdveshyabandhushu
Saadhushvapi cha paapeshu sambudhirvishishyate [9].

Meaning—He stands special who regards well wishers., friends, foes, neutrals, impartials, the hateful ones, kinsmen and the sinful alike.

Commentary—The quality of equality ('samatva') is again appreciated. This is especially in relation to persons. It is certainly to foster the sense of brotherhood among all people. Hatred, anger etc. are harmful for one's well-being so yogi regards friends and foes alike and does not hate even those who deserve hatred.

Yogi yunjeet statamaatamaanam rahasi sthitah
Ekaakee jatcitaatmaa niraashirparigrah [10].

Meaning—Let the yogi always concentrate (on the supreme) Himself remaining alone, his mind and soul subdued, expecting nothing and possessing nothing.

Commentary—The attempt begins to present in brief 'patanjal yog' as hinted at in the preceding chapter.

The first requirement for 'Pantajal yog'-practitioner is to find a secluded place and remain their without company of any kind. He is to keep noting with himself and expects no body to come to provide him any thing either material or immaterial. He must have complete control over mind and soul then only he can concentrate.

Shuchau deshe pratishthapya
sthirmaanasanamaatmanah,
Natyuchchritam naatineecham
chailaajinkushottaram [11].

Meaning—In a clear place having firmly placed his seat,

not very high or very low with kusha-grass, a dear-skin and cloth spread one upon the other.

Commentary—Explanation of the process and preparation for concentration continues. In the seclusion and aloofness explained in the preceding verse, one in a clean place, must form a firm seat which must not be imbalanced due to instability of the place he chooses to sit upon. Suppose it is a half hanging piece of stone, then it can not provide a firm ground. With the help of the sacred grass called 'kusha', dear-skin-with a piece of cloth spread over them one gets the comfort and so that the concentration is not disturbed.

Tatraikaagram manah kritvaa yatchittendriyakriyah
Upvishyaasane yumnjyaadyogmaatamvishudhaye [12].

Meaning—Siting there (on that seat) concentrating the mind and controlling the activation of thoughts and senses, he should practise yoga for self-purification.

Commentary—Explanation of the mechanism of 'patanjal-yog' continues. Having seated on the seat thus prepared (as described in the preceeding verse) one must control his mind and controlling the activities of thoughts and senses he should practise 'yoga' as it is self-purifying. How this 'patanjal yog' will be practised is explained in the following verses.

Samam kaayshirogrivam dhaaryannachalam sthirah,
Samprekshya naasikaagram svam dishashchaanavalokayan [13].

Meaning—Keeping the trunk, head and neck upright and steady, remaining firm and looking at the tip of his nose, not looking in other directions.

Commentary—This is about the posture of a yogi in readiness to meditate and realize Him. Its is really the mechanical process of 'patanjal yog'. He is to sit firm with trunk, neck and head straight. He should stop looking left-right or forward-backward rather fixed his gaze on the tip of his nose. This gives a state of stillness helpful in practising yoga.

Prashaantaatma bigatbhirbrhamachaarivrate sthitah
Manah sanyamya machchito yukt aaseet matparah [14].

Meaning—With is self peaceful, freed from fear, pledged to the vow of chastity, with mind controlled and fixed on

Me, he should sit realizing Me.

Commentary—The precaution prescribed so far, naturally leads to peace. What he is to do further is to become fearless and chaste. Fearlessness is necessary as it will allow one to remain peaceful. Fear and peace cannot co-exit. But there should be some way to become fearless. Fear is not easily to be eradicated. The way has not been prescribed here. But the just way is to surrender yourself to the Supreme. He is always, to take care of every thing including your enemies, so why to be afraid?

To be chaste is to direct your energy upward. This will strengthen your mental and spiritual faculties and help you in realizing Him.

The control of mind has been emphasized upon time and again and also its fixation on Him. With having accomplished all this, the yogi should sit in meditation feeling himself absorbed in Him.

Yunjannevam sadaatmaanam yogi niyatmaanasah
Shantim nirvaanhaparamaam matsansthamadhigachchati [15].

Meaning—Ever applying his mind to Me, the yogi of controlled mind attains the lasting peace including the supreme liberation which rests no where but in Me.

Commentary—The objective of yoga is thus realised, the lasting peace and the supreme liberation which are to be found but in Himself. It means he becomes one with Him. The conditions have been enumerated earlier, the two conditions mentioned here are the new. He having seated in the posture as explained above and on the seat prescribed, should constantly think of Him with pointed mind.

Natyashnatastu yog'sti na chaikaantmanashnatah
Na chaati svapnsheelasya jaagrato naiva chaarjun, [16].

Meaning—O Arjun, the yoga is not for one who eats too much, not for him who does not eat at all, it is not for him who is given to too much sleep nor for one who is ceaselessly awake.

Commentary—Emphasis is obviously on keeping the body fit for 'Patanjal yog'. Too much of food or sleep will make one lethargic. Similarly complete absence of them will render him sick. The correct approach is explained in the following verse.

Yuktaahaarvihaarasya yukta cheshtasya karmshu,
Yuktsvpnaavabodhasya yogo bhawati duhkhha [17].

Meaning—Yoga which destroys sorrow is for him who is moderate in food and recreation, moderate in efforts for action, moderate in sleeping and wake.

Commentary—The approach is defined as hinted earlier. Excess of any thing is bad. Extremes are to be avoided. The Gita does not prescribe a life of recluse to its followers, but it certainly advocates moderation. Eat and sleep moderately, even enjoy life moderately. Do not exert too much or too less in your day-to-day actions and the yoga is your's and it will provide a sorrow-free life.

Yadaa viniyatam chittamaatmnyevaavatisthate,
Nihsprih sarvkaamebhyo yukt etyuchyate tada, [18].

Meaning—When the mind under complete control is settled in the self alone then one who is free from yearning for all enjoyments is said to be united (yogi).

Commentary—Here is the ultimate result of 'Patanjal-yog.' After having settled himself in the posture prescribed and followed the methods described, one concentrates with in (on the Supreme) with a mind completely controlled and with no care for any kind of enjoyment, he succeeds in uniting himself with the supreme and becomes a real yogi.

Yathaa deepo nivaatastho nengata sopamaa smritaah
Yogino yatchittasya yunjato yogamaatmnah. [19].

Meaning—As lamp does not flicker in a windless place, analogous is stated to be the yogi of subdued mind, practising his yoga.

Commentary—The emphasis has time and again been laid on the control of mind or thoughts. The simile of a lamp not flickering in an airless place is also very original. The main thrust being that a practitioner of yoga must be steadfast in his concentration. This is certainly possible only with a mind which is completely under control and thoughts not running in different directions. In other words his mind though capable of being unsteady as a burning tip of a candle (say) becomes steady (which is not its nature) like the same burning tip of the candle which is placed where there is no air. This must be marked that what is meant by wind-lesseness, is not altogether absence of air but only the absence of its flow; no lamp can burn in a completly airless place as there will be no oxygen.

Yatroparamate chittam niruddham yogsevaya
Yatra chaivatmnatmaanam pashyaannatmani tushyati [20].

Meaning—The state in which the mind curbed through the practice of yoga comes to retire, in which seeing the self by the self itself (he) rejoices in the self.

Commentary—Whatever is, is with in one's self. The objective of the practice of yoga is to enable one to find contentment in himself (or soul) it self through the help of the self itself.

Such yogi does not seek pleasure out side but from the soul itself which is nothing but the part of the Super Soul of Self and which is all bliss. The first condition however, again is the control of mind and thought.

Sukhamaatyantikam yattadbudhigraahyamateendriyam
Vetti yatra Na chaivaayam sthitashchalti tattwatah. [21].

Meaning—Knowing that which is extreme joy not depending on the sense, is gained by the intellect and where established (the said yogi) does not deviate from the real truth.

Commentary—The truth is here on not moving from the real truth or God Himself as truth is God and god is truth. This is possible only when one knows that what is the highest bliss or joy is not gained through sense-enjoyments but by the intellect itself (united with self). When he is established himself in that intellect he stops wavering, running in direction in search of happiness.

Yam labdhva chaapram labham manyate nadhikam tatah,
Yasmin sthito na duhkhen gurunhapi vichalyate [22].

Meaning—Having gained which he does not reason any other gain as greater than that and established in which he is not moved even by a great grief.

Commentary—This is the result of the practice of this

(Patajal-yoga). The gain which he thus gets is the greatest. In other words no other gain is greater than this. The main advantage is that such a man is not moved by even great sorrow. How does it happen? As he is established himself in his self not affected by the dualities of life taking every, thing which comes in its stead, he remains unmoved even by the adverse circumstances of life

Tam vidyaad duhkhsamyogviyogam yogsamgitam
Sa nishchyen yoktbyo yogo'nirbinhachetasaa [23].

Meaning—This state which is termed as yoga free from the contact of grief should be known and this yoga must be practised with firm resolve and a pleasant mind.

Commentary—Here is a message by the Lord for the benefit of the mankind. Having explained the ways of practising this yoga and advantages accruing from it, He maintains that this yoga which is on the one side a union with the supreme and on the other a disunion with the wordly grief must be practised resolutely and with a pleasant mood.

Samkalpaprabhavankaamaanstyaktva sarvaanasheshatah,
Mansivendrinygraamam viniyamya samantatah [24].

Meaning—Completely a bandoning all desires arising from strong thoughts and fully controlling the senses on every side by the mind.

Commentary—This verse is a prelude to the following one. The emphasis here is again on abandoning all desires arising from the thoughts which are some times very resolute, and is also as much on controlling all senses without providing any of them any let up.

Shanaih, shanaihrupramedbudhya dhritigrihitaya,
Atmasamstham manah kritvaa na kinchidapi chintayet [25].

Meaning—Let him gradually attain tranquility through an intellect posscessed of patience and having established the mind in the self he should not think of any thing else.

Commentary—As stated earlier this is in continuation of the previous verse. With preparations outlined in the outgoing 'shloka' he should step by step try to achieve the state of bliss with the help of an intellect which is not impatient. Having gradually attained this blissful state he should concentrate and not think of any thing whatsoever.

yato-yato nishchurti manushchunchlumusthirum,
Tatasttato niyamayaiadaatmanyeva vasham nayet [26].

Meaning—Restraining the restless and unsteady mind from all those directions to which it runs, let him bring it under the sway of himself alone.

Commentary—This is just the injunction to control the mind. Mind is undoubtedly restless by nature. It has several objects of attraction.

The self or soul should exert and bring it under its control by all means. This helps in concentration.

Prashaantmanasam hycnam yoginam sukhamuttamam
Upaiti shaantrajasam brahmbbhootmakalmasham [27].

Meaning—The best happiness comes to the yogi whose mind is perfectly calm, who is sinless. Who is free from 'rajogunh' and who is identified with the supreme or Brahma.

Commentary—The objective of every human being is to achieve peace and happiness. The Lord maintains that the best or say the supreme happiness comes to him whose mind is at perfect rest, who commits no sin and who is far from 'rajas' or 'rajoguha' and is identified with he supreme or Brahma. 'Rajas' or 'rajogunha' is the cause behind all passions. Thus being free from 'rajogunha' he stands having subdued all passion. Thus one becomes identified with Brahma through concentration with the help of procedures defined in various preceding verses.

Yunjanevam sadaatmaanam yogi vigatkalmashah
Sukhen brahmsansparashamatyantam sukhamashnute. [28].

Meaning—Thus practising yoga always, the sinless yogi easily attains the eternal bliss of contact with Brahma.

Commentary—The infinite joy is the contact with the supreme or Brahma; there is no happiness beyond this. This is attained by one who ceaselessly practises yoga (Patanjal-yoga) and is sinless. What is meant by sin has been explained previously.

Sarvabhootasthmaatmaanam sarvanbhootaani chaatmani
Ekshate yogyuktaatmaa sarvatra samdarshanah. [29].

Meaning—One established in yoga who sees every

where equally and whose self is thus established in yoga sees himself in all beings and all beings in himself.

Commentary—'Samatvam Yog uchyate' (equality is yoga) the main message of the Gita is abundantly conveyed in this verse. A real yogi finds himself not at all different from others. He is in every being and every being is in him.

Yo maam pashyati sarvatra sarvam cha mayipashyati
Tasyaaham na pranhashyami sa cha me na pranhashyati [30].

Meaning—He who sees me every where and sees every thing in Me, I am never out of sight of him nor is he ever out of sight of Me.

Commentary—The almighty is all pervading; he is in every thing a in live (chetan) of life-less (jarh). Not only that every thing derives its sustenance from Him, if He is not, nothing remains. A person who is of this opinion, to him God is always in sight and he is also always in sight of Him.

The word 'Pranhashyati' has been interpreted by many commentators to mean destruction. According to them for such person God does not stand destructed to him nor does he stands destructed to Him. This interpretation is erroneous on its very face. God is certainly indestructible.

Sarvabhootasthitam yo maam bhajatyekatvamaasthitah,
Sarvaatha vartmano'pi sa yogi mayi vartate [31].

Meaning—Established in oneness who worships Me abiding in all beings, that yogi though living every where (any where in reality) lives in Me.

Commentary—Established in oneness here means believing only in one God, in Lord Krishna. He who believes in Him and worships Him and Him alone Who resides in every being, always lives in God though he may be moving from place to place living any or every where.

Atmoupamyen sarvatra samam pashyati yo Arjuna,
Sukham wa yadi wa duhkham sa yogi paramo matah. [32].

Meaning—O Arjun, he who looks on all as he looks on himself with the vision of equality, be it pleasure or pain he is the perfect yogi.

Commentary—To regard others as one regards oneself is the real message of this verse. One line of Sanskrit quoted during the commentary of some previous verse here is of much import. 'Aatmoupamyen sarveshu yah pashyati sa pashyati'—only he really sees, who sees others as he sees himself.

Here the reference to pleasure or pain is significant. For yogi the pleasure of others is the pleasure of his, similarly the pain of others is his pain. If one attains the above status, he is deemed to be a perfect yogi.

Arjun Uvaach :

Yo'yam yogastvaya proktah saamyen Madhusudan,
Etasayahm na pashyami chanchaltvatsthitim sthiram [33].

Meaning—Arjun said this yoga which you have taught based on equity, I do not perceive its state to be steady owing to unsteadiness (of mind).

Commentary—One can see equally on all only when one's mind is far from wavering. If that is not so a being who gets one's all sympathy at one moment loses it at the very next moment. This kid of 'yoga' is thus far from being steadfast. The unsteadiness of mind is dwelt upon in the next verse.

Chanchalam hi manah krishna pramathi balavaddriham
Tasyaaham nigraham manye vayuriva sudushkaram. [34].

Meaning—O 'Krishna' the mind is unsteady, turbulent, powerful and unyielding. I deem it as difficult to control as wind.

Commentary—Four clear characteristics of mind are outlined here :-

It is unsteady
It is turbulent
It is powerful
It is unyielding or tenacious

It is unsteady because which it likes today dislikes to morrow. It is turbulent because it is caught in the waves of thoughts—thoughts which compel to do even which is not worth doing. It is powerful because once it is bent upon having some thing it is very difficult to prevent it. It is tenacous or unyielding as it can not be compelled to act on the line you desire. In that case it is like an untamed horse refusing to follow your directions.

The simile with wind is also interesting, you have no control over a tempest. It comes and devastates, and you just look on helplessly.

Bhagavaanuvaach

Asansayam mahaabaaho manah durningraham chalam,
Abhyaasen tu kaunteya vairaagyen cha grihyate [35].

Meaning—The Lord said, O Arjun mind is undoubtedly hard to control and unsteady but O son of Kunti, it is controlled though practice and nonattachment.

Commentary—The Lord accepts the logic of Arjun about the mind but he does not accept its uncontrolability. It can be controlled if one practises to control and one does not allow it to remain attached to anything.

Asamyataatmana yogo dushpraapya iti me matih,
Vashyaatmanaa tu yatataa shakyo'vaaptumupaayath, [36].

Meaning—This is my conviction that for one who has not disciplined himself, yoga is hard to achieve but who has disciplined himself can attain it if he endeavors through proper means.

Commentary—Yoga is difficult to attain and Lord is not unaware of it. It is especially difficult for them whose self is not under control, whose thoughts are not disciplined; i.e. who are swayed away always and daily by stray thoughts.

But who has control over himself, is not under the sway of useless thoughts and tries by all means to attain it, he attains.

Arjun uvaach :

Ayatih shradhayopeto yogaachchalitmaanasah,
Aprapya yogsansidhim kaam gatim krishna gachhati [37].

Meaning—Arjun said O Krishna, what goal does he reach who is (certainly) full of faith (towards yoga) but whose mind is diverted from yoga (in the middle) due to lack of effort and he fails to achieve perfection in it.

Commentary—It is about them who almost leave the practice of yoga in the middle due to lack of proper effort though they have full faith in it.

Lord is about to explain that once one starts on the path of yoga, one is bound to attain it in lives to come even if he fails to do it in this life of his. This 'shloka' is one of the preambles to the significant statement He is about to make.

Kacchinnobhyavibhrashtaschchinnbhramiva nashyati,
Apratishtho Mahabaaho vimoodho brahmanhah pathi. [38].

Meaning—O Krishna (mightly armed!) Deluded on the path leading to Brahma and unstable does he not perish like a broken cloud deprived of both (world and God)?

Commentary—The preamble continues. Arjun wants to be clear if this man being almost dumbfoundded on the path leading to Brahma through yoga, having achieved nothing spiritual worth its name to bank upon does not perish like a cloud which is torn by wind and is he not deprived of both the worldly enjoyment and God-realisation?

Etanme samsayam Krishna chhettumarhasyasheshatah
Tvadanyah samshyaasya chhetta na hyupapadyate [39].

Meaning—O Krishna you are capable of dispelling my this doubt completely for none else than yourself is to be found who can clear this.

Commentary—Nothing particular. Arjun has by now been able to comprehend the power, the mind-power of Krishna and thus says that He Himself is the all pervading supreme. This and His knowledge of yoga which He has expounded so powerfully has led Arjun to the belief which has found expression in this verse.

Shri Bhagawaanuvaach

Parth naiveh naamutra vinaashastasya Vidyate
Na hi kalyaanhakritkashiddurgatim taat gachchati [40].

Meaning—O son of Pritha, their is no fall from him either here or there (after death). Who is involved in the act of welfare (or performing actions which is pure in nature) does not meet with evil destiny, O friend!

Commentary—After so many posers having extracted from Arjun, the Lord now replies them with the only objective of initiating him and others in yoga. Some does not start on the path of yoga out of fear that they may not complete it in this life and will forget it in the life after.

The Lord dispels this doubt. The act of practising yoga is a pious work and one who indulges in such works meets no misfortune. Whatever he achieves here is helpful in the life after death too. This the Lord will explain in the following verses.

The meaning of 'kalyan' is not necessarily welfare. As hinted above 'kalyaan' also stands for pious endeavor. Moreover words change meaning over ages. A word used five thousand years back does not necessarily carry the same meaning today.

Praapya punhyakritaam lokaanushitva shaashvatih samaah,
Shucheenaam shrimataam gehe yogbhrashtobhijaayate. [41].

Meaning—Having attained the world where the righteous live (after death) and having dwelt there for countless years, one who has fallen from yoga, takes birth in the house of pious and great men.

Commentary—Even the short practice of yoga or the fall from yoga does not go in vein. Such men after death are taken to the places (heavens) where right people reside. They dwell there for many years and then take birth in the house of those who are pure as well as well known and well to do.

Athawaa yoginaameva kule bhavati dheemtaam
Atadddhi durlabhataram loke janm yadeedrisham [42].

Meaning—Or he is born in the family of heightened yogis though this kind of birth is more difficult to have in this world.

Commentary—One fallen from 'yoga' may be born even in the family of yogis who are wise and certainly engaged in the practice of 'yoga'. Here he gets the ready facility to advance further on the path of yoga. It is why this kind of birth is described by the Lord to be more difficult to attain than the former one mentioned in the preceding verse.

Tatra tam budhisamyogam labhate paurbdehikam
Yatate cha tato bhooyah samsidhou Kurunandan [43].

Meaning—O joy of the kurus (Arjun) in the family (described in two previous verses) he regains the union of intellect (yoga) reached in the previous birth and through that he strives again for perfection.

Commentary—The experience gained in the previous

birth by the yogi who failed in that birth to reach perfection does not go in vein. He, born in the two types of families described in the preceding two verses regains the level of practice he had reached in that birth through what is called in Sanskrit 'sanskara' (say ideas imbedded from the past). With this background he again starts practising yoga to reach perfection which he failed to do in the previous birth. The Lord wants to stress that one should not hesitate in starting on the path of yoga with the fear that he may not attain perfection in this life.

Poorvaabhyaasen tenaiva hriyate hyabash'pi sah
Jigyaasurapi yogasya shabd brahmaativartate [44].

Meaning—By the former practice itself he is helplessly drawn towards (yoga). Even one curious about yoga, transcends the knowledge of the Vedas.

Commentary—The former experience serves as a propeller for him and be cannot check himself from practising yoga even if the wants. The Lord goes so far as to assert that yoga is so powerful that one who does not actually practises it but simply wants to know about it lifts his knowledge up even above the level of the knowledge of the Vedaas. 'Shabdbrahm' here naturally stands for the Vedaas and this meaning of it has been accepted by many commentators.

The Gita is basically against the Vedaas as it is the product of a period coming much after that of them and it teaches the importance of the absence of expectations of fruits of action while the Vedaas prescribe the methods to obtain results from actions.

Here, certainly, the Lord comes very heavily on the Vedaas. Even an apprentice in yoga, nay even an exquisitor of it is far above those who are well-versed in the Vedaas. The message of course, is that the Vedic practices are not worth pursuing whatever importance might have been attached to them in the past.

Prayatnaadyatamaanastu yogi samshudhkilbishah,
Anekjanmsamsidhastato yaati paraam gatim [45].

Meaning—The yogi who through endeavor practises

yoga is purged of all sins and perfected through many births, attains the supreme state.

Commentary—It thus may take many births for a man to reach the supreme state beyond which there is nothing to reach, as he is purified of all sins through the practice of yoga from birth to birth. He certainly endeavors ceaselessly for attaining higher levels in yoga and the endeavour is not forced but comes naturally due to experiences of the past practices.

Tapasvihhyo'dhilko yogi
gyaanibhyopimato'dlhikah,
Karmibhyaschaadliko yogi
tasmadyogi bhvaaraarjun [46].

Meaning—A yogi is superior to the ascetics, he is considered superior even to the man of knowledge. He is superior to those indulged in action. Therefore O Arjun be a yogi.

Commentary—The superiority of yog (indulging in constant actions without earning for results) is established over all kinds of practices including austerity, knowledge and actions performed with some motive.

Thus 'yoga' is superior to 'sanyas' even as some men of knowledge stand for those decrying actions and believing in renunciation.

Yoginaamapi sarveshaam madgatenaantraatmna,
Shradhavanbhajate yo maam sa me yuktatamo matah. [47].

Meaning—Of all yogis who devoutly worships Me with his innermost·self absorbed in Me, is adjudged to be the best by Me.

Commentary—True, a yogi is superior to all as stated in the previous verse but the best yogi is one who does not only practise yoga but also worships the Lord with full faith and knows none else, his self entrenched in Him and Him only.

Here, the Lord very intelligently introduces the concept of devotion (bhakti). The Gita might be believing in actions without expectations of fruits (Yoga) but it does not rejects devotion. One cannot reach any where without the help of the power that is supreme, here Krishna Himself; so, the importance of devotion to Him. **Yoga coupled with devotion is the best thing to have.**

"Om tatsaditi shrimadbhagavadgitaashoopanishashu brahmvidyayaam yogshaashtre Shrikrishnarjun sambaade aatmsamyam yogonaam shashtho'dhyaayah."

Thus is the Upanishad sung by the Lord, the science of Brahma the scripture of yoga, in the dialogue between Lord krishna and Arjuna ends the sixth chapter, entitled the "Yoga of self control."

CHAPTER VII

Shri Bhaawanuvaach

Mayyaasaktamanaah Parth Yagam yunjanmadaashryah,
Asanshayam Samagram maam yathaa gyaasyasi Tatchrinhu [1].

God Said—

Meaning—O Parth hear as to how with mind attached to Me, with Me as your only refuge, practising yoga you will undoubtedly know Me in entirity.

Commentary—The Lord is promising to Arjun that He will let him know how He can be known to him in His entirity. The only condition is that he should ever be attached to Him and dependent on Him and practise yoga as instructed by Him. In such case there is no doubt that he will know the Lord in **entirety** i.e. he will know His unlimited powers, splendour, wealth, prowess and His other qualities including His being the creator of all beings and also being their sustainer and provider.

Gyaanam Te'ham Savigyaanamidam vakshyamya sheshatah,
Yajgyaatvaa neh bhooyo'njgyaatavyamamavashishyate [2].

Meaning —I shall let you know in its **entirety** this knowledge along with the special knowledge (vigyaanam). Knowing which there remains nothing in this world to know.

Commentary—'Vigyaan' here is not to be confused with science. In fact, the term for science was token from the Gita and other scriptures.

'Vigyaan' here stands for the knowledge pertaining to soul and the supreme soul—God Himself.

Manushyaanhaam sahasreshu kashidyatati sidhaye
yattaamapi sidhaanaam kashchinmaam vetti tatwatah [3].

Meaning—Out of thousands of men hardly one tries

to realise Me. Of those endeavoring yogis only some one knows Me really.

Commentary—The emphasis is on knowing Him in reality, in His all dimensions. His real nature which is hard to be perceived is thus known only to some one in a million. To know Him superficially is not to know Him at all. He will however proceed in this and other succeeding chapters to introduce Himself to some extent. The manifestation of 'Viraat roop' will be the climax of it.

The painful realisation is that people even don't strive to know Him; what a pity!

Bhoomirapo'nalo vayuh kham mano budhireva cha,
Ahankaar iteeeyam me bhinna prakritirashtadha [4].

Meaning—Earth, water, fire, wind, ether, intellect, logic and also ego represent my nature divided eight fold.

Commentary—These eight characteristics of His nature certainly constitute the beginning of the enumeration of His real form.

Apareyamitastvanyaam prakritim vidhi me paraam,
jeevabhootaam mahaabaaho yayedam dhaaryate jagat [5].

Meaning—O mightly armed, this (enumerated in the preceding verses) is indeed My lower nature, the other by which universe is sustained know to be My higher nature in the form of the life-principle.

Commentary—Earth, Water, ether etc. are certainly the parts of His nature but they are declared by the Lord to be His lower form as indicated in the commentary of the preceding verse. He is really reflected in the form of numerous beings whom He sustains in this universe.

Nay, the universe is not only the collection of beings, it is much more than that. Sustaining this universe is only the work of God. None else is capable of it.

Atdyoneeni bhootaani sarvaanheetyupadhaaraya,
Aham Kritsnasya jagatah prabhavah pralayastatha [6].

Meaning—O Arjun, know that all beings are product of my two fold nature. I am the source of the entire world and also the end of it.

Commentary—His to fold nature is undoubtedly in the

root of the creation of all beings. The lower nature of His and the upper one both combine to produce this world. All created things ultimately perish so the creatures of the world and the world itself. Who is responsible for this? None but Krishna Himself.

Mattah partaram naanyatkinchidasti Dhananjay
Mayi sorvamidam proktam sootre manhiganha eva [7].

Meaning—O Danajyay (Arjun) there is nothing else than Me. As the clusters of yarn-beads are formed by knots on a thread so all these beings of the world is threaded in Me.

Commentary—The Lord declares in no uncertain terms that, there is nothing devoid of Him. He permeates every thing. As yarn and yarn only is present in the thread as well as in the knots, so the entire creation is threaded in Him.

Raso'hamapsu Kaunteya prabhasmi shashisooryooh
Pranhavah sarvvedeshu shabdah khe paurusham nrishu [8].

Meaning—O Arjuna, I am the sapidity found in water, I am the light of the moon and the sun. I am 'Om' in all the Vedas, the word in the sky and the manhood in men.

Commentary—The Lord proceeds to explain His splendour. Whatever the best or the main thing is in any thing or being, it is but his reflection. The water is nothing without its sapidity and the Lord claims that it is He in the form of this essence of water. A man is reduced to an almost pitiable existence if devoid of manliness which is nothing but He. The word or sound is the product and essence of the sky. This sound is He. Similar is the case of the moon and the sun. Deprived of their light what they are? And this light is but He.

Punhyo gandhah prithivyam cha tejashchasmi vibhavasau,
Jieevanam Sarvabhooteshu Tapashchaasmi tapasvishu [9].

Meaning—In the earth I am its flaw-less (or pure) odour, am the brightness (the very heat) of the fire, am the life-(force) in all beings, am the penance of the men of askesis.

Commentary—Nothing special. The meaning is very clear. The Lord goes on enumerating His qualities. The important point to note is that there is no life without Him as He himself is life of all beings both animate and inanimate.

Beejam maam sarvobhootanam viddhi parth sanatanam,
Budhirbudhimataamasmi tejastijasvinaamaham [10].

Meaning—O Parth! Know Me as the ever existent seed of all beings. I am the wisdom of the wise and the brightness of the bright.

Commentary—The Lord goes an enumerating his superb qualities found in different places as well as indifferent beings.

Balam balwataachaaham kamraagvivarjitam,
Dhirmaviruddho bhooteshu kaamo'smi Bgartarshabh [11].

Meaning—O Bhartarshabh (the best among Bharatas) I am the strength of the strong, divoid of desire and passion; I am the sexual power among the beings, if this power is not contrary to religion.

Commentary—He is the might of the mighty. There is nothing special about it. But He is also the sexual power of the beings. This may astonish some body. But the Lord hastens to clarify, he is only that sexual prowess which is endorsed by religion. It implies the following two :

(i) Sex with in the properly married couple is not sin; it is rather the root of creation.

(ii) Sex outside the wed-lock is not endorsed by the Lord rather it is this sex which has been decried in the Gita from time to time.

Ye chaiva saattvikaa bhaawa raajasaastaamasashch ye
Matt aveti taanvidhi na twaham teshu te mayi [12]

Meaning—Whatever other characteristics are, in form of 'sattva', 'rajas' and 'tamas' know them to have flowed from Me. I am not in them but they are in Me.

Commentary—'Sattva', 'rajas' and 'tanas'—the three modes of nature have been explained in previous pages. The Lord rightly claims that these entities have evolved from Him. Where else they can come from? But He is prompt to point out that they are in Him but He is not in them. True, God is free from all these modes of nature. He is above them all. Thus neither a 'saatvic' person nor a 'taamsic' person can clain that his charecteristics owe allegiance to Him. Once He already declared that He partakes neither the virtue nor the vice of any body.

Tribhirgunhamayairbhaavairebhih sarvamidam yagat, mohitam naabhijaanaati maanebhyah paramabyayam [13].

Meaning—This entire creation is deluded by these three entities, it is why, it does not recognise Me—the most imperishable.

Commentary—Do all people accept the existence of God (Who never perishes)? Some do, many do not. Why many do not recognise His existence? In other words why the people (most of them) during His time did not recognise Krishna as God. The people like, Duryodhan, Shishupaal etc? Because they like many others were deluded by these three modes of nature in other words by His (krishna) 'maaya'. He will come to this 'maaya' in the very next verse.

Daivi hyeshaa gunhamayee mam maaya duratyayaa, Maameva ye prapadyante maayaametaam taranti te [14].

Meaning—My 'maaya' of the modes (of nature) is divine and difficult to break through. Those who adore only Me are able to get through them.

Commentary—The most commonly used but most dreadful aspect of the Lord is His 'maaya' (veil or delusion) is said to be divine by Lord Krishna. It is divine because the modes creating them flow from Him. His this 'maayaa' as known to many has deluded even many a saint and seer including Narada who was very much curious to know about it.

But not all are its easy preys. Those who worship Krishna and Krishna alone escape its tentacles.

Na maam dushkritino moodah prapadyante naradhamaah, maayayaapahritgyaanaa aasuram bhaawamaa shritaah. [15]

Meaning—The vile fools of evil deeds whose thoughts have been carried away by 'maayaa' and are of demoniac nature do not adore Me.

Commentary—The Lord is vividly furious of them who fail to adore Him. They are called, 'dushkritinah' (engaged in pursuing evil deeds), 'moodhaah' (jack fools) and 'naraadha maah' (worst among men).

But He admits that being deluded by His 'maaya', they

are hardly at fault. Any way the best thing is to shun one's demonic nature and start adoring Him. The 'maayaa' will melt away.

Chaturvidhaa bhajante maam janaah sukritino'arjun,
Aarto jigyaasurthaarthee gyaanee cha Bhartarshabh [16].

Meaning—O Bhartarshabha four types of men of good deeds adore Me—the afflicted, the inquisitive, the seeker of wealth and the wise.

Commentary—They who adore the Lord has been identified by Him. We also know that usually these types remember Him. The afflicted are they who suffer from some disease. But the point to be noted is that not all such persons worship or remember Him but only they who are of noble deeds (Sukritinih). Other of opposite nature may suffer but will not bother to remember or worship Him faithless as they are.

Besides the afflicted one the rest types remember Him either for wealth or for knowledge (inquisitivity) or for wisdom.

Teshaam gyaanee nityazukt ekbhaktirvishishyate
Priyo hi gyaanino'tyarthaham so cha man priyah [17].

Meaning—Of them the wise is the best, he is ever united (with Me) he is devoted only to Me. It is why the wise is dear to Me and I am dear to Him.

Commentary—The man of wisdom has been declared to be the best of the four types enumerated in the preceding shloka. He is very dear to God as God is dear to Him.

The wise man here must not be confused with a 'Sanyasee'. This chapter is not devoted to 'gyaanyog'. The man of wisdom is the man who has gone through striptures and know on the strength of his study and experience the Lord to be all powerful.

Udaaraah sarva avaite gyaanee twaatmaiva me matan
Asthitah sa hi yuktatmaa maamevanuttamaam gatim [18].

Meaning—All of them are virtuous but 'gyaanee' with 'yoga' attached to Me is indeed firmly established in Me Who is the ultimate goal.

Commentary—The man with wisdom or wisdom itself

is being given preference by the Lord. He is always attached to Him knowing Him to be only worth attached with through his learning and practise of Yoga. As a result of it, Lord confesses, that he is firmly established in Him and this relation with the Lord is the aspiration of every body.

Bahoonaam janmaanante gyaanwanmaam prapodyate,
Vaasudevoh sarvamiti sa mahaatma sudurlabhah [19].

Meaning—At the end of many births the man of wisdom worships Me realizing that all this is Krishna. Such a great soul is very uncommon.

Commentary—It is not very easy to convince oneself even for an enlightened one that it is none but Lord Krishna Who is all pervasive and is in all animate and inanimate beings. It takes even for him many births to get this fact planted with in him. The Lord says that such a great soul is very rare.

It also emplieys that at the end of many births having attended the rank of enlightened devotee knowing all to be Shri Krishna, his cycle of birth and death stops.

Kaamaistaistairhritgyaanaah praapdyante'nya devataah,
Tam Tam niamamaasthaay prakrityaa niyatahaswaya [20].

Meaning—Those whose thinking has been carried away by this and that desire worship other gods according to the methods related to them having been prompted by their own nature.

Commentary—The different gods are selected by the nature of the worshipper. If a person worships 'kaali' and sacrifises animals on her **altar**, his nature is certainly 'taamasic.' If one worships Ganehsh or Hanuman who do not need such sacrifice, his nature is exalted i.e. sattvic. These worships are invariably done to get some desires fulfilled.

There are certainly different rules as well as 'mantraas' for the worship of different gods (and goddesses).

Yo yo yaam yaam tanu bhaktah
shradyaarchitumichchaati,
Tasya tasyaachalam shradhaam
taameva vidadhaamyaham [21].

Meaning—Whatever deity (god) the devotee wants to

worship with reverence I make stable the faith of that devotee in that particular god.

Commentary—It is not unknown to Krishna that many people worship different gods not Him. He is however not jealous. He being God of gods stabilizes the faith of such devotees in those gods so that he goes on worshipping them with deep faith.

Sataya shradhaya Yuktastasyaaraadhan meehate
Labhate cha totah kaamaanmayaiva vihitaanhi taan [22].

Meaning—With that faith made stable by Me He undertakes the worship of that particular god and undoubtedly obtains from him the desired needs which are (actually) ordained by Me.

Commentary—The message is very clear. The gods have not got their own powers. They are, anyway, helped by the Lord in two ways.

Firstly he establishes fimly the faith of their devotees in them. Thus worshipped through this firm faith they grant the desires of the devotees but here also they are helped by the Lord. Left alone they cannot grant anything. In other words their power of wishfulfilment flows from the all powerful, omnipotent Lord Krishna.

Antwanttu phalam teshaam tadbhavatyalpmedhasam,
Devaandevayajo yaanti madbhakta yaanti maamapi [23]

Meaning—The desires obtained by these men of small intellect do not end for ever. The worshippers of gods attain them (but) My devotees come to Me.

Commentary—The justice is dispensed in a very just way. After leaving this world the devotees of gods go to latters' abode while the devotees of the Lord go to His (eternal) abode.

The fruits obtained from the worship of gods shortly end. (So why not to worship the Lord instead of other gods?)

Abyaktam vyaktimaapannam manyante maambhudhyah,
param bhaavamajaananto mamaavyayamanuttamam [24]

Meaning—The fools not knowing My supreme nature which is beyond reach, unsurpassable and decaying regard me as (an ordinary) person (taking birth in and departing from the world).

Commentary—Krishna though in human form is not actually so. He is endless, beyond reach, unknown (not fully known to even men of wisdom and yogis) and of the supreme nature. The ignorant one (only) knows Him to be born in an ordinary human form.

Krishna is certainly an incarnation like Ram and others. But He differs from them as He is the full incarnation of the supreme while others are only partial. The 'Bhaagawat Puraana' bears it out 'Ete ansaavataaraahapunsaah Krishnastu Bhagawan svayam'—All these men are partial incarnations, Krishna is God Himself.'

So He rightly asserts that He is not an ordinary human being as the ignorant are inclined to consider Him.

Naaham prakaashah sarvasya yogmaayayaa samaavritah
Moodho'yam naabhijaanaati loko maamjamabyayan [25].

Meaning—The ignorant world does not know Me. The unborn and endless as I am not manifest to all; veiled by my yogmaaya (the divine delusion).

Commentary—Nothing special. The delusion called 'maaya' has occurred at many places. Here the Lord suffixes it with yog meaning there by that He creates this 'maaya' with the help of yoga which He either practises or is one of His qualities.

Vedaaham samateetaani vartmaanaani chaarjun,
Bhavishyaanhi cha blootani maam tu ved na kashchan [26].

Meaning—O Arjun I Know all the past, present and future beings but no body knows Me.

Commentary—It is certainly possible for the omnipresent and omniscient Lord to know who are here, who have been here and who are to be here. But how can the wisest of wise know Him fully?

Echchaadveshsamuthen dvandvamohen Bharat,
sarvabhootaani sammoham sarge yaanti parantap [27].

Meaning—O Bharat, O Parantap (chastiser of foes) due to delusion in form of pairs of opposites, born of desire and envy all beings in this world, are the victim of infatuation.

Commentary—People in this world are infatuated and deluded no doubt and it is why they exist. The cause of this infatuation, the Lord discloses is the pairs of opposites (pleasure and pain, love and hatred etc.). These opposites are born of desire and envy. One or another desire is always there; so is envy towards people appearing to be more prosperous, happy and successful.

Yesham tvantggyanam papam jananam punhyakarmnam
Te dvandvamohnirmukta bhajante maam drirhavrataah [28]

Meaning—The virtuous people whose sin has ended; are freed from the delusion of the pair of opposites and of firm resolve, worship Me.

Commentary—Virtue destroyes the sin. Such sinless people are not deluded by the pairs of opposites and it is they with firm resolve who are inclined to worship the Lord.

Jaraamaranha mokshaay mamashritya yatanti ye,
Te Brahm tadviduh kritasnamdhyatmam Karm chakhilam [29].

Meaning—Those striving for deliverence from old age, death, by taking refuge in Me, know the Brahm, entire adhyaatm as well as all actions.

Commentary—People who strive for deliverence of old-age and death strive by taking refuge in Him. But does any one escape the old age and death? Certaionly not. Then what does the Lord imply here? It is breaking away from the cycle of birth and death. When you are not born, where are the old age and death?

The real meaning of 'Brahma' and 'Adhyaatam' is provided by the Lord Himself in the I[st] shloka of the succeeding chapter. Wait till then.

As for (worth doing) actions are concerned they have been explained many a time.

Saadhibhootaadhidaivam maam saadhiyagyam cha ye vidhuh,
Prayaanhkaale'pi cha maam te viduryuktchetasah [30].

Meaning—They who know Me at the end of their worldly abode with 'adhibhoot', 'adhidaiva' and 'adhiyagya' and are of stiffest (mind full of yoga) know Me (really).

Commentary—To know Him really in fact is to merge with Him owing to the qualities enumerated here.

The meaning of 'adhibhoot,' 'adliyagya' 'adhyaatm' are given by the Lord Himself in the next chapter. They have been fully commented upon also.

Om tatsaditi Shrimadbhagawadgitaashoopnishatsu Brahmvidyayaam yogshahshtre Shri Krishnarjun Samvaade gyaanvigyaam yogo naam saptamo'dhyaayah.

Thus in the Upanishad sung (by Lord Krishna), the science of Brahma the scripture of yoga the dialogue between Shri Krishna and Arjun ends the Seventh chapter entitled 'gyan vigyaan yoga.'

CHAPTER VIII

Arjun Uvaach

Kimtadvrahm kimadhyaatammam kim karm purushottam, adhibhootam cha ki proktamdhidaivam kimuchyate [1].

Meaning—Arjuna asked, "O the best among men, what is that 'Brahma,' what is 'Adhyaatma' What is 'Karma' and what is termed as 'Adhibhoota' and 'adhidaiva'

Commentary—Arjuna's query continues in the next Shloka also, let us wait. They are merely questions or a request to explain some terms. Why should we explain them, before the Lord does it.' Yes, a new term karm which was not included in the last verse of the last chapter appears here. Let us see what the Lord is to say about it.

Adhiyagyah katham ko'tra dehe'sminmadhusoodan, prayaanhakaale cha katham gyeyo'shi niyataatmbhih [2].

Meaning—O killer of the demon Madhu, what is here 'adhiyagya' and how it is supposed to be in this body? How at the time of departure from this world you are known by those of exalted souls?

Commentary—Let us wait for the answer of the Lord which follows in the next verse.

Shri Bhagavaanuvaach :—

Aksharam Bhrahm Paramam svabhaavo'dhyaatmmuchyate, Bhootbhaavodhbhavakaaro visargah karmsamgditahatah [3].

Meaning—God said, Bhram is the supreme imperishable. One's own self is Adyaatma and the process of creating all these beings is karm i.e. action.

Commentary—The Lord follows the pattern of Arjun's

questions while rendering his explanations. First he takes Brahm. According to Him who is supreme indestructible is Brahma. The world supreme here is of significane. Not only Brahm is indestructible but even the lesser gods who are immortal are also endestructritable. But one who is supreme among them is Brahm.

So far as 'Adhyaatm' is concerned the Lord maintains in no uncertain term that it is one's own self. What does that mean? What is self? It is certainly the soul abiding in the body, as part or representative of God. Krishna has declared in the VIIth shloka of chapter XV that his own part dwells in all beings as the eternal soul (Mamaivaansho jeeva loke jeevahoottah sanaatanah). Thus the soul residing in this body which is called self is 'Adhyaatma' and is imperishable, being the part of the imperishable God.

Coming to 'Karma' i.e. action it is here different from the ordinary action of man. Here it is placed on an exalted platform. It is in reality the action of Supreme Himself as it is He who creates the beings of this world and the very process of creation is divine, the action of Lord and not that of any mortal. This creation is beyond him.

This process of creation is certainly automatic, done at the wish of the Lord. But the Lord himself is not actionsless. He believes in doing. He maintains in the 22nd shloka of the third chapter that though he has nothing to crave for or to obtain yet he indulges in actions.

Adhibhootam ksharo bhaavah purushashchaadhidvaivatam,
Adhyagyo'hamevatra dehe dehbritaam vara [4].

Meaning—O the best among the embodied beings! 'Adhibhoot' means all the perishable objects of this world (including certainly the human beings). As the world itself is perishable so everything here is not immune from destruction. 'Adhidaiva' is 'Purshah'. I am myself is 'Adhiyagya' in this body.

Commentary—The meaning of 'adhibhoota' has been fully elaborated above. Now who is this Purusha? He is not any ordinary mortal. Purush in the Gita is usually associated with Brahm. The Lord krishna is even above this Brahm. He is the 'Purushottama' as he maintains in the 18th shloka of the 15th canto.

So far as 'adhiyagya' is concerned it is He Himself. That is He is the 'yagyapurusha.' The question of Arjuna in this regard is two fold. Who is 'adhiyagya' and how does he dwell in this human form? Krishna answers these two questions in only one sentence, I myself is 'Adhiyagya' in this body. Now how 'Adhiyagya' dwells in the human body is taken care of. When the Lord Himself is the dweller, He knows best how to dwell.

He has maintained in shloka 29 of chapter IX that He is the enjoyer of all 'yagyas' (sacrifices), thus this is not surprising that He Himself declares to be 'Adhiyagya' here.

The readers must not over look the fact that the term 'Adhi' in all these words makes the difference. Bhoot becomes different from its usual form when it is 'Adhiboot' 'daiva' (usually a god) becomes the Supreme God or Brahm when it is 'Adhibhoot', 'yagya' is a usual scarifice but the moment 'adhi' is added to, it because Krishna Himself. Thus the importance of 'adhi' must not be lost upon the readers.

Antkale cha maameva smarnmuktva kalevaram,
Yah prayati sa madbhavam yati naastyatr sansayah. [5]

Meaning—At the times of finally leaving this body the person who thinks of Me and Me alone, he attains Me. There is no doubt about this.

Commentary—The Lord has made it clear in a pervious couplet that those who worship ancestors go to them, those who worship gods go to their abode and My devotees come to Me. Here is just underlined the last fact to augment the faith of Krishna-devotees. The expression here is no doubt ('nasyatra' samsayah) very assuring.

This also implies that the place and manner of death or even the past evil deeds do not matter. But it is clear that remembering the Lord through out the life is necessary other wise one will fail to remember Him at the time of departure from his worldly abode.

Yam Yam vaapi smaranbhaavam tyajtyante kalevaram
Tam tamevaiti konteya sada tadbhaavabhaavitah [6].

Meaning—O Son of kunti! Thinking of whatever entity one drops this body, that and that only he attains due to being always engrossed in that feeling.

Commentary—It is important that pure and Godly ideas are absorbed in at the time of death. Otherwise one's final alone will be decided by the mean ideas thinking which he departs from this world.

This also means that one must not continue to think about his unfulfilled cordial desires otherwise he will have to take birth to fulfill them and this birth may not be very exalted. This necessarily implies that if one dies thinking of devotion of the Lord he will he born as a staunch devotee of Shri Krishna or will go to His abode. This is borne out from the next 'shloka' :

Tasmaatsarveshu kaaleshu maamanusmar yudhya cha,
Mayyarpitmanobudhirmaamevaishyasanshayam. *[7]*

Meaning—So remember Me always and fight. When thus the mind and intellect are devoted to Me, you will undboubtedly come to Me.

Commentary—The Gita is sung to persuade Arjuna to take part in the ensuing battle which he wants not to indulge in for his own reasons which have been enunciated in the opening chapters.

Thus the Lord gives him another and sure temptation after preparing ground for it in the preceding shlokas. It is that if he fights remembering Him always, he will attain Him after death (eithter during the battle or after it).

Abhyaasyog yukten chetasaa naanyagaaminaa,
Paramam purusham divyam yati paarthaanuchintayan. [8]

Meaning—O son of Pritha! With yoga attained through constant practice and the mind not wandering (leaving Me) one attains the Supreme Divine Being i.e. the Lord Himself.

Commentary—The importance of 'yoga' comes again. It is to be noticed that in many a preceding verse the emphasis has been laid on the ways to attain the Lord at the time of death and this is the foremost attainment of a mortal being.

Here the 'yoga' is underlined to ensure this. But the fact is that this 'yoga' should be practised through out other wise at the time of crucial moment the mind will divert in other directions (as its nature is) and one will fail to attain the Supreme Divine Being i.e. Shri Krishna. If the mind is not diverted it will constantly remember Him ensuring His attainment.

Kavimpuraanhamanushaasitaar-
manhoranheeyansamanusmaredyah
Sarvasya Dhaataaramachintyaroopa
maadityavarnham Tanasah parastaat [9].

Meaning—Who that remembers the All wise, Ageless Ruler of the all and minute sustainer of every being whose form cannot be comprehended and whose colour is like that of the sun and who is beyond darkness.

Commentary—The idea is not complete, it will be completed in the following verse. Here the very speculations of the Supreme Being are enunciated. He is poet (kavi). But in Sanskrit poet is not only one who composes poetry. It stands for the learned. It has been explained earlier also.

He is Ageless. In this sense His origin is beyond trace. He is the oldest of the all (puraanhamm). He disciplines every body i.e. He is the ruler and guardian of all. And the most important, he is minuter than the minute. He can hardly be seen with these ordinary eyes and it is a scientific fact that more minute some thing is the more powerful it is. He is the sustainer of all in the sense that without Him here can not be any life. In other words He provides for all. His form or shape cannot be contemplated. Who knows how he looks? But he is as shining as the sun. His being beyond darkness does not imply that He is not dark. How the sun can be dark? It simply means that he is beyond 'Tamas' i.e.. the dark qualities-lethargy, ignorance, pride, deceit and impurity etc.

Prayaanha kaale manasaachalen
Bhaktyaa ukto yogbalen chaiva.
Bhruvormadhye pranhamaaveshya samyak
Sa tam param Puruhshamupaiti divyam [10].

Meaning—At the time of departure (from this world) with a steadfast mind, devotion and with the power of yoga who firmly holds the life-breath between the brows he attains that Divine Supreme Being (the Lord).

Commentary—It is for them who remember the Lord and the attributes enumerated in the preceding 'Shloka'

A method is shown to them how to attain that Supreme Being. It is actually a 'yogic' (pertaining to yoga) device.

According to the Lord a person should place the life-breath extracting from his whole body, between his eye-brows. How? By a steadfast mind, by the devotional attitude and by the power of yoga. Thus if he breathes his last in this way i.e. the life-force passes out through the space between the eyebrows (the most sacred place in the body on which yogis meditate) then one attains the Divine Supreme Being i.e. the Lord or Shri Krishna Himself.

Yadaksharam vedvido vadanti
Vishanti yadyatayo veetraagaah
Yadichchanto Brahmacharyam charanti,
Tatte padam sangrahenha pravakshye [11].

Meaning—Whom the knowers of the Vedas call indestructible, in Whom enter the striving ascetics free from passions and Whom desire the practitioners of celibacy, I will tell about in brief That (supreme) Goal.

Commentary—The Lord promises to describe in brief to Arjuna that He will tell about the supreme place whom the well versed in the Vedas describe as indestructible Which he really is, to Whom go the passionless striving saints and dwelling on Whom the celibates perform their difficult task i.e. of practising celibacy.

There is nothing new in His being indestructible. He has been described so in many a time. The Supreme place is His own abode and it is also therefore indestructible.

Now extra important attributes are added to Him in this verse.

First is that, those Who are passionless pure being (yatayah) struggle to reach His place and most importantly the practitioner of celibacy succeeds only by dwelling on that supreme abode of His.

Sarvadvaaranhi sanyamya mano hridi nirudhya cha,
Moordhanyadhayatmanah pranhamasthito yogdhaaranham [12].

Meaning—Having shut all the doors (of body i.e. senses), firmly placing the mind in the heart, who places his life-breath in the head and remains steadfastly in yogic concentration.

Commentary—Lord's statement will be completed in the next couplet. Here He describes first steps to attain the supreme goal He promised to be attained by the people with attributes described in the preceding verse :

The aspirant must do the following

- i He must shut off all senses i.e. they must be completely guarded (so that the life-breath does not escape through any of them)
- ii The mind (which is very unstable) should be confined in the heart.
- iii Establish the life-breath in the head.
- iv Remain steadfastly in the concept of 'yoga' (i.e. in its practice)

'Yoga' has been described earlier (in shloka 48, 49, 50 and 51 of the second canto). It is actually training the intellect so that it is free from all desires and the fruits of the actions performed. But here the Lord is talking of 'Patanjalyog.'

Omityekaakshram Brahm vyaaharanmaamnusmaran
Yah prayaati tyajandeham sa yaati paranaam gatim [13].

Meaning—He who departs (from this world) uttering 'Om' the indestructible Brahma as well as remembering Me, attains the supreme state.

Commentary—It has been uttered by the Lord previously also that who breathes last dwelling on Him reaches Him or in other words attains the supreme spiritual state.

Here in this 'Shloka' He also emphasises the importance of 'Om' which is always used in the beginning of all hymns and 'Shlokas'. It is nothing less then the indestructible Brahm, declares the Lord.

In fact some 'Upanishads' have pronounced 'Om' as Brahm Himself.

Ananyachetaah satatm yo maam smarati nityashah,
Tasyaaham sulabhah Parth nityayuktasya yoginah [14].

Meaning—O Son of Pritha I am easily approachable to

that yogi who constantly remembers Me with undivided mind and with the ceaseless attachment to Myself.

Commentary—The Lord is here underlining the importance of the following—

i Constant attachment to Him through yoga
ii Ceaseless remembrance of Him.

The first naturally is possible by a 'yogi'. It is why He says that He is easily available to such yogi. But one must not forget that yogi in the Gita is not an extraordinary person with supernatural powers or the member of a particular cult. Every one is a yogi if he performs his responsibilities in an indifferent way, indifferent towards the results and keeps himself ever attached to Shri Krishna.

Ever remembrance as required of in this verse is not that difficult even for an ordinary householder. Wise people have uttered many a time that go on doing your duties and keep the Lord in the mind remembering His glories, virtues and unlimited kindness.

Maamupetya punarjanm dukhalayamashaashvatam,
Naapnuvanti mahatmanah samsidhim paramam gataah [15].

Meaning—By attaining Me, the great souls who have achieved the highest perfection, are no more subject to rebirth which is the abode of suffering and is not permanent.

Commentary—This is in continuance of the former verse. The Lord had told as to who attain Him. Now He declares the bliss attaining Him which he attains. What is that bliss? The freedom from the painful circle of birth and death. He will not be reborn i.e. he will be one with the Lord and as a result of not being born he will also not die.

Aabrahmbhuwanaallokaah punraavartino'rjuna
Maamupetya tu kaunteya punarjanm na vidyate [16]

Meaning—O Arjuna, all the worlds right from the abode of Brahma and downwards, are subject to appearance and reappearance. By attaining Me there is no rebirth.

Commentary—The subject of rebirth continues. The Lord underlines its importance in many a way.

Here He declares that all the worlds from the abode of Brahma Himself and downwards appear and disappear and as a result reappear. Only by attaining Him one is free from the shackles of birth and death.

It thus implies that all these worlds even Brahmloka (the abode of Brahma) are born; created by the Lord Himself. Any thing born dies or anything created is destroyed. So all these are destructible and whoever residing in these worlds is subject to birth and rebirth. This follows that only the abode of the Lord Krishna is without beginning and end and it is why one who goes to Him is not subject to rebirth.

Sahasrayugaparyantmahayardbrahmanho vidhuh,
Raatrim Yugasahasraantaam te'horaatravido janaah [17].

Meaning—Brahma's day consists of a thousand yugas (ages) and so is his night, covering thousand ages. Those who know it are knowers of the time.

Commentary—The Lord here limits the age of Brahma. As he is perishable the time of his days and nights are determined though it may be considerably long. But this longevity has its end.

Commentary—According to Manusmriti, 4,32,00,00,000 human-years make a day of Brahma and the same length is of his night.

Avyaktaadvyakatyah sarvaah prabhavantyaharaagame,
Ratryaagame praleeyante tatraivaavyaktsangyake [18].

Meaning—All manifest (beings) emanate from the unmanifest at the appearance of the (celestial) day and merge in to the same at the (celestial) nightfall.

Commentary—The discussion is about Brahma's day and night and the resultant transitory nature of his and those created by him.

Here in fact the tell of the end and reappearance of world is subtly narrated; in other words 'pralaya' and the creation there-after are hinted upon. The fact of the end of creation is a phenomenon appearing in almost all religions. The resurgence of life there-after has also been described. The 'Noah's ark' is not imaginary.

The description here in the Gita is different only in the sense that it gives the exact period of dissolution and resurrection.

Bhootgramah sa evaayam bhootva bhootva praleeyate,
Raatryaagame'vashah parth prabhavatyaharahgame [19].

Meaning—O son of Pritha, this collection of beings emanates again and again and uncontrollably dissolves at the advent of the (cosmic) night and emerges again at the break of the (cosmic) day.

Commentary—Here the helplessness of the embodied beings has been highlighted. According to Krishna the multitude of these beings appears again and again but despite its wish it helplessly dissolves when the (cosmic) night falls. However it resurges again when the (cosmic) day arrives.

Parastasmaattu bhaavo'nyo'vyakto'vyakttaatsanaatanah,
Yah sa sarveshu bhooteshu nashyatsu na vinashyati [20].

Meaning—Another than this unmanifest there is a higher unmanifest which is eternal and which does not perish like all other beings.

Commentary—Here is emphasized the supremacy over the abode of Brahma of a higher and eternal unmanifest which while others perish, it does not. The next couplet will make clear that this higher or highest unmanifest power is none else than Lord Krishna Himself

Avyakto'kshar etuktastamaahuh paramaam gatim,
Yam prapya na nivartante taddhaam paramam mam [21]

Meaning—The indestructible unmanifest is called the supreme state. Attaining which one does not return back (to this world) is My supreme abode.

Commentary—This was hinted upon above that all worlds including the Brahma's abode are destructible, but the Lord had talked about an eternal imperishable unmanifest which does not perish though others do.

Here He maintains that the indestructible unmanifest is the supreme status and in a way it is My own abode attaining this, one need not return to this mortal world. In other words he is free from the cycle, of birth and death.

It implies that the only worth worshipping and remembering Being is Krishna Himself.

Purushah sa parah parth bhaktya labhyastvananyaya,
Yasyaantahsthaani bhootaani yen sarvamidam tatam. [22]

Meaning—O son of Pritha, that supreme Being (Purusha) in Whom all being reside and by Whom all this (creation) is pervaded is attainable through unparalleled devotion.

Commentary—Once Krishna is established as the supreme imperishable Lord it is appropriate to describe His other divine attributes. All beings reside in Him i.e. without Him none and nothing can exist. He is the very source of existence. And not only that, He pervades the entire creation.

Is He attainable? That, is Shri Krishna attainable?

Yes, says the Lord. How? Through devotion. What kind of devotion? Exclusive. One who knows and knows only Him and none else attains Him. Gets His divine and benign favour.

Mark the importance of devotion. Devotion to Lord Krishna. It is His greatness that He hands over the key to the attainment of Him to His devotees.

Yatra kaale tvanaavrittimaavrittim chaiva yoginah,
Prayaataa yaanti tam kaalam vakshyaami Bhartarsabh [23].

Meaning—O greatest among the Bharataas, I shall narrate that time departing from the world at which, 'yogis' do not return (to this mortal world) and also the time departing at which they do return.

Commentary—Certainly there are two kinds of time according to the Lord. One may be called auspicious and another unaususpicious.

Yogis breathing their last during the first do not return back to their earthly abode but those passing away during the next one do come back.

He will describe in the following two shlokas what are these two periods or span of times.

Agnirjyotirahah, Shuklah shanhmaasaa uttraaayanham,
Tatra prayata gachhanti Brahm Bhrahmvido janah [24].

Meaning—The first time or path is of which in-charge is the all effulgent fire god and there are the deities in charge of the daylight, the bright fortnight of the moon and the six months northward course (of the sun). By passing out through this those who know the Brahma reach him.

Commentary—In short those dying during the day,

during the bright fortnight of the moon and during the six months when the sun is in the northern hemisphere reach the Brahma. The only condition is that they must be the knower of Brahma.

It may be remembered that Bhishma layed himself bleeding on the arrow-bed waiting for the sun to take to its northern course, to breath his last, after pierced throughout his body with arrows by Arjuna in the Mahaabhaarat-battle.

Dhoomo ratristatha Krishnah sharhamasa dakshinhayanam,
Tatra chaandramasam jyotiryogee praapya nivartate. [25]

Meaning—The period of path full of smoke, night and falling in the dark fortnight and having the six months of southward course of the sun in which the yogi leaves this world returns back after enjoying the lusture of the moon.

Commentary—The death when the sun is on its southward journey of six months and there is the dark fortnight results is sending Yogi back; but before that he enjoys the good fruits of his 'yogic' actions by bathing in the soothing light of the moon who is supposed to be full of nectar.

The point is that though this period or path does not lead to the permanent abode (in the heavens) yet his practice of yoga does not go in vein and he enjoys the lusture of the moonshine for quite some time before he takes birth in this mortal world.

Shuklakrisnho gatee hyete Jagatah shaashwate mate,
Ekayaa yaatyanaavrittimanyayaavartate punah [26].

Meaning—For these twin paths of the world the bright and the dark are deemed to be eternal. Proceeding by one (i.e. the bright one) one attains the state from which there is no coming back but going by another he returns back again.

Commentary—The idea in the preceding 'Shloka' has been inunciated further making clear that these paths are of their own characteristics subject to no change. Going by one, one is not trapped in the vicious circle of birth and death but going by another one is.

Naite sritee paarth jaananyogi muhyati kashchan,
Tasmaatsarveshu kaaleshu yogukto bhavaarjun [27].

Meaning—O son of Pritha, knowing these two paths yogi is not deluded. Therefore, O Arjuna remain devoted to yoga at all times.

Commentary—The Gita is a book of 'Yoga' especially of 'karmyoga' (the yoga of desireless action). Shri Krishna, therefore, advises Arjuna to practise yoga always, Besides, other advantages described many times in the preceding and following shlokas one benefit is the path leading to the supreme abode from which there is no coming back to this world.

Vedeshu yagyeshu tapeshu chaiva,
daaneshu yatpunhyaphalam pradishtam
Atyeti tatsarvmidam viditva
Yogi param sthaanmupaiti chaadyam [28].

Meaning—The yogi having realized this (secret) undoubtedly transcends all fruits obtaining from the vedaas (their study) sacrifices, penances as well as charities and attain the eternal state.

Commentary—For a yogi who knows the importance of yoga (refer to the preceding shloka in which Arjuna is advised to practise yoga always) there is no need to read the Vedaas, indulge in sacrifices, perform penances and practise charity. Without all this he attains the supreme state by virtue of his yogic practices.

This chapter thus ends with highlighting the significance of 'yoga'.

Om tatsaditi Shri nandbhagwadgitaasoopanishatsu brahmividyaayaam yogshashtre Shri Krishna-arjunshamvade Aksharbrahmyogo naamashtamo'dhyaayah.

Thus in the upanishad Gita, the scripture of yog, in the knowledge of 'Bhramvidya' in the conversesion of Shri Krishna and Arjuna ends the eighth chapter entitled 'Aksharbrahmyog'.

CHAPTER IX

Shri Bhagavanuvaach

Edam tu te guhyatamam pravakshyaamyasasooyaye,
Gyaanam vigyaansahitim yajgyatva mokhyase'shubhat [1].

Meaning—The Lord said—Now, I shall tell you, the uncarping, the most secret thing, the knowledge together with the special knowledge by knowing which you will be released from the evil.

Commentary—'Vigyaan' these days stands for the physical sciences but it did not denote the same meaning in earlier days the word has just been borrowed from the scriptures like the Gita and others. It has been maintained earlier also.

'Vigyaan' in this verse stands for the knowledge superior to the ordinary knowledge found in the sacred books.

Here, the point to be noted is that even by knowing these two types of knowledge one is freed from evils. The emphasis thus suddenly shifts from 'yoga' to knowledge.

In fact the Gita tries to strike a balance among the most prevalent ways in those day, yoga, devotion and knowledge.

Raajvidyaa raajguhyam pavitramidamuttamam,
Pratyakshaavagamam dharmyam susukham kartumavyayam [2].

Meaning—This knowledge is a sovereign knowledge (knowledge of all knowledge) is sovereign, secret, holy, directly available, virtuous, easily practisable and imperishable.

Commentary—Let us see in the following verses what this knowledge of all knowledges is.

Ashraddadhanaah purusha dharmsyasya Paramtap,
Aprapya maam nivartante mrityusansar vartmani [3].

Meaning—O Parth, people having no faith in this religion, not attaining Me return to the paths of the world of death.

Commentary—Faith is the most important ingredient. Its importance has been realised in every religion. As said earlier the Bible is very specific about it. The new Testament clearly declares—

"And whatever you ask in prayer you will receive, if ye have faith". (James 21/22).

Thus the people who have no faith in the ways propounded by the Lord do not attain Him and as a consequence fail to free themselves from the cycle of birth and death.

Mayaa Tatamidam sarvam yagdavyaktamoortinaa,
Matsthaani sarvabhootaani na chaaham teshvasthitah [4].

Meaning—All this universe is permeated by Me—the unmanisfest. All beings are situated in Me, not I in them.

Commentary—It has been emphasised in the Gita, Time and again that every thing here is pervaded by Him. The term 'yen sarvamidam Tatam' has been used at least twice so for (Shloka 17, chapter II and shloka 22, chapter III).

The term here 'Mayaa tatamidam sarvam' is similar to the two quotations above. It is however direct. The doubt as to what or by him all this is permeated or pervaded is removed for ever by the term 'Mayaa' (By Me). So it is Krishna who permeates all.

The declaration that all beings are in Me and I am not in them is obvious. But it is contrrary to the declaration in shloka 7 chapter XV where the Lord declares that My own part resides in all beings (mamaivaansho jeeva loke jeevabhootah, sanaatanah).

The only explamation which appears to be convincing is that God does not reside in whole in the being but in part. As for example ocean is in its every wave, but only a part of it not the whole one itself. So, all the souls are the part of the Lord but the Lord as a whole is not in any of them.

Na cha matsthaani bhaotani pashya Me yogmaishvaram,

Bhootbhrinna cha bhootastho mamatma bhoot bhavavanah [5].

Meaning—Nay, these beings do not abide in Me, see My wonderful divine yoga, Myself is that which sustains all beings but Myself does not dwel in those beings.

Commentary—The apparent contradiction in two 'shlokas' is baffling on the face of it.

In the first He claims that all beings are situated in Him and here He denies His own statement. "Nay these beings do not abide in Me". The ordinary readers can easily be mistaken. But both statements are true in their own ways. All beings certainly reside in Him as He permeates everything in this universe. They do not reside in Him because due to His yoga (the very first principle of it is to be indifferent in all circumstances) He is careless in the sense that He does not care who reside in Him and who do not. He clearly confirms our interpretation when He says "See My wonderful divine yoga"—"Pashya Me yogaishwaram".

He is certainly the sustainer of all. It is not for nothing that the Bible says, "Therefore I tell you, do not be anxious about your life, what you shall eat or what you shall drink, nor about your body, what you shall put on" (Matthew 25, 1).

And again, "Look at the birds of the air, they neither sow nor reap nor gather in the barns but yet your heavenly father feeds them." (Same7/26).

Thus the both famous scriptures air the same view—He is the sustainer of all beings what to talk of men only?

He again asserts that 'Myself does not abide in them.' This has been taken care of in the commentary of the preceding verse.

Yathakaashsthito nityam vaayuh sarvatrago mahaan,
Tatha sarvaanhi bhootaani matshaaneetupadhaaraya [6].

Meaning—Just as the great and all pervading air always remains in the sky, so know that all things abide in Me.

Commentary—It is a known fact of science that where there is sky (in other words space) there is air. Air permeates every thing in a way. Sky is just a crude example. The only open space above is not sky. Anyway, the Lord is right in telling that as this air remains in the sky and its existence cannot be conceived about, so all beings are in Me.

One's attention is drawn towards the similar confession in the shloka four of this chapter where He clearly admits almost in the same language, all being abide in Me (matsthaani sarva bhootaani). Compare it with this "Know that all beings abide is me" (Matasthaaneetyupadhaaraya). The language is almost same in these both shlokas.

In fact this remains that all beings abide in Him whether He feels it or not due to His all powerful yoga and remains indifferent to all of them.

Sarvabhootaani kaunteya prakriti yaanti maamikaam,
Kalpakshaye punastaani kalpaadau vissrijaamyaham [7].

Meaning—O Arjun at the end of every 'kalpa' all beings enter my 'prakriti' and at the beginning of every kalpa, they are brought forth to Me.

Commentary—'Kalpa' means the day of 'Brahma', we have talked about it in shloka 12 of canto VIII. We have also talked about the 'pralaya' (when everything perishes) and the resurgence in shloka 18 of the same chapter.

Almost the same idea is expressed here. At the end of a Brahma-day, all being vanish in to nothingness and at the beginning of the Brahma-day they all reappear as from nowhere.

The conception of 'pralaya' is very old. The earth at least once suffered from it as it is evident from 'Noaha's Story,' indicated earlier. This is perhaps one reason that the Lord returns again and again to this complete disappearance of life from the earth and then to its resurgence.

Prakritim svaamavashtabhya visrijaami punah punah,
Bhaotgraamimam kritasnamavasham prakritervashaat [8].

Meaning—Taking hold of my nature, I bring forth again and again these all beings. Helplessly they come into being, in the control of this nature.

Commentary—He is the creator but His instrument is the nature itself which is His own part. He creates all beings again and again (after perhaps the 'pralaya¦). They are also helpless and are bound to come in this world controlled by the nature as they are.

Na cha maamtani karmanhi nibaghnanti Dhananjaya,
Udaaseenavadaaseenamasakatam teshu karmshu [9].

Meaning—O Arjun, these actions do not bind Me as I remain indifferent and unattached to them.

Commentary—The Lord returns to 'karmayog.' He asserts that though He performs such stupendous actions, He is not bound by them as He is indifferent and unattached to them. This 'karmyog', He has been preaching out time and again in this Gita and now He indirectly exhorts people to follow this example : doing everything but doing nothing.

Mayaadhyakshenha prakritih sooyate sacharaacharam,
Hetunaanen Kaunteya jagadviparivartate [10].

Meaning—I Am the controlling power of nature which produced both animate and inanimate. Due to this O Kaunteya, the wheel of the world is revolving.

Commentary—The fact that this world is the creation of the nature which is under the direct control of the Lord has been imphasised upon time and again. Here He makes it abundantly clear that He presides over this creation (coming in to being through the nature) of all which is animate or inanimate. It is thus that the cycle of the world revolves—beings come and go.

Avajaananti maam moodhaah maanushi tanumaashritam,
Param bhaavamajaananto mam bhaotmaheshwaram [11].

Meaning—Fools despise Me the Lord of all creation, lodged in the human body as they know not My supreme nature.

Commentary—Hint is certainly towards people like Duryodhan and Shishupaal etc. who just regarded Him as an ordinary being. While the former once tried to arrest Him and the latter went on abusing Him till he uttered his last abuse (the 101st one) and was killed by the Lord.

Moghaasha Moghkarmaanho moghgyaana vichetasah,
Raakshseemasureem chaiva, prakritim mohaneem shritaah, [12].

Meaning—All the hopes, actions and knowledge of such persons of deluded senses are vain. They dwell in a nature which is fiendish, demoniacal and delusive.

Commentary—This is about the people described in the

preceding verse. They who do not know God in His supreme nature and do not regard Him as the creator of all beings should vainly expect their hopes to be fulfilled, their actions to bear fruits, their knowledge and senses to be free from delusion. They are hardly human beings. What to talk of being near to God, their nature is that of demons and fiends.

It is thus clear that if one is to see one's hopes fulfilled, actions materialised and knowledge perfect, one should draw to God.

Mahatmanastu maam parth daivim prakritimashritah
Bhajantyananyamanaso gyatva bhootadimavyayam [13].

Meaning—O Parth ! the great soul possessing divine nature worship me solely knowing to Me as the creator of all beings, and imperishable.

Commentary—The point of the Lord being the creator of all existences and being imperishable has been imphasised upon in many preceding verses. The great souls only know His this nature and they turn to Him with undivided mind and heart full of love. To worship Him certainly does not mean to offer Him flowers, scented sticks and sweets (prasaadaas).

Satatam keertayanto maam yatantshcha dridhvrataah,
Namasyantashch maam bhaktya nityayukta upasate [14].

Meaning—Always chanting my names, steadfast in their endeavour, bowing down to My devotion, they worship Me constantly united with Me.

Commentary—It is a way of great souls, They remain always in yoga (i.e. united with Him).

They always chant His names and glories, always bow to Him in devotion and thus they worship Him.

Gyaanyagyen chaapyanye yojanto maamupaasate,
Ekatven, prithaktven, bahudhaa, vishvatomukham [15].

Meaning—Others also worship Me through offering of knowledge and betake themselves to Me in My oneness and in every separate being and in all My countless universal faces.

Commentary—Knowledge is not less than devotion. It enables the knowledgeable to see Him as One whole and also in different forms being lodged in different beings and also having countless faces looking in all directions in this universe.

The last sentence though a bit intrigue is supported in the chapter X where in shloka 33 He again declares Himself to be of universal face (vishvatomukhah). Almost same term 'vishvato mukham' is used in both shlokas.

Aham kraturaham yagyah svadhaahamahaushadham,
Mantro'halmevaajyamahamagniraham hutam [16].

Meaning—I am the ritual, I am the sacrifice, I am the offering to the departed, I am the herbage, I am the sacred words ('mantras') I am the processed butter ('ghee'—Aryam), I am the flame, I am the act of offering oblations in to the fire.

Commentary—With this shloka the Lord starts narrating His real and unparalleled nature, His supreme strength and His all pervding power.

As the sacrifice (yagaya) is supposed to be of much importance in wish-fulfilling (refer to chapter III and IV), the Lord first deals with it and declares Himself not only to be the very process of 'yagya' but also the things used in it including the fire in which oblations are offered and the 'mantra' (sacred or coded words) which are used to make gods accept the offerings.

Pitaahamasya jagato maataadhaataa Pitaamah,
Vedyam pavitramonkaar riksaam yajureva cha [17].

Meaning—I am the father of this world, the mother, the sustainer, the grand father, the object of knowledge, the scared syllable Om and the three vedas, Rig, Sama and yajuh.

Commentary—The Lord has fathered this world so it is natural for Him to call Himself father, So far 'as grand father, is concerned it means that as He has been fathering generations after generations He is naturally the Grand father. Rest is obvious.

Gatribharta prabuh saakshi nivasah sharanham suhrit,
Prabhavah pralayah sthanam nidhanam beejamabyayam [18].

Meaning—I am the goal, the supporter, the Lord, the witness, the abode, the refuge, the friends, the origin and the end (of the world), the place, the store-house and the imperishable seed.

Commentary—'Gatih' in Sanskrit means both the path and the goal. As the Lord is sought by every one, so the word here is interpreted as goal. What does the witness stands for? As the Lord overlooks all our deeds be the vicious or virtuous so He is the witness. Place is where one rests. The Lord's abode is the best resting place so He is described as the place. Refuge is clear. He is the ultimate shelter of all. If one is no where to go, one must seek the shelter of Him. He is the friend of friends. There cannot be a better friend than Him; All may refuse you in the hours of need but He will not. The abode stands for His own 'Loka' (a part of the universe where He does reside and where go they who are His devotees, after death). The store-house (nidhaanam) is in which all merge at the time when this universe is no more.

He is the seed in the sense that He is the cause of every being and as this universe arises, disappears and again comes in to being so this seed is imperishable.

Tapaamyahamaham varsham
nigrihnhaamyutsrijaami cha,
Amritam chaiva mriutushcha
sadasachchahamarjun, [19].

Meaning—O Arjun! I radiate heat (as the sun), I attract and send forth the rains. I am immortality and also death. I am existent as well as non-existent.

Commentary—The act of attracting and sending forth the rains is the explanation of the natural process of rains. It is every-body-knowledge that water of seas and rivers etc. are attracted by the sun and then the same is sent forth to earth as rains. He is the immortality as He is Himself immortal. He is the death as well because without Him death cannot be caused. He is all that exists and is also in that which is yet to come into existence.

Triavidyaa maam somapah pootapaapaa
Yagairishtva svargatim praarthayante,
Te punhyamaasaadya surendralok—

Mashnanti divyaandivi dewabhogaan [20].

Meaning—The knowers of the three Vedas who drink the sap of somaa-plant, purify themselves from sin, worshipping Me with 'yagyas' (sacrifices) seek access to heaven, attaining Indra's paradise due to their good deeds, enjoy the celestial pleasures in heaven.

Commentary—The emphasis here is on studying the Vedas and indulging in sacrifices. Also on drinking 'soma' which is supposed to be a purifying but nutritions drink. By all this the knowers of the Vedas get rid of themselves of sin and reach 'Indra-loka' where they enjoy themselves.

Indra is supposed to he the master of all gods and his abode is notorious for all kinds of pleasure.

Such people as described above of-course attain to the abode of Indra and enjoy the things to be enjoyed by gods but this bliss is not permanent as will be evident from the following verse.

Te tam bhuktvaa swarglokam bishaalam
Chhinhe punhye martyalokam vishanti,
Evam Trayidharmamanuprapannaa
gataagatam kaamkaama labhante [21].

Meaning—Having enjoyed the big heavenly world, they come back to mortal existence, the rewards of their merits being exhausted. Thus resorting to the virtues declared by the three Vedas, seeking the satisfaction of senses are caught in the cycle of birth and death.

Commentary—What was to follow in these lines was hinted at in the preceding verse itself. Message, the Lord wanted to convey is that the virtues acquired through the rituals of the 'Vedas' are not going to provide one with a permanent abode in the heaven.

The Vedic ritiuals—the sacrifice etc. are mainly for fulfilment of desires. Who indulge in them and not in the worship of the Lord may enjoy the heavenly bliss for a time but as soon as the fruits of their such efforts exhaust, they return again to this mortal world. They again die and again take birth. The way to get rid of the cycle of birth and death is not in the Vedas and is not provided by the rituals prescribed in them. The hint is clear—the only way is the one-pointed devotion to the Lord.

Ananyaashchintayanto mam ye yanaah paryupaasate,
Tesham nityabhiyuktanam yogkshemam vahamyaham. [22]

Meaning—Those who knowing no one else constantly worship Me, thinking only of Myself, to those ever united with Me I attend to their every need.

Commentary—This shloka is very important in the sense that it is supposed to be a promise made by the Lord.

This promise gains more significance as it is contained in the middle of the Gita (the very heart of the Lord). It is because the sacred book has eighteen chapters and this occurs in the IXth one.

They say that the Lord cannot breech this promise. The conditions are very simple :

(i) You are always to think about Him and about no other god or goddess.

(ii) Remaining in this state you are to worship Him in other words offer your prayers.

(iii) You are to feel that you are always united with Him. He is with you and you are with Him.

Having fulfilled these conditions you rest assure that God (or the Lord Krishna) is to take care of all your needs.

The line "yogakshemam Vahaamyaham" is very popular and it has been adopted by the Life Insurance Corporation of India as their slogan.

These lines of the Gita remind many a line of the Bible where similar promises are made. A few of them are quoted here :

(i) "Ask and it will be given you; seek, and you will find, knock and it will be opened to you". (Matthew—9/7).

(ii) With men this is impossible, but with God all things are possible (Matthew 19/20).

(iii) "And whatever you ask in paryer, you will receive, if you have faith". (Matthew 21/22).

(iv) Have no anxiety about anything but in everything by prayer and supplication with thanks-giving let your requests be made to God. (Colossians 4/6).

(v) Draw near no Got and He will draw near to you (james 4/18).

Let us add once more that this is the oft-quoted lines of the Gita and people with faith fully believe in it and having surrendered themselves to Him be free from all cares and anxieties about their needs as well as well-being.

Ye'pyanyadevataa bhaktaa yajante shradhyaanvitaah,
Tepi maameva Kauntey, yajantyavidlipoorvakam [23].

Meaning—O son of Kunti! Even those who worship other gods with devotion, they also worship Me only though unlawfully. Law here stands for divine law.

Commentary—All worships ultimately reach the Lord. Thus the proper way would have been to worship the Lord directly as the offers to other gods ultimately are indirect offers to Krishna Himself.

Aham hi sarvygyaanam bhokta cha probhumeva cha,
Na tu maambhijaananti tattvenaatashchyavanti te [24].

Meaning—It is I who am the enjoyer and the Lord of all sacrifices but they do not know Me in reality hence they fall.

Commentary—Sacrifices or 'yagyas' have their importance, it has been underlined again and again. But this is to be borne in mind that all worships go to the Lord so all sacrifices reach the Lord. They who do not know it in its deep reality they only fall i.e. they are subject to death and birth. Knowing the Lord to be the enjoyer and the Lord of all 'yagyas' is to develop profound esteem in Him and one knowing Him thus cannot be caught in the cycle of birth and death.

Yaanti devabrataa devaanpitirinyaanti pitrivrataah,
Bhootani yanti bhootejya janti madyajin'pi maam [25]

Meaning—Those who worship gods, go to gods, those who worship the ancestors go the ancestors, those who worship the spirits go to the spirits and My worshippers come to Me.

Commentary—It is thus prudent to worship the Lord (Krishna) only.

Patram pushpam phalam toyam yo Me bhaktyaa pray acchhati Tadaham bhaktyupa hritamashnuami pruyulutmunuh [26].

Meaning—Whatever is offered to me with devotion—a leaf, a flower, a fruit or even water I partake them offered with love by the striving soul.

Commentary—The Lord seeks devotion and love, nothing else, even a leaf is acceptable if offered with love.

He did not touch the delicious dishes of Duryodhan and ran to the dilapidated house of Vidur to partake a few bananas from the hands of his wife who was a great devotee of Him. She in her ecstasy gave only the covers of the fruits to him and let the content fall on the earth and the Lord ate all that uneatable with satisfaction and love.

'Prayataatmanah' is important here. It is for them who are striving for love and devotion of the Lord. Their offering is the real offering and acceptable to Him.

Yatkaroshi yadashnasi yajjuhoshi dadaasi yat,
Yattapasyasi kaunteya tatkurushva madarpanham [27].

Meaning—O son of Kunti! Whatever you do, whatever you eat, whatever you offer as sacrifices, whatever you give (in charity) whatever you perform as a form of penance offer it all to Me.

Commentary—It is the best way of not to be responsible for any action. Even good work bind you so the best way is to offer everything, your all deeds to Him.

There is one more advantage attached to it. If you are supposed to offer your all deeds to Him you will not indulge in bad deeds. If you are to offer to Him whatever you eat, you will not eat which must not be eaten and so on.

Shubhaashubhaphaluirevam mokshyase karmbandhanaih,
sannyaasyogyuktaatma vimukto mamupaishyasi [28].

Meaning—You will the liberated from good and evil results which constitute the bonds of action, with your soul in union with the Lord. Through renunciation you will become free and come to Me.

Commentary—The hint was provided in the commentary of the preceding 'shloka' that the Lord was providing the way to get oneself free from bondage. When one is offering to him all what he does he is certainly indulging in 'sanayas-yoga' and he is thus freed from all bonds and as a result of it attains to Him.

Samo'ham sarvbhooteshu na me dvesshyo'sti na priyah
Ye bhajanti tu mam bhaktya mayi te teshu chaapyaham [29].

Meaning—I am equal for all beings, none is dear to Me, none is hated by Me, they who worship Me with devotion, they are in Me and I am also in them.

Commentary—The Lord is generally quite indifferent. He hates none, he loves none. He has a sense of equality in all.

But He is not that indifferent. If one loves Him devoutedly he abides in Him and the Lord is also revealed in Him. This is the significance of devotion.

Api chetsuduraachaaro bhajate maamannyabhaak,
Saadhureva sa mantabyah samyagvyavasito hi sah [30].

Meaning—Even if a person of very evil conduct worships Me with exclusive devotion, he should be regarded as a saint as he is rightly resolved.

Commentary—A sinner no longer remains a sinner if he starts worshipping the Lord with exclusive devotion. He is nothing less than a saint as be has rightly resolved (to worship him devotedly.

Chhipram bhavati dharmaatmaa shaashwachchhantim Nigachchati,
Kaunteya pratijaneehi na me bhaktah pranhashyati [31].

Meaning—Swiftly he becomes a man of virtues and obtains eternal peace. This is My word of promise O son of Kunti, my devotee never perishes.

Commentary—This is about the person described in the previous verse, the vilest sinner. Even if he by virtue of his love to God, speedily becomes virtuous and enjoys the peace which is constant.

Here the Lord promises (remember his promise is shloka 22 of this very chapter) that his devotee is not subject to destruction. He survives for ever in Him. In simple language no one can do any harm to one who loves Him.

Maam hi parth vyapaashritya ye'pi suyh paapyonayah,
Shtriyo vaishyastatha shoadraste'pi, Yanti param gatim [32].

Meaning—O son of Pritha, by taking refuge in Me the born sinners in women, vaishyaas and shoodraas also attain the supreme goal.

Commentary—The Lord is not degrading the women-folk or 'vaishyas' or 'shoodras.' Then it will be at variance with our culture and tradition. Even if we leave aside 'shoodraas' 'vaishyaas' cannot be dumped as unacceptable to God. They are the trading community which gives much in charity and constructs temples and other places of worship.

The women folk had been regarded by many as worshipable—'yatra naaryastu poojyante ramante tatra devatah'—where women are worshipped, gods remain there.

The simple indication is that any of the three even if they are born of sin, or are sinner to be simple, attains the supreme goal if they take refuge in Him.

Kim punrbraahmnhah punhya bhakta rajarshayastatha,
Anityiamasukham lokamimam praapya bhajasva maam [33].

Meaning—How then 'braahmins', virtuous, devotees and kingsages (cannot attain the supreme?) You who have got this transient and joyless world worship Me.

Commentary—This shloka is an evident corollary to the preceding one. The Lord poses the question that when sinners in women, 'vaishyaas' and 'shoodraas' can attain the supreme goal why then, 'Brahmins,' the virtuous, my devotees, and the kings who are as good as super-saints (like janaka) cannot attain Me? It is why he asks Arjuna to worship Him and get rid of this unhappy transient world by attaining Him. He is being invited to be a devotee.

The word Brahmin here does not stand for any caste. It has been repeatedly maintained in the scriptures that one who knows 'Brahma' (the divine creator) is 'Braahman'—'Brahmam janaati eti Braahmanhah.'

The Gita has never laid emphasis on caste being decided by birth. It has been made amply clear in shloka 13 of chapter IV that the four 'varnhaas' or division of castes have been made by Him on the basis of men's merits and deeds (i.e. not on the basis of their birth)—

'Chaaturrvarnam mayaa srishtam gunha karm vibhaagashah'. (IV/13).

It can thus be easily inferred that if a man changes his nature and occupation, his caste will stand automatically changed. If for example a 'brahmin' idulges in vices and leaves his work of studying and teaching, he is no more a Braahmin. Similarly a man of any caste performing the duties of Braahman becomes Braahman. It has been xplained earlier also.

Manmana bhava madbhakto mdyaji maam namaskuru,
Maamevaishyasi yuktvaivamatmanam matparayanhah [34].

Meaning—Be My minded, be My devotee, adore Me, bow yourself to Me. Thus united with Me and completely depending on Me you shall attain Me.

Commentary—One is to be God's real devotee in every way (in Sanskrit it is called manasa, Vacha, karmanha by mind, by utterances and by deed) to attain Him i.e. to get free from the cycle of birth and death.

'Be My minded' needs an elaboration. It simply means that your mind be fixed always on Him. The rest are clear.

Om tatsaditi shrimdbhagavadgitasoopanishatsu Brahm vidyaayaam yogshastre Shrikrishnaarjun samvaade Raajvidyaaraajguhya yogo naam navamo'dhyaayah [35].

Thus in the upanishad sung by the Lord, the science of Brahma, the scripture on Yoga, the conversation between Shri Krishna and Arjuna ends the chapter IX entitled "The yoga of the sovereign knowledge and sovereign secret."

CHAPTER X

Shri Bhagvaanuvaach—
Bhooya eva mahabaho shrinhu me parmaam vachah,
Yattea'ham preeyamanhay vakshyami hitakamyaya [1].

Meaning—**The blessed Lord said**—O mighty-armed (Arjun) again listen to my supreme word which I will speak to you who are so loving, for your welfare.

Commentary—The Lord is going to tell something more of his supreme words with the only consideration of the welbeing of Arjuna whom He says to be very dear to Him.

Na me viduh suraganhaah prabhawam na maharshayah,
Ahamaadirihi devaanam maharasheenhaam cha sarvashah [2].

Meaning—Neither the gods nor the great seers know My birth as I am the origin in all respects of the gods and the great seers.

Commentary—The origin of the Lord is unknown. The divine is always the unborn eternal. Thus there is no question of gods or seers knowing His origin. Rather it is He without Whose all out efforts, there could have been neither the gods nor the seers.

Ya maamajamanaadi cha vetti lakmaheshawaram,
Asmoodhah sa mertyeshu sarvapaapaih pramuchyate [3].

Meaning—Whosoever knows Me as unborn and without any beginning and as the Supreme Lord of the universe, he umbiwildered among mortals is purged of all sins.

Commentary—To know the Lord in His real form and nature is enough to provide a man with balance of thinking and let him get rid of all sins and evils. About His being unborn and having no beginning and His being the supreme Lord of all worlds, He has talked often, so no further comments on his nature, form and powers.

Budhirgyaansammohah kshama satyam damah shamah,
Sukham duhkham bhavo'bhaavo bhayamchaabhayameva cha [4].
Ahinsaa samataa tushtistapo daanam yasho'yashah,
Bhavanti bhava bhootanam matt eva prithagvidhaih [5].

Meaning—Understanding, knowledge, freedom from delusion, forgiveness, truth, control over the senses, control over the mind, pleasure and sorrow, evolution (of beings) and dissolution, fear and absence of fear, non-violence, equality, contentment, authority, charity, glory and englorìousness—these diverse fellings of beings proceed from Me alone.

Commentary—Man vainly think that the emotions he is subjected to and conditions good or bad pleasant or unplesant he is caused to face are something of his own doing. They are really the wish of God and man is simply to abide by them taking as 'God's will.

One is here reminded of the very lines of the great saint Tulsidas in Ramcharitmaanas—

Sunahu Bharat bhaavi prabal
Vilakh kahe muninaath
Haani, laabh, jeevan maran
Yash upyash vidli haath

—The great saint (yagaya Valkya) told Bharat (the younger brother of Rama, who had gone to the jungle to get his eldest brother back) with grief—whatever is destined to happen is very strong (unavoidable); loss and gain, life and death, repute and disrepute are in the hands of God.

The Bible also asserts that you do not know what is going to happen tomorrow or the next moment to you—

"Come now who say" 'Today or tomorrow we will go into such and such a town and spend a year and trade and get gain, where as you do not know about tomorrow....in stead you aught to say, if the Lord wills we shall live and we shall do this or that (James-4/14-15).

Maharashayh sapt poorve chatvaaro manavastathaa,
Madbhaavaa manasa jaata yesham lok emaah prajah [6].

Meaning—The seven great seers, the seven ancients and the fourteen manus who all are devoted to Me are my mental becoming and to them belong all these creatures of the world.

Commentary—Here the Lord narrates the ancestry of the human beings. True, he is the creator of all, the seeds of all, claimed in different verses earlier. But it is just not accidental. It has a system and procedure of its own.

From the Lord emanated the seven great seers, the four ancients and fourteen manus. They in their turn produced the human beings on this earth.

The last ones have been called manus. The present manu is seventh one of which we are the progenies. He is called 'vaivasvat'. Let us forget the six who have already passed and the seven who are to come. There is much controversy regarding them.

We are, however, in a position to name the seven seers. They are—

1. Marichi
2. Angira
3. Atri
4. Pulastya
5. Pulah
6. Kratu
7. Bashishtha

The four ancients can also be named they are—

1. Sanak
2. Sanandan
3. Sanaatan
4. Sanatkumaar.

It may be of interest to know that in Sanskrit man is called 'manav'. It is because he is Manu. Who knows the word 'man' has also got something to do with 'Manu'?

Etaamveebhootim yogam cha mam yo vetti tattvatah,
So'vikampen yogen yuzyate naatra samshayah [7].

Meaning—Whosoever knows in reality this supreme glory of Mine and also My yoga, unites himself to Me by an unwavering yoga, undboubtedly.

Commentary—His glories have been enumerated above (many of them are yet to be enumerated).

The emphasis here is on 'yoga'. The first requirement

is to know 'yoga'. After knowing his glory and his yoga (His because this theory of yoga is propounded by Him), he is united with Him, with the Lord. This communion, this oneness with the Lord is perfect and fixed, once he is well-versed in the glory and the theory of yoga propounded by Him.

Aham sarvasya prabhavo mattah sarvam pravartate,
Eti matvaa bhajante maam budha bhaavasamanvitaah [8].

Meaning—I am the cause of the birth of all and due to Me all stir and act, knowing this the wise adore Me full of emotion (divine).

Commentary—He is the creator of all no doubt but the new fact added here is that without Him there is no efforts of any kind on the part of any being. He is thus the life-force and the source of all inspirations. If He does not want you may live but live a vegetable-existence without any will or effort to do any thing, to achieve any worth while goal.

Machchittaa madgatpraanhaa bodhayantah parasparam,
Kathyantashcha maam nityam tushyanti cha ramanti cha [9].

Meaning—With their mind concentrated on Me, with their lives surrendered to Me, mutually inlightening each other, talking of Me, they ever remain contented and delightful.

Commentary—It has been stressed upon earlier that the Gita is a way of life, a philosophy of life. Its only aim is to enable the man to lead a peaceful, cheerful and contented life.

Here is another recipe though not very different from the earlier ones. What is required to achieve this end is—

i. To fix one's mind always on the Lord.
ii. Surrender one's life to Him.
iii. To let know each other his glory and greatness
iv. To talk about Him.

With all this you receive His blessings and remain contented and delighted.

Teshaam satatayuktaanaam bhajataam preetipoorvakam,
Dadaami budhiyogam tam yen maamupayaanti te [10].

Meaning—On those who are in constant union with Me worshiping Me with love, I confer the yoga of mind by which they come to [10].

Commentary—The best that the Lord can confer on whom who love Him is this yoga which He every early termed as 'Budhi-yoga'. One is referred to chapter II where He elaborated in great details His 'Budhi-yoga' or yoga of mind. The mind to be trained in such a way that it becomes indifferent to pleasure and pain, gain and loss, success and failure and so on. This is the high road to happiness and peace which is the sole aim of the Gita's teaching.

The yoga of the Gita's is certainly and undoubtedly the yoga of mind. The Lord has certainly dwelt on Patanjai-yoga (the conservative form) for a short while in chapter VI but He has never forgotten his favourite version of yoga—'Mind-yoga'.

This yoga as He has stressed before also is not capable of only alleviating the sufferings one gets from fear and failure but if adhered to properly, it leads the practitioner to the Lord in the end. Remember shloka 39 of chapter II where he talks of both—the yoga of mind and its leading to the freedom from shackles of 'karmas' (thus naturally leading one to Him).

Teshaamevaanukampaarlthamahamgyaanajam Tamah,
Naashayamyaatmbhaavastho gyaandeepen bhaasvata [11].

Meaning—With a view to shower my grace upon them I dispel the darkness born of ignorance by the blazing lamp of wisdom having lodged Myself in their self.

Commentary—The Lord comes to wisdom (gyaan) for yoga. He has Talked a lot of devotion in the outgoing verses and will again talk in many of the coming ones. It is clear that though the main thrust is on yoga i.e. karm-yoga or yoga of mind, the Lord tries to strike a balance among the three prevalent schools of 'yoga'—'gyaana' 'karm' and 'bhakti' (devotion).

The Gita is here to set at rest all controversies regarding the three by producing a **syntheses** of all of them.

The shloko is important as it says that He showers His grace on the 'yogis' referred to in the preceding verse and in course of that He dispels the darkness of their ignorance with the lamp of wisdom. The perference goes to the 'yogis'—the 'mind—yogis', if one is allowed to coin this term.

So far his having remained lodged with in our selves is concerned, one is again refereed to His saying in chapter XIV shloka 7. Where be says 'manaivaansho jeevaloke jeeva bhootah sanaatanah, (the soul in the body is a portion of Myself). This saying has been often referred to in this book only to emphasise its supreme importance.

Arjun Uvaach—

Param Brahm poram dhaam pavitram paramam bhavaam,
Purusham shashvatam divymaadivevamajam vibhum [12].

Arjun Said—

You are the supreme eternal (Brahma), the ultimate resort, the greatest purifier, (God Himself), the original God-head and the all perveding one.

Commentary—Arjun having heard Krishna for so long about his specialities and divine nature fails to restrain himself and starts telling in what esteem he holds Him.

Ahustvaamrisayah sarve devarshirnaaradastathaa,
Asito Devalo vyaasah svayam chaiva braveeshi me [13].

Meaning—All the seers say this of you and the divine seer Narad, Devala, Vyasa and yourself as well say it to Me.

Commentary—Arjuna says that what he has said in the preceding 'shloka' is not of his saying. Many seers some of whom he has named maintain like this and even Krishna is testifying to it.

Let us introduce these, seers, in brief Narada and others.

Narada is a legendary figure always on some errand moving from place to place. He is almost omnipresent. At the same time he is a great devotee of the Lord always chanting 'Narayan', 'Narayan' (one of the names of Krishna). He is a life—long celibate.

Asit is the son of famous Kashyap. He finds a mention in 'koorm purana'. He also finds a mention in 'rigveda'

Vyas is a renowned seer. In fact the Gita is also a creation of Vyas in the sense that it was he who wrote Mahabharata of which the Gita forms a part. Krishna of course sung the Geeta but Vyas rendred it in to the written form. He is also the writer of 18 'puranas' as well as of the 'Brahmsutra' a famous scripture.

Sarvametadritam many yanmaam vadasi Keshava,
Na hi te Bhagavanvyaktim vidurdeva na daanavaah [14].

Meaning—O Keshava (Krishna) whatever you say I believe as true. O Lord neither the gods nor the demons are aware of your manifestation.

Commentary—True nature of his manifestations are not known to even the gods as well as demons who are supposed to possess more physical and mental strength than men.

Svayamevaatmanaatmaanam veth twam purushottam,
Bhootbhaavan, bhootesha devadeva jagatpate [15].

Meaning—You alone know your-self by yourself. You are best among the men (Purushottam), creator of beings, Lord of beings, God of gods and the master of the universe.

Commentary—When no body is capable of knowing Him only He can know Him through Himself (through His all powerful knowledge).

Vaktumahasyasheshenha divyaa hyaatmvibhootayah,
Yabhiribhootirlokenimanstvam vyaapya Tisthasi [15].

Meaning—You alone are capable of describing in full your divine glories by which you stand pervading these worlds.

Commentary—Nothing special.

Katham vidyaamaham yogimstvaam sadaa parichintayan,
Keshu keshu cha bhaaveshu chintyosi Bhagavanmaya [17].

Meaning—How should I know you O master of yoga by thinking of you at all time and in what becoming should I think of you O God?

Commentary—He is to be known by constantly thinking upon Him, but how to think so and on how many forms. This question Arjuna.

Vistarenaatmno yogam vibhootim cha Janardan,
Bhooyah kathay triptirhi Shrinvato naasti me'miritam [18].

Meaning—O Janardan, tell me again in detail, your yoga and your glory, for I am not satiated in hearing your words which are like nectar.

Commentary—Nothing special.

Shri Bhagavanuvaach,

Hant Te Kathayishyaami divyaa hyaatmvibhootayah,
Praadhaanyatah Kurushreshtha nastyanto vistarasya me [19].

Meaning—All right I shall let you know O best of the Kurus my divine glories but only the most important of them as there is no end to my extensions (in dirrerent forms and in countless directions).

Commentary—The Lord calls Arjun, 'Kurusreshtha'—best among the kurus. Though he is the son of Pandu so he is best addressed as a Pandava but as Kuru is the first man of Kauravaas and Pandavaas so Arjun is also a Kuru. He calls him kurushreshtha with a view to boost his morale otherwise there are many more superior to him in kuru-line including the great Bhishma.

Ahamaatma gudaakesha sarvbhootaashaysthitah,
Ahamaadishcha madhyam cha bhootanaamant eva cha [20].

Meaning—O Gudaakesha I am the self abiding in all beings. I am the beginning and middle and also the end of all beings.

Commentary—Gudakesha is one who has got complete control over sleep. Sleep is inaction and an important part of one's life is wasted in sleep doing nothing. Thus a man who can do for days without sleep is certainly praiseworthy.

As He is seated in the heart of all beings, He sees their beginning as well as their middle and end.

In other words with Him begins this world of beings with Him it reaches its maturity and it is due to Him that the beings attain their end.

Aadityaanaamaham vishnurjyotishaam raviransumaan,
Mareechirmarutaamashmi nakshtraanhaamaham shashee [21].

Meaning—I am Vishnu among the Adityaas and the radiant sun among luminaries, I am mareechi among maruts and the moon among stars.

Commentary—The Lord proceeds to narrate as to how He is the best among all kinds of beings or things whatsoever might be the case. Naturally He starts with the all powerful, ominpotent, omniscient and omnipresent, Lord Vishnu of Whom He is supposed to be the incarnation. The start is thus well considered and significant. Once he is Vishnu Himself, He may or may not be any thing else. From the very Vedic period Vishnu is supposed to be the God of gods.

He is said to be one among the several sons of Aditi and the most strongest and powerful among them. These sons are called 'Adityaas'. It is why the Lord says that He is Vishnu among Aadityaas.

These sons of Aaditis are as follows :

i. Dhaata
ii. Mitra
iii. Aryama
iv. Shakra
v. Varuna
vi. Ansh
vii. Bhag
viii. Vishvaman
ix. Pusha
x. Svita
xi. Tvasta
xii. Vishnu

There is nothing to tell about the importance of the sun among all which illuminates. He is the very source of heat and lIfe on this earth. Even the Rigveda says that the sun is the soul of the universe—'Soorya Atmajagatah'.

He thus equates Himself with this great life and light-giving force, the sun.

Mareechi is one of the forty nine sons of Diti, the sister of Aditi. These forty nine sons are called Maruts (Winds). Mareechi is the most powerful among his brothers. He is also called to be the life-breath itself.

The importance of moon needs no emphasis. Though to-day it is supposed to be a subplanet of the earth but formerly it was regarded as one of the stars. Whatever the case may be the moon is also the source of lives on earth and one of the most beautiful things nature ever created. He is the source of medicinal values in all herbs. He directly affects this earth more than any heavenly bodies which is evident from the tidal waves on moon-lit nights, when sea-waves rise so high as to touch the moon itself. The human body also contains 75%. water, thus the importance of moon and its effect on human beings can very easily be established.

Vedaanam saamvedo'smi devaanaamasmi vaasvah,
Indriyaanham manschaasmi bhootanamasmi chetana [22].

Meaning—Among the Vedaas I am the Samveda; among the gods I am Indra. Among the senses mind I am, I am the consciousness in living beings.

Commentary—Among the four vedas—Rig, Sam, Atharv and Yaju, Samveda is very dear to gods. It is musical as well and full of prayers to gods.

Indira is supposed to be the King of all gods. Many take to austerities to capture the throne of Indra. His famous weapon is 'vajra' which is capable of destroying any thing and any body. He is also the rain-god. Even to-day he is worshipped in many parts of this country when there is no rains.

The Vedaas have accorded Him much significance. In a way He is the presiding deity of the Vedas.

The mind has got its own significance. There are ten senses. Mind is the activating factor behind them. As for example among the ten senses are eyes, ears and nose also but they are useless unless mind is behind them. The eyes can hardly see if mind is occupied some where, ears can hardly hear if not associated with mind. Mind is also the king of body the very ruler. The physical aspect the body is only 75%, the rest is the mental one. If the mind is healthy, the body is all cheerful and full of health. If the mind is sick and discordant, body is useless.

It is thus in fitness of the things that Lord calls Himself the mind itself. Credit of all the scientific, literary and other achievements go to mind.

If there is no consciousness all beings are as good as dead. So He is the very life-force of all beings. Body may be created but if consciousness is not put in it, it is nothing better than a dead wood.

Rudranham Shankarashchaasmi vittesho yakshrakshsaam,
Vasoonaam paavakalshchaasmi meruh shikharinhaamaham [23].

Meaning—I am Shiva among the rudras, the Lord of wealth among yakhsaas and Raakhsaas (i.e. Kubera). I am the god of fire among the Vasus and I am Meru among the peaks of the world.

Commentary—There are eleven rudras namely—

1. Har
2. Bahurup
3. Tryambak
4. Aparaajit
5. Vrisakapi
6. Shambhu (Shankar)
7. Kapardi
8. Raivat
9. Mrigvyadh
10. Sharva
11. Kapali

The sixth rudra is the most powerful among them. According to 'Harvans Puran' this rudra, Shankar, is the god of gods—"So rudra mahadeva".

Shankar is also among the three most important Gods—Brahma, Vishnu and Mahesh (Shankar). While Brahma is the creator, Vishnu is the sustainer and Shankar is the destroyer of this universe.

Kubera is most wealthy among yakhsaas and raakhsaas as Indira is among the gods.

Fire is among the most important inventions of man. He is one among the eight vasus who are :

(i) Dhar
(ii) Dhruva
(iii) Sam
(iv) Ahah
(v) Anil
(vi) Anal (Agni-fire)
(vii) Pratyusa
(viii) Prabhasa

In Rigveda fire (agni) has got much significance, almost next to Indira. He is called the god of light—"Agnirhota Kavinratuh....." (Rigveda 1.1.5).

Meru is supposed to bė the highest among seven legendary peaks described among puraanaas. It was used to chur the ocean during the famous 'Samudra manthan' (Churning of the ocean) which produced among other things Laksmi (the goddess of wealth) and nectar and also the all devastating poison (Halaahal) which Shiva Kept in his throat and is thus called 'Neelkanth' (One whose throat is of 'nil' colour).

Purodhasaam cha mukhyam maam vidhi Parth Vrihaspatim,
Senaaneenaamaham skandah sarasaamasmi sagarah [24].

Meaning—O Parth ! Among priests know me to their chief Vrihaspati. Among generals I am Skanda, among the sheets of water, the ocean I am.

Commentary—Vrihaspati (Jupiter) is the most significant among the stars even according to the modern scientific studies. He has been given the most exalted position in astrology also. A man with strong Jupiter can reach any height and is bound to wallow in name and fame.

According to mythology he is the Guru (the reverend teacher) of Indra the master of gods and the learned priest of gods. In fact, he is the most learned among the gods; thus any body who is well versed in serval branches of knowledge is called as good and great as Vrihaspati.

Skand is the son of 'Shiva'. When 'Vritrasur' had become invincible, gods approached Shiva and requested him to give birth to a brave son to lead them in battle and kill Vrita. He thus naturally became the war-leader of gods and also killed that dreadful demon.

Ocean is certainly the largest among all sheets of water. It is the source of rains as well and a store-house of precious gems. The most part of the earth is formed by the ocean itself.

Maharsheenhaam Bhriguraham giraamasyekamaksharam,
Yagyaanam japyagyo'smi sthaavaraanhaam Himalayah [25].

Meaning—I am Bhrigu among the great seers, the sacred syllable 'Om' among the words. Among 'yagyas' I am the 'Jap-yagya', among the immovable I am the Himalayas.

Commentary—Bhirgu is supposed to be the most knowledgeable among the seers. He is the son of Brahma the supreme creator. He also finds references in the Rigveda as the knower of sacred 'manatras'.

'Om' is the most purifying among the words. It is used before any word and also before any mantra. It is supposed to be Brahma Himself.

The importance of 'yagyas' has been emphasised upon time and again in the Gita, 'Jap' is the recitation of names of God silently but constantly. It has been told that one becomes 'sidha' (all perfect) by japa—'japaat sidhi, japaat siddhi'.

It is thus the most important among all 'yagyas' especially explained in canto II and IV of the Gita.

Himalaya is undoubtedly the biggest and highest among immovables, epecially mountains. As the legend goes Paarvati who was wedded to Lord Shiva is the daughter of the Himalaya. Not to say that it is the origin of so many rivers including the ganges and is the respository of all kinds of medicinal plants and herbs.

Ashvathah sarvvrikshaanhaam devarsheenaam cha Naaradah,
Gandharbaanhaam Chitararathah, siddhaanam Kapilo munih [26].

Meaning—I am the Ashvatha among all trees, Narad among the divine sages, Chitraratha among gandharvaas, I am the sage Kapil among the 'siddhaas.'

Commentary—Ashvath is called 'peepal' in hindi and fig tree in English. It is supposed to be the most pious tree.

It finds special mention in Aatharvveda—'yashashva Vannaspatyaanaaroham krinheshuaadhaahan' (Atharv ved—3, 6, 6)—"The brave rises above all, as the Ashwatha tree which transcends all plants".

It is a known scientific fact that 'peepal' always emits oxygen—even during the night.

It is for nothing that it is worshipped with reverence in almost all parts of India especially by the women-folk.

Gandharvaas are known for their expertise in music. Chitrarath is their leader thus the most accomplished among the nusicians.

The sage Kapil is known for his 'sankhya' (knowledge) Darshan. He is the propounder of it. His philosophy has found references in the Gita also.

Uchchaihshravasamashvaanaam vidhi maamritodbhowam,
Airaavatam gajendrannham naranham cha naradhipam [27].

Meaning—Among horses know me as Uchchaishrava begotten along with nectar during the churning of the ocean, Among the mighty elephants I am Airavata. Among men I am the king.

Commentary—Uchchaishrava and Airavat both were found during the churning of the ocean. Airaavat was taken by Indira. As known nectar was also produced along with them.

The king from time immemorial has been called the representative of God. There was a divine theory prevalent mostly among western countries according to which king is selected by the divinity itself. He is thus best among the men.

Aayudhaanamaham vajram Dhenoonamasmi kamdhuk,
Prajanashchaasmi Kandarpah sarpaanhamasmi Vaasukih [28].

Meaning—Among weapons I am Vrjra among cows I am Kamdhenu, I am Kandarapa—The love-god—among the progenitors. Among the serpents I am Vasuki.

Commentary—Vajra is the weapon used my Indra. In common paralane it is called the thunder bolt.

Kamdhenu is the celestial cow who is capable of yielding measureless milk and also of fulfilling all desires.

Kardarp is called Kamdeo, the god of love and sex which leads to procreation.

Vasuki is the best known of serpents. He resides in the abode of Indra. Once Janamejaya, according to the legend started 'Sarp-yagya'-killing all serpents in sacrificial fire. Vasuki was also attracted by 'mantra' and was about to be fed to fire but it curled itself around one of the legs of the celestial throne of Indra. The 'mantra' was used to attract Indra along with his throne and 'vaasuki'. Any how the king of gods was saved form his firy grave and with him the most poisonous vaasuki.

Anantashchaasmi naagaanaam varunho yaadsaamahan
Pitreenhaamryamaa chaasmi yamah sanyataamaham [29].

Meaning—Among Nagas I am Ananta, Varuna among

creatures of water, Aryan among the fore-fathers-dead ancestors. Yama among rulers.

Commentary—Nag is a special variety of snake, deadly poisonous. Anant-nag is supposed to have many mouths and as the legend goes Lord Vishnu sleeps on the huge naga and this whole earth is resting on the huge head of this most powerful naga called Sheshnaag.

Varun is the water-god. He is thus also the lord of all which dwell in the water.

It is a coming belief among the Hindus that their fathers and grand fathers and grand—grand fathers who departed from this worldly abode protect and guide them in hours of need. Thus the importance of the ancestors.

Aryama is the oldest among men's ancestors. He finds mention in the Rigveda also "yamam raksranti prochetaso varuno, mitro, Aryama (Rigveda—1.90. 9); The meaning of this mantra is Aryama along with Varun and Mitra (Sun) protects us form the evil-doers.

There are seven famous ancestors according to scriptures—

1. Karyavaah,
2. Anal
3. Som
4. Yam
5. Aryama
6. Agnishvat
7. Varhishad.

'Yam' or Yamraj is the Lord of deads. Those who depart from this earth first appear before him and he decides with total indifference as to who deserves what—heaven or hell. He then lords upon them who dwell in hell and discipline them mercilessly.

Prahladashchaasmi daityanam kalah kalyataamaham,
Mrigaanham mrigendro'ham vainatheyashch pakshinham [30].

Meaning—I am Prahlad among the daityaas and Kal among the destroyers. Among quadruples I am the lion, the Garuda among birds.

Commentary—Daityas are demons who devour even

men. Prahlad was the son of a demon-King, Hiranya Kashipu, but he had no characteristics of a 'daitya'. He was devoted to God and at a very early age of fourteen or fifteen he caused God to appear in form of Nrisingh (half body being of lion and half of man) and kill Hiranyakashipu his own father who had become So egoistic, he declared himself as God.

Daityas are called daitya because they are according to legends son of Diti who was the full sister of Aditi who produced gods. The Time or 'Kal' is the great leveller. With it is destroyed everything gradually.

Lion is undisputedly the king of all animals. It is rightly said in the Sanskrit that lion himself became the lord of animals—'Svayameva mrigendrah' (Thus the leader among men himself becomes so, he awaits none to declare him as such).

Garuda is a big bird which flies very high in the sky. His food is supposed to be serpents and according to the legends he is so powerful and fast in flying that he serves as the carrier of Lord Vishnu.

Pavanah pavataamasmi Ramah Shashtrabhritaamaham,
Jhakshaanaam makarashchaami srotsaamasmi Jahnvi [31].

Meaning—Among purifiers I am the wind, Rama among the wielders of weapon, alligator among the beings of water and the Ganges among the rivers.

Commentary—The wind is certainly one of the most powerful purifiers along with water and fire, but while the latter even kill, the wind seldom does so.

There is nothing to tell about the bravery of Ram, the very incarnation of the Supreme Lord.

The Alligator is the most powerful among the creatures of water, Whale notwithstanding which may be known for its size but not for prowess.

Nothing to tell about the purity of the river Ganges. She is called 'jaahnvi' because according to the legend the seer 'jahnu' drank the whole of it on Her way to the sea and She was brought out operating on his thigh (Jahnu).

Sargaanhaamaadirantashcha madhyam chaivaahmarjun,
Adhyaatmavidya vidyaanam vaadah Pravadataamaham [32].

Meaning—O Arjuna, I am the beginning, the middle

and the end of all creations. Among knowledge I am the spiriitual knowledge, I am right reasoning among the disputants.

Commentary—The Lord has asserted it many times that He is the creator and the ultimate destroyer of this world. Here again it has been re-emphasised in the first line.

There is no denying the fact that spiritual knowledge is the real knowledge.

Upanishads have named two kinds of 'vidyas'—

i. Vidya

ii. Avidya

'Vidya' is the spirtual knowledge, avidya is the knowledge we generally learn. Upnishads say that they who indulge in 'avidya' go to a blinding dark place—"Andham Tamah pravishanti ye avidyaamupasate".

They also hold the view that 'avidya' the ordinary knowledge is just for survival it is 'vidya' (the spiritual knowledge) which provides one with immortality—'Avidyayaa mritym Tritva Vidyaamritam Asnute'.

Then the Lord is very right in claiming to be the spiritual knowledge and no other kinds of knowledge which are nothing than 'avidyas'.

Learned people often discuss and argue many things pertaining to scriptures and learning. Unless they reach some conclusion based on logic and right reasoning their arguments are futile. The Lord is thus the right reasoning itself.

Aksharaanhaamakaaro'smi dvandvah saamasikasya cha,
Ahmevaakshayah Kalo dhaataham visshvatomukham [33].

Meaning—Among the letter I am 'A', (अ) among compounds I am the dual, I am the imperishable time, I am the sustainer of all with focus on all sides.

Commenatary—Among letters 'A' (अ) naturally occupies much significance due to being the first among the alphabet. It is both in case of devanaagri script and the roman script. But in devanaagari it assumes much significance as it is in every letter. In Sanskrit a latter is incomplete unless it incorporates the 'A' sound. Without it the letter is only half. This is almost the same in Hindi. Let us take an example, the word 'म' is composed of म् and अ. It is why we do not write just म् for 'म' we have to write 'म'.

The letter has its spiritual importance too. It is of every body-knowledge that 'Om' is the most purifying word in Sanskrit. It is made of three words. 'A' 'U' and 'M', A being the first one.

Even other scriptures has dignified 'A' According to 'Aitreya Braahaman' A is all sound—*Akaaro vai sarva vak* (Aitreya Bra 3-6).

So far compounds or 'samasas' are concerned, they are used in Sanskrit to join two words. They are six in number—

1. Tatpurush
2. Bahuvrihi
3. Karmdhaaray
4. Dvigu
5. Dvandva
6. Abyayaibhaava

'Samaas' is very much is use in Sanskrit. Due to 'samaas' and 'sandhi' a sentence in Sanskrit can stretch to even four to six lines. **Unimaginable**? But it is has been demonstrated in a fiction-book called 'Kaadambari' authored by a famous prose-writer and poet, 'Vanhabhatta'.

'Dvandva' compound or 'samaas' is most important among them as it provides some significance to both the words it combines. Take for example day-night (Din—Rat). The compound 'dvandva' is here because we are are not calling day and night. One can give a lot of such examples—sukh-Dukh (pleasure and pain), Bhaavaabhaava (plenty and nothing) etc.

He is the imperishanble i.e. the everlasting time which has no origin and no end.

He has talked of 'kal' earlier also (shloka 30 of this very chapter) but that was in a different sense as explained in the commentary following the verse (30).

He is the sustainer of all and He has mouths in all directions. He has certainly made it amply clear in many preceding chapters that He creates and sustains all, so far as His having mouths in all directions is concerned, it will be clear when He will show His 'viraatroop' (the hugest form) in the next chapter.

Mrityuh sarvharshchahamudbhavashcha bhavishyatam
Keertih shrirvakcha naareenham smritirmedha dhritih, kshama [34].

Meaning—I am the all devouring death as well as the source of future beings. I am the fame, I am the sweet speech among the women. I am the memory, the intelligence, the steadfastness and the forgiveness.

Commentary—He is the death itself. He has already maintained at many places that He is the destroyer of all and all ultimately vanish in Him. He has also maintained earlier that He is the seed of all beings thus it is right to say that He is the source of all who are to come into being.

The second line has been often misunderstood. The qualities like sweet speech, glory, memory and intelligence etc. are here attributed to the woman only, but this is not the case. These qualities are possessed by men also. Only sweet speech can solely be attributed to the women. It is why I have interpreted this shloka in a non-conventional way. Nothing to comment on the qualities enumerated, they are all Godly.

Vrihatsaam taha saamnaam gaayatri chhaandasaamaham,
Maasaanaam maargsheersho'ahmritoonaam kusumaakarah [35].

Meaning—I am the great 'sama' among the sama hymns, the gaayatri among the metres (of verses). I am margsheersha among months (of Hindu calendar) and among the seasons I am the spring.

Commentary—Among the Vedas he has already declared to be the Saamveda, but here he is telling of something else. There are various hymns in the Saamved which are being sung in the praise of the gods. 'Vrihatsaam' is among such hymns. The very name indicates that it is the best or greatest of all such hymns. Many confused 'gaayatri' with the famous 'gaayatri' mantra (the sacred composition of letters) but here the lord is talking about one of the various metres of verses used in Sanskrit. Gayatri-metre is supposed to be the sacred of all. The sacred 'Durga saptshati' a book written in praise of the Lordess Kaali is mostly in 'gaayatri' metre.

'Naaraayan upnaishad calls 'gaayatri' as the mother of

all metres—'Gaayatri chhandsaam mateti'.

One must differentiate between a metre (chhand) and a hymn (mantra). Here the Lord is talking of 'Gaayatri' the metre.

The month known as maargshirsh was the first month of the calendar in the Mahabarat-period. It is composed of almost half of December and some part of January. It is why the Lord call Himself to be 'margshirsh' among the months—the first one.

There is nothing to comment upon the importance of the spring among the seasons. He calls it 'kusumaakar'—the repository of flowers. There are flowers and flowers every where in the spring.

Dutam chhalayataamasmi tejastejasvinaamaham,
Jayo'smi vyavasaayo'smi sattvam sattvavataamaham [36].

Meaning—I am the gambling in those practising fraud. The glory of those who are glorious, I am the victory, the resolution and the best quality of those who are the best.

Commentary—It is rather surprising that the Lord calls Himself the gambling. But he is to claim to be the strongest or best among all—good or evil. He is even the death. So He is right in calling Himself 'gambling' which is the fraud-uparlleled among the different frauds practised by the fraudulants.

Nothing to comment upon other qualities enumerated here, they are the most desirable.

The 'sattva' of course needs a bit elaboration. It is not certainly the best quality in real sense of the term. 'Sattva' stands for a truthful virtuous quality. There is no English synonim to it. Actually there are there qualities men are made of—

1. Sattva
2. Raj
3. and Tam.

Sattva is the first and therefore the best one. The righteous among men adhere to this 'sattva', the second to them is 'Raj' and the worst is Tam—the deplorable and the least desired one.

Vrishnheenaam Vasudeo'smi pandavanam Dhananjayah,
Muninaamapyaham vyasah kaveenamushana Kavih [37].

Meaning—I am Krishna among the vrishnh'clan, among the Pandvaas I am yourself. Among the seers I am Vyas. Among the poets I am Ashuna.

Commentary—The clan of Krishna is 'vrishnhi.' He rightly considers Himself the best of them. No doubt Arjun is the best among the Pandavaas. He calls him here Dhananjaya. According to Sanskrit one who wins wealths is dhanajaya. 'Dhanam jayati iti Dhananjayah.' It also indicates that Arjun in destined to win the battle of Mahbarat and thus asscumulate wealth.

About 'Vyas' we have previously told in details. The Lord says that He is 'Vyas' among 'Munis'. We have translated muni as seer. In fact according to Sanskrit one who always contemplates on things spiritual is Muni—'Mananaat Munih'.

Ashuna is here for Shukraachaarya. He was a great poet and the prist of Rakshsas (demons or man-eaters). In fact Shukraachaarya (or Ashuna) is a derivation from 'shukra'—the planet venus. Venus is known for its imaginative and artistic attributes. According to astrology whose Venus is strong in his astrological chart, is bound to be a great artist, writer or poet.

Dando dayataamasmi neetirasmi jigeeshataam,
Maunam chaivaasmi guhyaanam gyanam gyanavatamham [38].

Meaning—I am the punishing power among those who punish (are rulers), the policy of all who conquer, I am the silence of secret things (and thoughts). I am knowledge of the knowledgeable.

Commentary—So long as evils and evil-people are there, there is bound to be a rule-giver, one who punishes the evil-doers. The Lord claims to be the very quality of those who punish or must punish.

No body becomes a conqueror of war without a firm policy. History is full of examples in which kings without a firm policy and strategy have been vanquished though possessing much power in form of armies and resources. The

Lord is this very policy of victory.

If one is to keep secrets, the best course is to take recourse to silence. It is why silence is said to be silver.

Knowledgeable persons are powerful and respected. The Lord is this vary knowledge of them.

Yachchaapi sarvabhaotaanaam beejam tadahamarjun,
Na tadasti vina yatsyaanmaya bhootam charaacharam [39].

Meaning—O Arjun! I am even the seed of all beings. There is nothing animate or inanimate which can exist without Me.

Commentary—He has already proclaimed that He is the seed of all existence. Here He simply lists His this quality along with other specialities. There is nothing moving or immoving in which He is not.

Naant'sti mam divyaanaam vibhooteenaam parantap,
Esha Tooddeshatah prokto vibhootevistaro maya [40].

Meaning—O Arjun there is no end to My divine glories. This is just a brief description given be Me of the extent of My glories.

Commentary—God is all pervading and all powerful. Whatever there is, it is His manifestation. Whatever best is, it is He. Thus there is bound to be only a brief description of His powers and glories. Even He cannot narrate them in all details.

Yadyadvibhootimatsattvam Shreemadoorjitmeva va,
Tattadevaagacch tvam mam tejo' nshsambhavam [41].

Meaning—Whatever is full of glory, essence and beauty that is the product of a portion of my effulgence.

Commentary—Nothing special

Athava bahunaiten Kim gyaaten tavaarjun,
Vistabhyaahamidam kritasnamekaanshen sthito jagat [42].

Meaning—Or what is the need of you to know it in all details. Suffice it to know that I stand holding this entire existence with a single (infinitesimal) portion of Myself.

Commentary—The Lord ultimately summarises with the observation that it is only with a very infinitesimal part of His being that He has been holding together all this entire world of animate and inanimate beings. One can only imagine what the shape, size and qualities of this word would have been, had it retained the whole power of the Lord.

Om Tatsaditi Shrimadbhagavadgeetaashoopanishatsu Brahm vidyayaam yogshaashtre Krishnaarjun samvaade Vibhooti yog naam dashamo'dhyaayah.

Thus in the Upanishad sung by the Lord, the knowledge of Brahma, the scripture of yoga, the discussion between Shri Krishna and Arjuna ends the Xth chapter named "the yoga of divine golries."

CHAPTER XI

Arjun uvaach
Madanugrahaaya paramam guhyamadhyaatmsangitam
Yattvayoktam vachasten moho'yam vigato mam. [1].

Meaning —**Arjun said**—My delusion is dispelled by the most secret words of spiritual wisdom that have been spoken by you out of compassion for me.

Commentary—A gentleman as he is, Arjun expresses his gratitude to the Lord for all the best things He has said to him and he also admits that he is no more deluded.

Bhavaapyou he bhaotaanaam shrutau vistarshomaya,
Tvattah kamalpatraksh mahatmayamapi chaavyayam [2].

Meaning—O Lotus-eyed, I have heard from you in detail, accounts of the evolutions as well as the dissolution of beings and also your endless glory.

Commentary—Nothing special

Evametadyathaatth tvamaatmaanam parmesbwar,
Drashtumichchaami te roopmaishwaram Purushottam [3].

Meaning—O Lord so it is as you have declared yourself, I long to see your divine form O! Purushottam (the best among persons).

Commentary—Arjun, Admits that whatever the Lord has said about Himself is correct. Now he is naturally interested in looking at the divine body of the incarnation in human form, of one who is the Supreme Lord of the entire universe.

Manyase yadi tachchakyam maya drashtumiti prabho,
Yogesvhar tato me tvam darshayaatamaanamavyayam [4].

Meaning—O Lord, if yoy think that I am capable of beholding it, then O Master of yoga show me your imperishable self.

Commentary—Arjun is naturally in doubt if he can be able to fix his eyes on the divine form of Shri Krishna he, therefore says that he is not to make any such request which is difficult to be fulfilled. The divine form of the Lord could be materialized only when Arjun was able enough to behold it.

Shri Bhagavaan Uvaach

Pashya Me paarth roopaanhi shtasho'thsahasrashah,
Naanaavidhaani divyaani naanaavarnhakriteeni cha [5].

Meaning—The Blessed Lord said—O Son of Pritha, behold my hundreds and thousands of divine forms of diverse kinds, colours and shape.

Commentary—A hint at what is to materialise before Arjuna.

Pashyaadityaanvasoonroodraanshvinau Marutastathaa,
Bhoonyadrishtapoorvaani pashyaashcharyaanhi Bharat [6]

Meaning—O Bharat! Behold the Adityas, the vasus, the rudras, the two Ashwinis and the maruts. Behold many wonders never seen before

Commentary—Adityas, Vasus etc. have been explained in the preceding chapter. The Lord promises to show many more wonders which not have been seen before.

Ehaikastham jagatkritsnam pashyaadya sacharaacharam,
Mam dehe gudaakesh yachchaanyaddrashtumichchhasi [7].

Meaning—Behold O Gudakesh here itself, the entire creation consisting of both animate-inanimate beings unified in My body and whatever else you will to see.

Commentary—The Lord is about to manifest his supreme form and He invites Arjun to see Him as one who holds in Himself all that is in the universe moving or unmoving besides many such formations which were full of wonders and never beheld by the man-kind.

Na tu maam shakyase drashtumanenaiva svachakshusha
Divyam dadaami te chakshuh pashya Me yogamaishvaram [8].

Meaning—You can not see Me with these eyes of yours; therefore I provide you with the divine eyes with them you behold My divine yoga.

Commentary—The mention of the divine yoga is meaningful and significant; it implies that whatever the Lord is going to show is but the manifestation of the unparalleled yoga which is only His.

Sanjaya Uvaach

Evamuktvaatato raajanmahaayogeslvaro harih,
Darshyaamaas Parthaay paramam roopamaishvaram [9].

Meaning—Sanjaya Told—O king! Shri Krishna the Master of the great yoga having said thus, revealed to Arjuna His supreme divine form.

Commentary—Nothing Special

Anekvaktranayanmanekaadbhutadarshanam,
Anekdivyaabharanham divyaanekodyataayudham [10].

Meaning—(There was the supreme body) having many mouths, many eyes, presenting many wonderful sights, decorated with many divine ornaments, possessing many uplifted divine weapons.

Commentary—along with the next verse

Divyamaalyaambardharam divyagandhaanulepanam
sarvaashcharyamayam devamanantam visvatomukham [11].

Meaning—(It was) wearing divine garlands and clothes (it was) besmeared with divine perfume, full of all the wonders (of existence); it was an infinite divine body with faces every where.

Commentary—Lord, as promised to Arjuna, manifests Himself in a wonderful, magnificent as well as terrible form. This is His 'virat' (the unimaginably great) form full of wonder of wonders. The description continues.

Divi sooryasahasrasya bhavedyugapadutthitaa
yadi bhaah sadrishee saa syaadbhasastasya mahatmanah [12]

Meaning—If thousand suns rise simultaneously in the sky even their cumulated light would hardly meet the light of the Lord.

Commentary—The body of the gods is said to be made of light. It is just natural that the form of the Supreme Lord is also made of light. But this light is unimaginable. Even the splendour of one sun is beyond comprehension. One can only imagine the light created by thousand suns and the Lord's divine light surpasses even this combined light of suns thousand in number. It was very kind on the part of the Lord to bestow divine eyes to Arjuna other wise the fate that would have been of his ordinary mortal eyes can be well imagined.

Tatraikastham jagatkritasnam pravibhaktamanekadhaa
apashyaddevadevasya shareere paandvastada [13].

Meaning—Arjun, them beheld in the person of that supreme body the whole world multitudinously divided and yet unified is one limb (of the Lord).

Commentary—Outwardly the world is divided in manifold divisions but all these divisions rest in the being of the Supreme Lord Himself. They are not beyond Him. In other words all beings moving, unmoving are constantly emerging from only one source and that is the Lord Himself.

Tatah sa vishmyaavishto hrishtroma Dananjayah,
Pranhamya shirasa devam krihtaamjalirabhaashat [14].

Meaning—Then Dhananjaya (Arjuna) over come with wonder and with his hairs standing on their ends (a fear-effect) bowed down to the Lord and with clasped hands spoke thus.

Commentary—Nothing now.

Arjun Uvaaach

pashyaami devaanstva deva dehe
Srvaanstathaa bhoobtvishesha shamghaan,
Brahmanhameesham Kamlaasanasth-
mrishinshcha survaanuragaanshch divyaan [15].

Meaning—Arjuna said—O Lord! I see all the gods in your body and different companies of beings, Brahama seated on his lotus-seat, the Lord Shiva as well as all rishis and the divine serpents.

Commentary Being awed by seeing the ever unseen form of the Lord manifested in its full glory Arjuna starts praying to the Lord and in that process describes what he sees with the divine eyes so kindly bestowed on him by the Lord.

In this verse he sees all the gods in Him. This proves that even the gods are just part and parcel of His being. Clusters of different beings are there in His body. It has been made clear before that all beings emerge from Him—no wonder Arjun finds them lodged with in Himself. Brahma is seen perched on his lotus-seat. According to 'puranhaas' a lotus emerges from the navel of Lord Vishnu lying on his serpent-bed in the sea of milk and on that lotus-flower is seated Brahma who creates the whole universe from there itself.

As stated earlier Shiva is the Lord of destruction. Thus here is the representation of all the three important overlords, Brahma, the creator, Shiva the destroyer and Vishnu the sustainer (in the form of Lord Krishna Himself).

All 'rishis' are there in the body of the Lord. This also may mean that the 'rishis' ultimately attain to Him.

It must not be surprising that Arjun sees the divine serpents and also all reptiles. It has been explained how some of the serpents like Vaasuki and Sheshanaag are of immense importance. They are of course divine serpents and not those ordinary found on this earth. But the serpents in India have often been equated with the gods, there is a special day in every year called 'naagpanchami' when milk is offered to seprents. They are also supposed to be venerable as they are very dear to Lord Shiva and He is credited with ever wearing a garland of numerous serpents.

Anekbaahodarvaktranetram
Pashyaami tvam sarvato'anantrupam,
Naantam na madhyam na punastavaadim
pasyhaami Vishveshvar vishvarup [16].

Meaning—O ! Lord of universes, I see numerous arms and bellies and eyes and faces and your infinite forms on every side. I see not your end nor middle nor your beginning, O universe itself.

Commentary—The prayer being offered by Arjuna is spontaneous and full of adoration as well as awe. It is thus, natural, that some repetitions may occur here and there. Such repetitions can be marked in the following verses the repetitions may also show as to how He values some of the specialities and qualities of the Lord.

Arjuna calls Him the form of universe or the universe itself. This is remarkable. Truly speaking there is no difference between the creation and the creator. The latter himself has manifested as the former.

The Lord has neither beginning, nor middle, nor the end, similarly his 'Viraat roop' also appears to be dimensionless to Arjuna. He appears to have extended Himself in all directions, in all dimensions.

Here one is reminded of the famous line of the Gita quoted earlier which means; by Him is pervaded all that is here—'Yen sarvamidam tatam.' (The Gita chapter II Shloka—17.) Or Maya tatmam sarvam (IX-4).

Kireetinam gadinam charinam cha
tejoraashim sarvato diptimantam.
Pasyhaami tvam durnirikshyam samanta-
ddiptaanalarkdyutimaprameyam [17].

Meaning—I see you crowned, having mace (gada) and discus (chakra), you are in luminous mass of energy shining all around, an encompassing blaze, a sun-bright, firebright, hard to look and immeasurable on all sides.

Commentary—Diadem, mace and discus ('kirit', gada and chakra) are very favourite to Lord. While the first adds to His charms by decorating his head the 2nd and 3rd are his famous weapons. The most important is the last one. It is a legendary round weapon always moving fast in a circular way with sharp blade-like edge which can appear on His finger on command, can slay any thing and return back to His finger.

The most important point of this verse is His extraordinarily luminous form resembling burning fire and blazing sun, very hard to look at. This point has already been taken care of in shloka 12 of the same chapter.

Tvamaksharam paramam veditavyam
Tvamasya vishvasya param nidhaanam,
Tvamavyayah shaashvatadharmgopta,
Sanaatanastvam purusho mato me [18].

Meaning—You are the supreme immutable worthy of being realised, Thy are the ultimate resort of this world. You are the imperishable protector of the eternal laws (Dharma). You are the eternal Being according to me.

Commentary—Arjuna goes on offering prayer to the Lord with the adjectives we are already familiar by now. The only addition seems to be supreme protector of 'dharma.' This is also nothing new. He has already declared in chapter IV shloka 7 that whenever there is the fading of Dharm...he incarnets Himself (yada-yada he dharmsya...)

Anaadimadhyaantamanantvirya-
manantbaahum shashisooryanetram.
pasyhaami Tvaam Deepthutasha vaktram
Svatejasaa visvamidam tapantam [19].

Meaning—I behold you without end or middle or beginning having unlimited prowess and numberless arms. Your eyes are the sun and the moon. Your mouth is blazing fire. You are burning up the world with your radiance.

Commentary—The sun and the moon have often been described as God's eyes. The more important thing is that with His fire emitting mouth and His ever burning energy, He takes the form of the destroyer. With numberless arms He is capable of both embracing the world with divine love and destroying the same with these countless arms.

Dyaavaaprthivyoridamantaram hi
vyaaptam tvayaiken dishashcha sarvaah
Drishtvaadbhutam rupamugram tavedam,
Lokatrayam pravyathitam mahaatman [20].

Meaning—The space between heaven and earth including all quarters are filled by You alone. Seeing Your this fierce and astounding form all the three worlds feel uncontrollably alarmed, O Mighty Lord.

Commentary—It is clear that the Lord had laid imphasis on his destroyer-aspect while manifesting Himself. It is certainly so awe-provoking that nothing is left which is not filled up by His unimaginable endless form stretching in all directions and filling the distance between the haven and the earth.

This act of installing fear has a purpose behind it. One is reminded of a line from 'Sant Tuladsidas' that there is no love without fear—'Vinu bhay ho hi na preeti'.

Amee hi tvaam sursangha vishanti
Kechidbeetah praamjalayo grinhanti
Svasteetyuktva maharshisiddh sanghah
***Stuvanti twaam stutibhih pushklaabhih** [21].*

Meaning—These host of the gods are entering in to You, some of them with palms clasped chanting Your names out of fear, number of great seers and perfected souls saying that let there be wellbeing, are praising You with the best of prayers.

Commentary—The element of fear hinted at in the previous verse, is made amply clear in this verse, except the spectacle that many of the gods appear entering in to Him proving that He is God of gods, the rest of them are chanting His names.

It is the responsibility of the great seers (Maharshis) and perfected souls (siddhaas) to bring wellbeing where it is not. They are doing the same by heaping the best of praises on the Lord so that He becomes clam and His fury is gone.

Rudraadityaa vasavo ye cha saadhya
vishve'shvinau marutashchoshmapaashch,
Gandharvyakshaasursidhsamgha-
Veekshante tvaam vismitaashchaiva sarve. [22].

Meaning—The rudras, aadityas, vasus, sadhyas, vishvedeva, Ashvinikumaras, Maruts, manes and hosts of gandharvaas, yakshas, asuras, and siddhas all have their eyes fixed on You in amazement.

Commentary—We have talked of rudras, Adityas, vasus, Ashvinikumaras and maruts in the preceding chapter and enumerated their names.

The new terms we shall explain here.

Sadhyas are like the gods. They are the sons of sadhya the daughter of Dharm's wife who herself is the daughter of Daksh according to Vayupuranha. Their names are :—

1. Man
2. Anumanta
3. Praanha
4. Nar
5. Yam

6. Ehita
7. Haya
8. Naya
9. Hans
10. Narayan
11. Vibhu
12. Prabhu

Coming to vishvedeva they are also the sons of another wife of Dharm named Vishvaa. These ten vishvadevas are as follows.

1. Kratu
2. Daksha
3. Shravva
4. Satya
5. Kaal
6. Kaam
7. Dhuni
8. Kuruvan
9. Pranbhavaan
10. Rochmaan.

Manes are ascestors. They are called 'Ooshmapah' because they partake only warm foods,—'Oosmbhaagaah hi pitarah.'

Gandharvaas are said to be expert in singing and dancing; similarly 'yakshaas' are a community in itself just below the gods. Asurs are those who are just opposite to the gods (surs)

All of them are amazed at this 'virat roop' of the Lord.

Roopam mahatte vahuvaktranetram—
Mahaavaaho bahoobaahoorupaadam
Bahoodaram bahudanshtraakaraalam
Drishtvaalokaah pravyathitaastathaham [23].

Meaning—O mighty-armed, seeing Your great form of many mouths, and eyes, of many arms and thighs and feet and numerous bellies, of many terrible teeth all worlds are shaken as also am I.

Commentary—One can only imagine of a form with numerous bellies and terrible teeth and be terrified even while going through these lines.

Nabhasprisham deeptmanekvarnham—
Vyaattaananam Deeptvishaalnetram,
Drishtva hi tvaam provyathitaanataraatma,
Dhritim na vindaami samam cha Vishnho. [24].

Meaning—O Vishnhu (The Supreme Lord) having seen your form touching the heavens, blazing and of many hues, your mounths wide opened and enormous burning eyes, I with my soul troubled and in pains have lost self-control and there is no peace for me.

Commentary—Arjun in narrating his own state of affairs. It is significant that the 'virat-roop' witnessed by him has not been a source of pleasure but pain. The Lord is bent upon in showing His prowess in full.

Danshtraakaraalaani cha te mukhaani
Drishtaiva kaalaanalsannibhaani
Disho na jaane na labhe cha sharm
Praseed devesh Jagannivaas [25].

Meaning—Seeing Your mouths with awe-evoking teeth and full of fires of death, I lose sense of direction and find no peace. So be merciful to me o God of gods, and refuge of all the worlds.

Commentary—Seeing no other way Arjuna beseeches the Lord to be pleased (and to abandon His terrible form)

Amee cha tvaam Dhritaraashtrasya putraah
Sarve sahaivaavanipaalsamghaih,
Bhishmo Dranah sootputrastathaasau
Sahaasmdeeyairapi yodhmukhyaih [26]
Vaktraanhi te tvarmaanaa vishanti
Danshtra karalaani bhayaanakaani
Kechidvilagna dashanaantareshu
Sandrishyante choornhitairutktamaangaih [27].

Meaning—All these sons of Dhrtarshtra along with the multitude of kings as well as Bhishm, Dronha, Karna and the foremost warriors of our side also are hastening in Your fearful mouths with terrible teeth. Some are seen stuck up among your long teeth with their heads broken to pieces.

Commentary—Though the description is awesome, it

is highly prophetic too. The Lord in a way wants to assure Arjun about the outcome of war. Even Bhishm, Dronha and Karna, the arch rival of Arjuna are to enter the valley of death, of course along with a number of warriors of his side as well. But there is no mention of his and his brothers. This clearly shows which side the **victory** lies.

Yathaa nandeenaam bahavo'mbubegaah
Samudramevaabhimukha dravanti
Tatha tavaamee naarlokveera—
Vishanti vaktr'anhyabhivijvalanti [28].

Meaning—As many streams of rivers race towards the ocean so, all these heroes of the world of men are entering your mouths full of fierce fire.

Commentary—This is one of the finest verses so far uttered by Arjuna. The simile with rushing rivers is marvellous and suggestive. As the sure goal of all rivers is the ocean, so all the warriors (mentioned in the preceding verse) has death and destruction as their ultimate end.

Yatha pradiptam jvalanam patanga-
vishanti nashaay samriddhabegaah
Tathaiva nashaay vishanti loka-
stavaapi vaktraanhi samridhvegaah [29].

Meaning—As the moths with ever increasing speed just rush in to a blazing fire to their destruction, so the worlds are entering with rapid speed your mouths for their doom.

Commentary—The beauty of similes continues. The expression that all worlds are entering the mouths of the lord, blazing with the fire of hell is in no way prophetic. It simply hints at ultimate end of all beings.

Lelihyase grasamaanahsamanta—
llookaansamagraanvadanairjvaladbhih
Tejobhiraapoorya jagatsamagram—
Bhaasastavograh pratapanti Vishnho [30].

Meaning—O vishnho! Swallowing in your burning mouths, You are licking all these men on all sides. The entire world is full with the blaze of Thy energies. Your terrible light is unbearable and it burns the all.

Commentary—Through out almost all shlokas the blazing fire predominates, emphasizing the fact that fire is the strongest and surest desructive element.

Aakhyaahi me ko bhavanugraroopo
Namo'stu te devavar praseed,
vigyaatumichchaami bhavantamaadyam
Na hi prajaanaami tava pravrittim [31].

Meaning—Let me know who your are with a form so fierce. My obeisance to You, O great God-head; be pleased I want to know You O Primal being, I do not know what You intend at.

Commentary—Arjun terrified with this form of the Lord prays Him to be kind. He is afraid that He may destroy the whole world, so he clearly but politely wants to know about the purpose behind His assuming this form.

Shri Bhagavanuvaach—

Kalo'smi lokakshayakritpravriddho
Lokaansamaahartumih pravrittah
rite'pi tvaam na bhavishyanti sarve
ye'vasthitaah pratyaneekeshu yodhaah [32].

Meaning—The blessed Lord said; I am the death itself assuming huge statue capable of destroying the whole universe. My aim is to finish these worlds. Even without you, all these warriors shall be not who are arrayed in the opposite armies.

Commentary—The ego of Arjun stands deflated. He had abandoned his weapons with a vow not to kill those standing against him as if he was the only one capable of killing them all and without him there would be no war. Lord says they all stand slayed despite him.

Tasmaattvamutishth yasho labhasva
jitvaa shatroon bhumkshva raajyam samriddham
Mayaivaite nihataah poorvameva
Nimittmaatram bhava Savyasaachin, [33],

Meaning—Therefore you arise and get glory and after conquering enemies enjoy an opulent kingdom. By Me alone they stand slain already. You become only instrumental (in killing them) O Savyaasaachin!

Commentary—Every thing is predetermined. Nothing

is by accident. The enemies of Arjun already stand killed by Lord. Arjun is only to play his part in the ensuing drama. He was to be assured of his victory and having seen all his enemies being chewed by the Lord Himself he certainly feels less shaky and thus the Lord exhorts him to arise and fight and in the process gain both glory and a vast kingdom.

Savyasaachi is one who is capable of handling the bow with the left hand also.

Dronham cha Bhishmam cha Jayadratham cha,
Karnham, tathaanyaanapi yodhbeeraan
Maya hataanstvam jahi ma vyathishta-
Yudhyasva jetaasi ranhe saptnaan [34].

Meaning—Slay who are already slain by Me e. g. Dronh, Bhishm, jayadrath, Karnha and many other warriors. Do not be afraid. Fight as you will conquer the enemies in the battle.

Commentary—Nothing special

Samjaya uvaach

Etachchhrutvaa vachanam keshavasya,
Kritaamjalirvepamaanah kireetee
Namskritva bhooya evaah krishnam—
Sagadgadam bheetbheetah pranhamya [35].

Meaning—Sanjaya said

Having heard these words of Keshavaa (Krishna) kireetee (Arjuna) trembling and with clasped hands bowed to Him and bowing again in extreme terror spoke to Krishna in voice faltering like any thing.

Commentary—Kireetee is one who wears a crown on his head.

Arjun having been assured by the Lord in two above verses feels very obliged to Him but at the same time is very much afraid of His shape and therefore even though he bows and prays, his voice is not under much control.

Arjunuvaach

Sthaane Hrisheekesh tav prakeertya
jagatprahrishatyanurajyate cha,
Rakshaansi bheetaani disho dravanti
Sarve namasyanti cha siddh sanghah [36].

Meaning—Arjun Said, O Hrishikesh Krishna, it is but

in fitness of things that the world rejoice and takes pleasure in your name. Terrified demons are fleeing in all directions and all the hosts of the perfect souls are bowing to You.

Commentary—Having seen the power and prowess of the Lord, Arjun admits that it is no wonder that the world is rejoicing in the chanting of His names, virtues, and glories. He is worthy of any adoration. The evil forces like rakshasas flee from Him and the good forces like siddhas (those who have perfect souls) bow to Him with reverence.

Kasmaachha te na nameranmahaatman
Gareeyase Brahmnho'pyaadikartre,
Anant Devesh jagannivas
Tvamuksharam sadastattatparam yat [37].

Meaning—How should they not pay you homage O great spirit? You are the original creator and doer of works and greater even than Brahma himself. O Infinite Lord of the gods, O you abode of the universe you are what is and what is not and also that which is beyond the both i.e. the supreme Lord Himself.

Commentary—The lord deserves in the words of Arjun all the adorations and salutations, full of mighty powers just exhibited, as He is.

Tvamaadidevah purushah puraanha—
stvamasya vishvasya param nidhaanam
Vettaasi vedyam cha param cha dhaam
Tvaya tatam vishvamanantrup [38].

Meaning—You are the prime god, the most ancient person you are the ultimate resort of this universe. You are the known and that which is to be known and the highest abode. By You is pervaded the universe O ! endless in forms.

Commentary—All commented upon in earlier verses.

Vaayuryamognirvarunhah, shashaankah,
Projaapatistvam, Prapitaamahaschch
Namo namaste'stu sahasrakritvah,
Punashch bhooyo'pi namo namaste [39].
Namah purastaadath preishthataste
Namo'stu te sarvat eva sarva,
Anantveeryamitvikramastvam—

Sarvam samaapnohsi tato'si sarvah [40].

Meaning—You are vaayu, yam, agni, varunh, and moon. You are Brahma, nay the father of Brahma Himself. Salutations to You a thousand times, over and again and yet again, salutation in front and behind and from every side for You are infinite in might and immeasurable in strength. You are thus all.

Commentary—Vaayu is the wind—god, Yam is the god of death, Varunha is water-god. Agni is fire-god in Vedic literature, all these elements are termed as gods.

Sakheti matvaa prasabham yaduktam
He Krishna he yaadav he sakheti
Ajaanataa mahimaanam tavedam
Maya pramaadaatpranhayen vaapi [41].
Yachchavahaasaarthmasatkrito'si
Viharshayyasanbhojanehu
Eko'thavaapyachyut tatsamaksham
Tatkshaamaye tvamahamaprameyam [42].

Meaning—Having been ignorant of this greatness of Your and considering You only as a friend, I have addressed You in a wanton way, either through carelessness or through love, as Krishna, 'yadava', companion, and so on and whatsoever disrespect while playing, reposing in couch, sitting or dining either, alone or in presence of others. O faultless one, I pray forgiveness for all this from You the infinite.

Commentary—Arjun now realises how foolish it was on his part to behave with the Lord as if he was one like him.

Pitaasi lokasya charaacharasya
Tvamasya poojyashch gururgreeyaan,
Na tvatsamo'styabhyaadhikah kutonyo—
Loktraye'pyapratimaprabhaava [43].

Meaning—You are the father of all this world of the animate and inanimate creation. You are one to be worshipped and to be venerated. None is equal to you, O incomparable in might in all the three worlds, how can any one be greater then you?

Commentary—The three worlds generally stand for

heaven, earth and the world below the earth (Akash, dharati and patal)

Tasmaatpranhamya pranhidhaaya kaayam-
Prasaadaye tvaamahmeeshmeedyam,
Piteva putrasya sakheva sakhyuh
Priyah priyaayaarhasi deo sodhum [44].

Meaning—Therefore I lay my body at Your feet and prostrating beseech grace of You the adorable and the ruler of all. As a father to his son, as a friend to his friend, as a dear with her who he loves, You should bear with me.

Commentary—Full of reproach for his early behaviours Arjun seeks the grace and forgiveness of the Lord.

Adrishtapoorbam hrishito'smi drishtvaa,
Bhayen cha pravyathitam mano me,
Tadeva me darashay devaroopam
praseed devessh jagannivaas [45].

Meaning—I have beholden what never was seen before and I rejoice in it but my mind is tormented with fear, show to me your divine form. O Lord ! of the gods, abode of this universe, be pleased.

Commentary–The terrific form of the Lord is no longer bearable to Arjuna so he prays to the Lord to show His another but pleasant form which he will describe in the following verse.

Kireetinam gadinam chakrahast-
Michchhami tvaam drashtumaham tathaiva,
Tenaiva rupenha chaturbhujen
Sahasrabaaho bhava vishvamoorte [46].

Meaning—I like to see you as before with a didem on the head, holding the mace and the 'chakra', assume your four-armed form O ! thousand armed, O form of universe.

Commentary—The Lord Vishnhu has four arms. Arjun having realized that he is none other than Vishnhu the supreme lord of the universe, requests Him to assume not only His formal shape but also the most pleasing and gracious form of Vishnhu who holds 'sankh' 'gada,' 'chakra' and 'padma' (lotus-flower) in His four different hands. 'Sankh' stands for conch.

Shri Bhagavanuvaach
Maya prasannen Tavaarjunedam
Rupam param darshitamaatmyogaat,
Tejomayam vishvamanantmaadyam
Yanme tvadanyen na drishtpoorvam [47].

Meaning—The Blessed Lord said :—

Arjuna! As I was pleased with you so I showed you through My own power of yoga, this luminous, universal infinite and the primal form which was never seen by any one else in the past.

Commentary—This shows how favourite Arjuna is to the Lord. It is not for nothing that He has chosen to act as his charioteer.

Na vedayagyaadhyaayanairn danai-
rna cha kriyaabhiran tapobhirugraih,
Evamroopah shakya aham nriloke
Drashtum tvadanyen kurupraveer [48].

Meaning—O fore most of kurus! In this world of humans, I can not be seen in this form by any one else than you, either through the study of the Vedas or through sacrifices or through study (of scriptures), through gifts, action, or through austere penances.

Commentary—Nothing is equal to the grace of God, to His sheer pleasure which He showers upon him who is very dear to Him.

Maatevyathaa maa cha vimoodhabhaavo
Drishtva rupam ghormeedringmamedam,
Vyapetbheeh preetmanaah punastvam,
Tadeva me roopmidam prapashya [49].

Meaning—Having seen this fearful form of mine you should not feel pain, nor should you be deluded. You be fearless and rejoice and behold again the other form of Mine.

Commentary—The Lord has realized how terrified Arjun is on looking His 'Viraat-roop', therefore He asks him to cast away the fear, feel pleasant and be ready to behold His formal form.

Sanjay uvaach—

Etyarjunam Vaasudevastathoktvaa
Svaakam roopan darshayaamaas bhooyah,
ashvaasayaamaas cha bheetmenam-
Bhootva punah saumyavapurmahaatmaa [50].

Meaning—Sanjaya said :—

Krishna having thus spoken to Arjuna again manifested His pleasing appearance, the great souled consoled the terrified one.

Commentary—Nothing special

Arjun Uvaach—

Drishtvedam manusham roopam tava saumyam Janardan
Edaneemasmi samvrittah sachetah prakritim gatah [51].

Meaning—Arjuna said, Janardan beholding again Your pleasing human-form, I have now become composed and restored to my own nature.

Commentary—Nothing special

Shri Bhagavanuvaach—

Sudurdashamidam rupam drishtvaanasi yanmam.
Devaa apyasya rupasya nityam darshankamkshinhah [52].

Meaning—The Blessed Lord said—This four-armed form of mine which you have seen is very difficult to perceive. The gods themselves ever wish to behold it.

Naahan vedairan tapaasa na daanen na chejyayaa,
shakya evamvidho drashtum drishtvanasi mam yatha [53].

Meaning—I can not be seen as you have seen Me, by the study of the vedas nor by austerities nor by charity or worship.

Commentary—Nothing special

Bhaktyaa tvananyaya shakya ahamevamvidho'rjun
Gyaatum drastum cha tattven preveshtum cha parantap [54].

Meaning—O Valiant Arjuna, I can be seen in this form however with one pointed devotion and known in reality and even entered in to.

Commentary—Devotion and single-minded devotion to Krishna is emphasized upon.

Matkarmkrinmatparamo madbhaktah sangvarjitah,
Nirvairah sarvabhooteshu yah sa maameti Pandava [55].

Meaning—Arjun Be a doer of My works, depend on Me, be My devotee, has no attachment, be free from enmity to all beings, for such a man comes to Me.

Commentary—What is the work of the Lord? To propagate the theory He has propounded. To this we will come in a succeeding chapter.

Om Tatsaditi shrimadbhagvadgitasoopanishatsu Brahmvidyaayaam yogashashtre Shrikrishnaarjun-samvaade vishvaroop darshanyogo namaikadasho' dhyaayah.

Thus in the Upanishad sung by the Lord, the knowledge of Brahma, the scripture on yoga, the dialogue between Shrikrishna and Arjuna ends the eleventh chapter "The yoga of the vision of the universal shape."

CHAPTER XII

Arjun Uvaach

Evam satat yukta ye bhaktaastvaam paryupaasate,
Ye chaapyaksharamabyaktam tesham ke yog vittamaah [1].

Meaning—**Arjuna said :** Those devotees who thus by a constant union with You as shown in Your form and those who seek after Thee as unmanifest and immutable; which of these are the best knowers of yoga?

Commentary—Arjun now raises a vital question which concerns the 'Saakaar' (with form) and 'niraakaar' (formless) God. Some insist that devotion to the former is more desirable and some think that the devotees of the latter is doing the worth-doing.

Both are addressed here as yogi by Arjuna, the only question is, who is better.

The question of with form and without form has arisen only after the vision of 'virat-form' of the Lord.

Shri Bhagavanuvaach

Mayyaaveshya mano ye maam nityayukta upaasate
Shraddhya parayopetaaste me yuktatamaa matah [2].

Meaning—**The blessed Lord said**—

Those who with their mind centered on Me, are in constant union with Me and worship Me possessed of a supreme faith, they according to Me are the best yogis.

Commentary—The devotion to the Lord gets the upper hand. One with form is decided to be superior to the formless. This is the answer to the question posed by Arjuna in the preceding verse.

ye tvaksharmanirdeshyamavyaktam paryupaasate.
Sarvatragamchintyam cha kootshamachalam dhruvam [3].

Sanniyamyendriyagraaman sarvatra sambuddhayah,
***Te praapnuvanti maameva sarvabhoot hite rataah* [4].**

Meaning—But those who worship the indefinable, unmanifest, immutable, omnipresent, unhinkable, self-poised, immobile and constant, they too by controlling their senses and by being even minded towards all beings and by being engaged in doing good to all creatures, come to Me.

Commentary—Even those concentrating on the formless attain to the Lord. As stated earlier the main aim of the Gita is to strike a balance between divergent views. The Lord gives His approval to worship both the formless and the with form. But He will cartaintly show favour to the worship of one with form, not totally neglecting the former.

Klesho'dhikatarasteshaamavyaktasakatchetsaam,
***Avyakta hi gattriduhkam dehavadbhirvapyate* [5].**

Meaning—The path of those who have their mind attached to the formless is more difficult as for those who are centered in the body, self-identification with the formless is attained with difficulty.

Commentary—The easier path is to be devoted to the Lord who is manifest. Thus the superiority of worshiping the manifest over the unmanifest. This point will be emphasized upon further.

Ye tu sarvaanhi karmaanhi mayi sannyasya matparaah,
***Ananyenaiva yogen mam dhyaayant upaasate* [6].**
Teshamaham samuddharta mritusamsaarsaagarat,
***Bhavami nachiraatparth mayyaveshitchetsaam* [7].**

Meaning—Those who have surrendered their all actins to Me, are solely devoted to Me with an unswerving yoga and meditating on Me, worship Me with single minded devotion, O Parth, I speedily deliver them with their consciousness fixed on Me, out of the sea of the death-bound world.

Commentary—As indicated earlier, the devotion aspect is fully emphasized. This world has rightly been compared with a sea of death. Those devoted to Lord Krishna wholeheartedly and single-mindedly never fall again in this death sea.

Mayyeva man aadhatsva mayi budhimniveshaya, Nivasishyasi myyeva ata oordhvam na samsayah [8].

Meaning—Fix your mind on Me only, lodge your intellect in Me alone, you shall dwell in Me here-after.

Commentary—Hereafter stands for death, with mind as well as reasoning reposed in Him and Him only, there is no doubt that one will attain to Him after departing from this world.

Ath chittam samaadhaatum na shaknoshi mayi sthiram, abhyasayogen tato mamichchhaptum Dhananjaya [9].

Meaning—If you are not able to concentrate your mind on Me constantly then seek after Me by the yoga of practice.

Commentary—Practice makes perfect. It is not that easy to have a constant concentration on any thing including the Lord. One is therefore advised to take recourse to practice. Lord always lays emphasis on practice. Remember when Arjuna says that it is difficult to control the ever unstable mind. The Lord says it is possible through practice (Abhyasen tu kaunteya-VI 34).

Here this practice is also given the nomenclature of yoga to underline its importance. Sticking to constant practice is certainly that which may be called practice-yoga (Abhyaas yoga)

Abhyaase'pyasamartho'si matkarmparama bhava Madarthamapi karmanhi kurvansidhimavaapsyasi [10].

Meaning—If you are unable to practise even this then devote yourself fully to My work, by doing all actions for My sake you shall attain perfection.

Commentary—Again the question arises what are the works of the Lord which He is referring to. This question had arisen is the 55th shloka of the preceeding chapter also. There it was commented upon that to propagate the theory propouned by Him is His work. The theory of 'karmyog', performing, all works without attachment and never to remain inactive and perform whatever duty is allotted to one is the main message of the Gita or the Lord. Whoever practises this 'yoga' and more importantly make others to practise this is certainly performing His works.

Thus it can be said in short that to impart the teaching of the Lord is the work performed for Him, and this assertion is not unfounded. To realize its importance one will have to refer to a chapter yet to come—chapter XVII. In its 6th 'shloka' he clearly says "he who...shall impart this most secret teaching of Mine...shall reach Me doubtlessly.

Athaitadapyashakto'si kartum mdyogamaashritah,
Sarvkramphaltyaagam tattah kuru yataatmvaan [11].

Meaning—But if you are unable to do even this, then renounce all fruits of action with controlling your self and taking refuge in My yoga.

Commentary—The load is being made lighter. Even if one is not capable of doing His work as explained earlier let him do his own works without the hope of fruits. Certainly this is the yoga taught by Krishna and this verse gives the guarantee that by even indulging only in this, one becomes worthy to attain Him.

Shreyo hi gyanamabhyasangyanaddhyanam vishishyate
Dyaanatkarmphaltyaagstyaagaacchaantiranantaram [12].

Meaning—Knowledge is superior to practice, meditation is superior to knowledge and the renunciation of the fruit of action is superior to meditation as renunciation results in instant peace.

Commentary—Two terms need to be defined, 'practice' and 'knowledge'. The word practice has occurred earlier also but it was in different senses. The practice is always to achieve certain end. The Lord has talked of this in shloka nine of this chapter itself. In the commentary of it we have referred to shloka 34 of chapter VI.

But the word 'practice' used here has certainly a different connotation. Here it is used abruptly and independently with reference to nothing.

In the preceding context the practice was for some thing. But now the question arises to practise for what? In shloka 34 of chapter VI the practice was aimed at controlling the mind. In shloka 89 of this chapter the practice or what the Lord calls as practice-Yoga is to practise for concentrating on the Lord.

Here the word practice has no reference to any thing or any act. We shall have to find out the meaning attached to it here. This practice here must probably implies to take recourses to the practices generally required by the common man to seek the Lord. Such practice may include the chanting of the names of the Lord, worshiping his idols, visiting the places of pilgrimage etc. As we are not to impose our views on the readers, so it is upon them to accept or reject this interpretation. We have explained in the way we have thought to be the best.

'Knowledge' is certainly, knowledge of the 'Lord', of his vast powers, of his super human qualities, of his all, pervading nature.

The rest is clear. Knowledge is declared superior to practice by the Lord, meditation is superior to knowledge and the renunciation of fruits of works even superior to the meditation.

The sum and substance is that the yoga as propounded by the Lord is the golden path to reach Him.

Adveshta sarvabhootaanaam maitrah karunha eva cha,
Nirmamo nirhamkaarah, samduhkha, suhkhah kshami [13].
Santushtah satatam yogi yataatmaa dridhnishchayah,
Mayyarpitmanobudhiryo maddhaktah sa me priyah, [14].

Meaning—Who is free from jealousy towards all beings, has friendship and compassion for all, has attachment towards none and is free from ego and take the pain and pleasure in the same vein; is full of forgiveness and is always contented is a yogi and has conquered his soul and is of a firm resolve. That devotee who has surrendered his mind and intellect to Me is dear to Me.

Commentary—These are all conditions to be fulfilled if one is to be dear to God but at the same time he must be a devotee of Him. The importance of devotion has once again been reiterated in unequivocal way. But it is clear beyond an iota of doubt that a devotee of the Lord is expected to possess all virtues described above.

Yasmaannadvijate loko lakannodvijate cha yah,
Harshahamarshbhayodvegairmukto yah sa cha Me priyah [15].

Meaning—By whom the people are not disturbed and

who is not disturbed by people, who is free from the forces of pleasure and pain and fear is dear to Me.

Commentary—The Lord starting from the preceding shloka is going to nominate who are dear to Him and for what qualities.

Here, the first qualification of one dear to Him is very important. One shoul not behave in a way which perturbs or disturbs others nor one should be perturbed by the behaviour of some of the people who may try to disturb one's tranquillity. One should he calm and composed. This is the modern version of 'live and let live.'

Other qualifications do not need any elaboration.

Anapiekshah shuchirdaksha udaaseeno gatvyathah,
Sarvaarambhaparityagi yo madbhaktah sa Me priyah [16].

Meaning—He who expects nothing, is pure, expert, indifferent, above pain and who has given up all initiatives of action such a devotee of Mine is dear to Me.

Commentary—Experts here may stand for skillfull in every field. Above pain is the man who refuses to suffer come what may. To give up of all initiatives of action, is quite in accordance with the teaching of the Gita that all actions are being done by the forces of nature. Only the ignorant thinks that he is the doer (shloka 37, chapter III)

Yo na hrishyati na dveshti na shochati na kaankshati,
Shubhashubh parityagi bhaktimanyah sa me priyah [17].

Meaning—He who neither becomes pleased nor unpleased, nor grieves nor desires, who shuns both good and evil and who is full of devotion is dear to Me.

Commentary—Nothing special

Samah, shatrau cha mitre cha
tathamaanaapamaanayoh,
Shitoshnhsukhduhkeshu
samah, sangvivarjitah [18].

Meaning—Who is same to friend and foe, to honour and insult, to heat and cold, to pleasure and pain, non-attached (is dear to Me).

Commentary—The emphasis is on equanimity and equality. According to shloka 40 of chapter 2nd equality (itself) is yoga—'samatvam yog uchyate.'

Tulyanindaastutirmauni shantushto yen kenachit,
Aniketah, sthirmatirbhaktimaanme priyo narah [19].

Meaning—He who takes praise and blame alike, is silent, content with whatever is available, homeless, of fixed mind, given to devotion to Me that man is dear to Me.

Commentary—Not all the qualities need elaboration. Some of them do.

One should be content with whatever is available unasked for. He should not hanker after things for desire-fulfilment.

'Homeless' is important in the sense that it is the home which is the first love of many. Any body in a position to do so either builds a new house or rennovates the old one handed over to him from his ancestors. Moreover any body hardly wants to be driven out from his home where he lives with his near and dear ones who constitute another bondage. Besides, it is always better to meditate in jungles or in the caves of mountains where even today many sages and saints live and indulge in meditation.

One should be of fixed mind. Should not jump from one decision to another like monkey jumping from one tree to another.

Ye tu dharmyaamritmidam yathoktam paryupaasate,
Shraddhana matparama bhaktaaste'teeva Me priyaah [20].

Meaning—Extremely dear to Me are those devotees who take Me as their one supreme aim and who endowed with faith follow this immortal religion as set forth by Me.

Commentary—In the preceding verses the Lord talked of those dear to Him, in this He talks of him who is extremely dear to Him rather the dearest. Who is that fortunate one? Of course one who follows with faith the nectar like religion of 'karmyoga' propounded by Him.

Om tatsditi shrimadbhagavadgeetaasoopanishatsu Brahm vidyayaam yogshashtre Shrikrishnaarjun samvaade bhaktiyogo naam dvadasho'dhyayah,

Thus in the Bhagawadgita upanishad sung by the Lord, the knowledge of Brahma, the scripture on yoga, the dialogue between Shrikrishna and Arjuna ends the twelth chapter entitled "The yoga of Devotion".

CHAPTER XIII

Shri Bhagavanuvaach

Edam shareeram kaunteya kshetramityabhidheeyate
Atadyo vetti tam praahuh kshetragya eti tadvidah [1].

Meaning—The Blessed Lord said :—O son of kunti, this body is called field; one who knows this is called kshetragya by the sages.

Commentary—to compare this body with a field is a novel approach to show the working of 'karm-sidhaant', cause and effect relationship.

'As you sow so you reap' is an age-old proverb. Thus whatever you do becomes the seed for this body-field and you reap the harvest good or bad depending upon the nature of seeds you have sown. It is the soul which knows this body it is therefore, called 'kshetragya' i.e. one who knows the field.

As the soul is one which knows the field thoroughly so it is his duty to be careful in choosing the seed which is going to be sown in this field.

Keshetraygyam chaapi maam viddhisarvakshetreshu Bharat,
Keshetrkshetrakshetrgyorgyanam yattajgyaanam matam mam [2].

Meaning—O Bharat! Know Myself to be the knower of this field in all the fields. It is the knowledge of the field and knower which is considered to he the (real) knowledge.

Commentary—Certainly the soul residing in the body is not different from God. It is the part and parcel of the supreme soul i.e. God or the Lord Krishna Himself. He has also maintained is shloka 7 of chapter XV that His part is residing in all beings as their soul.

The Lord is thus very much justified in calling Himself the knower in every field. The knowledge of the field and its knower is the real knowledge according to Him as it explains the entire working of this world. Good or bad, pleasure or pain, are in our hands. As stated earlier what we are sowing we are reaping.

Tatkshetram yachcha yaadrikha yadvikaari yatashch Tat,
Sa cha yo yatprabhaavashch tatsamaasen Me shinhu [3].

Meaning—What that field is and what is that like and what are its deformations and what he (the knower) is, and what his powers are, hear all this from Me in brief.

Commentary—As He is the knower of this field He is certainly acquainted with its real character, both its good and bad aspects. At the same time being the Supreme Lord of the universe He knows the knower (the soul) also and its powers.

Rishibhirbahudhaa geetam chhanadobhirvividhaih prithak,
Brahmsootrapadaishchaiva hetumadbhirvinishchitaih [4].

Meaning—It has been sung by the seers in manifold ways, it has been described separately in different vedic chants and also in the rational and conclusive analysis of the Brahm-Sootraas.

Commentary—Nothing to say about the seers and the vedic chants. They have certainly done it in their different ways. We shall have to acquaint the readers with the Brahmsootraas.

The 'Brahmsoortraas' were propounded by the seer 'Vyas' himself. This is a book in which logic and examples have been taken recourse to, to explain the theories of Upanishads.

In fact the Upanishadas, the 'Brahmsootra' and the Gita are considered to be the three main pillars of hindu religion. They are termed to-gether in Sanskrit as 'prasthaan trayee' (the three important bases of knowledge).

Mahabhootanyahankaro buddirvyktmeva cha
Endriyaanhi dashaikam cha panch chendriyagocharaah. [5].
Echcha dveshah sukham duhkam samghaatshchetana dhritih
Etatkhsetram samaaseen savikaaramudaahritam [6].

Meaning—The five elements, the ego, the intellect, the unmanifest energy, the ten organs, the one (mind) and the five objects of senses, desire, aversion, pleasure, pain, the body, consciousness, patience, these briefly described constitute the field along with its deformations.

Commentary—Now the Lord describes what are the different factors constituting this field.

We shall have to explain some of them.

The five subtle elements are—

1. Ether
2. Fire
3. Water
4. Air
5. Earth

It is generally and rightly maintained that this body of ours is made of only these five elements. Even Tulsidas wrote in his Rama Charitmaanas.

Kshiti jal gagan sameeraah,
Panch rachit yah addham shareera
—This wretched body is composed of the five elements (enumerated above).

The unmanifest energy is certainly the power which has kept the body alive and functioning. It is just like electricity which is unmanifest but burn the bulbs and make many a machine and instruments perform. Without this the body is a dead lump.

The ten organs (say senses) are :—

1. Eyes
2. Ears
3. Nose
4. Tongue
5. Skin
6. Speech
7. Hands
8. Feet
9. Anus
10. Penis (the outlet of urine if we consider the women too).

Of these the first five are called to be knowledge-senses (gyaanendriya) as they let us know the world and its effects.

The last five are called "the senses of action" (karmendriya) as it is through them that we perform.

The five sense-object are :—

1. Sound
2. Touch
3. Colour
4. Taste
5. Smell

They are obviously related with the five knowledge-senses.

The body has also been included as one of the composition of the field which is the body itself. This invites clarification. The body here stands as the translation of 'sanghaat'. 'Samghaat' is the composition of the limbs and senses barring the spirit or the unmanifest energy so, the body here is not really the body a living being possesses. It is just the full frame minus the energy. It can be understood in a better way by the fact that once the energy or soul is gone the body remains but it is not the body we generally talk of. The former body is really what we mean here the 'sanghaataah'.

The deformations are certainly which have been enumerated in the 'shloka'—6. They are desire, aversion, pleasure and pain etc.

Amaanitvamadanbhitvamahinsa kchhaantiraarjavam,
Aacharyopaasanam shaucham sthairyamaatmvinigrah [7].

Meaning—No pride, no arrogance, non-violence, forgiveness, a candid soul, worship of the teacher, purity of mind and body, steadfastness, self-control.

Commentary—The Lord is here enumerating the qualities which He will later call the real knowledge.

Endriyaartheshu vairaagyamanahankaar eva chaa
Janammritujaraavyaadhiduhkhdoshaanudarshanam [8].

Meaning—Absence of attraction towards the objects of senses, no ego, constant remembrance of the pain and evil associated with birth, death, old age, disease.

Commentary—The enumeration continues. Most of the qualities need no explanation but some light needs to be thrown upon some of them.

The senses like eyes, etc. help in committing sin but they do so through their objects. The sense-objects have been mentioned in the commentaries earlier.

We shall exemplify how the senses become powerful through their objects. The object of eyes is colour and beauty. If it sees a colourful, beautiful being, it is easily lured and is liable to commit sin. Similarly the objects of ears is sound. If the ears hear a charming sound the whole being is attracted towards it. Deers are very much fund of music. The Killer attract them by playing flute etc.

If the senses are not attracted towards such objects, they are incapable of doing any harm.

If one always remembers the pain and evil connected with birth, death, old age etc. he or she will try to free himself or herself from the cycle of birth and death by taking recourse to the methods mentioned in the Gita from time to time.

Asaktiranabhishvangah putradoaraagrihaadishu
Nityam cha samchittatvamishtaunishtopapattishu [9].

Meaning—Non-attachment, no self identification with son, wife, home etc., constant equanimity in pleasant or unpleasant happenings.

Commentary—No quality needs elaboration.

Mayi chaananyyogen bhaktiravyabhichaarinhi,
Viviktdeshasevitvamaratirjanasansadi [10].

Meaning—An unswerving devotion to Me through steadfast yoga, living in solitude (in a secluded place), no pleasure in the company of people.

Commentary—Devotion to Lord through yoga simply means that the mind should constantly be concentrated on Him. Yoga in the Gita has different meanings at different places.

We have talked about being homeless i.e. living in a secluded place with no roof over head.

The company of diferent men and women detract you from the devotion to the Lord, moreover, they may be the source of many vices, it is thereofore to be avoided.

Adhyaatmgyaan nityatvam tattvagyaanarthdarshanam
Etajgyaanmiti proktamagyaanam yadatho'nyathaa [11].

Meaning—Always absorbed in spiritual knowledge, ability to perceive the real knowledge, all these are said to be the knowledge what is contrary to them is ignorance.

Commentary—The enumeration of constituents of knowledge ends.

The qualities mentioned here are not new.

The Lord opine that all these qualities starting from the verse 7 constitute knowledge and what is contrary to them constitute ignorance.

One can take a few examples to explain the last assertion—absence of pride is a part of knowledge, thus the presence of pride is a constituent of ignorance, non-violence is knowledge, violence is thus definitely ignorance.

Gyeyam yattatpravakhsyaami yajgyaatvaamritamashnute,
Anaadimatparam Bramh na sattannaasaduchyate. [12].

Meaning—I will let you know which ought to be known and on knowing which one attains immortality. That originless Brahm is under My control and is neither 'sat' (being) nor 'Asat' (no being).

Commentary—The Lord embarks upon imparting that knowledge which leads to immortality; he starts with the assertion that Brahm who is without beginning is not beyound Him and is neither being nor non-being i.e. the Brahma is absolute, possessing none of the deformities of the world and as he is dependent on Him, the Lord also possesses the qualities possessed by him. He is also without any beginning and He is also free from the deformities of the existence.

Sarvatah paanhipaadam tatsarvato'kshishiromukham
Sarvatah shrutimalloke sarvamaaviritya tishtati [13].

Meaning—It has hands, and feet in all directions, eyes, head and face all over the world. His ears are every where. He, fills and surrounds all this world.

Commentary—It is just a resumed description of the "Virat-roop" described earlier.

The fact that his feet and hands are every where, does not require Him to move from one place to another to eradicate the evil or to protect His devotees. Similarly His hands being every where implies that He is just to stretch his hands to eradicate the evil-doers and perform whatever is required. With eyes and ears every where, He sees and hears every thing including what we are indulged in—good or bad—and what we are praying for to him. The prayers, thus do not take time in reaching Him.

All this indicates that the Lord is omnipresent in the true sense of the term.

He is pervading all, is a fact emphasized upon time and again. One is again reminded of 'yen sarvamidam tatam' (see shloka 17 of chapter II).

Sarvendriyagunhaabhaasam sarvendriyavivarjitam
Asaktam sarvbhrichchaiva nirgunham gunhbhoktricha [14].

Meaning—He is the perceiver of all sense-objects but He is without senses. He is unattached yet all supporting, he is enjoyer of the 'gunhaas' (the three modes of the nature-prakriti) though not limited by them.

Commentary—Here the Lord is described as the representative of contradictions. This is the special quality of Him. It appears that he has all senses but actually he need not possesses any sense, though he is ever far from any kind of attachment, yet he sustains the whole universe.

A similar view has been expressed in 'Shvetaashvetar Upanishad'—

Apaanipaado gavano grahita
Pasyatyachakshu sa sirnhotyakarnhah
—He travels fast though he does not possess either feet or hands. He sees without eyes and hears without ears.

There is nothing to comment upon His being unattached when he Himself has been teaching the theory of non-attachment through out the Gita. His being the sustainer of the whole world cannot be questioned. Hindu poet Maluk das rightly observed :

'Ajagar karai na chaakari
Panchli karai na kaam
Das malukaa kah gaye
Sabake Daataa Ram.

—The big serpent known as 'ajager' does not serve any body to earn its livelihood, the birds do not work. Maluka das says that Ram (the Lord) is the sustainer of all.

The point to be made clear is that what is meant by His being the enjoyer of gunhas though not limited by them.

There are three 'gunhas' or the modas of 'prakriti' (the nature). They are :

i) Sattva
ii) Raj
iii) Tam

'Sattva' represents the best mode of the nature. All good things and qualities are the result of this e.g. a pious man engaged in the service of the gods or even of mankind possesses this mode, the 'sattva'.

'Raj' is next to 'sattva'. It is the representative of all that involves ego and other ruling or over-ruling qualities. A king is certainly possessed of 'Raj'.

'Tam' is the worst quality found in form of ignorance, anger, hate, vengeance etc. A killer, a theft, is possessed of 'Raj'.

Now the point is that though the Lord is above all these modes, yet He appears to possess or enjoy them all. Take the example of Krishna Himself. Being a man of truth and lover of justice, he possesses 'Sattva' in Him. Being he ruler of Dvarika he has got 'Raj' in Him as well. Being the sole factor behind the destruction of number of warriors in the battle of Mahabharat and given to occasional out-burst of anger during the same, He shows the symptom of possessing 'tam'. But every body knows that actually He is beyond all these three, completely unattached as He is to any thing or any body or any situation or circumstance.

Bahirantashcha bhootaanaamacharm charameva cha,
Sukhmtvaattdavigyeyam doorastham chantike cha tat. [14].

Meaning—That which is outside as well as the inside of all beings is He. He constitutes both animate and inanimate creation. He being the most subtle is beyond comprehension. He is both at far and very near.

Commentary—As He is all-pervading so there is no

doubt about his being both inside and outside the all beings may they be animate or inanimate.

He is subtle, so he is not seen or known. This need no explaination. The more subtle a thing is more invisible it is.

He is also far and very near. He is far for the ignorant and very near to His devotees and the knowledgeable.

These lines reflect to a great extent the idea contained in the following lines of 'Eshavasyopanishat' :—

'Tadejati' Tannaijati taddoore tadvantike. Tadantarasya sarvasyasya Aadu sarvaysa baahyatah' (Esa-5).

—He moves and does not move, He is far as well as near, He is within and without the whole world.

Avibhaktam cha bhooteshu vibhaktamiva cha sthitam,
Bhotbhartri cha tajgyeyam grasishnhu prabhavishnhu cha [16].

Meaning—Indivisible yet stands as divided among beings. He is the sustainer of beings, the destroyer and the creator, He must be known.

Commentary—God is in every being but He also stands as a whole. This point is very clear. His being in everything has been emphasized upon on many occasions till now.

'Vishnhu' being the sustainer, He is vishnhu, as the destroyer He is 'Shiva', being the creator he is 'Brahma.'

The Lord says He is worth-knowing i.e. It is our responsibility to know Him, to go near Him through knowledge, yoga or devotion, whatever suits us.

Jyotishaamapi tajjyotistamasah paramuchyate
Gyanam Gyeyam gyangamyam hridisarvasya visthitam [17].

Meaning—He is the light among all lights. He is beyond the 'tam', He is knowledge as well as the object of knowledge and He is to be known through knowledge. He is seated in the hearts of all.

Commentary—We have explained 'Tam' in the commentary of shloka 13 of this very chapter, rest is clear. The last line has often been emphasized upon.

The emphasis on knowledge is however to be noticed. He is knowledge and at the same time the only factor worth-knowing. But he is capable of being known through knowledge itself. This must not mislead any body that knowledge is the only way to know Him. As stated earlier, the Gita is a great work of synthesis. The Lord has also asserted that He is to be known by 'yoga' and also by devotion.

Thus knowledge is the one way to know Him. What is knowledge is explained in some of the preceding pages.

Eti kshetram tatha gyaanam gyeyam choktam samaasatah
Madbhakta etadvigyaaya madbhaavaayopapadyate [18].

Meaning—Thus the field, knowledge and the object of knowledge have been briefly described. My devotee thus knowing this attains My nature.

Commentary—Again the emphasis on devotion. The knowledge will lead to Him but not the knowledge of one who is not devoted to Him. Devotion is, therefore, the first and foremost condition. This is undoubtedly the undercurrent of the Gita.

To attain one's nature is to be like one. The devotee by knowing all this becomes like Him, God-like.

Sant Tulsidas told—

'Tum jaane tumhi hoi jaai'—Knowing you one become yourself.'

Prakritim purusham chaiva vidhyanaadee ubhaavapi
Vikaraananshch gunhanshchaiva vidhi prakritisambhavan [19].

Meaning—Know that both prakriti (nature) and Purush (the conroller of the nature the creator Himself) are both without origin and know the deformities and qualities to be born of nature.

Commentary—The supreme Lord the creator of this universe is without origin and so is the nature through which He creates. This means both of them were even before the universe came in to being otherwise it would have been hardly created.

Nature is the mother of all good and bad qualties i.e. it is nature which influences you to do good or bad. This is equally ture about the nature of a man as well.

Kaaryakaranhakartritve hetuh prakritiruchyate,
Purrushah sukhdukhaanaam bhoktritve heturuchyate [20].

Meaning—In the root of the creation of ceasue and effect (relations ship) is said nature. The supreme soul (Purush) is said to he in the root of the enjoyment of pleasure and pain.

Commentary—The entire universe is subject to the cause and effect relationship. Every effect has a cause behind it. Every action is followed by a reaction; this is the scientific truth. We enjoy pleasure or pain solely due to this law of cause and effect if we become a cause of pain we receive pain and so on.

The Lord says this cause and effect relation is created by nature itself. It is very true. Nature is under the supreme. He can not interfere every time in the affairs of beings, so has left it to the nature, to cause pleasure or pain to beings depending on the causes. Let us take a simple example, if one is drenched in rains, one is bound to catch cold, this is all due to nature. The cause (rains) the effect (cold) are both caused by the nature.

The point that the supreme is in the root of the enjoyment of pleasure and pain is to be pondered over. How is He is the root of this? He is because, had he not been no body would leave ordered the nature to indluge in this cause and effect relationship and let the beings relish or suffer. It is He afterall, who has ordained that you are to be awarded for a good cause and punished for a bad one.

Purusahah prakritishtho hi bhunkte prakritijangunhnhaan,
Kaaranham gunhasamgo'sya sadasdyonijanmasu [21].

Meaning—Purusha established in nature enjoys the qualities born of nature. Attachment to these qualities is in the root of His taking birth in good or bad creeds.

Commentary—Here the word Purush is the soul, the very part of the Supreme as the latter dwells in every being according to His own statement.

The soul thus being associated with nature enjoys one or all of its three 'gunhaas' (sattva, raj and tam explained earlier). It will again depend upon his own nature whether he enjoys the good or bad 'gunahaas.' The nature in itself provides only the base. The cause of being angry may be very much in the nature of a snake bitting to death your dear son. It is upon you to react in your own way (you may be subjected to 'tam', become angry and kill the snake) or you subject yourself to 'Sattva' not allowing to be angry yourself and let the serpent go away out of compassion towards it.

It is declared by the scriptures that there are so many 'yonis' (we prefer to call them creeds e.g. of men, animals, insects and plants etc.) It is your association with good or bad modes (gunhaas) of nature which decides where you are going to be a man or an animal after this life.

Some commentators have meant womb by yoni. This does not appear to be acceptable. A womb is not good or bad, a creed is.

Upadarshtanumanta cha bharta bhokta maheshwarah,
Paramaatmeti chaapyukto dehe'smin purushah parah [22].

Meaning—(He is) the witness, the guide, the sustainer, the enjoyer, the almighly Lord. He is God Himself, the supreme Purusha seated in this body.

Commentary—The substance of this verse is that the supreme Lord is very much seated in our body and we may cause Him pleasure and pain owing to our own activities. It is some thing else that none affects Him.

Ya evam vetti purusham prakritim cha gunhaih sah,
Sarvathaa vartmaano'pi na sa bhooyo'bhijaayate [23].

Meaning—He who thus knows purusha (the supreme) and 'prakriti' (Nature) along with its modes absorbed in all sorts of activities, he is not to be reborn.

Commentary—If one knows the Lord, it is itself suffcient to deliver him from the cycle of birth and death, knowing that naure and its three qualities or modes (already enumerated) he will try to absorb the good ones only and he will be doubly sure of escaping this vicious cycle.

Dhyaanenaatmani pashyanti kechidaatmanammaatmana
Anye saamkhyen yogen karmyogen chaapare [24].

Meaning—Some see this soul (supreme of course) with the help of their own self through meditation. Others behold Him by purusuing the path of knowledge and yet others by proceeding along the path of action without attachment.

Commentary—When He is seated in our body He may

be seen even. This is possible as the Lord states by 'Saankhya yog' that is by the help of knowledge. This knowledge (or 'sankhya'-pilosophyly) is also honoured by addressing it as 'yoga'. This is also possible through 'karm-yoga' which we all know is the action without attachment. What remains is the devotion. Let us wait, the Lord cannot neglect it.

Anye tvevamajaananatah shrutvanyebhya upaasate,
Te'pi chaatitarantyeva mrityum shrutiparayanhaah [25].

Meaning—Others not knowing thus (these two paths) engage in worship by hearing from others. They also thus intent on hearing conquer death.

Commentary—Those who do not know these two paths, learn about another path of worship or devotion from some knowledgeable people and they also get rid of the cycle of death and birth. The important thing is that they must be 'shrutiparayanah' i.e. quite attentive to hear about the different methods of worship and devotion.

Yaavatsamjaayate kimchitsattvam sthaavarjamgamam,
Kshetrakshetragyasamyogaattadviddhi Bhartarshabh [26]

Meaning—Whatever being, animate or inamate is born, know you the best of Bharataas, that is from the union between the field and the knower of the field.

Commentary—Field is 'kshetra' and also the representative of nature. 'Kshetragya' (knower of the field) is the Purush (supreme Lord Himself). The worlds of animate or inanimate is born out of the meeting of these forces of 'prakriti' and 'Purush.' They of course represent the femal and male in a way. This point will be dealt upon by the Lord again at length in a subsequent chapter.

Samam sarveshu bhooteshu tishttantam Parmesvaram,
Vinashyatsvavinasyhantam yah pashyati sa pashyati [27].

Meaning—The supreme Lord who is imperishable and equal for all is seated in all perishable beings. He who sees this is the only one who (really) sees.

Commentary—The Lord is kind to every being without distinction or discrimination. He abides in every body's soul. Who is able to see this equality of His is the only person who actually sees. Possessing the external eyes is not enough to see. They are blind though with eyes, who fail to see this marvel of the Lord.

Samam pashyanhi sarvatra samavasthitameeshvaram,
Na hinastyaatmanaatmaanam tato yati paraam gatim [28].

Meaning—Being the Lord given to equality and equally dwelling in all, one does not enjure his soul by his own soul and thus reaches the supreme status.

Commentary—One's soul is capable of injuriing one's self if it is not spiritually oriented. Injuring the self or to defile it is very much objected to by Upanishads.

'Esaavaasyopanishad' says this. They enter the blind darkness who defile their soul.

The best way not to degrade one's soul as envisaged in this verse is to see the undiscriminating Lord lodged in all beings with equal force. Thus he will injure no soul and save his soul from being degraded.

Prakrityaiva cha karmaanhi kriyamanhaani sarvashah,
Yah pashyati tathatmaanamakarataaram sa pashyati [29].

Meaning—He who sees all actions being done by nature and himself as non-doer, he really sees.

Commentary—Again the same poser, who sees? He who knows that all actions are done by nature itself and he is just a non-doer, sees.

So to see actually means to know the truth. And it is a truth which has been envisaged in the preceding verse and that which is being told here is also the truth.

The fact that all actions are done by the nature itself is emphasized in this verse of theGita also—

Prakriteh Kriyamaanhaani Gunhiah Karmaahi sarvashah
—'All actions are done by the modes of nature'
Yadaa bhootprithagbhaavamekasthamanupashyati,
Tat eva cha vistaaram Brahm sampadyate tada [30].

Meaning—When he perceives the diversified existence of beings as abiding in one (the entranal Being) and the projection of all beings from Him, then he attains 'Brahma.'

Commentary—All beings hare come forth from the supreme being as waves come out of the sea and as they are the projection of the sea itself, so all beings are the projections of the Supreme Being Himself. One who knows this fact, he attains the 'Brahma.'

Anaaditvaannirgunhatvaatparamatmaayamavyayah,
Shareerstho'pi kaunteya na karoti na lipyate [31].

Meaning—As it is without origin and is eternal and without attributes, this imperishable supreme soul though residing in the body O ! Kaunteya does not act nor is affected (by wordly actions).

Commentary—The emphasis on the Lord being completely inactive and unattached. He is just a silent spectator. Whatever is to be done is being done by the nature on His behalf.

Yatha sarvagatam saukhmyadaakaasham noplipyate,
sarvatraavasthito dehe tathaatmaa noplipyate [32].

Meaning—As the all prevading ether due to its subtle character is not contaminated so seated in all bodies the self is not contaminated.

Commentary—In a preceding verse we have talked about the power of the subtle.

The ether or better the sky is every where. Whereever there is open space, there is the sky. It is as good in a room or in a pot as in a field. But it cannot be touched so it cannot be contaminated. Similarly the self (say the supreme self it self as it seats in every body) is far from contamination despite having been lodged in every body.

Here the emphasis is on the pure and uncontaminated nature of the supreme.

Yathaa prakaashayatyekah kritsnam lokmimam ravih,
Kshetram kshetree tathaa kritsnam prakaashayati Bharat [33].

Meaning—O Arjun! As the one sun illuminates the entire world, so the Lord of the field (kshetri) illumines the entire field; (kshetra) Bharat!

Commentary—The Lord has already stated that He Himself is the kshetragya the master of the field so it certainly He Who focuses light on all parts of the body including the mind. It is why the body of a being comes into action.

Kshetrakshetragyorevamantaram gyaanchakshusha,
Bhootprakritimoksham cha ye viduryanti te param [34].

Meaning—They who with the eys of knowledge perceive the difference between the field and the knower of the field and the liberation of all beings from the rature, they go to the supreme.

Commentary—The body and soul are not the same entity. The importance of the soul is very much emphasised upon in chapter II.It is imperishable and immortal, without beginning and withut end while the body is perishable and with a beginning and a certain end. Moreover it is caught in the vicious cycle of birth and death. This is the difference betweeen the field (the body) and the 'kshetragya' (the soul or in the broader sense the supreme self Itself). Those who know this difference and are also not bound by the three modes of nature (because this is the way of liberation) they attain to the Supreme as they possess the real knowledge.

Om tatsaditi shrimadbhadga-
vadgeetaasoopanishatsu Brahm
vidyaayaam yogshashtre Shrikrishna-
arjun samvade kshetrakshetra
gya vibhag yogo nam traya-
dasho'dhyaayah.

Thus in the puanishad sung by the Lord, the knowledge of Braham the scripture on yoga, dialogue between Shri Krishna and Arjuna ends the thirteenth chapter entitled "The yoga of difference between the field and the knower of the field."

CHAPTER XIV

Shri Bhagavanuvaach

Param bhooyah pravakshyami gyananam gyanmuttamam,
Yajgyaatva munayah sarve param siddhimito gataah [1].

Meaning—The Blessed Lord said-I will again declare the supreme knowledge, the best of all knowledge, having known which all the sages have gone from here to the supreme perfection.

Commentary—Let us wait for that knowledge to be imparted by the Lord.

Edam gyaanamupaashritya mam saadharmyamaagataah,
Sarge'pi nopjaayante pralaye na vyathanti cha [2].

Meaning—Having acquired this knowledge and having acquired my nature, (people) are not born again even at the beginning of creation and are not troubled at the time of final dissolution.

Commentary—The knowledge is yet to be imparted, but one things is clear; having known this, one assumes the nature of the Lord Himself. We have dwelt upon this in shloka 18 of the last chapter.

Mam yonirmahadbrahm tasmingarbham dadhaaymyaham,
Sambhavah sarvabhotaanaam tato bhavati Bharat [3].

Meaning—My womb is the great Brahm, in to that I cast the seed, O Bharat! thence spring all beings.

Commentary—The supreme knowledge promised by the Lord has started to be imparted.

First he narrates the process through which this existance comes in to being.

He asserts that the great Braham Himself is the womb

in which the Lord casts his seed and thus comes in the existence all beings of the world.

So far we know that Brahma is the creator. Now it is clear that He does not create on His own. The Supreme Lord is behind this creation.

Sarvayonishu kaunteya moortayah sambhawantti yah,
Taasam Brahm mahadyoniraham beeejpradah pitaa [4].

Meaning—In all creeds whatever being are born their womb is the great Brahm and I being the provider of the seed am their father, o Son of Kunti.

Commentary—This verse is not very much different from the preceding one.

Sattvam rajastam eti gunhah prakritisambhavah
Nibadhnanti mahabaaho dehe dehinaamavyayam [5].

Meaning—O great armed one! the three modes of nature 'sattva', 'raj' and 'tam', bind the imperishable soul to the body.

Commantary—The imperishable soul is not supposed to be tied with the body but the three modes of nature already explained earlier bind it to the body.

Being compelled by these 'gunhaas' or modes of nature he indulges in actions good or bad and thus binds itself to the body.

Tatrasattvam nirmaltvaatprakashakamanaamayam
Sukhsamgen badhnaati gyansamgen chaanagha [6].

Meaning—O sinless! the 'Sattva' being pure, illuminating and not causing diseases, binds through happiness as well as knowledge.

Commentary—This verse confirms our view in the commentary of the preceding verse where we have stated that he "indulges in actions good or bad..."

The 'Sattva' gunha (mode) is representative of purity, light and health. It thus binds the soul by happiness and knowledge of scriptures. To be happy is also the cause of attachment. Similarly the inclination towards learning is also capable fo causing attachment. Whenever you enjoy or even suffer the soul is identified with body. This is how the immortal soul stands tied to the mortal body.

Rajo raagaatmakam viddhi trishnhaasangsamudbhavam,
Tannibadhnaati Kaunteya karmsamgen dehinaam [7].

Meaning—Know 'Rajas' having the nature of passion and born of desire as well as attachment. It binds the soul through actions.

Commentary—Action if performed with an eye on fruits is the strongest binding factor. 'Rajas' resembling the passion and action for fulfilment of desire. It is also propelled by the passion and attachment to things and objects it wants to acquire. This action thus binds the soul to the body.

Tamastvagyaanajam viddhi mohanam sarvdehinaam
Pramaadaalasyanidraabhistaannibadhnaati Bhaarat [8].

Meaning—Be it known to you that 'Tamas' is born of ignorance and it deludes all souls. It binds by negligence, indolence and sleep.

Commentary—Of the three modes of nature 'tamas' is decidedly the worst one. It is the product of ignorance. Where there is no knowledge, the ignorance is. It is thus the opposition of the first that is 'Sattva'. A man full of 'tamas' will hardly try to learn either from scriptures or from the masters of knowledge. The fool will consider himself to be all knowing. He will give preference to body over mind the source of knowledge and will thus through his foolishness bind the soul to the body.

'Tamas' deludes all souls in the sense that it will never allow any one to think in the right direction. To an illiterate fool even a rope will appear as a serpent.

A man full of 'Tamas' as full of negligence, sloth and sleep also. These other bind the soul to the body. A negligent man will avoid all important actions demanding immediate attention and soul and body will suffer together as a result of it. Similarly sloth or indolence will cause him forget his important tasks causing harm to the body and thus to the soul.

The sleep is the worst. When the body is slept what the soul is to worry about? The poor thing which is the master becomes the slave of an almost oversleeping being. It is how it is tied to the body.

Sattvam sukhe samjayati rajah karmanhi Bharat.
Gyaanamaavritya tu tamah pramaade samjayatyut [9].

Meaning—O Bharat it is thus told that 'sattva' attaches to happiness, Rajas to action and 'Thamas' to negligence.

Commentary—Commentaries on the two preceding verses suffice.

Rajastamashchaabhibhooya sattvam bhavati Bharat,
Rajah sattvam tamaschaiva tamah sattvam rajastatha [10].

Meaning—O Bharat, some times, 'Sattva' leads having over powred 'rajas' and 'tamas.' Some times 'Rajas' leads having overpowered 'sattva' and 'tamas' and sometimes 'Tamas' overpowers 'Sattva' and 'Rajas.'

Commentary—Being the prey of the three modes of nature one is not always guided by only one of them. Depending on the circumstances all the modes take their turn one by one.

Sarvadvaareshu dehe'sminprakaasha upjaayate,
Gyaanam yada tada Vidyadvivridham sattvamityut [11].

Meaning—When through all the doors of the body appears the light and knowledge then know that 'Sattva' is having predominence.

Commentary—It has already been stated that 'sattva' represents light and knowledge.

All doors mean all senses. When sttva prevails all these senses are lighted and thus become a source of knowledge. The darkness of ignorance is driven away.

Lobhah pravretiraarambhah karmanhaamashamah sprihaa,
Rajasyetaani jaayante vivriddhe Bharatarshabha [12].

Meaning—Greed, activity, undertaking of actions, unrest, desire, all these arise when 'Rajas' increases.

Commentary—**All clear.**

Aprakahso'pravritishcha pramado moh eva cha,
Tamasyetaani jaayante vivridhe kurunandan [13].

Meaning—Darkness (or ignorance) inertia, negligence and delusion these appear when 'Tamas' has got the upper hand O ! joy of the kurus!

Commentary—No need.

Yada sattve pravriddhe tu pralayam yati dehabhrit.
Tadottamvidaam lokaanamalaanpratipadyate [14].

Meaning—When one dies during the predominance of sattva then he goes to the spotless worlds where go seers.

Commentary—Quite clear

Rajasi pralayam gatvaa karmsangishu jaayate
Tathaa praleenastamasi moodhyonishu jaayate [15].

Meaning—When one dies during the ascendancy of 'Rajas' one is born among those attached to actin, similarly when 'Tamas' is predominant one is born among stupid creatures.

Commentary—Mark that those dying during the ascendancy of 'sattva' are not subjected to rebirth rather they go to divine places. They only are born in differenct circumstances who die during the supremacy of Rajas' and 'Tamas'.

karmanhah sukritasyahuh sattvikam niramalam phalam,
Rajasastu phalam duhkhamagyanam tamasah phalam [16].

Meaning—It is said that the fruits of the saattvic works are pure and faultless, pain is the counsequence of works done during the prevalence of 'Rajas' and the result of 'Tamas' is ignornace.

Commentary—Nothing

Sattvaavtsamjaayate gyanam rajaso lobha eva cha,
Pramaadmohau tamaso bhavato'gyaanmeva cha [17].

Meaning—Knowledge is born from 'Sattva' and greed from 'Rajas', negligence, delusion and also ignorance are the results of 'Tamas'

Commentary—All clear and explained earlier.

Oordhvam gachchhanti sattvastha madhye tishthanti rajasah,
Jaghanyagunhavrittistatha addho gachchhanti taamasoh [18].

Meaning—Those established in 'sattva' rise upwards (to heaven etc) those in 'Rajas' remain in the middle (the world itself) and those full of 'Tamas' and rooted in ignorance, inertia etc. go downward (to the world of demons etc).

Commentary—Sattva 'gunha' makes one's soul weightless having got rid of sins etc., it is why it ascends above. This is not the case with others.

Nanyam gunhebhyah kartaaram yada drashtaanupashyati
gunhebhyashch param vetti madbhaavam so'dhigachchati [19].

Meaning—When the seer (the man) does not see any agent of work other than these three modes of nature and knows that which is supreme and beyond the gunhaas, he attains My nature (becomes like Me).

Commentary—In the root of all worldly actions ordinary or extraordinary there are only these three modes of nature and the Lord is completely beyond them.

One who knows this fact becomes God like.

Gunhanetaaneteetya treendehi dehasamundbhavan
Janmmrityjaraadukhairvimukto'mritamashnute [20].

Meaning—The soul having transcended these three modes which are cause of this body is liberated from birth, death, old-age and pain attains the immortal state.

Commentary—The best way to attain immortatily is to avoid all these modes including the 'sattva' because as seen in the beginning all bind the soul to the body and make the attainment of immortality an impossibility.

Arjun Uvaach

kairlimgaishtreengunhaanetaanateeto bhavati prabho,
Kimaacharah katham chaitaanstreengunhaanativartate [21].

Meaning—Arjuna said :—What are the signs of one who has risen above these gunhas? How does he conduct himself and how does he surmount these gunhas?

Commentary—Quite clear.

Shri Bhagavaanuvach—

Prakasham cha prvritim cha mohmeva cha Pandava,
Na dveshti samprivrittani na nivrittaani kamkshati [22].

Meaning—The blessed Lord said :—O Pandava He who feels no aversion to light or activity or stupor when they are at hand and does not hanker after them when they are not.

Commentary—Not needed.

Udasheenvadaaseeno gunhairyo na vichalyate
Gunha vartant etyeva yo'avatishthanti nemgate [23].

Meaning—He who sitting indifferent is not moved by gunhaas and who seeing that it is 'gunhaas' that are in the root of actin remains established (in God) and is unshaken,

Commentary—The explanation by the Lord continues.

Samduhkhsukhah svasthah samloshtaashmakanchanah
Tulyapriyaapriyo dheerastulyanindaatmasamstutih [24].

Meaning—He who regards suffering and happiness alike is established in self, considers gold, mud and stone as equal in value, to whom pleasant and unpleasnt have no difference, who is patient and to whom praise and blame are alike.

Commentary—Explanation continues

Maanaapamaanyostulyastulyo nitraaripakshayoh,
Sarvaarambhparityaagee gunhaateetah sa uchyate [25].

Meaning—He who regards honour and insult alike, who favours equally the company of friends and enemies, who initiates no action is said to be above the 'gunhaas'.

Commentary—Ends the symptoms of those who are above 'gunhaas.'

Mam cha yo'vyabhicharenha bhaktiyogen sevate,
Sa gunhansamateetyaitaanbrahmbhooyaay kalpate [26].

Meaning—And he who loves Me with an undeviating yoga of devotion, transcends the three modes-'gunhaas' becomes eligible to attain Brahma.

Commentary—The importance of devotion is underlined again. Those devoted to the Lord with an unswerving faith does not only transcend all gunhas but gain more—become eligible to attain Brahma.

Brahmanho hi pratishthahamamritasyaavyayasya cha
Shashvatasya cha dharmasya sukhasyaikantikasya cha [27].

Meaning—I am the abode of Brahma, of immortality, of that which is imperishable, of the everlasting faith (dharm) of an utter bliss of happiness.

Commentary—Thus it is the Lord who is to be attained by any means which he has enumerated in many a preceding verse.

Om Tatsaditi shrimadbhagavadgeetaashoopanisatsu Brahm Vidyaayam yogshashtre Shrikrishnaarjun samvaade gunatraya vibhaag yogo naam chathurdasho'dhyaayah [14].

Thus in the upanishad sung by the Lord the knowlege of Brahma the, scripture of yoga, the dialogue between ShriKrishna and Arjuna ends the fourteenth chapter the yoga of classification of the three modes of the nature.

CHAPTER-XV

Shri Bhagavanuvaach—

Oordhvamoolamadhahshaakhamsvatsham praahuravyayam
Chhandansi yasya parnhaani yastam ved sa vedvit [1].

Meaning—**The Blessed Lord said :—**

There is (a tree) called Ashvatha (peepal in sanskrit). Its original root is above (in the Eternal). Its branches are stretching below. It is said to be imperishable; its leaves are the hymns of the Vedas. He who knows it, is knower of the Vedas.

Commentary—This is one of the most intricate verses of the Gita. It needs to be understood thoroughly.

Any way, this is nothing novel with the Gita itself.

In Kathopanisad also there is a reference to such a tree

Oordhvamoolo'vaakshaakh esho'svthaah sanaatanah (2.3.1)

—With root above and brances below there is an 'Ashvatth' which is eternal.

The first astounding thing is that one has never seen a tree which is just hanging up side down. Every tree has its roots in the earth and branches in the sky and not vice versa.

This is eartainly a peculiar tree.

But one is left with little doubt that this is nothing more or less than a simile.

It is of course.

This tree represents this worldly creation itself i.e. the world itself.

It means that the origin of the world is in the heavens itself. It is why it is imperishable in the sense also that it goes on as if for ever. If one dies another is born thus assuring the continuity of this world-tree.

Its branches are nothing but the different beings occupying this world especially the human folks. (This will be clear later).

The branches can not remain alive unless they have got leaves. What are the leaves of these branches? The numerous beings.

The Lord says the hymns of the Vedas are the leaves, the sustainer of these branches. As the hymns can be sung only by the human beings only, therefore it was maintained earlier in this commentary that by beings He especially means human beings.

The Vedas are thus the sustainer of this world of mankind.

One contradiction may attract readers' attention very easily. The Lord has not been favourably disposed towards the Vedas. He has often spoken against them. In shloka 42 of chapter II He has clearly denounced those believing in the Vedas calling them 'Vedvaadratah.' One is referred back to the meaning and commentary of that 'shloka'. There are a number of such instances.

But one need not worry. The Lord has not been against the Vedas themselves but to those rituals contained in them, which are indulged in by many to fulfil their worldy desires which in turn bind them to the world. This is certainly against the very theory propunded by the Lord.

One thing may also deserve mention. This tree can very well be compared with the human body itself as it is compared with the world at large. Its root is also in the heaven. Its different limbs are its branches and these branches are also best maintained through the hymns of the Vedas.

Adhashchordhvam prasristaastasya shakha,
Gunhapravriddhaa vishayapravaalaah,
Adhashch moolaanyanusantataani
Karmaanubandhaani manushyaloke [2].

Meaning—The branches of this tree are extended both below and above, they are nourished by the Gunhaas and sense-enjoyments are its foliage.

Its roots are spread below which bind (the soul) according to (his) actions in this world of human beings

Commentary—The Lord proceeds further and states two important facts. It is not that its branches are spread only below, they are also spread above, this is in form of higher beings like gods, gandharvas etc. These branches i.e. human and other beings below and celestial beings above are nourished by the three modes of natures-'Sattva' 'Rajas' and 'Tamas'. We have explained these modes earlier but it is worth mentioning that according to one's nature one injoys pleasure through these gunhas and is thus nourished e.g. a man having 'sattva,' will indulge in penance, Charity etc. and will feel contented. Similarly a man with the supremacy of 'Rajas' with in him will try to lord over others and sustain himself. A man with 'Tamas' many take to robbery tec. This is equally true for beings superior or inferior to men. There are innumerable examples of gods caught by 'Rajas' and 'Tanas' and performing actions not behoving them.

Let us come to the next statement 'sense enjoyments' are its foliage. Every tree needs foliage to survive its every branch so to say. Beings here and above indulge in enjoyment of sex etc. and be contented and thus flourish the foliage of this unique tree.

Not only the branches but also tree-roots are rooted both above and below. These roots are in the form of different actions which kep especially human beings (or say souls) tied to this world.

Na roopmasyeh tathopalabyate,
Naanto na chaardinacha sampratishtha,
Ashvatthamenam suviroodhmool-
masamgshashtrenha dridhen chhitva [3].
Tatah padam tatparimaargitavyam
yasmingata na nibvartanti bhooyah,
Tameva chaadyam purusham prapadye
Yatah pravrittih prasrita puraanhee [4].

Meaning—The real form of its is not perceived here. There is neither its beginning nor its end nor even stabliity.

Having cut down this Ashavatth which is firmly rooted,

with the formidable weapons of the detachment, one should seek that supreme state, having achieved which one never returns. 'I turn away (one should say) to seek that original Being (the Supreme Lord) alone from Whom has emanated this ancient urge to action.'

Commentary—It is not easy to state what the Lord means by maintaining that the tree is not seen here in this world, in its real form described by the Lord-with its feet above and the face below. Several interpretations have been given to this statement. But to my mind the Lord simply wants to say that such tree is not really available any where, He has just taken recourse to a simile to drive home the point He wants to drive.

The rest need no comments.

Nirmaanmoha jitsang doshaa-
Adhyaatmnitya vinivrittkamaah
Dvandvairvimuktaah sukh duhkhsamgyair-
Gachchhntyamoodhaah padamavyayam tat *[5].*

Meaning—Free from ego and infatuation, having conquered the vice of attachment, dwelling constantly in spiritualism, with desired stilled, free from the duality known as pleasure and pain, the wise, attain the supreme infinite.

Commentary—The ways to attain supreme-state are almost same here as narrated at different places earlier.

Na tadbhaasayate soorya na shashaanko na paavakah,
Yadgatvaa na nivartante tddhaam paramam mam *[6].*

Meaning—The sun does not illumine it nor the moon, nor the fire. That is my supreme state having reached which people do not comeback.

Commentary—That place of the Lord is illumined by his own supreme light. Remember the 'virat roop' of the Lord producing the light which thousand suns can not do.

Mamaivansho jeavaloke jeevabhootah sanaatanah,
Manah shashthanhindriyanhi prakrtisthani karshati *[7].*

Meaning—It is an eternal portion of Myself that takes form of the soul in the world of living beings. It attracts the mind and the five senses abiding in the nature.

Commentary—The Lord clearly admits in these lines

that He Himself resides in every being. Of course a part of His lives with in each and every being. He is just like an ocean which has many waves. In each wave there is nothing but the ocean itself. Similarly the Lord is a vast ocean and all the embodied souls are its waves. This simile has been taken recourse to by us at many places to make the picture clearer. This repetition is unavoidable.

The second line is important in the sense that mind and the five senses are drawn from nature itself. So far as the mind is concerned, it can be traced no where in the human-body. It is therefore very much in the nature itself—out side us. Other five senses are very much dependent on nature, you can not see any thing with your eyes, if there is no light, either from the sun or fire or electricity all of whom are the blessings of nature. Similarly the ears can not hear if there is no sky or ether. Words, cannot be produced in absence of sky similarly the dependence of all other senses can be traced to the nature.

Shareeram yadavaapnoti yachchaaputkraamteeshvarah,
***Greehitvaitaani sanyaati vaayurgandhanivaashayaat** [8].*

Meaning—As the Lord (the part of it) takes another body casting off the old one, He takes away all these senses with Him as the wind carries away adours where they exist from.

Commentary—The soul migrating to another body takes away with him the senses including mind and leaves behind the dead body. It is one reason why the body is dead. It is a scienctific fact that the body does not die till the mind is alive.

The soul has naturally been addressed as 'Eshwar' as it is nothing but the part of Him acording to His own ad mission.

Shrotram chakshuh sparshanam cha rasanam ghranhameva cha,
***Adhishthaay manashchaayam vishyaanupsevate** [9].*

Meaning—The ear, the eye, the touch, the taste and the smell using these and the mind too, it (the soul) enjoys the sense-objects.

Commentary—This is a bare statement of truth. The soul can not enjoy the objects of senses without their assistance. It is this enjoyment itself which also compels it to descend in to this world in different beings.

Utkraamantam sthitam vapi bhunjanam va gunhanvitam,
Vimoodhaa naanupashyanti pashyanti gyaanchakshushah [10].

Meaning—The eluded do not perceive the soul departing from or dweling in the body enjoying or its assuming the modes of nature, they only perceive, who have the eye of knowledge.

Commentary—All the attributes of the soul can be very easily seen or perceived by those possessing knowledge through penaness or study of scriptures. It is not just a fit of imagination of the Lord.

Yantanto yoginashchainam pashyantyaatmanyavasthitam,
Yatanto'pyakritaatmaano nainam pasyhantyachetasah [11].

Meaning—The yogis who strive, see it themselves but the ignorant even by striving do not see it because their hearts are not purified.

Commentary—So the both see Him—the part of the Lord—the knowers and the yogis. It is the privilege not limited to only one class.

[So for as the devotees are concerned, they least bother about it. They are content with their devotion to the Lord. They can see Him as a whole Itself instead of seing in parts.]

Yadadityhagatam tejo jagadbhaasayate'khilam,
Yachchandramasi yachchagnau tattejo viddhi mamakam [12].

Meaning—The effulgence in the sun, that illumines all this world, that which is in the moon and in the fire, that effulgence know to be Mine.

Commentary—God is the light-incarnate, he is supposed to be made of light itself, so there is no wonder if all the light emanates from Him, what to talk of the sun or the moon or the fire.

Gaamaavishya cha bhaotaani dhaarayaamyahamojasa,
Pusshnhaami chaushadheeh sarvah somo bhootva rasatmakah [13.]

Meaning—And residing in the earth, I sustain all beings by My power and becoming the moon full of sap I nourish all medicinal plants.

Commentary—The earth is the source of existence of

all beings living and unliving. God itself by entering the earth sustain these beings.

It is a known fact that the medicinal qualities of some plants are derived from the moon itself. Had there been no moon there would not have been any herb of medicine worth its name. The Lord says Himself, not to be different from the moon.

Aham vaishvaanaro bhootva pranhinam dehmashritah,
Pranhapansamayuktah pachaamyannam chaturvidham [14].

Meaning—I am the fire which dwels in the bodies of all beings and having united with 'prana' and 'apana' breaths, I digest the food of four kinds.

Commentary—The fire which exists in the body of all beings is called 'Jatharaagni'—fire in the belly. This fire with the help of the air we breath in and breath out helps in digesting the food we take. It is obvious that fire is of no use without air.

The four kinds of food are :—

i) That which is chewed.
ii) That which is sucked.
iii) That which is licked.
iv) That which is drunk.

Sarvasya chaaham hridi sannivsishto-
vattah smritirgyaanmapohanam cha.
Vedaishch sarvairahameva vedyo-
Vadaantkridvedavideva chaaham [15].

Meaning—I am lodged in the heart of all. Memory, wisdom and their absence are from Me. That which is known from the Vedas. I am indeed the author of the Vedanta and the knower of the Vedas.

Commentary—Vedantaas are the Upanishads and they are supposed to have been written by the sage Vyasa. But the Lord has already confessed that Vyasa is none also than Him.

So far the Vedas are concerned they are said to have descended from Himself. Thus he is certainly the knower of them.

Dvaavimau purushau loke Ksharshaakshar eva cha,
Ksharah sarvaanhi bhootaani kootashtho'kchar uchyate [16].

Meaning—There are two kinds of purush as (entities). One kind is perishable another is not. All the beings come in the former category. That which is lodged with in every being (and called soul) is imperishable.

Commentary—Quite clear.

Uttamah purushastvanyah paraatmetyudaahritah
Yo lokatrayamaavishya bibhartyavyaya Esvarah [17].

Meaning—But other than these two is that highest spirit called the Paramaatmaa (the Supreme self) Who enters the three worlds and upbears them. He is the imperishable Lord.

Commentary—The God is certainly different from both the body and the soul though the latter is a part of Himself.

Yasmaatksharamateeto'hamaksharadapi chottamah,
Ato'smi loke vede cha prathitah, Purushotamah [18].

Commentary—It was maintained in shloka 16 of this chapter that there are two kinds of Purusha He is the third and the best, the Purushottam.

Yo maamevasammoodho jaanaati Purushottamam
Sa sarvvidbhajati maam sarvbhaaven Bharat [19].

Meaning—O Bharat! the undeluded person who has knowledge of Me as the Purushottam adores Me with all knowledge and in all ways.

Commentary—Only the wise can recognize Him as the supreme person (Purushottam) and he full of all knowledge worships Him in every way.

Eti guhyatamam shaashtramidamuktam mayaanagh,
Etadbudhvaa buddhimanshyaatkritakrityashch Bharat [20].

Meaning—O sinlless one! thus by Me the most secret teaching has been imparted, O Bharat knowing this one becomes wise and attains utmost satisfaction.

Commentary—Lord has divulged the most secret of all 'shaashtraas' (this is nothing less than scripture). One must understand and believe it thoroughly to gain knowledge and attain supreme satisfaction.

Om tatsaditi shrimadbhagavadgeetaasoopanishasu Bhram vidyaayaam yogshashashtre shrikrishnarjun samvaade Purushotam yogo nam panchdasho'dhyayah [15].

Thus in the Upanishad knowledge of Brahma, the seripture of yoga, the dialogue between Shrikrishna and Arjuna ends the fifteenth chapter entitled 'Pursotam yoga.'

CHAPTER-XVI

Shri Bhagavanuvaach—

Abhayam sattvasanshuhddhirgyaanyogvyavasthitih,
Danam damashch yagyashcha svadhyaystap aarjavam [1]

Meaning—The Blessed Lord said--

Fearlessness, purity of soul, steadfastness in the yoga of knowledge, charity, control of senses, sacrifices, the study of scriptures, penances and simplicity.

Commentary—Enumeration of divine virtues commences.

Ahinsaa satyamakrodhastyaagah shantirapaishunam
Daya bhooteshvaloluptvam mardavam hreerachapalm [2].

Meaning—Non-violence, truthfullness, absence of wrath, renunciation, peacefulness, absence of faultfinding in others, kindness towards all beings, greedlessness, modesty, absence of restlessness.

Commentary—The enumeration continues. Commentary included in the succeeding verse also. We take up from the first shloka :

Fearlessness is certainly a rare quality. Even in the Vedas the most sacred and decidedly the most ancient intellectual achievement of the world, this quality has been underlined.

The Yajurved says 'Ma bhermaa mamviktha' (1.23)

-Do n't fear, do not be restless

The Upanishadas also underline its importance. The Taittireya Upanishad says—

Na vibheti kadaachaneti,
Na bibheti kootashchaneti
—Never fear, don't be afraid of any.

The fearlessness is such a quality that it has been compared with the 'Brahma' itself :

'Abhayam vai Brahm'. Fearlessness is Brahm Itself.

Let us now talk about charity. This has been emphasised upon in all religions. The Christians call it teething, to give away ten percent of their earning. In 'Islaam' also this provision exists.

In Hindu religion the very aim of earning is said to be the charity 'Daanaay Aryyati—Earns to give.'

If we turn to Upanishadas, it has been well said in the 'tattireya upanishad' that give with faith, even without faith, give in abundance, give with humility, give fearing God.'

Shradhaya deyam ashraddhayadeyam shriya deyam hriya deyam, bhiya deyam samvida deyam

Tejah, kshamaa dhritih shauchamadrohonatimanita
Bhavanti sampadam daivimabhijaatasya Bharat [3].

Meaning—Sublimity, forgiveness, patience, cleanness, absence of evvy as well as that of pride. Symptoms these are of the man born with divine wealth.

Commentary—In the above three verses twenty six symptoms of the men and women born with divine bliss or weath or to put is better with that nature have been enumerated. Some are very important and have found mention at other places also. We shall like to talk about them.

The first thing mentioned in the first verse itself is fearlessness. The entire Gita is aimed at rooting out fear. It has been comprehensibly commented upon on the previous page.

We need not dwel much upon the importance of sacrifice or 'Yagya'. The Lord has focussed sufficient light on it in chapter III of the Gita.

Thy study of scriptures or 'Svaadhyaay' is of course important; it does not only provide one with knowledge but it also purifies on's inner self. The Lord has Himself maintained that there is no purifying factor better than knowledge :

'Na hi gyaanen sadrisam
Pavitramih vidyate* (iv, *38).

He said about non violence. This has been considered to be the supreme religion in Hindu philosophy—

'Ahimsa paramo dharmah'

Patanjali said 'ahinsa 'vairtyaagah'µNon violence is absence of enmity.

Let us come to truth. It is said that it is truth which always wins **'satyameva jayate.'**

The scripture ordains that speak only that which is purified by truth **'Satyapootam vadet vaacham.'**

Anger has been denounced by every thinker. It has been scientifically proved that when in anger the entire inner system of a person is poisoned.

Vyas has rightly maintained in Mahabharat :

Krodho hi dharmam harati yateenaam duhkhsanchitam,
Tato dharmviheenaanaam ggatir na vidyate

—The anger destroyes the religion of the sages collected with great pain and there is no future for the irreligious.

The seer Vaalmiki says in his famous epic Ramayana that a man full of anger does not know what to speak and what to speak not.

'Vachyaavaachyam prakupito cha na vijaanti karhichit.'

So for as renumciation is concerned it has been emphasized time and again in the Gita itself according to shloka 12 of chapter 12, renunciation is in the root of peace,-

'Tyaagaat shanti' (12.12)

Dambho dorpo'bhimaanashch krodhah paarushyameva cha
agyanam chaabhijatasya Parth sampadamaasureem [4].

Meaning—O son of Pritha! pride, arrogance,excessive self esteem, anger, harshness, ignorance, these are the wealth of the man born with asuric (demoniac properties).

Commentary—These are six symptomps of people born with Asuric properties.

Most of them are easily understood. Absence of wrath was enumerated as one of 'saattvic' properties. Here presence of wrath is deemed as a demoniacal symptom. We had talked a lot about wrath and how it has been denounced by the scriptures. We must not repeat them.

Daivi sampadvimokshsaay nibandhaayasureemata
Ma shuchah sampadam daiveemabhijaato'si Pandava [5].

Meaning—The divine qualities lead to libearation and 'Asuric' towards bondage. Grieve not O Pandava! As you are born with divine qualities.

Commentary—Arjun was undoubtedly grief-stricken; it is why he had developed distaste towards duties. The Lord provides him with a shot in the arm that he is born with all divine gifts and is therefore, entitled to liberation also.

Dvau bhootsargau loke'smindaiv asur evaha,
Daiva vistarashah prokth aasuram Paarth Me shrinhu [6].

Meaning—There are two types of beings in this material world—daivic and aasuric. The daivic has been described at length, hear from me of Parth! the demonical (aasuri) also.

Commentary—Though shloka 4 of this chapter has been devoted to describing the aasuric or demoniacal symptoms, but it appears they have not been exhausted. So He returns to them again. It is worth remembering that while only six symptoms of 'Aasuric' tendencies have been mentioned, not less than twenty six qualities of persons born with 'Saattvic' wealth have been enumerted in the first three shlokas of this chapter. It was just expected that He would return to them again. The break is understandable. He could have narrated them in continuation of shloka 4 itself but He was in hurry to boost up the morale of Arjun therefore, he hastended to add that he is born with 'Saattvic' qualities.

Pravritim cha nivrtim cha jana na viduraasurah,
Na shaucham naapi chacharo na satyam teshu vidyate [7].

Meaning—Those belonging to 'aasuric' group do not know what is action or what is abstention. Thnere is no purity in them nor good conduct nor truth.

Commetary—Knowing the difference between activity or inactivity (or abstention) is very important. The Lord is quite aware of this fact and he asserted as back as in chapter IV shloka 16 that even wise men do not know the difference between what is action and what is inaction or inanctivity—

"Kim karm kimakrmeti kavayo'pyatra mohitaah."

There is no question of expecting external or internal purity from them. So far as conduct is concerned it is of course of immense importance. One must have a good conduct, must behave decently with people one come in contact. But it can hardly he expected of a man with Aasuric tendencies. They will behave burtally and indecently.

Good conduct i.e. 'aachaar' has been described in Hindu scriptures as the supreme religion "Achaarah pramo Dharmah"

A sanskrit stratement very well asserts :—

'Aacharheenam na punanti vedah, sarvasya tapaso moolmaachaaram—'

Those who are without conduct cannot appraise the vedas 'aachaar' is in the root of all penance.

Asatyamapratishtham te jagadaahuraneeshvaram,
Aparsparsambhootam kimanyatkaamhaitukam [8].

Meaning—They maintain that the world is altogether false and without any foundation. It has no God. It is brought up by mutual union (of males and females). The only purpose is to enjoy sex. What else?

Commentary—They consider the world to be just a chance-product, it has therefore, according to them no foundation to rest upon or no root at all. It is false because beings come and go, none is for ever.

They do not recognize God. Such people in Sanskrit are called 'naastick' (atheist)

Among Hindu Philosophers there has been a fomous atheist—Pilosopher named Chaarvaak. The shloka is perhaps an indirect reference to him and his followers. He went as far as to say,

Yaavat jeevet sukham jeevet,
Rinham kritvaa ghritam pivet,
Bhashmeebhootasya dehasya
Gamanaagamanam kutah."

—Live luxuriously as long as you are here. Raise even loan to eat ghee (purified butter). There is no coning in and going back of this body which is consumed by fire (thus no need to return even the loan you have raised).

Such people who do not believe in God has no scruples and they can go to any extent to denounce good qualities and embrance bad ones.

The most ridiculous part of it is that they believe this world to have come into being just as a result of sexual relationship, the fools do not know that many people go without progeny and they do not have issues depite their sex.

But topping all, they consider this world only a place to enjoy sex, there is no other use of it.

They are the worst kind of creatures. In sanskrit such a man in called 'Kaam-keet' (a sex-worm); one reveling in sex just like a disgusting worm. He hardly deserves to be called a human being.

In chapter IV of the Gita the Lord has very emphatically denounced this sex and has maintained that it is in the root of all evils and the dreadiest enemy of the mankind—Mahaasano, mahaapaapmaa viddyenamih vairinham (4.37) Readers are referred back to verses 37, 38, 39, 40 and 41 of Chapter IV in this connection.

Etaam drishtimavashtabhya nashtaatmaano'lpbuddhayah,
Prabhavantyugrakarmaanhah kshayaaya jagato'hitaah [9].

Meaning—Accepting this view they with their souls ruined and having little resoning and devoted to violent action are born they, with no sense of welfare, for the destruction of the world.

Commentary—The fact that they are with ruined souls is of importance. It has been imphasised earlier that soul must not be defiled. Shloka 5 of Chapter VI may be referred to which shows that soul must be upgraded and not allowed to deteriorate. It is our friend as well as foe.

In the case of 'Aasuric' people this soul becomes their enemy, nay the enemey of the whole world. Their demoniac activities only lead to the destruction of world. Can one forget the consequence of two world-wars? Who were behind the atomic destruction of 'Hiroshima' and Naagasaaki' and killing of millions of men? They were the people with Aasuric tendencies, with ruined soul and with little rather no understanding or reasoning. They had in mind well being of none in this world.

Kaamamaashritya dushpooram dambhamanmadanvitah,
Mohadgrahitvasadgraahanpravartante'shuchivratah [10].

Meaning—Resorting to never satiable sex, full of pride, self-esteem and arrogance, they pursue the worthless aims deluded and with impure resolution.

Commentary—The emphasis is again on the never to be satisfied sexual pursuits on which we have dwelt in the preceding verse.

They can not have other than impure resolutions with their mind deluded by sex, pride and false self-esteem, as well as arrogance.

Chintaamaparimeyaam cha pralayaantaamupaashritaah,
Kamopabhogparama etavaditi nishchitaah [11].

Meaning—They are driven to endless anxiety till their death. They consider the enjoyment of sensual pleasures to be the be end and all end of life.

Commentary—They are given to endless anxiety and the Gita's main purpose as stated earlier is to make man free from anxieties and care. To provide peace to man is the sole aim of the Gita. But unfortunate as they are, these men with Aasuric depositions never enjoy real pleasure through out their life.

It has been maintained earlier that they consider enjoyment of sensual pleasures as the only aim of their earthly existence.

The Lord is emphasizing the prevalence of sex in the life of some people only to show how dreadful this sex is.

Asshaapaashshatairbadhaah kaamkrodhparayahaah,
Eehante kaambhogaarthmanyaayenaarthsamchayan [12].

Meaning—Bound by a hundred ties of expectation given over to sex and anger, they desire to amaas wealth unjustly only to enjoy sensual pleasures.

Commentary—Expectation is the greatest cause of bondage. One thinks that if he or she has not succeeded to day, success will certainly arrive to-marrow. Fools depend on these uncertainties, wise man never indulges in false expectations. One sanskrit poct has rightly objserved :

"The limbs are mutilated, the hair has gone white, teeth have decayed but the man having grown old walking with the help of stick, sticks at his expectations"—

'Amgam galitam palitam mundam
Dasanviheenam jaatam tundam
Vriddho yati grihitva dandam
Tadapi na munchatyaasaahpimdam.

We have talked a lot about sex and anger. But the fact that such people strive to amass wealth dishonestly only with the sole aim of enjoyment of sensual pleasures is astounding. It means corruption is not the privilege of only modern times.

Edamadya maya labdhamimam prapsye manoratham,
Edamasteedamapi me bhavishyati punardhanam [13].

Meaning—(They think) "To day I have obtained this object of desire, that desire will be readied (shortly), to-day, I have this much of wealth, more I will accumulate again.

Commentary—This is a vivid description of greedy and overambitious man who is spotted every where these days. This greed leads him to any form of crime. To obtain what they desire, they can go to any length even to murder their onw men.

It has been rightly said in the scriptures that greed is the cause of sin—

"Lobhah paapasya kaaranham"

Saint Tulsidas rightly observed as the profit increases so the greed"—

'Jimi prati laabh lobh adlikaai'

Asau maya hatah shatrurhanishye chaaparaanapi
Eshvaro'hamaham bhogee siddho'ham balvaansukhi [14].

Meaning—They think this enemy is already salin by me, I shall slay others too. I am God (Himself), I am the enjoyer, am the perfected soul, I am strong and happy.

Commentary—These lines are some of the very beautiful lines of the Gita and they give an inimitable description of the greedy, proud and unscrupulous men of to-day and yonder days.

These fools indulge in heinous crimes. They slay their enemies (even when they may not be so) and plan to kill others. There is a proverb in English, nothing succeeds like success. So they move from one inglorious success to another.

They consider themelves to be God Himself. There is no dearth of such examples even in history what to talk of 'legends'? 'Hirnayakashipu' a legendary king declared himself to be God. Prahlad his own son opposed him and got him killed at the hands of God Himself. 'Kans' a historical figure and king of Mathura considered himself to be God. Even in these days of democracy there are despots who call themselves God. It was only recently that a Chief Minister of one of the northern Indian states declared himself to be Krishna Himself. And lo and behold his huge cut outs with 'Sankh' 'Chakra', 'Gada', 'Padm' (meanings of all these words have been given earlier) were exhibited at different places in the city.

One who can declare himself as God is bereft of all fears and he is certainly the only enjoyer, the only perfected soul and the strongest of all people.

Aadhyo'bhijanavaanasmi Ko'snyoasti sadrisho maya,
Ykshyedaasyaami modishya etyagyaànvimohitaah. [15].

Meaning—I am wealthy, I am of high birth, who is there like me, I will perform sacrifice, will give charity, I will enjoy.

Commentary—Not required.

Anekchittvibhraanta mohjaalsamaavritaah
Prasaktaah kaambhogeshu patanti narke'shuchau [16].

Meaning—Thus bewildered in mind in different ways, enmeshed in the web of delusion and indulged in the enjoyments of sensuous pleasures, they slide in to the hell which in impure.

Commentary—The sum and substance of this 'shloka' is that the persons of demoniacal nature go not to the heaven but to hell.

Their atrributes narrated in the verse have been directly or indirectly dwelt upon before.

Aatmsambhaavitaah stabdhaa dhanmaanmadaanvitaah,
Yajante naamyagyaiste danbhenaavidhipoorvakan [17].

Meaning—Full of (false) selfimportance, deluded, intoxicated with wealth and honour (bestowed on them by their flatterers) they perform the sacrifice (Yagya) of name-chanting, full of pride and without the method (prescribed by the scriptures).

Commentary—Their attributes need no elaboration. But the second part concerning with sacrifice (yagya) has been subjected to controversial commentaries.

By 'namyagyah' many mean indulging in sacrifice or 'yagyaa' only for the name sake or just only for show ('nam matra'). But we have differed from such commentators. It is an unnecessarily stretched explanation. The chanting of God's name especially in a covered rosary is also a kind of yagya. And this perfectly suits here as well. Many proud and ostentatious people can be seen in India and else where with their hands in a pocket conatining rosary as if they are always chanting the names of God though they will even indulge in all kinds of conversation and act simultaneously. It is one reason that it is said here that they do not perform this clanting of names according to rules prescribed. Had that been so they would have sat in some silent place and took the names of God, rosary or no rosary.

Ahankaaram balam darpam kamam krodham cha sanshritah,
Maamaatmapardeheshu pradvishanto'bhy asuyakaah [18]

Meaning—Over-powered by their ego, strength, arrogance, passion and anger they despise Me Who dwell in their as well other's bodies.

Commentary—Having declared himself as God it is but natural for them to despise and belittle God who resides with in them and others also.

The Gita has declared many a time that He lives in the bodies of beings. Even Upnishadas say so. We are not going to repeat them.

The only point to ponder over is why the Lord repeats the fact by telling that He lives in all bodies and also of theirs. It was suffice to say that He lives in all bodies.

It is because of the fact that due to their attribute they first harm themselves then others. For example one in anger certainly first harms himself then others against whom he is angry.

Taanaham dvishatah krooransansareshu naraadhamaan
Kshipamyajasramashubhaanasureeshveva yonishu [19].

Meaning—I cast down continually these haters (of God) evils, cruels and vilest among men in to the 'aasuric' creatures.

Commentary—They take birth again and again among those having demoniacal nature as they hardly get an opportunity to imporve themselves being creatures like animals including pigs and dogs etc. It is certainly what they deserve for their all hateful attributes.

Aasurim yonimaapanna moodha janmani janmani
Mamapraapaiva kaunteya tato yantyadhamaam gatim [20].

Meaning—cast in to aasuric creatures, these fools find Me not and attain lower depths.

Commentary—As stated in the previous commentary, they get little chance to improve themselves thus there is no chance of them attaining to the Lord or the supreme status, they sink to lower status say hell and what is called 'patallok' (the world below this world and dwelt by demons).

Trividham narakasyedam dvaram nashanamaatmanah,
kamah, krodhastatha lobhastasmdetattrayam tyajet {21]

Meaning—Sex, anger and greed are three different gates of hell. They are therefore to be avoided.

Commentary—The most vilest of the demoniacal tributes are these three which have been sufficiently commented upon in the last pages; the only hint left is to heed the advice of the Lord and get rid of them at any cost.

Etairvimuktah Kaunteya tamodvaaraishtribhirnarah,
Aacharatyaatmanah shryestato yati paraam gatim [22].

Meaning—O son of kunti! a person liberated from these dark doors, strives for his own good and reaches the supreme status.

Commentary—These three doors are called to be dark. It is but natural. Darkness is the opposite of light and the light represents the godly qualities. Those with 'Asuric' nature are bound to pass through paths full of darkness.

Darkness has been very much denounced in the upanishadas. They are almost allergic to it. Rember 'Andham tamah pravishanti' (Eshavashyopanisad) and Asurya nam te loka andhen tamasavritaah (Kathopanishad)—there are worlds devoid of the sun and filled with pitched darkness.

Needless to add that they who avoiding these three dark doors endeavour to improve themselves, they attain to the supreme status.

Yah shaashtra vidhimutsrijya vartate kaamkaaratah,
Na sa siddhimavaapnoti na sukham na paraam gatim [23].

Meaning—He who having cast aside the rule of scriptures, acts prompted by sensuous desire, attains neither perfection, nor happiness nor the supreme status.

Commentary—The message is clear. Act not driven by senses but according to the paths prescribed by scriptures and you will attain the supreme status (the Lord Himself).

Tasmaachchhaathram pramaanham te kaaryaakaaryavyavasthitau
Gyaatvaa shashravidhaanoktam karm kartumiharhasi [24].

Meaning—Therefore, let the scriptures be your authority in determining what aught to be done and what not aught to be done. Knowing what has been declared by the rules of the scriptures you act here, (in this world).

Commentary—It has been maintained earlier that it is difficult to decide what to do and what not to do. Reference has been made to shloka 16 of Chapter IV where the Lord Himself says "What is to be done and what is not to be done, even wise men do not know 'kim karm kimakarmeti kavayo'pitaramohitaah'.

But now the path is shown. Act as the scriptures ordain.

Om Tatsaditi srimadbhabhagavadgeetasoopanisatsu Brahm vidyaayaam yog shaastre shrikrishnaajun samvade daivaasursambaadvibhaag yogo naam shodasho'dhyaayah [16].

This in the Upanishad sung by the Lord, the Knowledge of Brahma, the scripture on yoga, this dialogue between Shrikrishna and Arjun ends the sixteenth chapter entitled the yoga of division between the divine and the demoniacal properties.

CHAPTER-XVII

Arjun Uvach

Ye shashtravidhimutsrijya yajante sraddhayaanvitaah,
Teshaam nishtha tu kaa krishnha sattvamaaho rajastamah [1].

Meaning—Arjun Said—O Krishna, the people who neglect the injuctions of scripture, but worship with full of faith, what is the category of their faith full of 'Sattva', 'Rajas' or 'Tamas'.

Commentary—Let us await the answer by the Lord.

Shri Bhagavan uvaach—

Trividhaa bhavati shraddha dehinaam saa svabhavajaa,
Saattviki, raajasee chaiva tamasee, cheti taam shrinhu [2].

Meaning—The blseed Lord said—The innate faith of begins is of triple kinds, saattvee, raajasee and taamasee. Hear them.

Commentary—We have by now known adequately about the there modes of the nature identified as 'Sattva', 'Rajas' and 'Tamas'. Depending on them the faith of beings (especially human beings) becomes of three kinds.

Sattvaanurupa sarvasya shradhaa bhavati Bharat,
Shradhamayo'ayam purushah yo yachchraddah eva Sah [3].

Meaning—O Bhaart! The faith of all is shaped according to every one's mental inclination. This man is made of faith, thus whatever his faith is, so is he.

Commentary—If the faith is full of 'Sattva', he will be 'saattvic', if he is full of 'Rajas' he will be 'Raajasic' and if full of 'Tamas' he will be 'Tamasic'. Faith the very inner nature of man is thus of utmost importance.

Yajante saattvikaa devaanyakshrakhsansi raajasaah,
Pretaanbhootganhaanshchaanye yajante taamasaa janaah [4].

Meaning—Those with 'Saattvic' qualities worship the gods, those having 'Raajasic' tendencies worship 'yakshan' and demons. The rest with 'Taamasic' nature worship spirits and ghosts.

Commentary—We have talked about 'yakshas' and 'Rakshasas' earlier. To refresh readers' memory it will be sufficient to add that 'yakshas' are semi celestial beings. They are supposed to be very wealthy. Kuber is the king of yakshas. He is famous for his fabulous weath, therefore any body very wealthy here, is called Kuber. 'Rakshsaas' are actually man-eating beings fuli of immeasurable strength. The demon is hardly the substitute of the word 'Raakhas' but in absence of any better substitute we are kneeling upon it.

It is easy to understand one worshiping the gods but why one does worship 'yakshas' and 'Raakshaas.' For weath and strength necessarily. Being pleased they are supposed to guarantee these things.

Similarly there is still no lack of people who worship spirits and ghosts. It is futile to discuss wheather they exist or not. They do exist. The readers are referred to the best known theosophical literature, especially of Lade Beater, they may also refer to my book 'Bandhak aatmaayen' (Rajesh prakasan, G-62 street no. 5 Arjun Nager, Delhi) for authentic description of spirits and ghosts.

The point is why the people of 'Taamsic' tendency worship them. It is because they are also capable to some extent, to fulfil the desires of man and they are easily to be propitiated.

Ashaashtravihitam ghoram tapyante ye tapo janaah,
Dambhaahamkarasamyuktaahkamrag balaanvditaah [5].
Karshayantah, shareerastham bhootgraamchetasah,
Mam chaivantah shareerastham tanviddhyasurnishchayaan [6].

Meaning—The people who perform difficult penances not sanctioned by the scripture, being full of pride and ego and impelled by the forces of sex and passion, they devoid of thinking, torment the aggregated elements forming the body and Me residing in their hearts; know them to be 'Aasuric' in their resolve.

Commentary—The difficult penance which unnecessarily subject the bodies and thus the elements like (earth, water, air, fire, and ether) to unnecessary hardships, naturally torment the soul also in process of tormenting the body, the soul which is nothing but a part of the Lord Himself as maintained at different places is the Gita. They are called by the Lord ignorant and indulge in nothing but 'Aasuric' resolves, being propelled by arrogance, pride, sex, passion etc.

Aaharastvapi sarvasya trividho bhavati priyah,
Yagyastapahstatha danam tesham bhedamimam shrihu [7].

Meaning—The food also which is favourite to all (according to their nature) is of triple character and so the sacrifice, penance and charity, hear their distinction.

Commentary—No need.

Ayah sattvabalaarogya sukh preeti vivardhanaaha,
Rashyaah, snigdhaah, sthiraa, hridya, aahaarah saattvikpriyaah [8].

Meaning—Foods promoting longevity, soul-power, strength, freedom from diseases; happiness, taste (of the food itself) and succulent, soft, nourishing and satisfying are favourites of the people with saattvic disposition.

Commentary—Wait

Katvamlalavanhaatyushnateeksnharookshvidaahinah,
Aaharaa raajasasyeshtaa duhkhshokaamaypradaah. [9]

Meaning—The 'rajasic' type of men prefer foods which are bitter, acids, salted, very hot, pungent, rough and burning, they give rise to pain, grief, and ailments.

Commentary—Wait

Yaatyaamam gatrasam pooti paryushitam cha yat,
Uchchlishtamapi chamedhyam bhojanam Tamaspriyam [10].

Meaning—The food which is cold, insipid, full of bad odour, stale and left-over are favourite of those with 'taamasic' nature.

Commentary—We sum up the commentaries to all the above three verses here. It is certain that what you eat you are. Foods not only shape your body but also your thoughts and feelings.

There is an interesting story that the priest of a king stole away the golden ornaments of the deity. It was never expected of him pious as he has always been. A probe was set up to find the cause which made the priest indulge in such an action. It was ultimately discovered that while on his way to palace a day back, he halted at the place of a thief and ate the food offered by him.

It has been well stated in Chhaandogya Upanishad that with the purity of foods the thinking becomes pure and with it becoming pure,the memory becomes strong and all complexes are also gone—

"Aahaarsuddhau sattvasuddh, sattva suddhau dhruva smritih, smrtilabhe sarvgrantheenaam vimokshah (chh. 7. 26. 2).

Aphala kamkshiviryagyo vidhidrishto sa ejyate
Yashtavyameveti manah samadfhay sa saattvikah [11].

Meaning—The 'saattvic' sacrifce is that which is offered with a firm belief that it is a duty must to be performed and is offered according to the way prescribed by the scriptures and without desire for fruits.

Commentary—Nothing special

Abhisandhaay tu phalam dambhaarthamapi chaiva yat,
Ejyate Bharatshreshtha tam yagyam viddhi raajasam [12].

Meaning—O Bharat! know that sacrifice to be of raajasic nature which is offered with a desire for fruit and also for ostentation.

Commentary—The men of 'raajasic' tendency perform sacrifice (yagya) mainly to get some desire fulfilled and also to learn name and fame. It is more for show than for really pleasing God or the gods.

Vidhiheenamasrishtaannam mantraheenamadakshinham,
Shradha virahitam yagyam taamasam parichakshate [13].

Meaning—Tasmasic is that sacrifice which is performed not based on the method prescribed by the scriptures, with no food offered to the hungry; without mantra (sacred syllables), without fees (to the performing priests) and without faith.

Commentary—Offering of food is an essential part of yagya, it satisfies the hungry. Pleases the priests.

'Anna' (food) has been deemed as Brahma itself in Hindu

scriptures when they ordain—

'Annam Brahm. Annen jaataani jeevaanti'—Food is Brahm. Beings live on food.

Devadvijgurupraagyapoojanam shauch maarjavam,
Brahmcharyamahinsa cha shaareeram tap uchyate [14].
Anudvegakaram vaakyam satyam priyahitam cha yat
Svadhyayabhyasanan chaiva vamgamayam tap uchyate [15].
Manahprasaadah saumatvam maunamaatmavinigrahah
Bhaavasamsuddhirityetattapo maanasmuchyate [16].

Meaning—Three kinds of penance are being described in the above shlokaas :

The worship of gods, the twice borns (Brahmanas) guru (the spiritual guide), cleanness, candid dealing, celibacy, non-violence, these are the austerity of body [14].

Speech not tormenting others, truthful, pleasing and beneficial and practice of the study of scriptures constitute the austerity of speech. [15]

Delightfulness of mind, gentleness, silence, self-control and purity of feeling, these are called to be the austerity of the mind [16].

Commentary—It is evident that austerity or penance is not concerned with body alone. Speech and mind can also be subjected to it and it has been amply explained as what the three kinds of sacrifice stand for.

Some points in these three verses need to be commented upon.

The penance which is the subject-matter of these three shlokas is in itself of immense significance. It is said that it is due to penance that 'Brahma' becomes capable of bringing in to existence this creation. It is due to penance that Vishnu becomes able to sustain all beings of the creation. The Lord Shiva is known for his constant penance and thus He gathers the energy to serve as the Destroyer of all that is created.

The 'Taitreya Upanishad says that the absolute Being (Brahma) can be known through austerity (or penance), nay penance is Brahma Himself.

'Tapasaa Brahm vijigyaasasva, tapo Brahmeti (T.u.s. 5.1)

There is a mention of worshiping 'Dvij' and Guru. Dvij'

we have described as Brahmans because they are supposed to be twice born. First when they are really born to this earth and next when they are provided with the sacred thread ('Yagyopavit').

By Guru we do not necessarily mean a spiritual guide. Mother, father and Aacharya (Guru) have been placed under the same category and all of them have been equated with gods. Upanishad syas, treat mother as god, father as God and Aacharya as God :—

'Matri deo bhava, pitri deo Bhava, Aachaarya deo bhava (Taithirieya up 1.11.2)

These are some of the salient features of the austerity or penance of the body.

Let us turn over to the penance of speech. This is in a way more important than the austerity of body.

Its significance has been realised right from the vedic period.

The yajurved says, may the protector of speech sweeten our speech—Vaachaspatih vacham nah svadaatu (Yajurved).

The Upanishad says, 'May my tongue be sweetest—

Jihvaa me madhu mattam (taittireeya u.).

A pleasing sweet speech is very welcomed. A harsh tongue is the cause of enmity.

The Bible has very nicely expressed this in the following lines : 'every kind of beast and bird, of reptile and sea creature can be tamed and has been tamed by humankind but no human can tame the tongue a restless evil full of deadly poison.' We can only say, what a pity? The Bible proceeds to reveal rightly, "with it we bless the Lord, Father and with it we curse men who are made in the likeness of God" (James 3/ to 9).

The conrol of tongue is the real autsterity of speech.

Now let us come to mind. Mind is every thing. It is the king and controller of the body. If mind is well, body is well. If mind is ill body is ill. It is now a scientific fact that 90% of our diseases originate in the mind. They call them psychosomatic diseases pertaining to both psyche (mind) and soma (body). This has been hinted upon earlier also.

Thus a mind purified through penance or austerity is very helpful. A saying in the sanskrit rightly says—Mind is the cause of bondage as well as liberation—

'Man eva manushyanaam kaaranam bandhmokshyoh'

Shraddhaya parayaa taptam tapastatrividham naraih,
Aphalakamkshibhiryuktaih satvikam parichakshate [17].

Meaning—The three fold penances performed with surpreme faith and union (with God) by men who have no desire for fruits is said to be saattvic.

Commentary—Not needed.

Satkaaramaanpoojaartham tapo dambhen chaivya yat,
kriyate tadih, proktam raajasam chalamadhruvam [18].

Meaning—The askesis which is udertaken to get respect, honour and worship and for ostentation is said to be 'raajasic.' It is unstable and fleeting in nature.

Commentary—The world to day is full of such hypocrates. By smarting a yellow robe and long beard along with a few lines of scripture on their tongue these self-styled 'gurus' go on chitting people left and right.

Moodhgraahenhaatmno yatpeedaya kriyate tapah,
Parasyotasaadanaartham va tattmaasmudaahritam [19].

Meaning—The askesis which is pursued under a deluded understanding with torture (to body) and with the object of harming others is said to be 'taamasic'.

Commentary—There is no dearth of examples in which men have lived on only water and air, subjected their body to fierce heat in the summer and to the chilling cold in winter.

Similarly there are people who take to austerities to harm others.

The Lord demeans all such kinds of austerities.

Daatvyamiti yadddaanam deeyate'nupkaarinhe,
Deshe kaale cha paatre taddaanam saativikam smritam [20].

Meaning—The charity which is given as having decided as it is to be given (as a part of dury) to one from whom nothing is expected in return and with due regard to place, time and recipient, that charity is deemed to be 'saatvic'.

Commentary—The Lord suddenly switches over to charity. Rightly so, as charity is also a form of penance.

The last line, needs to be commented upon. What are of importance and worth consideration are :

1. Place—the charity given at a suitable place bears much fruits. Given at a place of worship or 'Tirthas' (the places of religious pilgrimage) the gifts given return to the giver with much more than what he gives.

2. Time—this is also important. Providing drinking water at different places in the summer is one sush example. Distributing grains during draughts and famines is another.

3. Recipient or the person who receives the charity. What is the use of giving food to a person who is well fed? What is the meaning of giving money to a man who will gamble it out or run to the nearest bar to be drunk. Give to the needy, the deserving.

Yattu pratyupkaaraartham phalamuddishya va punah,
Deeyate cha pariklishtam taddaanam raajasam smritam [21].

Meaning—The giving which is done with the hope of getting something in return or with a view to gain some fruit (in form of blessings of gods) or with a repentant mood is 'raajasic' in nature.

Commentary—There are a lot of people who repent or grudge after giving, especially when nothing comes back immediately in return.

Adeshakaale yaddaanamapaatrehyashch deeyate,
Asatkritamavagyaatam tattaamasmudaahritam [22].

Meaning—The giving done at not a suitable place and time and to an undeserving person and also in disrespectful manner is said to be 'taamasic'.

Commentary—We have dwelt at length on the place, time and recipient. What is added here is that no charity should be made in an insulting and disrepectful manner. Many of us must have seen many people throwing handful of coins among the beggars who run helter-skelter and even quarrel among themselves to collect them. This is one example of giving disrespectfully. On some doors the beggars are of course given some coins but driven away hurriedly to get rid of their ugly and deformed body. This is an example of giving with insult.

Om tatsaditi nirdesho brahmbhanhastribvidhah smritah,
Brahmanhasten vedaashch yagyashch vihitaah pura [23].

Meaning—Om, Tat, Sat, is the triple designation, according to the Brahma (The absolute). It is by him that Brahmanhas, the Vedas and sacrifices were created in the past (at the beginning of the creation).

Commentary—Brahma is the creator of this universe. Om is Brahma Himself. It is thus either Brahma or Om, tat, sat, who created first the Braahmanhas, the Vedas, the sacrifices. By Braahmanhas we do not necessarily mean a particular caste; as stated earlier, whoever knows Brahma the absolute, is Braahmanha—'Brahmam janati eti Braahmanhah.'

Tasmaadomityudahritya yagyadaantapah kriyaah,
Pravartante vidhanoktaah satatam Brahmvaadinaam [24].

Meaning—Therefore with the pronunciation of Om the acts of 'yagya' charity and penance as laid down in the rules (of the scriptures) are always commenced by them who know the Brahma.

Commentary—Om is therefore, generally used before chanting the mantras (the sacred syllables).

The vedas have also declared om tat, sat as Brahma—

"Om iti Brahm, tat tvam asi sat, eva samyedamagno aaseet."

"Om is Brahma himself, you are the same sat that was in the beginning of all".

Tadityanabhismdhaay phalam yagyatapah kriyaah,
Dankriyaashch vividhhah kriyante mokshkaamkshibhih [25].

Meaning—With the pronunciation of tat and without any desire of fruit are performed the various acts of sacrifice, askesis and charity by those who long for liberation.

Commentary—First the use of Om was emphasised. In this shloka the importance of 'tat' has been dwelt upon.

Sabbhaavae saadhubhaave cha sadityetatprayujyate
Prashaste karmanhi tatha sachhabdhah Parth yujyate [26].

Meaning—Sat is employed in the sense of truth and virtue and O Parth ! the word 'sat' is also used to denote a praiseworthy act.

Commentary—No need.

Yagyae, Tapasi dane cha sthitih saditi chochyate
Karm chaiva tadartheeyam sadityevabhidheeyate [27].

Meaning—All (virtues) abiding in sacrifice, penance and charity are also designated as 'sat' and the action for the sake of Him is (also termed as) sat.

Commentary—'Sat' is actually the synonim of satya i.e. truth. Truth is God Himself, it is why so much importance is attached to sat.

Ashraddhaya hutam dattam tapastaptam kritam cha yat,
Asadityuchyate Parth na cha tatpretya no eha [28].

Meaning—O Parth, oblation, charity, and askesis and any other action performed without faith, is referred as asat, it is simply naught here or after.

Commentary—The significance of faith is once more emphasised. Any action either worship or sacrifice or any action aimed at pleasing the gods or God must be backed by adequate faith other wise it will be of no use here or here after. We have talked a lot about faith in previous pages.

Om tatsaditi shrimadbhagawadgeetasoopanishatsu
Brahm vidyaayaam yog-shaastre
shrikrishnaajun samvaade shraddhaatraya
vibhaag yogo naamsaptdasho'dhyaayah [17].

Thus is the Upanishad sung by the Lord, the knowledge of Brahma, the scripture on yoga the dialogue between ShriKrishna and Arjuna ends the seventeenth chapter entitled the yoga of the division of the three fold faith.

CHATER—XVIII

Arjun Uvaach :

Sannyaasasya mahaabhaaho tattvamichchaami veditum
Tyaagasya cha Hrisheekesha prithakkeshinishoodan [1].

Meaning—O mighty-armed I desire to know the essence of 'sannyaas' and also that of 'tyaag' explained separately.

Commentary—Arjun is convinced by now that 'sanyas' is quite different from 'tyaag.' But as it appears he is still confused so he wants the Lord to explain them one by one differentiating one from another.

Shri Bhagavanuvaach—

Kamyanam karmanhaam nyasam sannyasam kavayo viduh,
Sarvakarmphaltyaagam prahustyagam vichakshanhah [2].

Meaning—The Blessed Lord said :—

Some scholars say 'sannyaas' to be renunciation of actions promoted by desire, the really learned ones say 'tyaag' to be the relinquishment of the fruit of all actions.

Commentary—The Lord very much denounces 'sannyaas' in its prevalent form i.e. the renunciation of works themselves. He is in no case in favour of leaving the human-habitation and marching to the forests, therefore He says 'sannyaas' to be only the renunciation of desire-prompted actions.

As far as 'tyaag' is concerned, he refers to this by now well known 'karmyoga.' It is the relinquishment of the fruit of all actions.

Tyajyam doshavadityeke karm praahurmaeeshnhah,
Yagyadaantapah karm na tyaajyamiti chaapare [3].

Meaning—All actions are evil and as such should be relinquished say some wisemen while others maintain that actions like sacrifice, charity, penanace should not be abandoned.

Commentary—Nothing

Nishchayam shrinhu me tatra tyaage Bharatsattam
Tyaago hi Purubyaaghra trividhah samprakeertitah [4].

Meaning—O best of Bharatas, hear my own decision regarding 'tyaaga' O lion among men, relinquishment (Tyaag) is described to be of three kinds.

Commentary—Let us see what these three kinds are.

Yagyadan tapah karm na tyajyam karyameva tat,
Yagya danam tapas chaiva pavanani maneeshinhaam [5].

Meaning—Acts of sacrifice, charity and penance outgh not to be renounced rather they must be performed, for sacrife, charity, and penance purfiy the wise.

Commentary—The question which naturally arises is why the acts of sacrifice, charity and penance purify only the wise and not all. The answer is simple; the Lord has told a lot in the preceding chapter as to how to indulge in such actions—without ostentation, without pride, according to the rituals prescribed by the scriptures. Only the wise are capable of acting according to the instructions of the Lord. So they only are in a position to be purified.

Etanyapi tu karmaanhi samgam tyaktva phalaani cha,
Kartabyaaneeti me parth nishchitam matmuttamam [6].

Meaning—O son of Pritha even these actions are to be performed without attachment and without any expectation of fruit, this is My considered opinion.

Commentary—By these actions Lord means those of sacrifice, charity and penance. His 'karmyoga' gets its upper hand here also. As they are the exalted acts, so it never means that they can be performed with attachment and with an eye on fruits.

Niyatasya tu sannyaasah karmonho nopapadyate
Mohattasya parityaagastaamasah parikeertitah [7].

Meaning—Those actions which are fixed or prescribed, their renunciation is not advisable, to renounce them due to delusion is said to be 'tamas.'

Commentary—The prescribed actions are in no way to be relinquished. A man who does so is deemed to be of 'tamasic' tendency.

The question arises as to what are the prescribed actions. The answer is whatever you are indulged in, is your fixed or prescribed duty. You are bound to perform them other wise as told by the Lord you cannot maintain even your life (sharir yatraapi cha te na prasiddhyet akarmaanha (shloka 8th of chapter iii).

In chapter III this 'nitya' or prescribed action finds its reference. Readers are referred back to the commentary of the above mentioned shloka to avoid repetition.

Duhkhmityeva yatkarm kaayakleshabhayattyajet
Sa kritva rajasam tyagam naiva tyag phalam labhet [8].

Meaning—He who pretends that all action is painful and forsakes his prescribed action for fear of trouble to the flesh, he practises the 'rajas' relinquishment and does not get the fruits of renunciation.

Commentary—There are idle people who say that all actions are exhaustive and painful and set a good excuse for not to act. They of course relinquish the actions but they are not entitled to the fruit of renunciation as their relinquishment is mere 'Tamasic'.

Kaaryamityeva yat karm niyatam kriyte'rjun,
Sangam tyaktva phalam chaiva sa tyagah sattviko matah [9].

Meaning—A prescribed work, which is performed, because it has to be performed and is performed without any attachment or expectation of fruit is said to be 'sattvic.'

Commentary—'Karm-Yoga' again.

Na dvestyakushalam karm kushale naanushajjate,
Tyaagi sattvasamavishto medhaavi chhinnasansayah [10].

Meaning—The wise man who has no aversion to unpleasnt action and no attachment to pleasant action, that person with 'sattvic' mind, attains fredom from doubts and is a man of (true) renunciation.

Commentary—The emphasis is again on doing one's prescribed duty which may be good or bad, pleasant or unpleasnt. He is certainly not deluded about what to do and what not to do. His doubts are removed as he knows that whatever is his prescribed duty is to be performed.

Na hi dehbhrita shakyam tyakatum karmanhyasheshatah,
Yastu karmphaltyagi sa tyageetyabhidheeyate [11].

Meaning—As it is not possible for those having bodies to renounce actions, thus who gives up the fruit of action is said to be a render.

Commentary—It has bee said earlier also that even one's survival is impossible without action. The message is here very clear and simple. You become a renouncer without renouncing works if you just renounce the fruits of works i.e. you do not bother about the fruits.

Anishtmishtam mishram cha Trividham karmanhah phalam,
Bhawatyatyaaginaam pretya na tu sannyaasinaam kvachit [12]

Meaning—There are three kinds of fruit—welcome, unwelcome and mixed, that accrue from actions after death to unrenouncing, but not to 'sannyaasis.'

Commentary—The nature of two words here—'atyaaginaam' and 'sannyasinaam' is to be marked. Thus the 'shloka' is not actually related to 'sannyas.' It simply means that they who renounce (the fruits) do not get these results, those who do not, get them. The emphasis certainly is on karm-yoga.

Pancfhaitaani Mahaabaaho kaarnhaani nibodh me,
Sankhye kritante proktani siddyaye sarvkarmnhaam [13].

Meaning—O Mighty armed! learn of Me these five causes laid by believers in 'sankhya' for the accomplishment of all works by neutralising all actions.

Commentary—'Saankhya' as we know is that branch of philosophy which emphasizes the supremacy of knowledge. Let us see what the Lord has to pick up from it.

Adhisthaanam tatha karta karanham cha prithagvidham,
Vividhashch prithakcheshta daivam chaivaatra pamchamam. [14].

Meaning—The base (i.e. the body it self), the doer (the soul with in) and the different organs, the divergent efforts of various kinds and the fifth being the luck.

Commentary—Let us understand these five factors

which are respobsible for the accomplishment of any action. It is indeed very scientific.

i) The body is to be certainly there. It does all the running about, without it no action can be conceived.

ii) The doer is really some thing else than the body. The body may prefer to lay idle and do nothing. It is certainly the power with in called soul or spirit which propels the body to act. Once this spirit is gone after death, the body despite its shape intact, cannot perform anything.

iii) The different organs are of course important. What action can be done without eyes or hands?

iv) Next comes the efforts of different kinds. It you do not make efforts you cannot accomplish any thing. You are to meet the influential people, go to places and even to exert hard.

Shareervaamgmanobhiryatkarm praarabhate narah.
Nyaayyam va vipareetam va panchaite tasyhetavah. [15]

Meaning—Whatever action is performed by man by his body, speech and mind whether just or unjest, these are the five factors behind it.

Commentary—These five factors are responsible for all kinds of action just or unjust. Good or bad. It is thus for the doer to ensure that only commendable works are performed with the assistance of them and that too without attachment. This is the very philosophy of the Gita.

Tatraivam sati kartaaramaatmaanam kevalam tu yah,
Pashyatyakritbuddhitvaanna sa pashyati durmatih. [16]

Meaning—That being so, he who due to impure reasoning regards himself as the doer is of perverted mind and does not see (understand) at all.

Commentary—Emphasis is again on the fact that man alone is not capable of doing any thing. Even the factor of luck mentioned in the preceding shloka is worth consideration. It may be called chance or anything but it is more than once that while every thing is going farourable the aim is not achieved in the end. What can be concluded from it? The message here is clear that one must get rid of the ego that he is the master of circumstances and can perform any action he is intent upon.

Yasyanaahamkrito bhaavo buddhiryasya na lipyate,
Hatvaapi sa immamlokaanna hanti na nibadhyate [17].

Meaning—Once, who is free from the ego, whose intelligence remains unattached, even though he slays all these worlds, he does not slay, nor is bound by sin.

Commentary—Bereft of egoism and keeping himself his mind unattached to what he is doing, he can slay the people of world and really does not slay them nor he is bound by even this kind of action. This is the real 'karm yoga' of the Lord.

Gyaanam gyeyam parigyaataa trividhaa karmchodana,
Karanham karm karteti trividhah karm samgrahah [18].

Meaning—Knowledge, the objects of knowledge and the knower these three constitute the mental inspiration, the cause of actions, the action itself and the doer, these three are the constitutents of action.

Commentary—Any work is first constituted in mind. If there are no mental stimuli, there can be hardly any work. The question is how these three, knowledge, the objects of knowledge and the knower serve as mental stimuli. The explanation is simple, the knowledge is the only factor which can help you in knowing the worth knowing i.e. the object of knowledge. Without any object one can not imagine of having the knowledge of a thing which is very fascinating, useful and worthy. Thus both the knowledge and the object to be known are certainly important for the mental impulse to work. The remaining third is the knower. Who is the knower, the body does not know; the mind do. Thus mind is the knower and it is decidedly the best stimulus. It is the kingpin. Thus mind along with the rest two serves as the stimulus to work as without work there is no knowledge. Similarly there are three consittuents of work-organs of actions, work itself and the doer. This is also quite clear. It there are no organs i.e. five 'gyaanendriyaas (senses imparting knowledge like eyes, ears etc) and five 'Karmendriyas' (i.e. senses of work, i.e. hands, feet etc.) no work can be done. We have talked about them earlier also. The action or work itself is one of the constituents. If there is no work what will you perform? During the days of depression there are no works and people go without work, starve and suffer. Last but not the least without the doer no work can take shape, it cannot simply materialize. Who is the doer? This is certainly not the body. It is the self or spirit with in the body, without the latter the former is worthless. We have also dwelt at length upon these points.

Gyaanam karm cha kartaa cha tridhaiva gunhabhedatah,
Prochyate gunhasamkyane yathavachhrinhu taanyapi [19].

Meaning—Knowledge, work and the doer are said to be as the there kinds of 'gunhas' in the texts devoted to classification of gunhas, hear them as they are.

Commentary—The three kinds of gunhas—'Sattva', 'Rajas' and 'Tamas' are talked about in this as usual. The three worth knowing are :

i) Knowledge
ii) Action
iii) Doer.

Sarvbhooteshu yenaikam bhaavamavyaymeekshate,
Avibhaktam bivhakteshu tajgyanam viddhi sattvikam [20].

Meaning—That by which one imperishable being is seen in all beings, one indivisible being in all these divisions, know that knowledge to be 'Rajasic.'

Commentary—There is no doubt that body though perishable has with in it the part of the impreshable Supreme being. Similary the supreme force which is ever undivisible is being divided in all bodies (remember the simile of ocean and waves).

If one possesses this much of the knowledge, one is the possessor of 'sattvic' knowledge.

Prilthaktven tu yajgyaanam naanaabhavaanpriethagvidhaan,
Vetti sarveshu bhooteshu tajgyaanam viddhi raajasam [21].

Meaning—The Knowledge which sees different existences in different beings due to (apparent) differences, know that knowledge to be 'rajasic'.

Commentary—All beings appear separate on the face of them. He who is deluded by it and considers all of them as separate identities though in really they are not so, his knowledge is deemed to be 'raajasic'.

Yattu kritsnavadekasminkaarye saktamahaitukam,
Atattvaarthvadalpam cha tattaamasmudaahritam [22].

Meaning—That knowledge which clings to one cause as if it were the whole, which (knowledge) is devoid of reasons, of any real object and of little value is called as 'taamasic.'

Commentary—This knowledge does not prefer any important action, it gves importance to the body itself and one who thinks that the body is every thing and there is nothing beyond that and it is not dwelt in by a part of the supreme being, possesses 'tamasic' knowledge.

Niyatam samgrahitamaraagdveshatah kritam,
Aphalprepsunaa karm yattsaattvikamuchyate [23].

Meaning—That action which is prescribed as duty and which is performed without attachment, without liking or disliking, by the undesirous of fruit, is said to be 'saattvic.'

Commentary—This is real 'karmyog' which has been abudantly expalained in the preceding pages.

Yattu kamepsuna karm saahamkaarenha va punah,
Kriyate bahulaayaasam tadrajasamudaahritam [24].

Meaning—The action which is here driven by desire, is prompted by egoism and involves much strain is said to be 'rajas'.

Commantary—Desire and egoism have always been condemned by the Lord. It has also been declared that even penance which means unnecessary pain to body and consequently to the soul is not desirable. Here it is clearly maintained that the action which demands much of strain is only but 'raajasic'.

Anubandham kshayam hinsamanvekshya cha paurusham,
Mohaadaarabhyate karm yatttattaamasmuchyate [25].

Meaning—The action undertaken under delusion (devoid of understanding) without an eye on the result, loss, voilence and without regard to the capacity is declared to be 'taamasic.'

Commentary—The people of 'taamasic' tendency plunge in to any action without caring for the loss and viloence it may cause to them or to others.

It implies that before undertaking any action one must assess his strength, must guess about the outcome and see to it that it is not unnecessarily strenuous and is not capable of harming the doer himself and others as well.

Muktasamgo'nahmvaadi dhrityutsaahsamanvitah,
Sidhyasidhyornirvikaarah karta saattvik uchayate [26].

Meaning—That doer is deemd to be 'sattvic' who is free from attachmnent and ego and is full of patience as well as enthusiasm and unaffected by success and failure.

Commentary—Needs no elaboration. All of the points discussed earlier.

Raageekarmphalprepsurlubdho hinsaatmako'shuchih,
Harshshokaanvitah kartaa raajasah parikeertitah, [27].

Meaning—Attached, desirious of fruits, greedy, given to violence, impure, affected by plesure and pain, the doer is said to be of 'rajasic' nature.

Commentary—Not needed.

Ayuktah praakritah stabdhah shatho naishkritiko'lasah,
Vishadee Deerghsootri cha kartaa taamas Uchyate [28].

Meaning—Not united (with the self), vulgar, arrogant, deceitful, inclined to humiliate other, lazy, slothful, despondent and procrastinating, the doer is called taamasic.

Commentary—Not needed.

Buddherbhedam dhriteshchaiva gunhatastrividham shrinhu,
Prochyamanamasheshenha prithaktven Dhananjaya [29].

Meaning—O Dhananjaya! reason as also patience are of three kinds depending upon the qualities, hear them as described fully and severally.

Commentary—Reason and patience as depending on the three modes (or gunhas) are also of three kinds, hear them one by one and and also in totality.

Pravrtim cha nivrtim cha kaaryaakaarye bhayaabhaye,
Bandam moksham cha ya vetti buddhih sa parth saattviki [30].

Meaning—O son of Pritha, the reason which knows what is faith and what is opposite. Of what is to be done what is not to be done, what is fear and what is absence of fear, what is bondage and what is liberation, is 'saattvic.'

Commentary—This verse of the Gita is one of the best and it contains in itself the very essence of the Lord's message. His real 'Karmyog.'

The words 'pravriti' and 'nivriti' have been subjected to different interpretations. Some have called them right action and right cessation of action or abstention of action. Others have called them indulgence in faith and non indulgence in faith. We have subscribed to the latter.

There are two factors which support our stand. 'Pravriti' has often been used in connection with faith or in other word religion. One is reminded of a famous line of Sanskrit 'Jaanaami Dharmam na che me 'Pravritim.' "I Know the religion but I am not inclined towards it".

The second and most important point of support is contained in the very first words of the next verse. It starts with religion (Faith) and the opposite of it. This certainly makes evident what the Lord is dwelling on the start of both these verses. Moreover action and cessation of action are taken care of in the very following word—'Karyaakarya' thus if we approve of the first interpretation then we shall have to approve of the repetition which does not appear just especially when the words are attributed to the Lord Himself.

Yayaa dharmamadharmam cha karyam chaakaryameva cha,
Ayathaavatprajanaati buddhih saa Parth Raajasi [31].

Meaning—O Parth! The reason by which one does not correctly discern what is faith and what is opposite of it, what is worth doing and what is not worth doing, that is 'rajasic' (in nature).

Commentary—No need.

Adharmam dharmmiti ya manyatc tamasaavrita
Sarvarthaanvipreetanshch buddhih sa Parth 'taamsee' [32].

Meaning—O Parth, the reason enveloped in darkness (of ignorance) regards irreligion as religion and see all things contrary to what they mean is 'taamasic.'

Commentary—A man full of 'Tamas' cannot differentiate between right and wrong (faith and absence of it), rather consideres right to be worng and is so deluded that takes contrary view of every thing, the poor fellow is full of 'tamas.'

He is very certainly apt to consider a foe as a friend and a friend as a foe.

Dhritya yaya dharyate manah pranhen driyakriyaah,
Yogenavyabhicharinhya dhritih, sa Parth 'sattviki' **[33].**

Meaning—The patience by which through uncorrupt yoga one controls the activities of the mind, life-breaths and senses, that patience is called 'saattvic.'

Commentary—As promised earlier, Lord returns to patience again. Patience is of utmost importance in the field of faith, rather in the life itself. You are ship without radar, when you lack in patience. Here the Lord talks of 'sattvic' patience by which one controls the activities of mind, breaths and senses. Mind as we know is very unsteady, breaths are also like that, their proper regulation is necessary, nothing to talk about the escapades of senses. One requires patience to control all these three and such patience is termed as 'Saattvic.'

Yayaa tu dharmkaamaarthaandhritya dhaarayate'rjun,
Prasamgen phalaakankshi dhritih saa Parth raajasi **[34].**

Meaning—O Parth, the patience by which one (due to attachments to wordly pleasures) and desire of fruits (of action) sticks to faith, wealth and sensual enjoyment, is called 'raajasi'.

Commentary—Dharm (Faith) Arth (Weath) and 'kaam' (sex) these are called 'purushaarth' (the worth endeavouring aims) in sanskrit. The men of 'raajasic' nature try to obtain and enjoy with wherever in their powers.

The weath and sex have not been very much relegated in original Hindu philosophy, the religion is rather considered capable of providing the rest two. This is confirmed, by a very famous statement of Vyas in Mahaabhaarat.

Oordhva baahuviraumesha na kaschi shrinotimam
Dharmaadarthashch kamashch sa dharmam kim na sevyate.'

I declare by raising my hand that faith (religion) is in the root of wealth as well as sex so why this religion is not adhered to.

By sex one must not understand rampant and uncontrolled and unjustified sexual indulgence. But it is not at all a deplorable thing if indulged in justifiably. Even. the Lord declares in this very Gita that I am the sex which is not against religion (i.e. religious sanctions)—'Dharmaviruddho bhooteshu kamo'smi Bharatarshabh (vii-ii).

Yayaa svapnam bhayam shokam vishaadam madmeva cha,
Na vimunchati durmedhaa dhritih sa Parth 'tamasi' [35].

Meaning—O Parth, that patience by which a dolt does not abandon sleep, fear, grief, despondence and also arrogance, is 'taamasic.'

Commentary—The undesirable faculties enumerated above are worth abandoning.

Sukham tvidanim trividham shrinhu me Bhartarshabha,
Abhyasaadramate yatra duhkhantam cha nigachhati [36].

Meaning—Hear from Me O great of of Bharatas the three kinds of enjoyment one obtains through practice and puts an end to pain (is saatvic).

Commentary—The word practice here is important. This practice certainly refers to practice of faith, chanting of names, charity, worship, prayer etc. Such parctice of course is capable of generating pleasure and such practice alone can put an end to pains.

Yatdagre vishmiva parinhaame'mritopamam,
Tatsukham saattvikam roktamaatmbuddhiprasaadajam [37].

Meaning—Which at first is as poison but in the end is like nectar that pleasure is said to be 'saatvic' and received as the gift of the knowledge of God.

Commentary—The real pleasure is certainly which is born of soul, the very representative of the supreme residing in every being. This supreme is nothing but pleasure itself. The scripture has rightly maintained 'Raso vaih sah' he is the pleasure-incarnate.

This pleasure is certainly as nectar. This can be testified by them only who have realized the bliss of soul. There is how much pleasure in meditating, in worshipping, in serving the poor and diseased. But why this pleasure is like poison in the beginning? Because it is very difficult in the beginning to control the mind and senses, who consider the real pleasure to be the be all and end all of life and regard other pleasures as useless, nothing better them poison which mars the real pleasure, they are to be supposed really enjoying.

Vishayendriyasamyogadyattadafre'mritopam,
Parinhame vishamiva tatsukham raajasam smritam [38].

Meaning—That pleasure which is derived from the contact of the senses with their objects, which appears first as nectar, but in the end is like poison is known as 'raajasic.'

Commentary—This is the real description of sexual pleasures. This verse is an unpleasant statement of a hard reality. The beauty of woman to take a simple example, appears to be nothing less them nectar in the beginning. One even falls in what is erroneously called love. Love is something very pure and has got little to do with lust. The end result is often well known. One is either deserted and greives all over his life or finds himself in differnt kind of troubles better imagined then narrated. What is it if not like nectar in the beginning and like poison in the end if some of the young men and women first enjoy sensually and in many cases even end their life (if not both at least one of them) due to frustration, deceit, social disapproval and many a time of unwelcome conceptions?

This verse may serve as a deterent especially to the wayward modern generation.

Yadagre chaanubandhe cha sukham mohanamaatmanah,
Nidralasyapramaadottham tattaamasmudahritam [39].

Meaning—The pleasure that deludes the soul both in the beginning and in the end and that which is derived from sleep, indolence and negligence, is called 'taamas.'

Commentary—There are of course pleasures which delude the mind as well as soul. Drinking or durg-taking may be taken as an example. The drug-takers' pathetic conditions need not be mentioned. They are never happy neither while taking the drugs nor after it. They take to drugs because they cannot live without them. They are restless and their mind and soul are always deluded, body always tortured. Where is the pleasure then? And to defile the soul as stated earlier is the grçatest crime, man commits on himself. Neither the Gita nor the Upanishads lag behind in condemning this act.

Some one derives pleasure from sleep, they can go on sleeping for any length of time. They arise only to eat and again they slip in to the sleep. They are legendary, Kumbhakarna, who used to sleep for six months continuously.

The pleasure derived from sleep is of ourse deluding to the soul as it allows the sleeper to do nothing to uplift it. Similar is the case of indolent and negligent people. They derive pleasure in doing nothing and nothing is accomplished by them in any field including spiritual. Their spirit is dead, their soul deluded. This pleasure is deceptive, it is simply delusion.

Na tadasti prethivyaam vaa divi deveshu va punah,
Sattvam prakrtijairmuktam yadebhihsyaattribhirgunhaiha [40].

Meaning—There is no entity either on the earth or in the heavens or among the gods which is free from these three modes (gunhaas) of nature.

Commentary—This is vary important as man cannot be conceived of only physical body with blood, flesh and bones. So no one either in this world or others can be without three gunhaas. It is different that in some 'Sattva' is prominent, in some 'rajas' and in some 'tamas.' Most of them possess an equally proportioned quantity of all these three.

Whatever has been said about gods is equally true. Even the 'gods' have been seen slipping due to predominance of 'tamas', some times in their life. The story of 'Ahlya' is very much known. She was unnkowingly subjected to the lust of 'Indra' the king of the gods who soiled her taking the form of her husband and the poor lady was turned in to stone due to the anger of rishi Gautama who thought her to be equally guilty.

Braahmanhakshatriyavisham shoodranham cha parantap,
karmaanhi pravibhaktaani svabhaavaprabhavairgunhaih [41].

Meaning—O Arjùn! The work of Brahmins, kshatriyas vaishyas and shoodras are divided according to the modes (gunhaas) born of their own inner nature.

Commentary—The castesystom prevalent in India was

not so previously as it is to day. It was never based on birth. It is made abundantly clear in these lines that the people of different 'castes' used to get their works on the basis of qualities (or 'guanhas') they possessed.

This is not for the first time that the Lord is emphasizing it. He maintained in shloka 13 of chapter IV that the castes were created by Himself, based on works and 'gunhas' of the peoples **(Chaturvarnam maya sristhtam gunha karma vibhaagashah).**

Shamo damastapah shaucham kshaantiraarjavameva cha,
Gyanam vigyanamaastikyam Brahmkarn svabhavajam [42].

Meaning—Calm, self-control, purity, tolerance, simplicity, and knowledge, super knowledge (regarding the soul and the supreme being) belief in God are the works of Brahmans born of (his) nature.

Commentary—These are the 'sattvic' 'Gunhas' and who have them in their very nature are Brahmans despite their birth and background).

Shauryam, tejo dhrtirdakhsyam yuddhe chapyapalayanam,
Danmeesvarbhaavashch kshaatram karm svabhavajam [43].

Meaning—Heriosm, majesty, patience, ability, not fleeing from the battle, charity, lordship are the duty of kshatriya born of (his) nature.

Commentary—These are the 'rajasic' tendencies and whoever possessing them, is a kshatriya. There is also a hint here by the Lord to Arjun that he must not desist from battle as he is a 'kshatriya.'

Krishigauraksyavanhijyam vaishya karm svabhavajam,
Paricharyatmakam karm shoodrasyapi svabhavajam [44].

Meaning—Agriculture, protection of cows, trade are the natural works of 'Vaishya' due to his born nature; service (to others) is the work of 'shoodra' owing to his own nature.

Commentary—These duties are based on 'taamasic' 'gunhaas'

Sve sve karmanhyabhiratah samsidhim labhate narah,
Svakarmniratah siddhim yatha vindati tacshrinhu [45].

Meaning—Men intent on their different natural works attain perfection. Listen how perfection is attained by him who is intent on the work born of his nature.

Commentary—This verse is very significant and it under lines the importance of work which is the essence of the Lord's 'karmyoga.' This is asserting that one by only attending to one's duty is capable of attaining perfection. No penance, no austerity, no knowledge mundane or spiritual, nothing of the kind.

It has been maintaind that persons like king 'Janak' (who came to be known as 'Rajarshi' seer among kings) attained perfection by only performing wholeheartedly their duties.

Yatah pravrittirbhootaanaam yen sarvamidam tatam,
Svakaramanha tamabhyarchya siddhim vindati manavah [46].

Meaning—He from whom all beings originate, by Whom all this is pervaded, by worshipping Him by his own duty, man attains perfection.

Commentary—The term 'yen sarvamidam tattam' has often been used in the Gita. It simply implies that the Lord is all pervading, all permeating. The Lord again insists on his new founded theory that by worshipping Him just by performing his duty (deveotedly) man is capable of attaining freedom.

This verse is just the extension of the former one.

Shreyaansvadharmo vigunhah pardharmatsvanushthitat,
Svabhaav niyatam karm kurvannapnoti kilvisham [47].

Meaning—One's work though in itself faulty is better than another's duty well wrought out. He who performs duty decided according to his nature never incurs sin.

Commentary—The word Dharm has been erroneously taken to be as religion by many commentators. Dharm more often than not means duty as for example the 'Dharm' of fire is to burn, the water to drench. This has been indicated earlier also.

The Lord decries the nature of men to think the pasture on the other sied of fence to be greener. Every one must be satisfied with the work he has got to do and perform it without grudge. In reality what happens is one thinks his job inferior to that of another. A doctor thinks that an engineer is better and an engineer thinks that the doctor is better-placed.

This creates unecessary tension and restlessness and the

main purpose of the Gita is to free the mankind from all kinds of tension and make his life peaceful. Thus even if one's work is really inferior to another, he should be satisfied with it and perform it with all abilities at his command. This fact has partly been dealt wilh in a previous shloka also.

Sahajam karm kaunteya sadoshmapi na tyajet,
Sarvarmabha hi doshen dhoomenaagnirivavritah [48]

Meaning—The work easily (and naturally) allotted to one should not be abandoned even if it is defective. All actions indeed are clouded by defects as fire by smoke.

Commentary—Emphasis on one's own alloted duty continues. All actions are to more or less extent full of defects as fire is never without sumke so why to worry about one's work and be tempted by others?

Asaktbuddhih sarvatra jitaatma vigatsprihah,
Naishkarmyasiddhim parmaam sannyaasenaadhigachchhati [49].

Meaning—He whose mind is unattached in all cases, has self control and is empty of desire, he attains through 'sannyas' (renunciation) the highest perfection born of actionlessness.

Commentary—The subject registers a change and the Lord switches over to the description of perfection through other means also. So long he was concentrating on one's allotted duties, now he goes on to dwell on more intricate subjects.

The theory of non-attachment and of being desireless is nothing novel in it, what is important is that the Lord, tells that by 'sannyas' one reaches the supreme perfection obtainable through actionlessness, it means that the importance of renunciation of works also finds place in his scheme of works. Let us wait for his further assertions.

Siddlim praapto yathaa Brahm tathaapnoti nibodh me,
Samaasenaiva kaunteya nishtha gyaanasya ya para [50].

Meaning—O son of Kunti, hear from Me in brief how having attained this perfection, one thus attains to Brahm, which is the supreme state of knowledge.

Commentary—Perfection leads to Brahma which is the perfection of knowledge.

Buddhya vishudhyayukto dhrityatmaanam niyamya cha,
Shabdaadeenvishayanstyaktva ragdveshau vyudasya cha [51].
Vivikthsevi ladhvaasi yatvakkayamaanashah.
Dhyanyogparo nityamvairagyam samupaashritah [52].
Ahamkarm balam darpam kamam krodham parighraham,
Vimuchya mirmamah shanto Brahmbhooyaya kalpate [53].

Meaning—United with the purified intelligence, conrolling oneself through persistent efforts, having renounced sound and other objects of the sense withdrawing from all likings and dislikings, living in solitude, partaking very little food, having conrolled speech and mind, constantly absorbed in yoga of meditation, given to renouncement, having put away egoism, strength (that harms others), arrogance, sex, anger and instrument of possession, free from compassion, such a calm man becomes; fit to become the Brahma.

Commentary—All these qualifications have been enumerated in more or less details earlier. One possessing all of them to-gether becomes nothing less than Brhama.

Brahmbhootah prasannaatma na shochati na kankshati
Samah sarveshu bhooteshu madbhaktim labhate paraam [54].

Meaning—Having become one with the Brahma (the Supreme and etenal being) and happy with in the self, he neither grives nor long for anything. Equal to all beings, he obtains my supreme devotion.

Commentary—Conditions to his devotion mentioned. They have been emphasized earlier also. The emphasis on equality is the very essence of 'karmyoga.' It has already been stated, as mentioned earlier also, that according to the 'Gita' 'equality is yoga' (Samatvam yog Uchyate—shloka 48 Chapter II).

Perhaps being infuleuced by this statement the scriptures rightly observed :

"Praanhah yathaatmaano abheeshta Bhotaanaamapi te tatha, atmaupamyen bhoteshu yah pashyati sa pashyati."

—As our life is dear to us so the life of all beings are dear to them. One who sees other beings as compared to himself, he really sees.

Bhaktya mamabhijaanaati yavanyashchasmi tattvatah,

Tato mam tattvato gyaatva vishate tadanantaram [55].

Meaning—Through devotion he comes to know Me, how and what I am and having known Me in essence, he enters Him (the supreme Being).

Commentary—Not needed.

Sarvakarmaanhyapi sadaa kurvanho madvyapashrayah,
Matprasadadavapnoti shashvatam padamavyayam [56].

Meaning—By doing actions also, always having taken refuge in me, he attains through my grace the eternal and imperishable status.

Commentary—The emphasis is again on actions with devotion. As already maintained earlier by actions alone, according, to the Lord, one is capable of attaining perfection.

Chetasa sarvakarmaanhi mayi sannyasya matparah,
Budhi yogamupashritya machchittah statam bhav [57].

Meaning—Surrendering all actions to Me through cautious effort and depending fully on Me and resorting to yoga he is always one in consciousness with Me.

Commentary—The yoga propounded in the Gita is really 'Buddhi-yoga', the yoga of intelligence. This new concept of yoga is explained in chapter II itself. Readers are referrad back to it for full comprehension, for immediate consumption it may be told that according to this 'yoga' the intelligence is to be trained and applied in such a way that one performs all actions without attachment. It is why the Lord says that yoga is nothing but the real skill to perform (Yogah karmshu kaushalam (the Gita 50-II).

Machhittah sarvadurgaanhi matprasaadaattarishyasi,
Ath chevamahamkaraanna shroshyasi vinamkshyasi [58].

Meaning—If you are one in consciousness with Me, You shall pass through all difficulties (all perilous passages) but if you due to egoism will not listen to Me then you will be perished.

Yadahamkaarmaashritya na yostya eti manyase,
Mithyaisha vyavasaayaste prakritstvam niyo kshyati [59].

Meaning—If owing to egoism you think that you wil not fight, vain is your resolve, nature will engage you (in the act of fighting).

Commentary—Ego has been constantly decried by the Lord.

Once again the point is being emphasized that we do not do any thing, the forces and modes of the nature are performing every thing. This point has been referred to in the commentaries of many a preceding verse.

Svabhaavajen kaunteya nibaddhah sven karmanhaa,
Kartunechchasi yanmohaatkarishyasyavasho'pi tat [60].

Meaning—O son of Kunti that which from delusion you do not desire to do, that bound by your own duty born of your nature you will helplessly do.

Commentary—The Lord in this chapter is now endeavouring to come to his main purpose that is to prepare Arjun to fight.

Eshvarah sarvabhootaanaam hariddeshe'rjun tishthati
Bhraamayan sarvabhootani yantraroodhani maayaya [61].

Meaning—God, O Arjun is seated in the heart of the beings, revolving all beings through his illusive power as if they are mounted upon a (revolving) machine.

Commentary—The fact that God dwells in the heart of every being is very clearly stated in the very first hymn of Eshaavaasyopanishad—**'Eshaavaasyamidam sarvam yatkimchitjagatyaam jagat (Esa (1.1)** God dwells in every thing existing in this world. It has been quoted by us before also.

So for as revolving the being mounted on a machine is concerned it refers to their different endevavours and efforts which are really the product of the nature as empshsised many a time earlier. It also indicates that such machines were available in India even five thousand years back.

Tameva Sharaanaham gachchh sarv bhaaven bhaarat
Tatprasadatparam shantim sthanam praapsyasi shashwatam [62].

Meaning—O Bharat! take refuge in Him in all ways. By His grace you shall obtain supreme peace and the eternal abode (after this life).

Commentary—It is easy to take refuge in One Who is very much with in you. Recognize it and surrender to it. It grants both, the supreme peace and the eternal status.

Eti te gyaanamaakhyaatam guhyaadguhyataram maya, Vimrishyaitadasheshenha yathechchasi tathaa kuru [63]

Meaning—Thus I have expounded to you knowledge more secret than secrecy itself. Having reflected on it fully do as you wish.

Commentary—Nothing special.

Sarvguhyatamam bhooyah shrinhu Me paraman vachah, Eshto'si me dridhamiti tato vakshyaami te hitam [64]

Meaning—Further hear My supreme word, the most secret of all. You are my unwavering dearest, therefore, I shall tell which is conducive to you.

Commentary—Let us await the secret.

Manmana bhava madhakto madyaji maam namaskuru, Mamevaishyasi satyam te pratijano priyosi me [65]

Meaning—Your mind is to be full of Me, you are to be My devotee, you should worship Me, bow before Me, then you shall come to Me. This is My true promise to you as you are dear to Me.

Commentary—Full devotion to Lord Krishna with one-pointed love, this is the secret. This leads to Him. More important is the pledge made by Him. Any one with his mind only on Him and who is fully devoted to Him, is bound to mingle with Him ultimately.

Commentary—One is again reminded of a pledge made in sloka 22 of chapter ix.

Sarvdharmaan parityajya maamekam sharanam vraj Aham tvaam sarvapapebhyo mokshyishyami ma suchah [66]

Meaning—Abondaning all Dharmas, take refuge in Me, I will deliver you from all sins, do not grieve.

Commentary—'Dharm' here really means religion or faith. The Lord is asking Arjun to abandon all other religions and come to Him. In other words to adopt Krishna-dharm that was gradually known as Narayani Dharma. The Lord again promises that who comes under His shelter, his all sins are removed. It is just like Christ. Christ was born and crucified to take away the sins of others.

The fact that one is relieved of all griefs has been emphasized in upanishadas also.

"Tatra ko mohah kah shokah ekatvamanupashyatah" (Eshavaasyopanishad)

—Where is the grief and delusion once you are with him.

Idam te naatapaskaay naabhaktaay kadaachan,
Na chashushrooshave vachyam na cha maam yo'bhyasooyati [67]

Meaning—Never is this to be spoken to one without askesis, nor to one who is not devotee (of the Lord), not even to him who is not willing to hear, nor again to him who belittles Me.

Commentary—The message of the Gita is about to end, the Lord has imparted it to Arjun, now he cautions him to not let it be known to them who are not deserving. Such people have been indentified by Him.

One important factor is that He warns him not to impart this knowledge to them also who despise Him or speak against Him.

It is not that Lord has any hatred against them, it is because they will simply not believe it. The Lord is aware that there are people who speak against Him, who are non-believers.

Ya emam paramam guhyam
madbhakteshvabhidhaashyati
Bhaktim mayi paraam kritvaa
mamevaisyatyasamsayah, [68]

Meaning—He who will impart this most secret teaching of mine to my devotees, he having thus indulged in supreme devotion of Mine will undoubtedly come to Me.

Commentary—This verse is very important including the following one. The dearest to Lord is that person and he is the real devotee of His who spreads His message among His devotees.

Na cha tasmanmanushyeshu kashchinme priyakritamah,
Bhavita na cha me tasmaadanyah priyataro bhuvi [69]

Meaning—And there is none among men who does Me a more loving service than he; and there will be none else dearer to Me on this earth.

Commentary—The point is to be pondered over, forget

all 'yoga', 'sannyas', and devotion. Engage yourself only in propagating the message conveyed by the Lord among His devotees and you're the dearest to Him.

So, one must do whatever is with in one's power to spread the message of the Gita far and wide. It can be done in divergent ways :

(i) By distributing the book freely
(ii) By preaching on it; by quoting it.
(iii) By printing the copies of it even for considerations.
(iv) By writing books on it.
(v) By translating it in to as many languages as possible
(vi) By preparing its tapes and so an.

Adhyeshate cha ya eman dharmyam samvadamaavayoh, Gyanyagyen tenaahamishtah syaamitit Me matih [70]

Meaning—And he who shall study this religious dialogue of ours. By him I shall be worshipped through gyanyagyam (yagya devoted to knowledge). This is my view.

Commentary—Coming from propagating the message of the Gita, one that studies it, is also the worshipper of the Lord, he may not have to take recourse to other forms of worship.

Shraddhaavaananasooyashcha shrinhuyaadapi yo narah, So'pi muktah shubhaamllokaanpraapnuyaatpunhyakarmnhaam [71]

Meaning—Also man who full of faith and uncaring, listens to it is liberated and attains to the pleasing worlds of the righteous.

Commentary—Not only preaching of the Gita, not only studying it but also listening to it with faith gurantees the supreme place to the men.

The practice of reading the Gita to the dying people, perhaps, is based on this 'shloka.'

kachchidetshchrutam Parth tvaikaagrenha chetasa, Kachidagyaansammohah pranashtaste Dhananjaya. [72]

Meaning—O son of Kunti has this been heard by you with concentrated mind, has your delusion cuased by ignorance been dispelled of?

Commentary—The entire message of the Gita was delivered to prepare Arjun for battle, who deluded by ignorance had relinquished his weapon and declared not to fight.

After lecturing to him on various aspects of life and plilosophy, the Lord naturally wants to know if his bewildered disciple could listen to his lectures attentively and whether his delusion is gone. In other words whether he is ready to fight now.

Arjun Uvaach

Nashto mohah smirtirlabdhva tvatprasaadanmayaachut,
Sthito'smi gatsamdehah karishye vachanam tava. [73]

Meaning—Arjun Said, Achyut my delusion stand destroyed, I have gained widsom through your grace, I stand free from doubts, I shall therefore, obey your words.

Commentary—Arjun admits that knowledge he gained through the lectures of his God-charioteer, has dispelled his all doubts and he is ready to carry out his bidding.

Sanjaya Uvaach

etyaham Vasudevasya Paarthasya cha mahaatmanah,
Samvadamimamashraushamadbhutam romharshanham [74]

Meaning—Sanjay said—Thus I heard this wonderful discourse of Vasudeva and of high souled Arjuna causing my hairs to stand on end.

Commentary—Sanjay testifies to the standard of the dialogue between the Lord and Arjuna which is nothing but the Gita itself.

Vyasprasaadachchrutavanetadguhyamaham param
Yogam yogesvaratkrishnatsakshatkathayatah svayam [75]

Meaning—Through the grace of Vyasa I heard this supreme secret yoga directly from Krishna the Master of yoga, who delivered it Himself.

Commentary—Sanjaya is naturally overwhelmed that he heard the principles of yoga enunciated by the Master of yoga Himself, i.e. the Lord Krishna.

The grace of Vyas is being given its due by Him as it was the former, who supplied Sanjaya with divine power to see and naturally hear what was going on in the battlefield of kurukshetra.

Raajan samsmritya samsamritya samvaadamimadbhutam
Keshavarjunayoh punhyam hrishyaami cha muhurmuhuh [76]

Meaning—O king rememhering again and again this wonderful and sacred dialouge between Keshava (Krishna) and Arjuna, I become overwhelmed again and again.

Commentary—The dialogue is capable of creating constant pleasure and joy which makes Sanjay rejoice again and again.

Tachcha sansmritya sansmritya roopamadyadbhutam Hareh,
Vismayo me maha rajan hrishyami cha punah, punah **[77]**

Meaning—O king recollecting again and again also of that most wonderful form of Hari (Krishna) I am greatly wonder-struck and I rejoice again and again.

Commentary—No less important than the Gita is the Virat-roop, of Shrikrishna

Yatra yogesvaro Krishnho yatra Partho Dhanurdharah,
Tatra shrirvijayo bhootirdhruvaa neetirmatirmam **[78]**

Meaning—Wherever is Krishna the Lord of yoga and wherever is Arjuna, the archer (the wielder of the Gandeeva bow) assured are there; glory, victory, prosperity and there is also the overriding law of right, this is may view.

Commentary—This shloka is not ordinary. It says indirectly that where there is Lord Krishna to guide one who is prepared with all means at his command to fight through the battle of life, he is bound to come out victorious.

Om tatsaditi srimadbhagavadgeetaasoopanishatsu Brahm vidyaayaam yogshashtre shrikrishnarjun samvaade moksh sannyaas yogo mamashtadasho'dhyaayah [79]

Thus in the upanishad sung by the Lord, the knowledge of Brahma, the scripture on yoga, the dialogue between Shrikrishna and Arjuna ends the eighteenth chapter entitled the yoga of liberation through the path of knowledge and self-surrender.

The Gita—Original

ॐ श्री परमात्मने नमः

अथ श्रीमद्भगवद्गीता

अथ प्रथमोऽध्यायः

धृतराष्ट्र उवाच

धर्मक्षेत्रे कुरुक्षेत्रे समवेता युयुत्सवः।
मामकाः पाण्डवाश्चैव किमकुर्वत संजय ॥1॥

संजय उवाच

दृष्ट्वा तु पाण्डवानीकं व्यूढं दुर्योधनस्तदा।
आचार्यमुपसङ्गम्य राजा वचनमब्रवीत् ॥2॥
पश्यैतां पाण्डुपुत्राणामाचार्य महतीं चमूम्।
व्यूढां द्रुपदपुत्रेण तव शिष्येण धीमता ॥3॥
अत्र शूरा महेष्वासा भीमार्जुनसमा युधि।
युयुधानो विराटश्च द्रुपदश्च महारथः ॥4॥
धृष्टकेतुश्चेकितानः काशिराजश्च वीर्यवान्।
पुरुजित्कुन्तिभोजश्च शैब्यश्च नरपुङ्गवः ॥5॥
युधामन्युश्च विक्रान्त उत्तमौजाश्च वीर्यवान्।
सौभद्रो द्रौपदेयाश्च सर्व एव महारथाः ॥6॥
अस्माकं तु विशिष्टा ये तान्निबोध द्विजोत्तम।
नायका मम सैन्यस्य संज्ञार्थं तान्ब्रवीमि ते ॥7॥
भवान्भीष्मश्च कर्णश्च कृपश्च समितिंजयः।
अश्वत्थामा विकर्णश्च सौमदत्तिस्तथैव च ॥8॥

अन्ये च बहवः शूरा मदर्थे त्यक्तजीविताः।
नानाशस्त्रप्रहरणाः सर्वे युद्धविशारदाः ॥9॥
अपर्याप्तं तदस्माकं बलं भीष्माभिरक्षितम्।
पर्याप्तंत्विदमेतेषां बलं भीमाभिरक्षितम् ॥10॥
अयनेषु च सर्वेषु यथाभागमवस्थिताः।
भीष्ममेवाभिरक्षन्तु भवन्तः सर्व एव हि ॥11॥
तस्य संजनयन्हर्षं कुरुवृद्धः पितामहः।
सिंहनादं विनद्योच्चैः शङ्खंदध्मौ प्रतापवान् ॥12॥
ततः शङ्खाश्च भेर्यश्च पणवानकगोमुखाः।
सहसैवाभ्यहन्यन्त स शबदस्तुमुलोऽभवत् ॥13॥
ततः श्वेतैर्हयैर्युक्ते महति स्यन्दने स्थितौ।
माधवः पाण्डवश्चैव दिव्यौ शङ्खौ प्रदध्मतुः ॥14॥
पाञ्चजन्यं हृषीकेशो देवदत्तं धनंजयः।
पौण्ड्रं दध्मौ महाशङ्खं भीमकर्मा वृकोदरः ॥15॥
अनन्तविजयं राजा कुन्तीपुत्रो युधिष्ठिरः।
नकुलः सहदेवश्च सुघोषमणिपुष्पकौ ॥16॥
काश्यश्च परमेष्वासः शिखण्डी च महारथः।
धृष्टद्युम्नो विराटश्च सात्यकिश्चापराजितः ॥17॥
द्रुपदो द्रौपदेयाश्च सर्वशः पृथिवीपते।
सौभद्रश्च महाबाहुः शङ्खान्दध्मुः पृथक्पृथक् ॥18॥
स घोषो धार्तराष्ट्राणां हृदयानि व्यदारयत्।
नभश्च पृथिवीं चैव तुमुलो व्यनुनादयन् ॥19॥
अथव्यवस्थितान्दृष्ट्वा धार्तराष्ट्रान् कपिध्वजः।
प्रवृत्ते शस्त्रसंपाते धनुरुद्यम्य पाण्डवः ॥20॥

अर्जुन उवाच

हृषीकेशं तदा वाक्यमिदमाह महीपते।
सेनयोरुभयोर्मध्ये रथं स्थापय मेऽच्युत ॥21॥
यावदेतान्निरीक्षेऽहं योद्धुकामानवस्थितान्।
कैर्मया सह योद्धव्यमस्मिन्रणसमुद्यमे ॥22॥

योत्स्यमानानवेक्षेऽहं य एतेऽत्र समागताः।
धार्तराष्ट्रस्य दुर्बुद्धेर्युद्धे प्रियचिकीर्षवः ॥23॥

संजय उवाच

सवमुक्तो हृषीकेशो गुडाकेशेन भारत।
सेनयोरुभयोर्मध्ये स्थापयित्वा रथोत्तमम् ॥24॥
भीष्मद्रोणप्रमुखतः सर्वेषां च महीक्षिताम्।
उवाच पार्थ पश्यैतान्समवेतान्कुरूनिति ॥25॥
तत्रापश्यत्स्थितान्पार्थः पितॄनथ पितामहान्।
आचार्यान्मातुलान्भ्रातॄन्पुत्रान्पौत्रान्सखींस्तथा ॥26॥
श्वशुरान्सुहृदश्चैव सेनयोरुभयोरपि।
तान्समीक्ष्य स कौन्तेयः सर्वान्बन्धूनवस्थितान् ॥27॥

अर्जुन उवाच

कृपया परयाविष्टो विषीदन्निदमब्रवीत्।
दृष्ट्वेमं स्वजनं कृष्ण युयुत्सुं समुपस्थितम् ॥28॥
सीदन्ति मम गात्राणि मुखं च परिशुष्यति।
वेपथुश्च शरीरे मे रोमहर्षश्च जायते ॥29॥
गाण्डीवं स्रंसते हस्तात्त्वक्चैव परिदह्यते।
न च शक्नोम्यवस्थातुं भ्रमतीव च मे मनः ॥30॥
निमित्तानि च पश्यामि विपरीतानि केशव।
न च श्रेयोऽनुपश्यामि हत्वा स्वजनमाहवे ॥31॥
न काङ्क्षे विजयं कृष्ण न च राज्यं सुखानि च।
किं नो राज्येन गोविन्द किं भोगैर्जीवितेन वा ॥32॥
येषामर्थेकाङ्क्षितं नो राज्यं भोगाः सुखानि च।
त इमेऽवस्थिता युद्धे प्राणांस्त्यक्त्वा धनानि च ॥33॥
आचार्याः पितरः पुत्रास्तथैव च पितामहाः।
मातुलाः श्वशुराः पौत्राः श्यालाः सम्बन्धिनस्तथा ॥34॥
एतान्न हन्तुमिच्छामि घ्नतोऽपि मधुसूदन।
अपि त्रैलोक्यराज्यस्य हेतोः किं नु महीकृते ॥35॥
निहत्य धार्तराष्ट्रान्नः का प्रीतिः स्याज्जनार्दन।
पापमेवाश्रयेदस्मान्हत्वैतानाततायिनः ॥36॥

तस्मान्नार्हा वयं हन्तुं धार्तराष्ट्रान्स्वबान्धवान्।
स्वजनं हि कथं हत्वा सुखिनः स्याम माधव ॥37॥
यद्यप्येते न पश्यन्ति लोभोपहतचेतसः।
कुलक्षयकृतं दोषं मित्रद्रोहे च पातकम् ॥38॥
कथं न ज्ञेयमस्माभिः पापादस्मान्निवर्तितुम्।
कुलक्षयकृतं दोषं प्रपश्यद्भिर्जनार्दन ॥39॥
कुलक्षये प्रणश्यन्ति कुलधर्माः सनातनाः।
धर्मे नष्टे कुलं कृत्स्नमधर्मोऽभिभवत्युत ॥40॥
अधर्मोभिभवात्कृष्ण प्रदुष्यन्ति कुलस्त्रियः।
स्त्रीषु दुष्टासु वार्ष्णेय जायते वर्णसंकरः ॥41॥
संकरो नरकायैव कुलघ्नानां कुलस्य च।
पतन्ति पितरो ह्येषां लुप्तपिण्डोदकक्रियाः ॥42॥
दोषैरेतैः कुलघ्नानां वर्णसंकरकारकैः।
उत्साद्यन्ते जातिधर्माः कुलधर्माश्च शाश्वताः ॥43॥
उत्सन्नकुलधर्माणां मनुष्याणां जनार्दन।
नरकेऽनियतं वासो भवतीत्यनुशुश्रुम ॥44॥
अहो बत महत्पापं कर्तुं व्यवसिता वयम्।
यद्राज्यसुखलोभेन हन्तुं स्वजनमुद्यताः ॥45॥
यदि मामप्रतीकारमशस्त्रं शस्त्रपाणयः।
धार्तराष्ट्रा रणे हन्युस्तन्मे क्षेमतरं भवेत् ॥46॥

संजय उवाच

एवमुक्त्वार्जुनः संख्ये रथोपस्थ उपाविशत्।
विसृज्य सशरं चापं शोकसंविग्नमानसः ॥47॥

ॐ तत्सदिति श्रीमद्भगवद्गीतासूपनिषत्सु ब्रह्मविद्यायां
योगशास्त्रे श्रीकृष्णार्जुनविषादयोगो
नाम प्रथमोऽध्यायः ॥1॥

अथ द्वितीयोऽध्यायः

संजय उवाच

तं तथा कृपयाविष्टमश्रुपूर्णाकुलेक्षणम्।
विषीदन्तमिदं वाक्यमुवाच मधुसूदनः ॥1॥

श्रीभगवानुवाच

कुतस्त्वा कश्मलमिदं विषमे समुपस्थितम्।
अनार्यजुष्टमस्वर्ग्यमकीर्तिकरमर्जुन ॥2॥
क्लैब्यं मा स्म गमः पार्थ नैतत्त्वय्युपपद्यते।
क्षुद्रं हृदयदौर्बल्यं त्यक्त्वोत्तिष्ठ परंतप ॥3॥

अर्जुन उवाच

कथं भीष्ममहं संख्ये द्रोणं च मधुसूदन।
इषुभिः प्रति योत्स्यामि पूजार्हावरिसूदन ॥4॥
गुरूनहत्वा हि महानुभावान्
श्रेयो भोक्तुं भैक्ष्यमपीह लोके।
हत्वार्थकामांस्तु गुरुनिहैव
भुञ्जीय योगान्रुधिरप्रदिग्धान् ॥5॥
न चैतद्विद्मः कतरन्नो गरीयो।
यद्वा जयेम यदि वा नो जयेयुः।
यानेव हत्वा न जिजीविषाम-
स्तेऽवस्थिताः प्रमुखे धार्तराष्ट्राः ॥6॥
कार्पण्यदोषोपहतस्वभावः
पृच्छामि त्वां धर्मसंमूढचेताः।
यच्छ्रेयः स्यान्निश्चितं ब्रूहि तन्मे
शिष्यस्तेऽहं शाधि मां त्वां प्रपन्नम् ॥7॥
न हि प्रपश्यामि ममापनुद्याद्
यच्छोकमुच्छोषणमिन्द्रियाणाम्।
अवाप्य भूमावसपत्नमृद्धं
राज्यं सुराणामपि चाधिपत्यम् ॥8॥

संजय उवाच

एवमुक्त्वा हृषीकेशं गुडाकेशः परंतप।
न योत्स्य इति गोविन्दमुक्त्वा तूष्णीं बभूव ह ॥9॥
तमुवाच हृषीकेशः प्रहसन्निव भारत।
सेनयोरुभयोर्मध्ये विषीदन्तमिदं वचः ॥10॥

श्रीभगवानुवाच

अशोच्यानन्वशोचस्त्वं प्रज्ञावादांश्च भाषसे।
गतासूनगतासूंश्च नानुशोचन्ति पण्डिताः ॥11॥
न त्वेवाहं जातु नासं न त्वं नेमे जनाधिपाः।
न चैव न भविष्यामः सर्वे वयमतः परम् ॥12॥
देहिनोऽस्मिन्यथा देहे कौमारं यौवनं जरा।
तथा देहान्तरप्राप्तिर्धीरस्तत्र न मुह्यति ॥13॥
मात्रास्पर्शास्तु कौन्तेय शीतोष्णुसखदुः खदाः।
आगमापायिनोऽनित्यास्तांस्तितिक्षस्व भारत ॥14॥
यं हि न व्यथयन्त्येते पुरुषं पुरुषर्षभ।
समदुःखसुखं धीरं सोऽमृतत्वाय कल्पते ॥15॥
नासतो विद्यते भावो नाभावो विद्यते सतः।
उभयोरपि दृष्टोऽन्तस्त्वनयोस्तत्त्वदर्शिभिः ॥16॥
अविनाशि तु तद्विद्धि येन सर्वमिदं ततम्।
विनाशमव्ययस्यास्य न कश्चित्कर्तुमर्हति ॥17॥
अन्तवन्त इमे देहा नित्यस्योक्ताः शरीरिणः।
अनाशिनोऽप्रमेयस्य तस्माद्युध्यस्व भारत ॥18॥
य एनं वेत्ति हन्तारं यश्चैनं मन्यते हतम्।
उभौ तौ न विजानीतो नायं हन्ति न हन्यते ॥19॥
न जायते म्रियते वा कदाचि-
न्नायं भूत्वा भविता वा न भूयः।
अजो नित्यः शाश्वतोऽयं पुराणो
न हन्यते हन्यमाने शरीरे ॥20॥
वेदाविनाशिनं नित्यं य एनमजमव्ययम्।
कथं स पुरुषः पार्थ कं घातयति हन्ति कम् ॥21॥

वासांसि जीर्णानि यथा विहाय
नवानि गृह्णाति नरोऽपराणि।
तथा शरीराणि विहाय जीर्णा-
न्यन्यानि संयाति नवानि देही ॥22॥
नैनं छिन्दन्ति शस्त्राणि नैनं दहति पावकः।
न चैनं क्लेदयन्त्यापो न शोषयति मारुतः ॥23॥
अच्छेद्योऽयमदाह्योऽयमक्लेद्योऽशोष्य एव च।
नित्यः सर्वगतः स्थाणुरचलोऽयं सनातनः ॥24॥
अव्यक्तोऽयमचिन्त्योऽयमविकार्योऽयमुच्यते।
तस्मादेवं विदित्वैनं नानुशोचितुमर्हसि ॥25॥
अथ चैनं नित्यजातं नित्यं वा मन्यसे मृतम्।
तथापि त्वं महाबाहो नैवं शोचितुमर्हसि ॥26॥
जातस्य हि ध्रुवो मृत्युर्ध्रुवं जन्म मृतस्य च।
तस्मादपरिहार्येऽर्थे न त्वं शोचितुमर्हसि ॥27॥
अव्यक्तादीनि भूतानि व्यक्तमध्यानि भारत।
अव्यक्तनिधनान्येव तत्र का परिदेवना ॥28॥
आश्चर्यवत्पश्यति कश्चिदेन-
माश्चर्यवद्वदति तथैव चान्यः।
आश्चर्यवच्चैनमन्यः शृणोति
श्रुत्वाप्येनं वेद न चैव कश्चित् ॥29॥
देही नित्यमवध्योऽयं देहे सर्वस्य भारत।
तस्मात्सर्वाणि भूतानि न त्वं शोचितुमर्हसि ॥30॥
स्वधर्ममपि चावेक्ष्य न विकम्पितुमर्हसि।
धर्म्याद्धि युद्धाच्छ्रेयोऽन्यत्क्षत्रियस्य न विद्यते ॥31॥
यदृच्छया चोपपन्नं स्वर्गद्वारमपावृतम्।
सुखिनः क्षत्रियाः पार्थ लभन्ते युद्धमीदृशम् ॥32॥
अथ चेत्त्वमिमं धर्म्यं संग्रामं न करिष्यसि।
ततः स्वधर्मं कीर्तिं च हित्वा पापमवाप्स्यसि ॥33॥
अकीर्तिं चापि भूतानि कथयिष्यन्ति तेऽव्ययाम्।
संभावितस्य चाकीर्तिर्मरणादतिरिच्यते ॥34॥

भयाद्रणादुपरतं मंस्यन्ते त्वां महारथाः।
येषां च त्वं बहुमतो भूत्वा यास्यसि लाघवम् ॥35॥
अवाच्यवादांश्च बहून्वदिष्यन्ति तवाहिताः।
निन्दन्तस्तव सामर्थ्यं ततो दुःखतरं नु किम् ॥36॥
हतो वा प्राप्स्यसि स्वर्गं जित्वा वा भोक्ष्यसे महीम्।
तस्मादुत्तिष्ठ कौन्तेय युद्धाय कृतनिश्चयः ॥37॥
सुखदुःखे समे कृत्वा लाभालाभौ जयाजयौ।
ततो युद्धाय युज्यस्व नैवं पापमवापस्यसि ॥38॥
एषा तेऽभिहिता सांख्ये बुद्धिर्योगे त्विमां शृणु।
बुद्ध्या युक्तो यया पार्थ कर्मबन्धं प्रहास्यसि ॥39॥
नेहाभिक्रमनाशोऽस्ति प्रत्यवायो न विद्यते।
स्वल्पमप्यस्य धर्मस्य त्रायते महतो भयात् ॥40॥
व्यवसायात्मिका बुद्धिरेकेह कुरुनन्दन।
बहुशाखा ह्यनन्ताश्च बुद्धयोऽव्यवसायिनाम् ॥41॥
यामिमां पुष्पितां वाचं प्रवदन्त्यविपश्चितः।
वेदवादरताः पार्थ नान्यदस्तीति वादिनः ॥42॥
कामात्मानः स्वर्गपरा जन्मकर्मफलप्रदाम्।
क्रियाविशेषबहुलां भोगैश्वर्यगतिं प्रति ॥43॥
भोगैश्वर्यप्रसक्तानां तयापहृतचेतसाम्।
व्यवसायात्मिका बुद्धिः समाधौ न विधीयते ॥44॥
त्रैगुण्यविषया वेदा निस्त्रैगुण्यो भवार्जुन।
निर्द्वन्द्वोनित्यसत्त्वस्थो निर्योगक्षेम आत्मवान् ॥45॥
यावानर्थ उदपाने सर्वतः संप्लुतोदके।
तावान्सर्वेषु वेदेषु ब्राह्मणस्य विजानतः ॥46॥
कर्मण्येवाधिकारस्ते मा फलेषु कदाचन।
मा कर्मफलहेतुर्भूर्मा ते सङ्गोऽस्त्वकर्मणि ॥47॥
योगस्थः कुरु कर्माणि सङ्गं त्यक्त्वा धनंजय।
सिद्ध्यसिद्ध्योः समो भूत्वा समत्वं योग उच्यते ॥48॥
दूरेण ह्यवरं कर्म बुद्धि योगाद्धनंजय।
बुद्धौ शरणमन्विच्छ कृपणाः फलहेतवः ॥49॥

बुद्धियुक्तो जहातीह उभे सुकृतदुष्कृते।
तस्मायोगाय युज्यस्व योगः कर्मसु कौशलम् ॥50॥
कर्मजं बुद्धियुक्ता हि फलं त्यक्त्वा मनीषिणः।
जन्मबन्धविनिर्मुक्ताः पदं गच्छन्त्यनामयम् ॥51॥
यदा ते मोहकलिलं बुद्धिर्व्यतितरिष्यति।
तदा गन्तासि निर्वेदं श्रोतव्यस्य श्रुतस्य च ॥52॥
श्रुतिविप्रतिपन्ना ते यदा स्थास्यति निश्चला।
समाधावचला बुद्धिस्तदा योगमवाप्स्यसि ॥53॥

अर्जुन उवाच

स्थितप्रज्ञस्य का भाषा समाधिस्थस्य केशव।
स्थितधीः किं प्रभाषेत किमासीत ब्रजेत किम् ॥54॥

श्रीभगवानुवाच

प्रजहाति यदा कामान्सर्वान्पार्थ मनोगतान्।
आत्मन्येवात्मना तुष्टः स्थितप्रज्ञस्तदोच्यते ॥55॥
दुःखेष्वनुद्विग्नमनाः सुखेषु विगतस्पृहः।
वीतरागभयक्रोधः स्थितधीर्मुनिरुच्यते ॥56॥
यः सर्वत्रानभिस्नेहस्तत्तत्प्राप्य शुभाशुभम्।
नाभिनन्दति न द्वेष्टि तस्य प्रज्ञा प्रतिष्ठिा ॥57॥
यदा संहरते वायं कूर्मोऽङ्गानीव सर्वशः।
इन्द्रियाणीन्द्रियार्थेभ्यस्तस्य प्रज्ञा प्रतिष्ठिता ॥58॥
विषया विनिवर्तन्ते निराहारस्य देहिनः।
रसवर्जं रसोऽप्यस्य परं दृष्ट्वा निवर्तते ॥59॥
यततो ह्यपि कौन्तेय पुरुषस्य विपश्चितः।
इन्द्रियाणि प्रमाथीनि हरन्ति प्रसभं मनः ॥60॥
तानि सर्वाणि संयम्य युक्त आसीत मत्परः।
वशे हि यस्येन्द्रियाणि तस्य प्रज्ञा प्रतिष्ठिता ॥61॥
ध्यायतो विषयान्पुंसः सङ्गस्तेषूपजायते।
सङ्गात्संजायते कामः कामात्क्रोधोऽभिजायते ॥62॥
क्रोधाद्भवति संमोहः संमोहात्स्मृतिविभ्रमः।
स्मृतिभ्रंशाद्बुद्धिनाशो बुद्धिनाशात्प्रणश्यति ॥63॥

रागद्वेषयियुक्तैस्तु विषयानिन्द्रियैश्चरन्।
आत्मवश्यैर्विधेयात्मा प्रसादमधिगच्छति ॥64॥
प्रसादे सर्वदुःखानां हानिरस्योपजायते।
प्रसन्नचेतसो ह्याशु बुद्धिः पर्यवतिष्ठते ॥65॥
नास्ति बुद्धिरयुक्तस्य न चायुक्तस्य भावना।
न चाभावयतः शान्तिरशान्तस्य कुतः सुखम् ॥66॥
इन्द्रियाणां हि चरतां यन्मनोऽनुविधीयते।
तदस्य हरति प्रज्ञां वायुर्नावमिवाम्भसि ॥67॥
तस्माद्यस्य महाबाहो निगृहीतानि सर्वशः।
इन्द्रियाण्यीन्द्रियार्थेभ्यस्तस्य प्रज्ञा प्रतिष्ठिता ॥68॥
या निशा सर्वभूतानां तस्यां जागर्ति संयमी।
यस्यां जाग्रति भूतानि सा निशा पश्यतो मुनेः ॥69॥
आपूर्यमाणमचलप्रतिष्ठं
समुद्रमापः प्रविशन्ति यद्वत्।
तद्वत्कामां यं प्रविशन्ति सर्वे
स शान्तिमाप्नोति न कामकामी ॥70॥
विहाय कामान्यः सर्वान्पुमांश्चरति निःस्पृहः।
निर्ममो निरहंकारः स शान्तिमधिगच्छति ॥71॥
एषा ब्राह्मी स्थितिः पार्थ नैनां प्राप्य विमुह्यति।
स्थित्वास्यामन्तकालेऽपि ब्रह्मनिर्वाणमृच्छति ॥72॥

ॐ तत्सदिति श्रीमद्भगवद्गीतासूपनिषत्सु ब्रह्मविद्यायां
योगशास्त्रे श्रीकृष्णार्जुनसंवादे सांख्ययोगो
नाम द्वितीयोऽध्यायः ॥2॥

ॐ श्रीपरमात्मने नमः

अथ तृतीयोऽध्यायः

अर्जुन उवाच

ज्यायसी चेत्कर्मणस्ते मता बुद्धिर्जनार्दन।
तत्किं कर्मणि घोरे मां नियोजयसि केशव ॥1॥

व्यामिश्रेणेव वाक्येन बुद्धिं मोहयसीव मे।
तदेकं वद निश्चित्य येन श्रेयोऽहमाप्नुयाम् ॥2॥

श्रीभगवानुवाच

लोकेऽस्मिन्द्विविधा निष्ठा पुरा प्रोक्ता मयानघ।
ज्ञानयोगेन सांख्यानां कर्मयोगेन योगिनाम् ॥3॥
न कर्मणामनारम्भान्नैष्कर्म्यं पुरुषोऽश्नुते।
न च संन्यसनादेव सिद्धिं समधिगच्छति ॥4॥
न हि कश्चित्क्षणमपि जातु तिष्ठत्यकर्मकृत्।
कार्यते ह्यवशः कर्म सर्वः प्रकृतिजैर्गुणैः ॥5॥
कर्मेन्द्रियाणि संयम्य य आस्ते मनसा स्मरन्।
इन्द्रियार्थान्विमूढात्मा मिथ्याचारः स उच्यते ॥6॥
यस्त्विन्द्रियाणि मनसा नियम्यारभतेऽर्जुन।
कर्मेन्द्रियैः कर्मयोगमसक्तः स विशिष्यते ॥7॥
नियतं कुरु कर्म त्वं कर्म ज्यायो ह्यकर्मणः।
शरीरयात्रापि च ते न प्रसिद्ध्येदकर्मणः ॥8॥
यज्ञार्थात्कर्मणोऽन्यत्र लोकोऽयं कर्मबन्धनः।
तदर्थं कर्म कौन्तेय मुक्तसङ्गः समाचर ॥9॥
सहयज्ञाः प्रजाः सृष्ट्वा पुरोवाच प्रजापतिः।
अनेन प्रसविष्यध्वमेष वोऽस्त्विष्टकामधुक् ॥10॥
देवान्भावयतानेन ते देवा भावयन्तु वः।
परस्परं भावयन्तः श्रेयः परमवाप्स्यथ ॥11॥
इष्टान्भोगान्हि वो देवा दास्यन्ते यज्ञभाविताः।
तैर्दत्तानप्रदायैभ्यो यो भुङ्क्ते स्तेन एव सः ॥12॥
यज्ञशिष्टाशिनः सन्तो मुच्यन्ते सर्वकिल्बिषैः।
भुञ्जते ते त्वघं पापा ये पचन्त्यात्मकारणात् ॥13॥
अन्नाद्भवन्ति भूतानि पर्जन्यादन्नसंभवः।
यज्ञाद्भवति पर्जन्यो यज्ञः कर्मसमुद्भवः ॥14॥
कर्म ब्रह्मोद्भवं विद्धि ब्रह्माक्षरसमुद्भवम्।
तस्मात्सर्वगतं ब्रह्म नित्यं यज्ञे प्रतिष्ठितम् ॥15॥

एवं प्रवर्तितं चक्रं नानुवर्तयतीह यः।
अघायुरिन्द्रियारामो मोघं पार्थ स जीवति ॥16॥
यस्त्वात्मरतिरेव स्यादात्मतृप्तश्च मानवः।
आत्मन्येव च संतुष्टस्तस्य कार्यं न विद्यते ॥17॥
नैव तस्य कृतेनार्थो नाकृतेनेह कश्चन।
न चास्य सर्वभूतेषु कश्चिदर्थव्यपाश्रयः ॥18॥
तस्मादसक्तः सततं कार्यं कर्म समाचर।
असक्तो ह्याचरन्कर्म परमाप्नोति पुरुषः ॥19॥
कर्मणैव हि संसिद्धिमास्थिता जनकादयः।
लोकसंग्रहमेवापि संपश्यन्कर्तुमर्हसि ॥20॥
यद्यदाचरति श्रेष्ठस्तत्तदेवेतरो जनः।
स यत्प्रमाणं कुरुते लोकस्तदनुवर्तते ॥21॥
न मे पार्थास्ति कर्तव्यं त्रिषु लोकेषु किंचन।
नानवाप्तमवाप्तव्यं वर्त एव च कर्मणि ॥22॥
यदि ह्यहं न वर्तेयं जातु कर्मण्यतन्द्रितः।
मम वर्त्मानुवर्तन्ते मनुष्याः पार्थ सर्वशः ॥23॥
उत्सीदेयुरिमे लोका न कुर्यां कर्म चेदहम्।
संकरस्य च कर्ता स्यामुपहन्यामिमाः प्रजाः ॥24॥
सक्ताः कर्मण्यविद्वांसो यथा कुर्वन्ति भारत।
कुर्याद्विद्वांस्तथासक्तश्चिकीर्षुर्लोकसंग्रहम् ॥25॥
न बुद्धिभेदं जनयेदज्ञानां कर्मसङ्गिनाम्।
जोषयेत्सर्वकर्माणि विद्वान्युक्तः समाचरन् ॥26॥
प्रकृतेः क्रियमाणानि गुणैः कर्माणि सर्वशः।
अहंकारविमूढात्मा कर्ताहमिति मन्यते ॥27॥
तत्त्ववित्तु महाबाहो गुणकर्मविभागयोः।
गुणा गुणेषु वर्तन्त इति मत्वा न सज्जते ॥28॥
प्रकृतेर्गुणसंमूढाः सज्जन्ते गुणकर्मसु।
तानकृत्स्नविदो मन्दान्कृत्स्नविन्न विचालयेत् ॥29॥
मयि सर्वाणि कर्माणि संन्यस्याध्यात्मचेतसा।
निराशीर्निर्ममो भूत्वा युध्यस्व विगतज्वरः ॥30॥

ये मे मतमिदं नित्यमनुतिष्ठन्ति मानवाः।
श्रद्धावन्तोऽनसूयन्तो मुच्यन्ते तेऽपि कर्मभिः ॥31॥
ये त्वेतदभ्यसूयन्तो नानुतिष्ठन्ति मे मतम्।
सर्वज्ञानविमूढांस्तान्विद्धि नष्टानचेतसः ॥32॥
सदृशं चेष्टते स्वस्याः प्रकृतेर्ज्ञानवानपि।
प्रकृतिं यान्ति भूतानि निग्रहः किं करिष्यति ॥33॥
इन्द्रियस्येन्द्रियस्यार्थे रागद्वेषौ व्यवस्थितौ।
तयोर्न वशमागच्छेत्तौ ह्यस्य परिपन्थिनौ ॥34॥
श्रेयान् स्वधर्मो विगुणः परधर्मात्स्वनुष्ठितात्।
स्वधर्मे निधनं श्रेयः परधर्मो भयावहः ॥35॥

अर्जुन उवाच

अथ केन प्रयुक्तोऽयं पापं चरति पूरुषः।
अनिच्छन्नपि वार्ष्णेय बलादिव नियोजितः ॥36॥

श्रीभगवानुवाच

काम एष क्रोध एष रजोगुणसमुद्भवः।
महाशनो महापाप्मा विद्ध्येनमिह वैरिणम् ॥37॥
धूमेनाव्रियते वह्निर्यथादर्शो मलेन च।
यथोल्बेनावृतो गर्भस्तथा तेनेदमावृतम् ॥38॥
आवृतं ज्ञानमेतेन ज्ञानिनो नित्यवैरिणा।
कामरूपेण कौन्तेय दुष्पूरेणानलेन च ॥39॥
इन्द्रियाणि मनो बुद्धिरस्याधिष्ठानमुच्यते।
एतैर्विमोहयत्येषु ज्ञानमावृत्य देहिनम् ॥40॥
तस्मात्त्वमिन्द्रियाण्यादौ नियम्य भरतर्षभ।
पाप्मानं प्रजहि ह्येनं ज्ञानविज्ञाननाशनम् ॥41॥
इन्द्रियाणि पराण्याहुरिन्द्रियेभ्यः परं मनः।
मनसस्तु परा बुद्धिर्यो बुद्धेः परतस्तु सः ॥42॥
एवं बुद्धेः परं बुद्ध्वा संस्तभ्यात्मानमात्मना।
जहि शत्रुं महाबाहो कामरूपं दुरासदम् ॥43॥

ॐ तत्ससदिति श्रीमद्भगवद्गीतासूपनिषत्सु ब्रह्मविद्यायां
योगशास्त्रे श्रीकृष्णार्जुनसंवादे कर्मयोगो
नाम तृतीयोऽयाययः ॥3॥

अथ चतुर्थोऽध्यायः

श्रीभगवानुवाच

इमं विवस्वते योगं प्रोक्तवानहमव्ययम्।
विवस्वान्मनवे प्राह मनुरिक्ष्वाकववेऽब्रवीत् ॥1॥
एवं परम्पराप्राप्तमिमं राजर्षयो विदुः।
स कालेनेह महता योगो नष्टः परंतप ॥2॥
स एवायं मया तेऽद्य योगः प्रोक्तः पुरातनः।
भक्तोऽसि मे सखा चेति रहस्यं ह्येतदुत्तमम् ॥3॥

अर्जुन उवाच

अपरं भवतो जन्म परं जन्म विवस्वतः।
कथमेतद्विजानीयां त्वमादौ प्रोक्तवानिति ॥4॥

श्रीभगवानुवाच

बहूनि मे व्यतीतानि जन्मानि तव चार्जुन।
तान्यहं वेद सर्वाणि न त्वं वेत्थ परंतप ॥5॥
अजोऽपि सन्नव्ययात्मा भूतानामीश्वरोऽपि सन्।
प्रकृतिं स्वामधिष्ठाय संभवाम्यात्ममायया ॥6॥
यदा यदा हि धर्मस्य ग्लानिर्भवति भारत।
अभ्युत्थानमधर्मस्य तदात्मानं सृजाम्यहम् ॥7॥
परित्राणाय साधूनां विनाशाय च दुष्कृताम्।
धर्मसंस्थापनार्थाय संभवामि युगे युगे ॥8॥
जन्म कर्म च मे दिव्यमेवं यो वेत्ति तत्त्वतः।
त्यक्त्वा देहं पुनर्जन्म नैति मामेति सोऽर्जुन ॥9॥
वीतरागभयक्रोधा मन्मया मामुपाश्रिताः।
बहवोज्ञानतपससा पूता मद्भावमागताः ॥10॥
ये यथा मां प्रपद्यन्ते तांस्तथैव भजाम्यहम्।
मम वर्त्मानुवर्तन्ते मनुष्याः पार्थ सर्वशः ॥11॥

काङ्क्षन्तः कर्मणां सिद्धिं यजन्त इह देवताः।
क्षिप्रं हि मानुषे लोके सिद्धिर्भवति कर्मजा ॥12॥
चातुर्वर्ण्यं मया सृष्टं गुणकर्मविभागशः।
तस्य कर्तारमपि मां विद्ध्यकर्तारमव्ययम् ॥13॥
न मां कर्माणि लिम्पन्ति न मे कर्मफले स्पृहा।
इति मां योऽभिजानाति कर्मभिर्न स बध्यते ॥14॥
एवं ज्ञात्वा कृतं कर्म पूर्वैरपि मुमुक्षुभिः।
कुरु कर्मैव तस्मात्त्वं पूर्वैः पूर्वतरं कृतम् ॥15॥
किं कर्म किमकर्मेति कवयोऽप्यत्र मोहिताः।
तत्ते कर्म प्रवक्ष्यामि यज्ज्ञात्वा मोक्ष्यसेऽशुभात् ॥16॥
कर्मणो ह्यपि बोद्धव्यं बोद्धव्यं च विकर्मणः।
अकर्मणश्च बोद्धव्यं गहना कर्मणो गतिः ॥17॥
कर्मण्यकर्म यः पश्येदकर्मणि च कर्म यः।
स बुद्धिमान्मनुष्येषु स युक्तः कृत्स्नकर्मकृत् ॥18॥
यस्य सर्वे समारम्भाः कामसंकल्पवर्जिताः।
ज्ञानाग्निदग्धकर्माणं तमाहुः पण्डितं बुधाः ॥19॥
त्यक्त्वा कर्मफलासङ्गं नित्यतृप्तो निराश्रयः।
कर्मण्यभिप्रवृत्तोऽपि नैव किञ्चित्करोति सः ॥20॥
निराशीर्यतचित्तात्मा त्यक्तसर्वपरिग्रहः।
शारीरं केवलं कर्म कुर्वन्नाप्नोति किल्बिषम् ॥21॥
यदृच्छालाभसंतुष्टो द्वन्द्वातीतो विमत्सरः।
समः सिद्धावसिद्धौ च कृत्वापि न निबध्यते ॥22॥
गतसङ्गस्य मुक्तस्य ज्ञानावस्थितचेतसः।
यज्ञायाचरतः कर्म समग्रं प्रविलीयते ॥23॥
ब्रह्मार्पणं ब्रह्म हविर्ब्रह्माग्नौ ब्रह्मणा हुतम्।
ब्रह्मैव तेन गन्तव्यं ब्रह्मकर्मसमाधिना ॥24॥
दैवमेवापरे यज्ञं योगिनः पर्युपासते।
ब्रह्माग्नावपरे यज्ञं यज्ञेनैवोपजुह्वति ॥25॥
श्रोत्रादीनीन्द्रियाण्यन्ये संयमाग्निषु जुह्वति।
शब्दादीन्विषयानन्य इन्द्रियाग्निषु जुह्वति ॥26॥

सर्वाणीन्द्रियकर्माणि प्राणकर्माणि चापरे ।
आत्मसंयमयोगाग्नौ जुह्वति ज्ञानदीपिते ॥27॥
द्रव्ययज्ञास्तपोयज्ञा योगयज्ञास्तथापरे ।
स्वाध्यायज्ञानयज्ञाश्च यतयः संशितव्रताः ॥28॥
अपाने जुह्वति प्राणं प्राणेऽपानं तथापरे ।
प्राणापानगती रुद्ध्वा प्राणायामपरायणाः ॥29॥
अपरे नियताहाराः प्राणान्प्राणेषु जुह्वति ।
सर्वेऽप्येते यज्ञविदो यज्ञक्षपितकल्मषाः ॥30॥
यज्ञशिष्टामृतभुजो यान्ति ब्रह्म सनातनम् ।
नायं लोकोऽस्त्ययज्ञस्य कुतोऽन्यः कुरुसत्तम ॥31॥
एवं बहुविधा यज्ञा वितता ब्रह्मणो मुखे ।
कर्मजान्विद्धि तान्सर्वानेवं ज्ञात्वा विमोक्ष्यसे ॥32॥
श्रेयान्द्रव्यमयाद्यज्ञाज्ज्ञानयज्ञः परंतप ।
सर्वं कर्माखिलं पार्थ ज्ञाने परिसमाप्यते ॥33॥
तद्विद्धि प्रणिपातेन परिप्रश्नेन सेवया ।
उपदेक्ष्यन्ति ते ज्ञानं ज्ञानिनस्तत्त्वदर्शिनः ॥34॥
यज्ज्ञात्वा न पुनर्मोहमेवं यास्यसि पाण्डव ।
येन भूतान्यशेषेण द्रक्ष्यस्यात्मन्यथो मयि ॥35॥
अपि चेदसि पापेभ्यः सर्वेभ्यः पापकृत्तमः ।
सर्वं ज्ञानप्लवेनैव वृजिनं संतरिष्यसि ॥36॥
यथैधांसि समिद्धोऽग्निर्भस्मसात्कुरुतेऽर्जुन ।
ज्ञानाग्निः सर्वकर्माणि भस्मसात्कुरुते तथा ॥37॥
न हि ज्ञानेन सदृशं पवित्रमिह विद्यते ।
तत्स्वयं योगसंसिद्धः कालेनात्मनि विन्दति ॥38॥
श्रद्धावाँल्लभते ज्ञानं तत्परः संयतेन्द्रियः ।
ज्ञानं लब्ध्वा परां शान्तिमचिरेणाधिगच्छति ॥39॥
अज्ञश्चाश्रद्दधानश्च संशयात्मा विनश्यति ।
नायं लोकोऽस्ति न परो न सुखं संशयात्मनः ॥40॥
योगसंन्यस्तकर्माणं ज्ञानसंछिन्नसंशयम् ।
आत्मवन्तं न कर्माणि निबध्नन्ति धनंजय ॥41॥

तस्मादज्ञानसंभूतं हृत्स्थं ज्ञानासिनात्मनः।
छित्त्वैनं संशयं योगमातिष्ठोत्तिष्ठ भारत ॥42॥

ॐ तत्सदिति श्रीमद्भगवद्गीतासूपनिषत्सु ब्रह्मविद्यायां
योगशास्त्रे श्रीकृष्णार्जुनसंवादे ज्ञानकर्मसंन्यास-
योगो नाम चतुर्थोऽध्यायः ॥4॥

अथ पञ्चमोऽध्यायः

अर्जुन उवाच

संन्यासं कर्मणां कृष्ण पुनर्योगं च शंससि।
यच्छ्रेय एतयोरेकं तन्मे ब्रूहि सुनिश्चितम् ॥1॥

श्रीभगवानुवाच

संन्यासः कर्मयोगश्च निःश्रेयसकरावुभौ।
तयोस्तु कर्मसंन्यासात्कर्मयोगो विशिष्यते ॥2॥
ज्ञेयः स नित्यसंन्यासी यो न द्वेष्टि न काङ्क्षति।
निर्द्वन्द्वो हि महाबाहो सुखं बन्धात्प्रमुच्यते ॥3॥
सांख्ययोगौ पृथग्बालाः प्रवदन्ति न पण्डिताः।
एकमप्यास्थितः सम्यगुभयोर्विन्दते फलम् ॥4॥
यत्सांख्यैः प्राप्यते स्थानं तद्योगैरपि गम्यते।
एकं सांख्यं च योगं च यः पश्यति स पश्यति ॥5॥
संन्यासस्तु महाबाहो दुःखमाप्तुमयोगतः।
योगयुक्तो मुनिर्ब्रह्म नचिरेणाधिगच्छति ॥6॥
योगयुक्तो विशुद्धात्मा विजितात्मा जितेन्द्रियः।
सर्वभूतात्मभूतात्मा कुर्वन्नपि न लिप्यते ॥7॥
नैव किंचितकरोमीति युक्तो मन्यतेत तत्त्ववित्।
पश्यञ्शृण्वन्स्पृशञ्जिघ्रन्नश्नन्गच्छन्स्वपञ्श्वसन् ॥8॥
प्रलपन्विसृजन्गृह्णन्नुन्मिषन्निमिषन्नपि।
इन्द्रियाणीन्द्रियार्थेषु वर्तन्त इति धारयन् ॥9॥
ब्रह्मण्याधाय कर्माणि सङ्गंत्यक्त्वा करोति यः।
लिप्यते न स पापेन पद्मपत्रमिवाम्भसा ॥10॥

कायेन मनसा बुद्ध्या केवलैरिन्द्रियैरपि।
योगिनः कर्म कुर्वन्ति सङ्गं त्यक्त्वात्मशुद्धये ॥11॥
युक्तः कर्मफलंत्यक्त्वा शान्तिमाप्नोति नैष्ठिकीम्।
अयुक्तः कामकारेण फले सक्तो निबध्यते ॥12॥
सर्वकर्माणि मनसा संन्यस्यास्ते सुखं वशी।
नवद्वारे पुरे देही नैव कुर्वन्न कारयन् ॥13॥
न कर्तृत्वं न कर्माणि लोकस्य सृजति प्रभुः।
न कर्मफलसंयोगं स्वभावस्तु प्रवर्तते ॥14॥
नादत्ते कस्यचित्पापं न चैव सुकृतं विभुः।
अज्ञानेनावृतं ज्ञानं तेन मुह्यन्ति जन्तवः ॥15॥
ज्ञानेन तु तदज्ञानं येषां नाशितमात्मनः।
तेषामादित्यवज्ज्ञानं प्रकाशयति तत्परम् ॥16॥
तद्बुद्धयस्तदात्मानस्तन्निष्ठास्तत्परायणाः।
गच्छन्त्यपुनरावृत्तिं ज्ञाननिर्धूतकल्मषाः ॥17॥
विद्याविनयसंपन्ने ब्राह्मणे गवि हस्तिनि।
शुनि चैव श्वपाके च पण्डिताः समदर्शिनः ॥18॥
इहैव तैर्जितः सर्गो येषां साम्ये स्थितं मनः।
निर्दोषं हि समं ब्रह्म तस्माद्ब्रह्मणि ते स्थिताः ॥19॥
न प्रहृष्येत्प्रियं प्राप्य नोद्विजेत्प्राप्य चाप्रियम्।
स्थिरबुद्धिरसंमूढो ब्रह्मविद् ब्रह्मणि स्थितः ॥20॥
बाह्यस्पर्शेष्वसक्तात्मा विन्दत्यात्मनि यत्सुखम्।
स ब्रह्मयोगयुक्तात्मा सुखमक्षयमश्नुते ॥21॥
ये हि संस्पर्शजा भोगा दुःखयोनय एव ते।
आद्यन्तवन्तः कौन्तेय न तेषु रमते बुधः ॥22॥
शक्नोतीहैव यः सोढुं प्राक्शरीरविमोक्षणात्।
कामक्रोधोद्भवं वेगं स युक्तः स सुखी नरः ॥23॥
योऽन्तः सुखोऽन्तरारामस्तथान्तर्ज्योतिरेव यः।
स योगी ब्रह्मनिर्वाणं ब्रह्मभूतोऽधिगच्छति ॥24॥
लभन्ते ब्रह्मनिर्वाणमृषयः क्षीणकल्मषाः।
छिन्नद्वैधा यतात्मानः सर्वभूतहिते रताः ॥25॥

कामक्रोधवियुक्तानां यतीनां यतचेतसाम् ।
अभितो ब्रह्मनिर्वाणं वर्तते विदितात्मनाम् ॥26॥
स्पर्शान्कृतवा बहिर्बाह्यांश्चक्षुश्चैवान्तरे भ्रुवोः ।
प्राणापानौ समौ कृत्वा नासाभ्यन्तरचारिणौ ॥27॥
यतेन्द्रियमनोबुद्धिर्मुनिर्मोक्षपरायणः ।
विगतेच्छाभयक्रोधो यः सदा मुक्त एव सः ॥28॥
भोक्तारं यज्ञतपसां सर्वलोकमहेश्वरम् ।
सुहृदं सर्वभूतानां ज्ञात्वा मां शान्तिमृच्छति ॥29॥

ॐ तत्सदिति श्रीमद्भगवद्गीतासूपनिषत्सु ब्रह्मविद्यायां
योगशास्त्रे श्रीकृष्णार्जुनसंवादे कर्मसंन्यासयोगो
नाम पञ्चमोऽध्यायः ॥5॥

ॐ श्रीपरमात्मने नमः

अथ षष्ठोऽध्यायः

श्रीभगवानुवाच

अनाश्रितः कर्मफलं कार्यं कर्म करोति यः ।
स संन्यासी च योगी च न निरग्निर्न चाक्रियः ॥1॥
यं संन्यासमिति प्राहुर्योगं तं विद्धि पाण्डव ।
न ह्यसंन्यस्तसंकल्पो योगी भवति कश्चन ॥2॥
आरुरुक्षोर्मुनेर्योगं कर्म कारणमुच्यते ।
योगारूढस्य तस्यैव शमः कारणमुच्यते ॥3॥
यदा हि नेन्द्रियार्थेषु न कर्मस्वनुषज्जते ।
सर्वसंकल्पसंन्यासी योगारूढस्तदोच्यते ॥4॥
उद्धरेदात्मनात्मानं नात्मानमवसादयेत् ।
आत्मैव ह्यात्मनोबन्धुरात्मैव रिपुरात्मनः ॥5॥
बन्धुरात्मात्मनस्तस्य येनात्मेवात्मना जितः ।
अनात्मनस्तु शत्रुत्वे वर्ततात्मैव शत्रुवत् ॥6॥
जितात्मनः प्रशान्तस्य परमात्मा समाहितः ।
शीतोष्णसुखदुःखेषु तथा मानापमानयोः ॥7॥

ज्ञानविज्ञानतृप्तात्मा कूटस्थो विजितेन्द्रियः ।
युक्त इत्युच्यते योगी समलोष्टाश्मकाञ्चनः ॥8॥
सुहृन्मित्रार्युदासीनमध्यस्थद्वेष्यबन्धुषु ।
साधुष्वपि च पापेषु समबुद्धिर्विशिष्यते ॥9॥
योगी युञ्जीत सततमात्मानं रहसि स्थितः ।
एकाकी यतचित्तात्मा निराशीरपरिग्रहः ॥10॥
शुचौ देशे प्रतिष्ठाप्य स्थिरमासनमात्मनः ।
नात्युच्छ्रितं नातिनीचं चैलाजिनकुशोत्तरम् ॥11॥
तत्रैकाग्रं मनः कृत्वा यतचित्तेन्द्रियक्रियः ।
उपविश्यासने युञ्ज्याद्योगमात्मविशुद्धये ॥12॥
समं कायशिरोग्रीवं धारयन्नचलं स्थिरः ।
संप्रेक्ष्य नासिकाग्रं स्वं दिशश्चानवलोकयन् ॥13॥
प्रशान्तात्मा विगतभीर्ब्रह्मचारिव्रते स्थितः ।
मनः संयम्य मच्चित्तो युक्त आसीत मत्परः ॥14॥
युञ्जन्नेवं सदात्मानं योगी नियतमानसः ।
शान्तिं निर्वाणपरमां मत्संस्थामधिगच्छति ॥15॥
नात्यश्नतस्तु योगोऽस्ति न चैकान्तमनश्नतः ।
न चाति स्वप्नशीलस्य जाग्रतो नैव चार्जुन ॥16॥
युक्ताहारविहारस्य युक्तचेष्टस्य कर्मसु ।
युक्तस्वप्नावबोधस्य योगो भवति दुःखहा ॥17॥
यदा विनियतं चित्तमात्मन्येवावतिष्ठते ।
निःस्पृहःसर्वकामेभ्यो युक्त इत्युच्यते तदा ॥18॥
यथा दीपो निवातस्थो नेङ्गते सोपमा स्मृता ।
योगिनो यतचित्तस्य युञ्जतो योगमात्मनः ॥19॥
यत्रोपरमते चित्तं निरुद्धं योगसेवया ।
यत्र चैवात्मनात्मानं पश्यन्नात्मनि तुष्यति ॥20॥
सुखमात्यन्तिकं यत्तद्बुद्धिग्राह्यमतीन्द्रियम् ।
वेत्ति यत्र न चैवायं स्थितश्चलति तत्त्वतः ॥21॥
यं लब्ध्वा चापरं लाभं मन्यते नाधिकं ततः ।
यस्मिन्स्थितो न दुःखेन गुरुणापि विचाल्यते ॥22॥

तं विद्याद्दुःखसंयोगवियोगं योगसंज्ञितम्।
स निश्चयेन योक्तव्यो योगोऽनिर्विण्णचेतसा ॥23॥
संकल्पप्रभवान्कामांस्त्यक्त्वा सर्वानशेषतः।
मनसैवेन्द्रियग्रामं विनियम्य समन्ततः ॥24॥
शनैः शनैरुपरमेद्बुद्ध्या धृतिगृहीतया।
आत्मसंस्थं मनः कृत्वा न किञ्चिदपि चिन्तयेत् ॥25॥
यतो यतो निश्चरति मनश्चञ्चलमस्थिरम्।
ततस्ततो नियम्यैतदात्मन्येव वशं नयेत् ॥26॥
प्रशान्तमनसं ह्येनं योगिनं सुखमुत्तमम्।
उपैति शान्तरजसं ब्रह्मभूतमकल्मषम् ॥27॥
युञ्जन्नेवं सदात्मानं योगी विगतकल्मषः।
सुखेन ब्रह्मसंस्पर्शमत्यन्तं सुखमश्नुते ॥28॥
सर्वभूतस्थमात्मानं सर्वभूतानि चात्मनि।
ईक्षते योगयुक्तात्मा सर्वत्र समदर्शनः ॥29॥
यो मां पश्यति सर्वत्र सर्वं च मयि पश्यति।
तस्याहं न प्रणश्यामि स च मे न प्रणश्यति ॥30॥
सर्वभूतस्थितं यो मां भजत्येकत्वमास्थितः।
आत्मौपम्येन सर्वत्र समं पश्यति योऽर्जुन।
सर्वथा वर्तमानोऽपि स योगी मयि वर्तते ॥31॥
आत्मौपम्येन सर्वत्र समं पश्यति योऽर्जुन।
सुखं वा यदि वा दुःखं स योगी परमो मतः ॥32॥

अर्जुन उवाच

योऽयं योगस्त्वया प्रोक्तः साम्येन मधुसूदन।
एतस्याहं न पश्यामि चञ्चलत्वात्स्थितिं स्थिराम्
चञ्चलं हि मनः कृष्ण प्रमाथि बलवद्दृढम्।
तस्याहं निग्रहं मन्ये वायोरिव सुदुष्करम् ॥34॥

श्रीभगवानुवाच

असंशयं महाबाहो मनो दुर्निग्रहं चलम्।
अभ्यासेन तु कौन्तेय वैराग्येण च गृह्यते ॥35॥

असंयतात्मना योगो दुष्प्राप इति मे मतिः।
वश्यात्मना तु यतता शक्योऽवाप्तुमुपायतः ॥36॥

अर्जुन उवाच

अयतिः श्रद्धयोपेतो योगाच्चलितमानसः।
अप्राप्य योगसंसिद्धिं कां गतिं कृष्ण गच्छति ॥37॥
कच्चिन्नोभयविभ्रष्टाश्छिन्नाभ्रमिव नश्यति।
अप्रतिष्ठो महाबाहो विमूढो ब्रह्मणः पथि ॥38॥
एतन्मे संशयं कृष्ण छेत्तुमर्हस्यशेषतः।
त्वदन्यः संशयस्यास्य छेत्ता न ह्युपपद्यते ॥39॥

श्रीभगवानुवाच

पार्थ नैवेह नामुत्र विनाशस्तस्य विद्यते।
न हि कल्याणकृत्कश्चिद्दुर्गतिं तात गच्छति ॥40॥
प्राप्य पुण्यकृतां लोकानुषित्वा शाश्वतीःसमाः।
शुचीनां श्रीमतां गेहे योगभ्रष्टोऽभिजायते ॥41॥
अथवा योगिनामेव कुले भवति धीमताम्।
एतद्धि दुर्लभतरं लोके जन्म यदीदृशम् ॥42॥
तत्र तं बुद्धिसंयोगं लभते पौर्वदेहिकम्।
यतते च ततो भूयः संसिद्धौ कुरुनन्दन ॥43॥
पूर्वाभ्यासेन तेनैव ह्रियते ह्यवशोऽपि सः।
जिज्ञासुरपि योगस्य शब्दब्रह्मातिवर्तते ॥44॥
प्रयत्नाद्यतमानस्तु योगी संशुद्धकिल्बिषः।
अनेकजन्मसंसिद्धस्ततो याति परां गतिम् ॥45॥

तपस्विभ्योऽधिको योगी
ज्ञानिभ्योऽपि मतोऽधिकः।
कर्मिभ्यश्चाधिको योगी
तस्माद्योगी भवार्जुन ॥46॥

योगिनामपि सर्वेषां मद्गतेनान्तरात्मना।
श्रद्धावान्भजते यो मां स मे युक्ततमो मतः ॥47॥

ॐ तत्सदिति श्रीमद्भगवद्गीतासूपनिषत्सु ब्रह्मविद्यायां
योगशास्त्रे श्रीकृष्णार्जुनसंवादे आत्मसंयमयोगो
नाम षष्ठोऽध्यायः ॥6॥

अथ सप्तमोऽध्यायः

श्रीभगवानुवाच

मय्यासक्तमनाः पार्थ योगं युञ्जन्मदाश्रयः।
असंशयं समग्रं मां यथा ज्ञास्यसि तच्छृणु ॥1॥
ज्ञानं तेऽहं सविज्ञानमिदं वक्ष्याम्यशेषतः।
यज्ज्ञात्वा नेह भूयोऽन्यज्ज्ञातव्यमवशिष्यते ॥2॥
मनुष्याणां सहस्रेषु कश्चिद्यतति सिद्धये।
यततामपि सिद्धानां कश्चिन्मां वेत्ति तत्त्वतः ॥3॥
भूमिरापोऽनलो वायुः खं मनो बुद्धिरेव च।
अहंकार इतीयं मे भिन्ना प्रकृतिरष्टधा ॥4॥
अपरेयमितस्त्वन्यां प्रकृतिं विद्धि मे पराम्।
जीवभूतां महाबाहो ययेदं धार्यते जगत् ॥5॥
एतद्योनीनि भूतानि सर्वाणीत्युपधारय।
अहं कृत्स्नस्य जगतः प्रभवः प्रलयस्तथा ॥6॥
मत्तः परतरं नान्यत्किञ्चिदस्ति धनंजय।
मयि सर्वमिदं प्रोतं सूत्रे मणिगणा इव ॥7॥
रसोऽहमप्सु कौन्तेय प्रभास्मि शशिसूर्ययोः।
प्रणवः सर्ववेदेषु शब्दः खे पौरुषं नृषु ॥8॥
पुण्यो गन्धः पृथिव्यां च तेजश्चास्मि विभावसौ।
जीवनं सर्वभूतेषु तपश्चास्मि तपस्विषु ॥9॥
बीजं मां सर्वभूतानां विद्धि पार्थ सनातनम्।
बुद्धिर्बुद्धिमतामस्मि तेजस्तेजस्विनामहम् ॥10॥
बलं बलवतां चाहं कामरागविवर्जितम्।
धर्माविरुद्धो भूतेषु कामोऽस्मि भरतर्षभ ॥11॥
ये चैव सात्त्विका भावा राजसास्तामसाश्च ये।
मत्त एवेति तान्विद्धि न त्वहं तेषु ते मयि ॥12॥

त्रिभिर्गुणमयैर्भावैरेभिः सर्वमिदं जगत्।
मोहितं नाभिजानाति मामेभ्यः परमव्ययम् ॥13॥
दैवी ह्येषा गुणमयी मम माया दुरत्यया।
मामेव ये प्रपद्यन्ते मायामेतां तरन्ति ते ॥14॥
न मां दुष्कृतिनो मूढाः प्रपद्यन्ते नराधमाः।
माययापहृतज्ञाना आसुरं भावमाश्रिताः ॥15॥
चतुर्विधा भजन्ते मां जनाः सुकृतिनोऽर्जुन।
आर्तो जिज्ञासुरर्थार्थी ज्ञानी च भरतर्षभ ॥16॥
तेषां ज्ञानी नित्ययुक्त एकभक्तिर्विशिष्यते।
प्रियो हि ज्ञानिनोऽत्यर्थमहं स च मम प्रियः ॥17॥
उदाराः सर्व एवैते ज्ञानी त्वात्मैव मे मतम्।
आस्थितः स हि युक्तात्मा मामेवानुत्तमां गतिम् ॥18॥
बहूनां जन्मनामन्ते ज्ञानवान्मां प्रपद्यते।
वासुदेवः सर्वमिति स महात्मा सुदुर्लभः ॥19॥
कामैस्तैस्तैर्हृतज्ञानाः प्रपद्यन्तेऽन्यदेवताः।
तं तं नियममास्थाय प्रकृत्या नियताः स्वया ॥20॥
यो यो यां यां तनु भ : श्रद्धयार्चितुमिच्छति।
तस्य तस्याचलां श्रद्धा तामेव विदधाम्यहम् ॥21॥
स तया श्रद्धया युक्तस्तस्याराधनमीहते।
लभते च ततः कामान्मयैव विहितान्हि तान् ॥22॥
अन्तवत्तु फलं तेषां तद्भवत्यल्पमेधसाम्।
देवान्देवयजो यान्ति मद्भक्ता यान्ति मामपि ॥23॥
अव्यक्तं व्यक्तिमापन्नं मन्यन्ते मामबुद्धयः।
परं भावमजानन्तो ममाव्ययमनुत्तमम् ॥24॥
नाहं प्रकाशः सर्वस्य योगमायासमावृतः।
मूढोऽयं नाभिजानाति लोको मामजमव्ययम् ॥25॥
वेदाहं समतीतानि वर्तमानानि चार्जुन।
भविष्याणि च भूतानि मां तु वेद न कश्चन ॥26॥
इच्छाद्वेषसमुत्थेन द्वन्द्वमोहेन भारत।
सर्वभूतानि संमोहं सर्गे यान्ति परंतप ॥27॥

येषां त्वन्तगतं पापं जनानां पुण्यकर्मणाम्।
ते द्वन्द्वमोहनिर्मुक्ता भजन्ते मां दृढव्रताः ॥28॥
जरामरणमोक्षाय मामाश्रित्य यतन्ति ये।
ते ब्रह्म तद्विदुः कृत्स्नमध्यात्मं कर्म चाखिलम् ॥29॥
साधिभूताधिदैवं मां साधियज्ञं च ये विदुः।
प्रयाणकालेऽपि च मां ते विदुर्युक्तचेतसः ॥30॥

ॐ तत्सदिति श्रीमद्भगवद्गीतासूपनिषत्सु ब्रह्मविद्यायां योगशास्त्रे श्रीकृष्णार्जुनसंवादे ज्ञानविज्ञानयोगो नाम सप्तमोऽध्यायः ॥7॥

अथाष्टमोऽध्यायः

अर्जुन उवाच

किं तद्ब्रह्म किमध्यात्मं किं कर्म पुरुषोत्तम।
अधिभूतं च किं प्रोक्तमधिदैवं किमुच्यते ॥1॥
अधियज्ञः कथं कोऽत्र देहेऽस्मिन्मधुसूदन।
प्रयाणकाले च कथं ज्ञेयोऽसि नियतात्मभिः ॥2॥

श्रीभगवानुवाच

अक्षरं ब्रह्म परमं स्वभावोऽध्यात्ममुच्यते।
भूतभावोद्भवकरो विसर्गः कर्मसंज्ञितः ॥3॥
अधिभूतं क्षरो भावः पुरुषश्चाधिदैवतम्।
अधियज्ञोऽहमेवात्र देहे देहभृतां वर ॥4॥
अन्तकाले च मामेव स्मरन्मुक्त्वा कलेवरम्।
यः प्रयाति स मद्भावं याति नास्त्यत्र संशयः ॥5॥
यं यं वापि स्मरन्भावं त्यजत्यन्ते कलेवरम्।
तं तमेवैति कौन्तेय सदा तद्भावभावितः ॥6॥
तस्मात्सर्वेषु कालेषु मामनुस्मर युध्य च।
मय्यर्पितमनोबुद्धिर्मामेवैष्यस्यसंशयम् ॥7॥
अभ्यासयोगयुक्तेन चेतसा नान्यगामिना।
परमं पुरुषं दिव्यं याति पार्थानुचिन्तयन् ॥8॥

कविं पुराणमनुशासितार-
मणोरणीयांसमनुस्मरेद्यः ।
सर्वस्य धातारमचिन्त्यरूप-
मादित्यवर्णं तमसः परस्तात् ॥9॥
प्रयाणकाले मनसाचलेन
भक्त्या युक्तो योगबलेन चैव।
भ्रुवोर्मध्ये प्राणमावेश्य सम्यक्
स तं परं पुरुषमुपैति दिव्यम् ॥10॥
यदक्षरं वेदविदो वदन्ति।
विशन्ति यद्यतयो वीतरागाः।
यदिच्छन्तो ब्रह्मचर्यं चरन्ति
तत्ते पदं संग्रहेण प्रवक्ष्ये ॥11॥
सर्वद्वाराणि संयम्य मनो हृदि निरुध्य च।
मूर्ध्न्याधायात्मनः प्राणमास्थितो योगधारणाम् ॥12॥
ओमित्येकाक्षरं ब्रह्म व्याहरन्मामनुस्मरन्।
यः प्रयाति त्यजन्देहं स याति परमां गतिम् ॥13॥
अनन्यचेताः सततं यो मां स्मरति नित्यशः।
तस्याहं सुलभः पार्थ नित्ययुक्तस्य योगिनः ॥14॥
मामुपेत्य पुनर्जन्म दुःखालयमशाश्वतम्।
नाप्नुवन्ति महात्मानः संसिद्धिं परमां गताः ॥15॥
आब्रह्मभुवनाल्लोकाः पुनरावर्तिनोऽर्जुन।
मामुपेत्य तु कौन्तेय पुनर्जन्म न विद्यते ॥16॥
सहस्रयुगपर्यन्तमहर्यद्ब्रह्मणो विदुः।
रात्रिं युगसहस्रान्तां तेऽहोरात्रविदो जनाः ॥17॥
अव्यक्ताद्व्यक्तयः सर्वाः प्रभवन्त्यहरागमे।
रात्र्यागमे प्रलीयन्ते तत्रैवाव्यक्तसंज्ञके ॥18॥
भूतग्रामः स एवायं भूत्वा भूत्वा प्रलीयते।
रात्र्यागमेऽवशः पार्थ प्रभवत्यहरागमे ॥19॥
परस्तस्मात्तु भावोऽन्योऽव्यक्तोऽव्यक्तात्सनातनः
यः स सर्वेषु भूतेषु नश्यत्सु न विनश्यति ॥20॥

अव्यक्तोऽक्षर इत्युक्तस्तमाहुः परमां गतिम्।
यं प्राप्य न निवर्तन्ते तद्धाम परमं मम ॥21॥
पुरुषः स परः पार्थ भक्त्या लभ्यस्त्वनन्यया।
यस्यान्तः स्थानि भूतानि येन सर्वमिदं ततम् ॥22॥
यत्र काले त्वनावृत्तिमावृत्तिं चैव योगिनः।
प्रयाता यान्ति तं कालं वक्ष्यामि भरतर्षभ ॥23॥
अग्निर्ज्योतिरहः शुक्लः षण्मासा उत्तरायणम्।
तत्र प्रयाता गच्छन्ति ब्रह्म ब्रह्मविदो जनाः ॥24॥
धूमो रात्रिस्तथा कृष्णः षण्मासा दक्षिणायनम्।
तत्र चान्द्रमसं ज्योतिर्योगी प्राप्य निवर्तते ॥25॥
शुक्लकृष्णे गती ह्येते जगतः शाश्वते मते।
एकया यात्यनावृत्तिमन्ययावर्तते पुनः ॥26॥
नैते सृती पार्थ जानन्योगी मुह्यति कश्चन।
तस्मात्सर्वेषु कालेषु योगयुक्तो भवार्जुन ॥27॥

वेदेषु यज्ञेषु तपः सु चैव
दानेषु यत्पुण्यफलं प्रदिष्टम्।
अत्येति तत्सर्वमिदं विदित्वा
योगी परं स्थानमुपैति चाद्यम् ॥28॥

ॐ तत्सदिति श्रीमद्भगवद्गीतातासूपनिषत्सु ब्रह्मविद्यायां
योगशास्त्रे श्रीकृष्णार्जुनसंवादे अक्षरब्रह्मयोगो
नामाष्टमोऽध्यायः ॥8॥

अथ नवमोऽध्यायः

श्रीभगवानुवाच

इदं तु ते गुह्यतमं प्रवक्ष्याम्यनसूयवे।
ज्ञानं विज्ञानसहितं यज्ज्ञात्वा मोक्ष्यसेऽशुभात् ॥1॥
राजविद्या राजगुह्यं पवित्रमिदमुत्तमम्।
प्रत्यक्षावगमं धर्म्यं सुसुखं कर्तुमव्ययम् ॥2॥
अश्रद्दधानाः पुरुषा धर्मस्यास्य परंतम।
अप्राप्य मां निवर्तन्ते मृत्युसंसारवर्त्मनि ॥3॥

मया ततमिदं सर्वंजगदव्यक्तमूर्तिना।
मत्स्थानि सर्वभूतानि न चाहं तेष्ववस्थितः ॥4॥
न च मत्स्थानि भूतानि पश्य मे योगमैश्वरम्।
भूतभृन्न च भूतस्थो ममात्मा भूतभावनः ॥5॥
यथाकाशस्थितो नित्यं वायुः सर्वत्रगो महान्।
तथा सर्वाणि भूतानि मत्स्थानीत्युपधारय ॥6॥
सर्वभूतानि कौन्तेय प्रकृतिं यान्ति मामिकाम्
कल्पक्षये पुनस्तानि कल्पादौ विसृजाम्यहम् ॥7॥
प्रकृतिं स्वामवष्टभ्य विसृजामि पुनः पुनः।
भूतग्राममिमं कृत्स्नमवशं प्रकृतेर्वशात् ॥8॥
न च मां तानि कर्माणि निबध्नन्ति धनंजय।
उदासीनवदासीनमसक्तं तेषु कर्मसु ॥9॥
मयाध्यक्षेण प्रकृतिः सूयते सचराचरम्।
हेतुनानेन कौन्तेय जगद्विपरिवर्तते ॥10॥
अवजानन्ति मां मूढा मानुषीं तनुमाश्रितम्।
परं भावमजानन्तो मम भूतमहेश्वरम् ॥11॥
मोघाशा मोघकर्माणो मोघज्ञाना विचेतसः।
राक्षसीमासुरीं चैव प्रकृतिं मोहिनीं श्रिताः ॥12॥
महात्मानस्तु मां पार्थ दैवीं प्रकृतिमाश्रिताः।
भजन्त्यनन्यमनसो ज्ञात्वा भूतादिमव्ययम् ॥13॥
सततं कीर्तयन्तो मां यतन्तश्च दृढव्रताः।
नमस्यन्तश्च मां भक्त्या नित्ययुक्ता उपासते ॥14॥
ज्ञानयज्ञेन चाप्यन्ये यजन्तो मामुपासते।
एकत्वेन पृथक्त्वेन बहुधा विश्वतोमुखम् ॥15॥
अहं क्रतुरहं यज्ञः स्वधाहमहमौषधम्।
मन्त्रोऽहमहमेवाज्यमहमग्निरहं हुतम् ॥16॥
पिताहमस्य जगतो माता धाता पितामहः।
वेद्यं पवित्रमोंकार ऋक्साम यजुरेव च ॥17॥
गतिर्भर्ता प्रभुः साक्षी निवासः शरणं सुहृत्।
प्रभवः प्रलयः स्थानं निधानं बीजमव्ययम् ॥18॥

तपाम्यहमहं वर्षं निगृह्णाम्युत्सृजामि च।
अमृतं चैव मृत्युश्च सदसच्चाहमर्जुन ॥19॥

त्रैविद्या मां सोमपाः पूतपापा
यज्ञैरिष्ट्वा स्वर्गतिं प्रार्थयन्ते।
ते पुण्यमासाद्य सुरेन्द्रलोक-
मश्नन्ति दिव्यान्दिवि देवभोगान् ॥20॥

ते तं भुक्त्वा स्वर्गलोकं विशालं
क्षीणे पुण्ये मर्त्यलोकं विशन्ति।
एवं त्रयीधर्ममनुप्रपन्ना
गतागतं कामकामा लभन्ते ॥21॥

अनन्याश्चिन्तयन्तो मां ये जनाः पर्युपासते।
तेषां नित्याभियुक्तानां योगक्षेमं वहाम्यहम् ॥22॥

येऽप्यन्यदेवता भक्ता यजन्ते श्रद्धयान्विताः।
तेऽपि मामेव कौन्तेय यजन्त्यविधिपूर्वकम् ॥23॥

अहं हि सर्वयज्ञानां भोक्ता च प्रभुरेव च।
न तु मामभिजानन्ति तत्त्वेतानश्च्यवन्ति ते ॥24॥

यान्ति देवव्रता देवान्पितॄन्यान्ति पितृव्रताः।
भूतानि यान्ति भूतेज्या यान्ति मद्याजिनोऽपि माम् ॥25॥

पत्रं पुष्पं फलं तोयं यो मे भक्त्या प्रयच्छति।
तदहं भक्त्युपहृतमश्नामि प्रयतात्मनः ॥26॥

यत्करोषि यदश्नासि यज्जुहोषि ददासि यत्।
यत्तपस्यसि कौन्तेय तत्कुरुष्व मदर्पणम् ॥27॥

शुभाशुभफलैरेवं मोक्ष्यसे कर्मबन्धनैः।
संन्यासयोगयुक्तात्मा विमुक्तो मामुपैष्यसि ॥28॥

समोऽहं सर्वभूतेषु न मे द्वेष्योऽस्ति न प्रियः।
ये भजन्ति तु मां भक्त्या मयि ते तेषु चाप्यहम् ॥29॥

अपि चेत्सुदुराचारो भजते मामनन्यभाक्।
साधुरेव स मन्तव्यः सम्यग्व्यवसितो हि सः ॥30॥

क्षिप्रं भवति धर्मात्मा शश्वच्छान्तिं निगच्छति
कौन्तेय प्रति जानीहि न मे भक्तः प्रणश्यति ॥31॥

मां हि पार्थ व्यपाश्रित्य येऽपि स्युः पापयोनयः।
स्त्रियोवैश्यास्तथा शूद्रास्तेऽपि यान्ति परां गतिम् ॥32॥
किं पुनर्ब्राह्मणाः पुण्या भक्ता राजर्षयस्तथा।
अनित्यमसुखं लोकमिमं प्राप्य भजस्व माम् ॥33॥
मन्मना भव मद्भक्तो मद्याजी मां नमस्कुरु।
मामेवैष्यसि युक्त्वैवमात्मानं मत्परायणः ॥34॥

ॐ तत्सदिति श्रीमद्भगवद्गीतासूपनिषत्सु ब्रह्मविद्यायां योगाशास्त्रे श्रीकृष्णार्जुनसंवादे राजविद्याराजगुह्य-योगो नाम नवमोऽध्यायः ॥9॥

अथ दशमोऽध्यायः

श्रीभगवानुवाच

भूय एव महाबाहो शृणु मे परमं वचः।
यत्तेऽहं प्रीयमाणाय वक्ष्यामि हितकाम्यया ॥1॥
न मे विदुः सुरगणाः प्रभवं न महर्षयः।
अहमादिर्हि देवानां महर्षीणां च सर्वशः ॥2॥
यो मामजमनादिं च वेत्ति लोकमहेश्वरम्।
असंमूढः स मर्त्येषु सर्वपापैः प्रमुच्यते ॥3॥
बुद्धिर्ज्ञानमसंमोहः क्षमा सत्यं दमः शमः।
सुखं दुःखं भवोऽभावो भयं चाभयमेव च ॥4॥
अहिंसा समता तुष्टिस्तपो दानं यशोऽयशः।
भवन्ति भावा भूतानां मत्त एवं पृथग्विधाः ॥5॥
महर्षयः सप्त पूर्वे चत्वारो मनवस्तथा।
मद्भावा मानसा जाता येषां लोक इमाः प्रजाः ॥6॥
एतां विभूतिं योगं च मम यो वेत्ति तत्त्वतः।
सोऽविकम्पेन योगेन युज्यते नात्र संयशः ॥7॥
अहं सर्वस्य प्रभवो मत्तः सर्वं प्रवर्तते।
इति मत्वा भजन्ते मां बुधा भावसमन्विताः ॥8॥
मच्चित्ता मद्गतप्राणा बोधयन्तः परस्परम्।
कथयन्तश्च मां नित्यं तुष्यन्ति च रमन्ति च ॥9॥

तेषां सततयुक्तानां भजतां प्रीतिपूर्वकम्।
ददामि बुद्धियोगं तं येन मामुपयान्ति ते ॥10॥
तेषामेवानुकम्पार्थमहमज्ञानजं तमः।
नाशयाम्यात्मभावस्थो ज्ञानदीपेन भास्वता। ॥11॥

अर्जुन उवाच

परं ब्रह्म परं धाम पवित्रं परमं भवान्।
पुरुषं शाश्वतं दिव्यमादिदेवमजंविभुम् ॥12॥
आहुस्त्वामृषयः सर्वे देवर्षिर्नारदस्तथा।
असितो देवलो व्यासः स्वयं चैव ब्रवीषि मे ॥13॥
सर्वमेतदृतं मन्ये यन्मां वदसि केशव।
न हि ते भगवन्व्यक्तिं विदुर्देवा न दानवाः ॥14॥
स्वयमेवात्मनात्मानं वेत्थ त्वं पुरुषोत्तम।
भूतभावन भूतेश देवदेव जगत्पते ॥15॥
वक्तुमर्हस्यशेषेण दिव्या ह्यात्मविभूतयः।
याभिर्विभूतिभिर्लोकानिमांस्त्वं व्याप्य तिष्ठसि ॥16॥
कथं विद्यामहं योगिंस्त्वां सदा परिचिन्तयन्।
केषु केषु च भावेषु चिन्त्योऽसि भगवन्मया ॥17॥
विस्तरेणात्मनो योगं विभूतिं च जनार्दन।
भूयः कथय तृप्तिर्हि शृण्वतो नास्ति मेऽमृतम् ॥18॥

श्रीभगवानुवाच

हन्त ते कथयिष्यामि दिव्या ह्यात्मविभूतयः।
प्राधान्यतः कुरुश्रेष्ठ नास्त्यन्तो विस्तरस्य मे ॥19॥
अहमात्मा गुडाकेश सर्वभूताशयस्थितः।
अहमादिश्च मध्यं च भूतानामन्त एव च ॥20॥
आदित्यानामहं विष्णुर्ज्योतिषां रविरंशुमान्।
मरीचिर्मरुतामस्मि नक्षत्राणामहं शशी ॥21॥
वेदानां समावेदोऽस्मि देवानामस्मि वासवः।
इन्द्रियाणां मनश्चास्मि भूतानामस्मि चेतना ॥22॥
रुद्राणां शंकरश्चास्मि वित्तेशो यक्षरक्षसाम्।
वसूनां पावकश्चास्मि मेरुः शिखरिणामहम् ॥23॥

पुरोधसां च मुख्यं मां विद्धि पार्थ बृहस्पतिम् ।
सेनानीनामहं स्कन्दः सरसामस्मि सागरः ॥24॥
महर्षीणां भृगुरहं गिरामस्म्येकमक्षरम् ।
यज्ञानां जपयज्ञोऽस्मि स्थावराणां हिमालयः ॥25॥
अश्वत्थः सर्ववृक्षाणां देवर्षीणां च नारदः ।
गन्धर्वाणां चित्ररथः सिद्धानां कपिलो मुनिः ॥26॥
उच्चैःश्रवसमश्वानां विद्धि माममृतोद्भवम् ।
ऐरावतं गजेन्द्राणां नराणां च नराधिपम् ॥27॥
आयुधानामहं वज्रं धेनूनामस्मि कामधुक् ।
प्रजनश्चास्मि कन्दर्पः सर्पाणामस्मि वासुकिः ॥28॥
अनन्तश्चास्मि नागानां वरुणो यादसामहम् ।
पितॄणामर्यमा चास्मि यः संयमतामहम् ॥29॥
प्रह्लादश्चास्मि दैत्यानां कालः कलयतामहम् ।
मृगाणां च मृगेन्द्रोऽहं वैनतेयश्च पक्षिणाम् ॥30॥
पवनः पवतामस्मि रामः शस्त्रभृतामहम् ।
झषाणां मकरश्चास्मि स्रोतसामस्मि जाह्नवी ॥31॥
सर्गाणामादिरन्तश्च मध्यं चैवाहमर्जुन ।
अध्यात्मविद्या विद्यानां वादः प्रवदतामहम् ॥32॥
अक्षराणामकारोऽस्मि द्वन्द्वः सामासिकस्य च ।
अहमेवाक्षयः कालो धाताहं विश्वतोमुखः ॥33॥
मृत्युः सर्वहरश्चाहमुद्भवश्च भविष्यताम् ।
कीर्तिः श्रीर्वाक्य नारीणां स्मृतिर्मेधा धृतिः क्षमा ॥34॥
बृहत्साम तथा साम्नां गायत्री छन्दसामहम् ।
मासानां मार्गशीर्षोऽहमृतूनां कुसुमाकरः ॥35॥
द्यूतं छलयतामस्मि तेजस्तेजस्विनामहम् ।
जयोऽस्मि व्यवसायोऽस्मि सत्त्वं सत्त्ववतामहम् ॥36॥
वृष्णीनां वासुदेवोऽस्मि पाण्डवानां धनंजयः ।
मुनीनामप्यहं व्यासः कवीनामुशना कविः ॥37॥
दण्डो दमयतामस्मि नीतिरस्मि जिगीषताम् ।
मौनं चैवास्मि गुह्यानां ज्ञानं ज्ञानवतामहम् ॥38॥

यच्चापि सर्वभूतानां बीजं तदहमर्जुन ।
न तदस्ति विना यत्स्यान्मया भूतं चराचरम् ॥39॥
नान्तोऽस्ति मम दिव्यानां विभूतीनां परंतप ।
एष तूद्देशतः प्रोक्तो विभूतेर्विस्तरो मया ॥40॥
यद्यद्विभूतिमत्सत्त्वं श्रीमदूर्जितमेव वा ।
तत्तदेवावगच्छ त्वं मम तेजोंऽशसंभवम् ॥41॥
अथवा बहुनैतेन किं ज्ञातेन तवार्जुन ।
विष्टभ्याहमिदं कृत्स्नमेकांशेन स्थितो जगत् ॥42॥

ॐ तत्सदिति श्रीमद्भगवद्गीतासूपनिषत्सु ब्रह्मविद्यायां
योगशास्त्रे श्रीकृष्णार्जुनसंवादे विभूतियोगो
नाम दशमोऽध्यायः ॥10॥

ॐ श्रीपरमात्मने नमः

अथैकादशोऽध्यायः

अर्जुन उवाच

मदनुग्रहाय परमं गुह्यमध्यात्मसंज्ञितम् ।
यत्त्वयोक्तं वचस्तेन मोहोऽयं विगतो मम ॥1॥
भवाप्ययौ हि भूतानां श्रुतौ विस्तरशो मया ।
त्वत्तः कमलपत्राक्ष माहात्म्यमपि चाव्ययम् ॥2॥
एवमेतद्यथात्थ त्वमात्मानं परमेश्वर ।
द्रष्टुमिच्छामि ते रूपमैश्वरं पुरुषोत्तम ॥3॥
मन्यसे यदि तच्छक्यं मया द्रष्टुमिति प्रभो ।
योगेश्वर ततो मे त्वं दर्शयात्मानमव्ययम् ॥4॥

श्रीभगवानुवाच

पश्य मे पार्थ रूपाणि शतशोऽथ सहस्रशः ।
नानाविधानि दिव्यानि नानावर्णाकृतीनि च ॥5॥
पश्यादित्यान्वसून्रुद्रानश्विनौ मरुतस्तथा ।
बहून्यदृष्टपूर्वाणि पश्याश्चर्याणि भारत ॥6॥

इहैकस्थं जगत्कृत्स्नं पश्याद्य सचराचरम्।
मम देहे गुडाकेश यच्चान्यद्द्रष्टुमिच्छसि ॥7॥
न तु मां शक्यसे द्रष्टुमनेनैव स्वचक्षुषा।
दिव्यं ददामि ते चक्षुः पश्य मे योगमैश्वरम् ॥8॥

संजय उवाच

एवमुक्त्वा ततो राजन्महायोगेश्वरो हरिः।
दर्शयामास पार्थाय परमं रूपमैश्वरम् ॥9॥
अनेकवक्त्रनयनमनेकाद्भुतदर्शनम्।
अनेकदिव्याभरणं दिव्यानेकोद्यतायुधम् ॥10॥
दिव्यमाल्याम्बरधरं दिव्यगन्धानुलेपनम्।
सर्वाश्चर्यमयं देवमनन्तं विश्वतोमुखम् ॥11॥
दिवि सूर्यसहस्रस्य भवेद्युगपदुत्थिता।
यदि भाः सदृशी सा स्याद्भासस्तस्य महात्मनः ॥12॥
तत्रैकस्थं जगत्कृत्स्नं प्रविभक्तमनेकधा।
अपश्यद्देवदेवस्य शरीरे पाण्डवस्तदा ॥13॥
ततः स विस्मयाविष्टो हृष्टरोमा धनंजयः।
प्रणम्य शिरसा देवं कृताञ्जलिरभाषत ॥14॥

अर्जुन उवाच

पश्यामि देवांस्तव देव देहे
सर्वांस्तथा भूतविशेषसङ्घान्।
ब्रह्माणमीशं कमलासनस्थ-
मृषींश्च सर्वानुरगांश्च दिव्यान् ॥15॥
अनेकबाहूदरवक्त्रनेत्रं
पश्यामि त्वां सर्वतोऽनन्तरूपम्।
नान्तं न मध्यं न पुनस्तवादिं
पश्यामि विश्वेश्वर विश्वरूप ॥16॥
किरीटिनं गदिनं चक्रिणं च
तेजोराशिं सर्वतो दीप्तिमन्तम्।
पश्यामि त्वां दुर्निरीक्ष्यं समन्ता-
द्दीप्तानलार्कद्युतिमप्रमेयम् ॥17॥

त्वमक्षरं परमं वेदितव्यं
त्वमस्य विश्वस्य परं निधानम्।
त्वमव्ययः शाश्वतधर्मगोप्ता
सनातनस्त्वं पुरुषो मतो मे ॥18॥

अनादिमध्यान्तमनन्तवीर्य-
मनन्तबाहुं शशिसूर्यनेत्रम्।
पश्यामि त्वां दीप्तहुताशवक्त्रं
स्वतेजसा विश्वमिदं तपन्तम् ॥19॥

द्यावापृथिव्योरिदमन्तरं हि
व्याप्तं त्वयैकेन दिशश्च सर्वाः।
दृष्ट्वाद्भुतं रूपमुग्रं तवेदं
लोकत्रयं प्रव्यथितं महात्मन् ॥20॥

अमी हि त्वां सुरसङ्घा विशन्ति
केचिद्भीताः प्राञ्जलयो गृणन्ति।
स्वस्तीत्युक्त्वा महर्षिसिद्धसङ्घाः
स्तुवन्ति त्वां स्तुतिभिः पुष्कलाभिः ॥21॥

रुद्रादित्या वसवो ये च साध्या
विश्वेऽश्विनौ मरुतश्चोष्मपाश्च।
गन्धर्वयक्षासुरसिद्धसङ्घा
वीक्षन्ते त्वां विस्मिताश्चैव सर्वे ॥22॥

रूपं महत्ते बहुवक्त्रनेत्रं
महाबाहो बहुबाहूरुपादम्।
बहूदरं बहुदंष्ट्राकरालं
दृष्ट्वा लोकाः प्रव्यथितास्तथाहम् ॥23॥

नभःस्पृशं दीप्तमनेकवर्णं
व्यात्ताननं दीप्तविशालनेत्रम्।
दृष्ट्वा हि त्वां प्रव्यथितान्तरात्मा
धृतिं न विन्दामि शमं च विष्णो ॥24॥

दंष्ट्राकरालानि च ते मुखानि
दृष्ट्वैव कालानलसन्निभानि।
दिशो न जाने न लभे च शर्म
प्रसीद देवेश जगन्निवास ॥25॥

अमी च त्वां धृतराष्ट्रस्य पुत्राः
सर्वे सहैवावनिपालसङ्घैः ।
भीष्मो द्रोणः सूतपुत्रस्तथासौ
सहास्मदीयैरपि योधमुख्यैः ॥26॥

वक्त्राणि ते त्वरमाणा विशन्ति
दंष्ट्राकरालानि भयानकानि ।
केचिद्विलग्ना दशनान्तरेषु
संदृश्यन्ते चूर्णितैरुत्तमाङ्गैः ॥27॥

यथा नदीनां बहवोऽम्बुवेगाः
समुद्रमेवाभिमुखा द्रवन्ति ।
तथा तवामी नरलोकवीरा
विशन्ति वक्त्राण्यभिविज्वलन्ति ॥28॥

यथा प्रदीप्तं ज्वलनं पतङ्गा
विशन्ति नाशाय समृद्धवेगाः ।
तथैव नाशाय विशन्ति लोका-
स्तवापि वक्त्राणि समृद्धवेगाः ॥29॥

लेलिह्यसे ग्रसमानः समन्ता-
ल्लोकान्समग्रान्वदनैर्ज्वलद्भिः ।
तेजोभिरापूर्य जगत्समग्रं
भासस्तवोग्राः प्रतपन्ति विष्णो ॥30॥

आख्याहि मे को भवानुग्ररूपो
नमोऽस्तु ते देववर प्रसीद ।
विज्ञातुमिच्छामि भवन्तमाद्यं
न हि प्रजानामि तव प्रवृत्तिम् ॥31॥

श्रीभगवानुवाच

कालोऽस्मि लोकक्षयकृत्प्रवृद्धो
लोकान्समाहर्तुमिह प्रवृत्तः ।
ऋतेऽपि त्वां न भविष्यन्ति सर्वे
येऽवस्थिताः प्रत्यनीकेषु योधाः ॥32॥

तस्मात्त्वमुत्तिष्ठ यशो लभस्व
जित्वा शत्रून् भुङ्क्ष्व राज्य समृद्धम्।
मयैवैते निहताः पूर्वमेव
निमित्तमात्रं भव सव्यसाचिन् ॥33॥

द्रोणं च भीष्मं च जयद्रथं च
कर्णं तथान्यानपि योधवीरान्।
मया हतांस्त्वं जहि मा व्यथिष्ठा
युध्यस्व जेतासि रणे सपत्नान् ॥34॥

संजय उवाच

एतच्छ्रुत्वा वचनं केशवस्य
कृताञ्जलिर्वेपमानः किरीटी।
नमस्कृत्वा भूय एवाह कृष्णं
सगद्गदं भीतभीतः प्रणम्य ॥35॥

अर्जुव उवाच

स्थाने हृषीकेश तव प्रकीर्त्या
जगत्प्रहृष्यत्यनुरज्यते च।
रक्षांसि भीतानि दिशो द्रवन्ति
सर्वे नमस्यन्ति च सिद्धसङ्घाः ॥36॥

कस्माच्च ते न नमेरन्महात्मन्
गरीयसे ब्रह्मणोऽप्यादिकर्त्रे।
अनन्त देवेश जगन्निवास
त्वमक्षरं सदसत्तत्परं यत् ॥37॥

त्वमादिदेवः पुरुषः पुराण-
स्त्वमस्य विश्वस्य परं निधानम्।
वेत्तासि वेद्यं च परं च धाम
त्वया ततं विश्वमनन्तरूप ॥38॥

वायुर्यमोऽग्निर्वरुणः शशाङ्कः
प्रजापतिस्त्वं प्रपितामहश्च।
नमो नमस्तेऽस्तुसहस्रकृत्वः
पुनश्च भूयोऽपि नमो नमस्ते ॥39॥

नमः पुरस्तादथ पृष्ठतस्ते
नमोऽस्तु ते सर्वत एव सर्व।
अनन्तवीर्यामितविक्रमस्त्वं
सर्वं समाप्नोषि ततोऽसि सर्वः ॥40॥

सखेति मत्वा प्रसभं यदुक्तं
हे कृष्ण हे यादव हे सखेति।
अजानता महिमानं तवेदं
मया प्रमादात्प्रणयेन वापि ॥41॥

यच्चावहासार्थमसत्कृतोऽसि
विहारशय्यासनभोजनेषु।
एकोऽथवाप्यच्युत तत्समक्षं
तत्क्षामये त्वामहमप्रमेयम् ॥42॥

पितासि लोकस्य चराचरस्य
त्वमस्य पूज्यश्च गुरुर्गरीयान्।
न त्वत्समोऽस्त्यभ्यधिकः कुतोऽन्यो
लोकत्रयेऽप्यप्रतिमप्रभाव ॥43॥

तस्मात्प्रणम्य प्रणिधाय कायं
प्रसादये त्वामहमीशमीड्यम्।
पितेव पुत्रस्य सखेव सख्युः
प्रियः प्रियायार्हसि देव सोढुम् ॥44॥

अदृष्टपूर्वं हृषितोऽस्मि दृष्ट्वा
भयेन च प्रव्यथितं मनो मे।
तदेव मे दर्शय देव रूपं
प्रसीद देवेश जगन्निवास ॥45॥

किरीटिनं गदिनं चक्रहस्त-
मिच्छामि त्वां द्रष्टुमहं तथैव।
तेनैव रूपेण चतुर्भुजेन
सहस्रबाहो भव विश्वमूर्ते ॥46॥

श्रीभगवानुवाच

मया प्रसन्नेन तवार्जुनेदं
रूपं परं दर्शितमात्मयोगात्।

तेजोमयं विश्वमनन्तमाद्यं
यन्मे त्वदन्येन न दृष्टपूर्वम् ॥47॥
न वेदयज्ञाध्ययनैर्न दानै-
र्न च क्रियाभिर्न तपोभिरुग्रैः।
एवंरूपः शक्य अहं नृलोके
द्रष्टुं त्वदन्येन कुरुप्रवीर ॥48॥
मा ते व्यथा मा च विमूढभावो
दृष्ट्वा रूपं घोरमीदृङ्‌मेदम्।
व्यपेतभीः प्रीतमनाः पुनस्त्वं
तदेव मे रूपमिदं प्रपश्य ॥49॥

संजय उवाच

इत्यर्जुनं वासुदेवस्तथोक्त्वा
स्वकं रूपं दर्शयामास भूयः।
आश्वासयामास च भीतमेनं
भूत्वा पुनः सौम्यवपुर्महात्मा ॥50॥

अर्जुन उवाच

दृष्ट्वेदं मानुषं रूपं तव सौम्यं जनार्दन।
इदानीमस्मि संवृत्तः सचेताः प्रकृतिं गतः ॥51॥

श्रीभगवानुवाच

सुदुर्दर्शमिदं रूपं दृष्टवानसि यन्मम।
देवा अप्यस्य रूपस्य नित्यं दर्शनकाङ्क्षिणः ॥52॥
नाहं वेदैर्न तपसा न दानेन न चेज्यया।
शक्य त्वनन्यया शक्य अहमेवंविधोऽर्जुन। ॥53॥
भक्त्या त्वनन्यया शक्य अहमेवंविधोऽर्जुन।
ज्ञातुं द्रष्टुं च तत्त्वेन प्रवेष्टुं च परंतप ॥54॥
मत्कर्मकृन्मत्परमो मद्भक्तः सङ्गवर्जितः।
निर्वैरः सर्वभूतेषु यः स मामेति पाण्डव ॥55॥

ॐ तत्सदिति श्रीमद्भगवद्गीतासूपनिषत्सु ब्रह्मविद्यायां
योगशास्त्रे श्रीकृष्णार्जुनसंवादे विश्वरूपदर्शनयोगो

नामैकादशोऽध्यायः ॥11॥

ॐ श्रीपरमात्मने नमः

अथ द्वादशोऽध्यायः

अर्जुन उवाच

एवं सततयुक्ता ये भक्तास्त्वां पर्युपासते।
ये चाप्यक्षरमव्यक्तं तेषां के योगवित्तमाः ॥1॥

श्रीभगवानुवाच

मय्यावेश्य मनो ये मां नित्ययुक्ता उपासते।
श्रद्धया परयोपेतास्ते मे युक्ततमा मताः ॥2॥
ये त्वक्षरमनिर्देश्यमव्यक्तं पर्युपासते।
सर्वत्रगमचिन्त्यं च कूटस्थमचलं ध्रुवम् ॥3॥
संनियम्येन्द्रियग्रामं सर्वत्र समबुद्धयः।
ते प्राप्नुवन्ति मामेव सर्वभूतहिते रताः ॥4॥
क्लेशोऽधिकतरस्तेषामव्यक्तासक्तचेतसाम्।
अव्यक्ता हि गतिर्दुःखं देहवद्भिरवाप्यते ॥5॥
ये तु सर्वाणि कर्माणि मयि संन्यस्य मत्पराः।
अनन्येनैव योगेन मां ध्यायन्त उपासते ॥6॥
तेषामहं समुद्धर्ता मृत्युसंसारसागरात्।
भवामि नचिरात्पार्थ मय्यावेशितचेतसाम् ॥7॥
मय्येव मन आधत्स्व मयि बुद्धिं निवेशय।
निवसिष्यसि मय्येव अत ऊर्ध्वं न संशयः ॥8॥
अथ चित्तं समाधातुं न शक्नोषि मयि स्थिरम्।
अभ्यासयोगेन ततो मामिच्छाप्तुं धनंजय ॥9॥
अभ्यासेऽप्यसमर्थोऽसि मत्कर्मपरमो भव।
मदर्थमपि कर्माणि कुर्वन्सिद्धिमवाप्स्यसि ॥10॥
अथैतदप्यशक्तोऽसि कर्तुं मद्योगमाश्रितः।
सर्वकर्मफलत्यागं ततः कुरु यतात्मवान् ॥11॥
श्रेयो हि ज्ञानमभ्यासाज्ज्ञानाद्ध्यानं विशिष्यते।
ध्यानात्कर्मफलत्यागस्त्यागाच्छान्तिरनन्तरम् ॥12॥

अद्वेष्टा सर्वभूतानां मैत्र करुण एव च।
निर्ममो निरहंकारः समदुः खसुखःक्षमी ॥13॥
संतुष्टः सततं योगी यतात्मा दृढनिश्चयः।
मय्यर्पितमनोबुद्धिर्यो मद्भक्तः स मे प्रियः ॥14॥
यस्मान्नोद्विजते लोको लोकान्नोद्विजते च यः।
हर्षामर्षभयोद्वेगैर्मुक्तो यः स च मे प्रियः ॥15॥
अनपेक्षः शुचिर्दक्ष उदासीनो गतव्यथः।
सर्वारम्भपरित्यागी यो मद्भक्तः स मे प्रियः ॥16॥
यो न हृष्यति न द्वेष्टि न शोचति न काङ्क्षति।
शुभाशुभपरित्यागी भक्तिमान्यः स मे प्रियः ॥17॥
समः शत्रौ च मित्रे च तथा मानापमानयोः।
शीतोष्णसुखदुःखेषु समः सङ्गविवर्जितः ॥18॥
तुल्यनिन्दास्तुतिर्मौनी संतुष्टो येन केनचित्।
अनिकेतः स्थिरमतिर्भक्तिमान्मे प्रियो नरः ॥19॥
ये तु धर्म्यामृतमिदं यथोक्तं पर्युपासते।
श्रद्दधाना मत्परमा भक्तास्तेऽतीव मे प्रियाः ॥20॥

ॐ तत्सदिति श्रीमद्भगवद्गीतासूपनिषत्सु ब्रह्मविद्यायां
योगशास्त्रे श्रीकृष्णार्जुनसंवादे भक्तियोगो
नाम द्वादशोऽध्यायः ॥12॥

अथ त्रयोदशोऽध्यायः

श्रीभगवानुवाच

इदं शरीरं कौन्तेय क्षेत्रमित्यभिधीयते।
एतद्यो वेत्ति तं प्राहुः क्षेत्रज्ञ इति तद्विदः ॥1॥
क्षेत्रज्ञं चापि मां विद्धि सर्वक्षेत्रेषु भारत।
क्षेत्रक्षेत्रज्ञयोर्ज्ञानं यत्तज्ज्ञानं मतं मम ॥2॥
तत्क्षेत्रं यच्च यादृक्च यद्विकारि यतश्च यत्।
स च यो यत्प्रभावश्च तत्समासेन मे शृणु ॥3॥
ऋषिभिर्बहुधा गीतं छन्दोभिर्विविधैः पृथक्।
ब्रह्मसूत्रपदैश्चैव हेतुमद्भिर्विनिश्चितैः ॥4॥

महाभूतान्यहंकारो बुद्धिरव्यक्तमेव च।
इन्द्रियाणि दशैकं च पञ्च चेन्द्रियगोचराः ॥5॥
इच्छा द्वेषः सुखं दुःखं संघातश्चेतना धृतिः।
एतत्क्षेत्रं समासेन सविकारमुदाहृतम् ॥6॥
अमानित्वमदम्भित्वमहिंसा क्षान्तिरार्जवम्।
आचार्योपासनं शौचं स्थैर्यमात्मविनिग्रहः ॥7॥
इन्द्रियार्थेषु वैराग्यमनहंकार एव च।
जन्ममृत्युजराव्याधिदुःखदोषानुदर्शनम् ॥8॥
असक्तिरनभिष्वङ्गः पुत्रदारगृहादिषु।
नित्यं च समचित्तत्वमिष्टानिष्टोपपत्तिषु ॥9॥
मयि चानन्ययोगेन भक्तिरव्यभिचारिणी।
विविक्तदेशसेवित्वमरतिर्जनसंसदि ॥10॥
अध्यात्मज्ञाननित्यत्वं तत्त्वज्ञानार्थदर्शनम्।
एतज्ज्ञानमिति प्रोक्तमज्ञानं यदतोऽन्यथा ॥11॥
ज्ञेयं यत्तत्प्रवक्ष्यामि यज्ज्ञात्वामृतमश्नुते।
अनादिमत्परं ब्रह्म न सत्तन्नासदुच्यते ॥12॥
सर्वतःपाणिपादं तत्सर्वतोऽक्षिशिरोमुखम्।
सर्वतःश्रुतिमल्लोके सर्वमावृत्य तिष्ठति ॥13॥
सर्वेन्द्रियगुणाभासं सर्वेन्द्रियविवर्जितम्।
असक्तं सर्वभृच्चैव निर्गुणं गुणभोक्तृच ॥14॥
बहिरन्तश्च भूतानामचरं चरमेव च।
सूक्ष्मत्वात्तदविज्ञेयं दूरस्थं चान्तिके च तत् ॥15॥
अविभक्तं च भूतेषु विभक्तमिव च स्थितम्।
भूतभर्तृ च तज्ज्ञेयं ग्रसिष्णु प्रभविष्णु च ॥16॥
ज्योतिषामपि तज्जयोतिस्तमसः परमुच्यते।
ज्ञानं ज्ञेयं ज्ञानगम्यं हृदि सर्वस्य विष्ठितम् ॥17॥
इति क्षेत्रं तथा ज्ञानं श्रेयं चोक्तं समासतः।
मद्भक्त एतद्विज्ञाय मद्भावायोपपद्यते ॥18॥
प्रकृतिं पुरुषं चैव विद्ध्यनादी उभावपि।
विकारांश्चगुणांश्चैव विद्धि प्रकृतिसंभवान् ॥19॥

कार्यकरणकर्तृत्वे हेतुः प्रकृतिरुच्यते ।
पुरुषः सुखदुःखानां भोक्तृत्वे हेतुरुच्यते ॥20॥
पुरुषः प्रकृतिस्थो हि भुङ्क्ते प्रकृतिजान्गुणान् ।
कारणं गुणसङ्गोऽस्य सदसद्योनिजन्मसु ॥21॥
उपद्रष्टानुमन्ता च भर्ता भोक्ता महेश्वरः ।
परमात्मेति चाप्युक्तो देहेऽस्मिन्पुरुषः परः ॥22॥
य एवं वेत्ति पुरुषं प्रकृतिं च गुणैः सह ।
सर्वथा वर्तमानोऽपि न स भूयोऽभिजायते ॥23॥
ध्यानेनात्मनि पश्यन्ति केचिदात्मानमात्मना ।
अन्ये सांख्येन योगेन कर्मयोगेन चापरे ॥24॥
अन्ये त्वेवमजानन्तः श्रुत्वान्येभ्य उपासते ।
तेऽपि चातितरन्त्येव मृत्युं श्रुतिपरायणाः ॥25॥
यावत्संजायते किंचित्सत्त्वं स्थावरजङ्गमम् ।
क्षेत्रक्षेत्रज्ञसंयोगात्तद्विद्धि भरतर्षभ ॥26॥
समं सर्वेषु भूतेषु तिष्ठन्तं परमेश्वरम् ।
विनश्यत्स्वविनश्यन्तं यः पश्यति स पश्यति ॥27॥
समं पश्यन्हि सर्वत्र समवस्थितमीश्वरम् ।
न हिनस्त्यात्मनात्मानं ततो याति परां गतिम् ॥28॥
प्रकृत्यैव च कर्माणि क्रियमाणानि सर्वशः ।
यः पश्यति तथात्मानमकर्तारं स पश्यति ॥29॥
यदा भूतपृथग्भावमेकस्थमनुपश्यति ।
तत एव च विस्तारं ब्रह्म संपद्यते तदा ॥30॥
अनादित्वान्निर्गुणत्वात्परमात्मायमव्ययः ।
शरीरस्थोऽपि कौन्तेय न करोति न लिप्यते ॥31॥
यथा सर्वगतं सौक्ष्म्यादाकाशं नोपलिप्यते ।
सर्वत्रावस्थितो देहे तथात्मा नोपलिप्यते ॥32॥
यथा प्रकाशयत्येकः कृत्स्नं लोकमिमं रविः ।
क्षेत्रं क्षेत्री तथा कृत्स्नं प्रकाशयति भारत ॥33॥
क्षेत्रक्षेत्रज्ञयोरेवमन्तरं ज्ञानचक्षुषा ।
भूतप्रकृतिमोक्षं च ये विदुर्यान्ति ते परम् ॥34॥

ॐ तत्सदिति श्रीमद्भगवद्गीतासूपनिषत्सु ब्रह्मविद्यायां योगशास्त्रे श्रीकृष्णार्जुनसंवादे क्षेत्रक्षेत्रज्ञविभागयोगो नाम त्रयोदशोऽध्यायः ॥13॥

अथ चतुर्दशोऽध्यायः

श्रीभगवानुवाच

परं भूयः प्रवक्ष्यामि ज्ञानानां ज्ञानमुत्तमम्।
यज्ज्ञात्वा मुनयः सर्वे परां सिद्धिमितो गताः ॥1॥
इदं ज्ञानमुपाश्रित्य मम साधर्म्यमागताः।
सर्गेऽपि नोपजायन्ते प्रलये न व्यथन्ति च ॥2॥
मम योनिर्महद्ब्रह्म तस्मिन्गर्भं दधाम्यहम्।
संभवः सर्वभूतानां ततो भवति भारत ॥3॥
सर्वयोनिषु कौन्तेय मूर्तयः संभवन्ति याः।
तासां ब्रह्म महद्योनिरहं बीजप्रदः पिता ॥4॥
सत्त्वं रजस्तम इति गुणाः प्रकृतिसंभवाः।
निबध्नन्ति महाबाहो देहे देहिनमव्ययम् ॥5॥
तत्र सत्त्वं निर्मलत्वात्प्रकाशकमनामयम्।
सुखसङ्गेन बध्नाति ज्ञानसङ्गेन चानघ ॥6॥
रजो रागात्मकं विद्धि तृष्णासङ्गसमुद्भवम्।
तन्निबध्नति कौन्तेय कर्मसङ्गेन देहिनम् ॥7॥
तमस्त्वज्ञानजं विद्धि मोहनं सर्वदेहिनाम्।
प्रमादालस्यनिद्राभिस्तन्निबध्नाति भारत ॥8॥
सत्त्वं सुखे संजयति रजः कर्मणि भारत।
ज्ञानमावृत्य तु तमः प्रमादे संजयत्युत ॥9॥
रजस्तमश्चाभिभूय सत्त्वं भवति भारत।
रजः सत्त्वं तमश्चैव तमः सत्त्वं रजस्तथा ॥10॥
सर्वद्वारेषु देहेऽस्मिन्प्रकाश उपजायते।
ज्ञानं यदा तदा विद्याद्विवृद्धं सत्त्वमित्युत ॥11॥
लोभः प्रवृत्तिरारम्भः कर्मणामशमः स्पृहा।
रजस्येतानि जायन्ते विवृद्धे भरतर्षभ ॥12॥
अप्रकाशोऽप्रवृत्तिश्च प्रमादो मोह एव च।
तमस्येतानि जायन्ते विवृद्धे कुरुनन्दन ॥13॥

यदा सत्त्वे प्रवृद्धे तु प्रलयं याति देहभृत्।
तदोत्तमविदां लोकानमलान्प्रतिपद्यते ॥14॥
रजसि प्रलयं गत्वा कर्मसङ्गिषु जायते।
तथा प्रलीनस्तमसि मूढयोनिषु जायते ॥15॥
कर्मणः सुकृतस्याहुः सात्त्विकं निर्मलं फलम्।
रजसस्तु फलं दुःखमज्ञानं तमसः फलम् ॥16॥
सत्त्वात्संजायते ज्ञानं रजसो लोभ एव च।
प्रमादमोहौ तमसो भवतोऽज्ञानमेव च ॥17॥
ऊर्ध्वंगच्छन्ति सत्त्वस्था मध्ये तिष्ठन्ति राजसाः
जघन्यगुणवृत्तिस्था अधो गच्छन्ति तामसाः ॥18॥
नान्यं गुणेभ्यः कर्तारं यदा द्रष्टानुपश्यति।
गुणेभ्यश्च परं वेत्ति मद्भावं सोऽधिगच्छति ॥19॥
गुणानेतानतीत्य त्रीन्देही देहसमुद्भवान्।
जन्ममृत्युजरादुःखैर्विमुक्तोऽमृतमश्नुते ॥20॥

अर्जुन उवाच

कैर्लिङ्गैस्त्रीन्गुणानेतानतीतो भवति प्रभो।
किमाचारः कथं चैतांस्त्रीन्गुणानतिवर्तते ॥21॥

श्रीभगवानुवाच

प्रकाशं च प्रवृत्तिं च मोहमेव च पाण्डव।
न द्वेष्टि संप्रवृत्तानि न निवृत्तानि काङ्क्षति ॥22॥
उदासीनवदासीनो गुणैर्यो न विचाल्यते।
गुणा वर्तन्त इत्येव योऽवतिष्ठति नेङ्गते ॥23॥
समदुःखसुखः स्वस्थः समलोष्टाश्मकाञ्चनः।
तुल्यप्रियाप्रियो धीरस्तुल्यनिन्दात्मसंस्तुतिः ॥24॥
मानापमानयोस्तुल्यस्तुल्यो मित्रारिपक्षयोः।
सर्वारम्भपरित्यागी गुणातीतः स उच्यते ॥25॥
मां च योऽव्यभिचारेण भक्तियोगेन सेवते।
स गुणान्समतीत्यैतान्ब्रह्मभूयाय कल्पते ॥26॥

ब्रह्मणो हि प्रतिष्ठाहममृतस्याव्ययस्य च।
शाश्वतस्य च धर्मस्य सुखस्यैकान्तिकस्य च ॥27॥

ॐ तत्सदिति श्रीमद्भगवद्गीतासूपनिषत्सु ब्रह्मविद्यायां योगशास्त्रे श्रीकृष्णार्जुनसंवादे गुणत्रयविभागयोगो नाम चतुर्दशोऽध्यायः ॥14॥

ॐ श्रीपरमात्मने नमः

अथ पञ्चदशोऽध्यायः

श्रीभगवानुवाच

ऊर्ध्वमूलमधःशाखमश्वत्थं प्राहुरव्ययम्।
छन्दांसि यस्य पर्णानि यस्तं वेद स वेदवित् ॥1॥
अधश्चोर्ध्वं प्रसृतास्तस्य शाखा
गुणप्रवृद्धा विषयप्रवालाः।
अधश्च मूलान्यनुसंततानि
कर्मानुबन्धीनि मनुष्यलोके ॥2॥
न रूपमस्येह तथोपलभ्यते
नान्तो न चादिर्न च संप्रतिष्ठा।
अश्वत्थमेनं सुविरूढमूल-
मसङ्गशस्त्रेण दृढेन छित्त्वा ॥3॥
ततः पदं तत्परिमार्गितव्यं
यस्मिन्गता न निवर्तन्ति भूयः।
तमेव चाद्यं पुरुषं प्रपद्ये
यतः प्रवृत्तिः प्रसृता पुराणी ॥4॥
निर्मानमोहा जितसङ्गदोषा
अध्यात्मनित्या विनिवृत्तकामाः।
द्वन्द्वैर्विमुक्ताः सुखदुःखसंज्ञै-
र्गच्छन्त्यमूढाः पदमव्ययं तत् ॥5॥
न तद्भासयते सूर्यो न शशाङ्को न पावकः।
यद्गत्वा न निवर्तन्ते तद्धाम परमं मम ॥6॥

ममैवांशो जीवलोके जीवभूतः सनातनः।
मनः षष्ठानीन्द्रियाणि प्रकृतिस्थानि कर्षति ॥7॥
शरीरं यदवाप्नोति यच्चाप्युत्क्रामतीश्वरः।
गृहीत्वैतानि संयाति वायुर्गन्धानिवाशयात् ॥8॥
श्रोत्रं चक्षुः स्पर्शनं च रसनं घ्राणमेव च।
अधिष्ठाय मनश्चायं विषयानुपसेवते ॥9॥
उत्क्रामन्तं स्थितं वापि भुञ्जानं वा गुणान्वितम्।
विमूढा नानुपश्यन्ति पश्यन्ति ज्ञानचक्षुषः ॥10॥
यतन्तो योगिनश्चैनं पश्यन्त्यात्मन्यवस्थितम्।
यतन्तोऽप्यकृतात्मानो नैनं पश्यन्त्यचेतसः ॥11॥
यदादित्यगतं तेजो जगद्भासयतेऽखिलम्।
यच्चन्द्रमसि यच्चाग्नौ तत्तेजो विद्धि मामकम् ॥12॥
गामाविश्य च भूतानि धारयाम्यहमोजसा।
पुष्णामि चौषधीः सर्वाः सोमो भूत्वा रसात्मकः ॥13॥
अहं वैश्वानरो भूत्वा प्राणिनां देहमाश्रितः।
प्राणापानसमायुक्तः पचाम्यन्नं चतुर्विधम् ॥14॥

सर्वस्य चाहं हृदि संनिविष्टो
मत्तः स्मृतिर्ज्ञानमपोहनं च।
वेदैश्च सर्वैरहमेव वेद्यो
वेदान्तकृद्वेदविदेव चाहम् ॥15॥

द्वाविमौ पुरुषौ लोके क्षरश्चाक्षर एव च।
क्षरः सर्वाणि भूतानि कूटस्थोऽक्षर उच्यते ॥16॥
उत्तमः पुरुषस्त्वन्यः परमात्मेत्युदाहृतः।
यो लोकत्रयमाविश्य बिभर्त्यव्यय ईश्वरः ॥17॥
यस्मात्क्षरमतीतोऽहमक्षरादपि चोत्तमः।
अतोऽस्मि लोके वेदे च प्रथितः पुरुषोत्तमः ॥18॥
यो मामेवमसंमूढो जानाति पुरुषोत्तमम्।
स सर्वविद्भजति मां सर्वभावेन भारत ॥19॥
इति गुह्यतमं शास्त्रमिदमुक्तं मयानघ।
एतद्बुद्ध्वा बुद्धिमान्स्यात्कृतकृत्यश्च भारत ॥20॥

ॐ तत्सदिति श्रीमद्भगवद्गीतासूपनिषत्सु ब्रह्मविद्यायां
योगशास्त्रे श्रीकृष्णार्जुनसंवादे पुरुषोत्तमयोगो
नाम पञ्चदशोऽध्यायः ॥15॥

अथ षोडशोऽध्यायः

श्रीभगवानुवाच

अभयं सत्त्वसंशुद्धिर्ज्ञानयोगव्यवस्थितिः।
दानं दमश्च यज्ञश्च स्वाध्यायस्तप आर्जवम् ॥1॥
अहिंसा सत्यमक्रोधस्त्यागः शान्तिरपैशुनम्।
दया भूतेष्वलोलुप्त्वं मार्दवं ह्रीरचापलम् ॥2॥
तेजः क्षमा धृतिः शौचमद्रोहो नातिमानिता।
भवन्ति संपदं दैवीमभिजातस्य भारत ॥3॥
दम्भो दर्पोऽभिमानश्च क्रोधः पारुष्यमेब च।
अज्ञानं चाभिजातस्य पार्थ संपदमासुरीम् ॥4॥
दैवी संपद्विमोक्षाय निबन्धायासुरी मता।
मा शुचः संपदं दैवीमभिजातोऽसि पाण्डव ॥5॥
द्वौ भूतसर्गौ लोकेऽस्मिन्दैव आसुर एव च।
दैवो विस्तरशः प्रोक्त आसुरं पार्थ मे शृणु ॥6॥
प्रवृत्तिं च निवृत्तिं च जना न विदुरासुराः।
न शौचं नापि चाचारो न सत्यं तेषु विद्यते ॥7॥
असत्यमप्रतिष्ठं ते जगदाहुरनीश्वरम्।
अपरस्परसंभूतं किमन्यत्कामहैतुकम् ॥8॥
एतां दृष्टिमवष्टभ्य नष्टात्मानोऽल्पबुद्धयः।
प्रभवन्त्युग्रकर्माणः क्षयाय जगतोऽहिताः ॥9॥
काममाश्रित्य दुष्पूरं दम्भमानमदान्विताः।
मोहाद्गृहीत्वासद्ग्राहान्प्रवर्तन्तेऽशुचिव्रताः ॥10॥
चिन्तामपरिमेयां च प्रलयान्तामुपाश्रिताः।
कामोपभोगपरमा एतावदिति निश्चिताः ॥11॥
आशापाशशतैर्बद्धाः कामक्रोधपरायणाः।
ईहन्ते कामभोगार्थमन्यायेनार्थसञ्चयान् ॥12॥
इदमद्य मया लब्धमिमं प्राप्स्ये मनोरथम्।
इदमस्तीदमपि मे भविष्यति पुनर्धनम् ॥13॥

असौ मया हतः शत्रुर्हनिष्ये चापरानपि।
ईश्वरोऽहमहं भोगी सिद्धोऽहं बलवान्सुखी ॥14॥
आढ्योभिजनवानस्मि कोऽन्योऽस्ति सदृशो मया
यक्ष्ये दास्यामि मोदिष्य इत्यज्ञानविमोहिताः ॥15॥
अनेकचित्तविभ्रान्ता मोहजालसमावृताः।
प्रसक्ताः कामभोगेषु पतन्ति नरकेऽशुचौ ॥16॥
आत्मसंभाविताः स्तब्धा धनमानमदान्विताः।
यजन्ते नामयज्ञैस्ते दम्भेनाविधिपूर्वकम् ॥17॥
अहंकारं बलं दर्पं कामं क्रोधं च संश्रिताः।
मामात्मपरदेहेषु प्रद्विषन्तोऽभ्यसूयकाः ॥18॥
तानहं द्विषतः क्रूरान्संसारेषु नराधमान्।
क्षिपाम्यजस्रमशुभानासुरीष्वेव योनिषु ॥19॥
आसुरीं योनिमापन्ना मूढा जन्मनि जन्मनि।
मामप्राप्यैव कौन्तेय ततो यान्त्यधमां गतिम् ॥20॥
त्रिविधं नरकस्येदं द्वारं नाशनमात्मनः।
कामः क्रोधस्तथा लोभस्तस्मादेतत्त्रयं त्यजेत् ॥21॥
एतैर्विमुक्तः कौन्तेय तमोद्वारैस्त्रिभिर्नरः।
आचरत्यात्मनः श्रेयस्ततो याति परां गतिम् ॥22॥
यः शास्त्रविधिमुत्सृज्य वर्तते कामकारतः।
न स सिद्धिमवाप्नोति न सुखं न परां गतिम् ॥23॥
तस्माच्छास्त्रं प्रमाणं ते कार्याकार्यव्यवस्थितौ.।
ज्ञात्वा शास्त्रविधानोक्तं कर्म कर्तुमिहार्हसि ॥24॥

ॐ तत्सदिति श्रीमद्भगवद्गीतासूपनिषत्सु ब्रह्मविद्यायां
योगशास्त्रे श्रीकृष्णार्जुनसंवादे दैवासुर-
संपद्विभागयोगो नाम षोडशोऽध्यायः ॥16॥

अथ सप्तदशोऽध्यायः

अर्जुन उवाच

ये शास्त्रविधिमुत्सृज्य यजन्ते श्रद्धयान्विताः ।
तेषां निष्ठा तु का कृष्ण सत्त्वमाहो रजस्तमः ॥1॥

श्रीभगवानुवाच

त्रिविधा भवति श्रद्धा देहिनां सा स्वभावजा ।
सात्त्विकी राजसी चैव तामसी चेति तां शृणु ॥2॥
सत्त्वानुरूपा सर्वस्य श्रद्धा भवति भारत ।
श्रद्धामयोऽयं पुरुषो यो यच्छ्रद्धः स एव सः ॥3॥
यजन्ते सात्त्विका देवान्यक्षरक्षांसि राजसाः ।
प्रेतान्भूतगणांश्चान्ये यजन्ते तामसा जनाः ॥4॥
अशास्त्रविहितं घोरं तप्यन्ते ये तपो जनाः ।
दम्भाहंकारसंयुक्ताः कामरागबलान्विताः ॥5॥
कर्षयन्तः शरीरस्थं भूतग्राममचेतसः ।
मां चैवान्तः शरीरस्थं तान्विद्ध्यासुरनिश्चयान् ॥6॥
आहारस्त्वपि सर्वस्य त्रिविधो भवति प्रियः ।
यज्ञस्तपस्तथा दानं तेषां भेदमिमं शृणु ॥7॥

आयुः सत्त्वबलारोग्य-
सुखप्रीतिविवर्धनाः ।
रस्याः स्निग्धाः स्थिरा हृद्या
आहाराः सात्त्विकप्रियाः ॥8॥

कट्वम्ललवणात्युष्णतीक्ष्णरूक्षविदाहिनः ।
आहारा राजसस्येष्टा दुःखशोकामयप्रदाः ॥9॥
यातयामं गतरसं पूति पर्युषितं च यत् ।
उच्छिष्टमपि चामेध्यं भोजनं तामसप्रियम् ॥10॥
अफलाकाङ्क्षिभिर्यज्ञो विधिदृष्टो य इज्यते ।
यष्टव्यमेवेति मनः समाधाय स सात्त्विकः ॥11॥
अभिसंधाय तु फलं दम्भार्थमपि चैव यत् ।
इज्यते भरतश्रेष्ठ तं यज्ञं विद्धि राजसम् ॥12॥
विधिहीनमसृष्टान्नं मन्त्रहीनमदक्षिणम् ।
श्रद्धाविरहितं यज्ञं तामसं परिचक्षते ॥13॥

देवद्विजगुरुप्राज्ञपूजनं शौचमार्जवम् ।
ब्रह्मचर्यमहिंसा च शारीरं तप उच्यते ॥14॥
अनुद्वेगकरं वाक्यं सत्यं प्रियहितं च यत् ।
स्वाध्यायाभ्यसनं चैव वाङ्मयं तप उच्यते ॥15॥
मनःप्रसादः सौम्यत्वं मौनमात्मविनिग्रहः ।
भावसंशुद्धिरित्येतत्तपो मानसमुच्यते ॥16॥
श्रद्धया परया तप्तं तपस्तत्त्रिविधं नरैः ।
अफलाकाङ्क्षिभिर्युक्तैः सात्त्विकं परिचक्षते ॥17॥
सत्कारमानपूजार्थं तपो दम्भेन चैव यत् ।
क्रियते तदिह प्रोक्तं राजसं चलमध्रुवम् ॥18॥
मूढग्राहेणात्मनो यत्पीडया क्रियते तपः ।
परस्योत्सादनार्थं वा तत्तामसमुदाहृतम् ॥19॥
दातव्यमिति यद्दानं दीयतेऽनुपकारिणे ।
देशे काले च पात्रे च तद्दानं सात्त्विकं स्मृतम् ॥20॥
यत्तु प्रत्युपकारार्थं फलमुद्दिश्य वा पुनः ।
दीयते च परिक्लिष्टं तद्दानं राजसं स्मृतम् ॥21॥
अदेशकाले यद्दानमपात्रेभ्यश्च दीयते ।
असत्कृतमवज्ञातं तत्तामसमुदाहृतम् ॥22॥
ॐ तत्सदिति निर्देशो ब्रह्मणस्त्रिविध स्मृतः ।
ब्राह्मणास्तेन वेदाश्च यज्ञाश्च विहिताः पुरा ॥23॥
तस्मादोमित्युदाहृत्य यज्ञदानतपःक्रियाः ।
प्रवर्तन्ते विधानोक्ताः सततं ब्रह्मवादिनाम् ॥24॥
तदित्यनभिसंधाय फलं यज्ञतपःक्रियाः ।
दानक्रियाश्च विविधाः क्रियन्ते मोक्षकाङ्क्षिभिः ॥25॥
सद्भावे साधुभावे च सदित्येतत्प्रयुज्यते ।
प्रशस्ते कर्मणि तथा सच्छब्दः पार्थ युज्यते ॥26॥
यज्ञे तपसि दाने च स्थितिः सदिति चोच्यते ।
कर्म चैव तदर्थीयं सदित्येवाभिधीयते ॥27॥
अश्रद्धया हुतं दत्तं तपस्तप्तं कृतं च यत् ।
असदित्युच्यते पार्थ न च तत्प्रेत्य नो इह ॥28॥

ॐ तत्सदिति श्रीमद्भगवद्गीतासूपनिषत्सु ब्रह्मविद्यायां योगशास्त्रे श्रीकृष्णार्जुनसंवादे श्रद्धात्रयविभागयोगो नाम सप्तदशोऽध्यायः ॥17॥

अथाष्टादशोऽध्यायः

अर्जुन उवाच

संन्यासस्य महाबाहो तत्त्वमिच्छामि वेदितुम् ।
त्यागस्य च हृषीकेश पृथक्केशिनिषूदन ॥1॥

श्रीभगवानुवाच

काम्यानां कर्मणां न्यासं संन्यासं कवयो विदुः ।
सर्वकर्मफलत्यांग प्राहुस्त्यागं विचक्षणाः ॥2॥
त्याज्यं दोषवदित्येके कर्म प्राहुर्मनीषिणः ।
यज्ञदानतपः कर्म न त्याज्यमिति चापरे ॥3॥
निश्चयं शृणु मे तत्र त्यागे भरतसत्तम ।
त्यागो हि पुरुषव्याघ्र त्रिविधः संप्रकीर्तितः ॥4॥
यज्ञदानतपःकर्म न त्याज्यं कार्यमेव तत् ।
यज्ञो दानं तपश्चैव पावनानि मनीषिणाम् ॥5॥
एतान्यपि तु कर्माणि सङ्गं त्यक्त्वा फलानि च ।
कर्तव्यानीति मे पार्थ निश्चितं मतमुत्तमम् ॥6॥
नियतस्य तु संन्यासः: कर्मणो नोपपद्यते ।
मोहात्तस्य परित्यागस्तामसः परिकीर्तितः ॥7॥
दुःखमित्येव यत्कर्म कायक्लेशभयात्त्यजेत् ।
स कृत्वा राजसं त्यागं नैव त्यागफलं लभेत् ॥8॥
कार्यमित्येव यत्कर्म नियतं क्रियतेऽर्जुन ।
सङ्गं त्यक्त्वा फलं चैव स त्यागः सात्त्विको मतः ॥9॥
न द्वेष्ट्यकुशलं कर्म कुशले नानुषज्जते ।
त्यागी सत्त्वसमाविष्टो मेधावी छिन्नसंशयः ॥10॥
न हि देहभृता शक्यं त्यक्तुं कर्माण्यशेषतः ।
यस्तु कर्मफलत्यागी स त्यागीत्यभिधीयते ॥11॥
अनिष्टमिष्टं मिश्रं च त्रिविधं कर्मणः फलम् ।
भवत्यत्यागिनां प्रेत्य न तु संन्यासिनां क्वचित् ॥12॥

पञ्चैतानि महाबाहो कारणानि निबोध मे।
सांख्ये कृतान्ते प्रोक्तानि सिद्धये सर्वकर्मणाम् ॥13॥
अधिष्ठानं तथा कर्ता करणं च पृथग्विधम्।
विविधाश्च पृथक्चेष्टा दैवं चैवात्र पञ्चमम् ॥14॥
शरीवाङ्मनोभिर्यत्कर्म प्रारभते नरः।
न्याय्यं वा विपरीतं वा पञ्चैते तस्य हेतवः ॥15॥
तत्रैवं सति कर्तारमात्मानं केवलं तु यः।
पश्यत्यकृतबुद्धित्वान्न स पश्यति दुर्मतिः ॥16॥
यस्य नाहंकृतो भावो बुद्धिर्यस्य न लिप्यते।
हत्वापि स इमाँल्लोकान्न हन्ति न निबध्यते ॥17॥
ज्ञानं ज्ञेयं परिज्ञाता त्रिविधा कर्मचोदना।
करणं कर्म कर्तेति त्रिविधः कर्मसंग्रहः ॥18॥
ज्ञानं कर्म च कर्ता च त्रिधैव गुणभेदतः।
प्रोच्यते गुणसंख्याने यथावच्छृणु तान्यपि ॥19॥
सर्वभूतेषु येनैकं भावमव्ययमीक्षते।
अविभक्तं विभक्तेषु तज्ज्ञानं विद्धि सात्त्विकम् ॥20॥
पृथक्त्वेन तु यज्ज्ञानं नानाभावान्पृथग्विधान्।
वेत्ति सर्वेषु भूतेषु तज्ज्ञानं विद्धि राजसम् ॥21॥
यत्तु कृत्स्नवदेकस्मिन्कार्ये सक्तमहैतुकम्।
अतत्त्वार्थवदल्पं च तत्तामसमुदाहृतम् ॥22॥
नियतं सङ्गरहितमरागद्वेषतः कृतम्।
अफलप्रेप्सुना कर्म यत्तत्सात्त्विकमुच्यते ॥23॥
यत्तु कामेप्सुना कर्म साहंकारेण वा पुनः।
क्रियते बहुलायासं तद्राजसमुदाहृतम् ॥24॥
अनुबन्धं क्षयं हिंसामनवेक्ष्य च पौरुषम्।
मोहादारभ्यते कर्म यत्तत्तामसमुच्यते ॥25॥
मुक्तसङ्गोऽनहंवादी धृत्युत्साहसमन्वितः।
सिद्ध्यसिद्ध्योर्निर्विकारः कर्ता सात्त्विक उच्यते ॥26॥
रागी कर्मफलप्रेप्सुर्लुब्धो हिंसात्मकोऽशुचिः।
हर्षशोकान्वितः कर्ता राजसः परिकीर्तितः ॥27॥

अयुक्तः प्राकृतः स्तब्धः शठो नैष्कृतिकोऽलसः।
विषादी दीर्घसूत्री च कर्ता तामस उच्यते ॥28॥
बुद्धेर्भेदं धृतेश्चैव गुणतस्त्रिविधं शृणु।
प्रोच्यमानमशेषेण पृथक्त्वेन धनंजय ॥29॥
प्रवृत्तिं च निवृत्तिं च कार्याकार्ये भयाभये।
बन्ध मोक्षं च या वेत्ति बुद्धिः सा पार्थ सात्त्विकी ॥30॥
यया धर्ममधर्मं च कार्यं चाकार्यमेव च।
अयथावत्प्रजानाति बुद्धिः सा पार्थ राजसी ॥31॥
अधर्मं धर्ममिति या मन्यते तमसावृता।
सर्वार्थान्विपरीतांश्च बुद्धिः सा पार्थ तामसी ॥32॥
धृत्या यया धारयते मनःप्राणेन्द्रियक्रियाः।
योगेनाव्यभिचारिण्या धृतिः सा पार्थ सात्त्विकी ॥33॥
यया तु धर्मकामार्थान्धृत्या धारयतेऽर्जुन।
प्रसङ्गेन फलाकाङ्क्षी धृतिः सा पार्थ राजसी ॥34॥
यया स्वप्नं भयं शोकं विषादं मदमेव च।
न विमुञ्चति दुर्मेधा धृतिः सा पार्थ तामसी ॥35॥
सुखं त्विदानीं त्रिविधं शृणु मे भरतर्षभ।
अभ्यासाद्रमते यत्र दुःखान्तं च निगच्छति ॥36॥
यत्तदग्रे विषमिव परिणामेऽमृतोपमम्।
तत्सुखं सात्त्विकं प्रोक्तमात्मबुद्धिप्रसादजम् ॥37॥
विषयेन्द्रियसंयोगाद्यत्तदग्रेऽमृतोपमम्।
परिणामे विषमिव तत्सुखं राजसं स्मृतम् ॥38॥
यदग्रे चानुबन्धे च सुखं मोहनमात्मनः।
निद्रालस्यप्रमादोत्थं तत्तामसमुदाहृतम् ॥39॥
न तदस्ति पृथिव्यां वा दिवि देवेषु वा पुनः।
सत्त्वं प्रकृतिजैर्मुक्तं यदेभिः स्यात्त्रिभिर्गुणैः ॥40॥
ब्राह्मणक्षत्रियविशां शूद्राणां च परंतप।
कर्माणि प्रविभक्तानि स्वभावप्रभवैर्गुणैः ॥41॥
शमो दमस्तपः शौचं क्षान्तिरार्जवमेव च।
ज्ञानं विज्ञानमास्तिक्यं ब्रह्मकर्म स्वभावजम् ॥42॥

शौर्यं तेजो धृतिर्दाक्ष्यं युद्धे चाप्यपलायनम्।
दानमीश्वरभावश्च क्षात्रं कर्म स्वभावजम् ॥43॥
कृषिगौरक्ष्यवाणिज्यं वैश्यकर्म स्वभावजम्।
परिचर्यात्मकं कर्म शूद्रस्यापि स्वभावजम् ॥44॥
स्वे स्वे कर्मण्यभिरतः संसिद्धिं लभते नरः।
स्वकर्मनिरतः सिद्धिं यथा विन्दति तच्छृणु ॥45॥
यतः प्रवृत्तिर्भूतानां येन सर्वमिदं ततम्।
स्वकर्मणा तमभ्यर्च्य सिद्धिं विन्दति मानवः ॥46॥
श्रेयान्स्वधर्मो विगुणः परधर्मात्स्वनुष्ठितात्।
स्वभावविनयं कर्म कुर्वन्नाप्नोति किल्बिषम् ॥47॥
सहजं कर्म कौन्तेय सदोषमपिं न त्यज्येत्।
सर्वारम्भा हि दोषेण धूमेनाग्निरिवावृताः ॥48॥
असक्तबुद्धिः सर्वत्र जितात्मा विगतस्पृहः।
नैष्कर्म्यसिद्धिं परमां संन्यासेनाधिगच्छति ॥49॥
सिद्धिं प्राप्तो यथा ब्रह्म तथाप्नोति निबोध मे।
समासेनैव कौन्तेय निष्ठा ज्ञानस्य या परा ॥50॥
बुद्ध्या विशुद्धया युक्तो धृत्यात्मानं नियम्य च।
शब्दादीनिवषयांस्त्यक्त्वा रागद्वेषौ व्युदस्य च ॥51॥
विविक्तसेवी लघ्वाशी यतवाक्कायमानसः।
ध्यानयोगपरो नित्यं वैराग्यं समुपाश्रितः ॥52॥
अहंकारं बलं दर्पं कामं क्रोधं परिग्रहम्।
विमुच्य निर्ममः शान्तो ब्रह्मभूयाय कल्पते ॥53॥
ब्रह्मभूतः प्रसन्नात्मा न शोचति न काङ्क्षति।
समः सर्वेषु भूतेषु मद्भक्तिं लभते पराम् ॥54॥
भक्त्या मामभिजानाति यावान्यश्चास्मि तत्त्वतः।
ततो मां तत्त्वतो ज्ञात्वा विशते तदनन्तरम् ॥55॥
सर्वकर्माण्यपि सदा कुर्वाणो मद्व्यपाश्रयः।
मत्प्रसादादवाप्नोति शाश्वतं पदमव्ययम् ॥56॥
चेतसा सर्वकर्माणि मयि संन्यस्य मत्परः।
बुद्धियोगमुपाश्रित्य मच्चित्तः सततं भव ॥57॥

मच्चित्तः सर्वदुर्गाणि मत्प्रसादात्तरिष्यसि।
अथ चेत्त्वमहंकारान्न श्रोष्यसि विनङ्क्ष्यसि ॥58॥
यदहंकारमाश्रित्य न योत्स्य इति मन्यसे।
मिथ्यैष व्यवसायस्ते प्रकृतिस्त्वां नियोक्ष्यति ॥59॥
स्वभावजेन कौन्तेय निबद्धः स्वेन कर्मणा।
कर्तुं नेच्छसि यन्मोहात्करिष्यस्यवशोऽपि तत् ॥60॥
ईश्वरः सर्वभूतानां हृद्देशेऽर्जुन तिष्ठति।
भ्रामयन्सर्वभूतानि यन्त्रारूढानि मायया ॥61॥
तमेव शरणं गच्छ सर्वभावेन भारत।
तत्प्रसादात्परां शान्तिं स्थानं प्राप्स्यसि शाश्वतम् ॥62॥
इति ते ज्ञानमाख्यातं गुह्याद्गुह्यतरं मया।
विमृश्यैतदशेषेण यथेच्छसि तथा कुरु ॥63॥
सर्वगुह्यतमं भूयः शृणु मे परमं वचः।
इष्टोऽसि मे दृढमिति ततो वक्ष्यामि ते हितम् ॥64॥
मन्मना भव मद्भक्तो मद्याजी मां नमस्कुरु।
मामेवैष्यसि सत्यं ते प्रतिजाने प्रियोऽसि मे ॥65॥
सर्वधर्मान्परित्यज्य मामेकं शरणं व्रज।
अहंत्वा सर्वपापेभ्यो मोक्षयिष्यामि मा शुचः ॥66॥
इदं ते नातपस्काय नाभक्ताय कदाचन।
न चाशुश्रूषवे वाच्यं न च मां योऽभ्यसूयति ॥67॥
य इमं परमं गुह्यं मद्भक्तेष्वभिधास्यति।
भक्तिं मयि परां कृत्वा मामेवैष्यत्यसंशयः ॥68॥
न च तस्मान्मनुष्येषु कश्चिन्मे प्रियकृत्तमः।
भविता न च मे तस्मादन्यः प्रियतरो भुवि ॥69॥
अध्येष्यते च य इमं धर्म्यं संवादमावयोः।
ज्ञानयज्ञेन तेनाहमिष्टः स्यामिति मे मतिः ॥70॥
श्रद्धावाननसूयश्च शृणुयादपि यो नरः।
सोऽपि मुक्तः शुभाँल्लोकान्प्राप्नुयात्पुण्यकर्मणाम् ॥71॥
कच्चिदेतच्छ्रुतं पार्थ त्वयैकाग्रेण चेतसा।
कच्चिदज्ञानसंमोहः प्रनश्टस्ते धनंजय ॥77॥

अर्जुन उवाच

नष्टो मोहः स्मृतिर्लब्धा त्वत्प्रसादान्मयाच्युत ।
स्थितोऽस्मि गतसन्देहः करिष्ये वचनं तव ॥73॥

संजय उवाच

इत्यहं वासुदेवस्य पार्थस्य च महात्मनः ।
संवादमिममश्रौषमद्भुतं रोमहर्षणम् ॥74॥
व्यासप्रसादाच्छ्रुतवानेतद्गुह्यमहं परम् ।
योगं योगेश्वरात्कृष्णात्साक्षात्कथयतः स्वयम् ॥75॥
राजन्संस्मृत्य संस्मृत्य संवादमिममद्भुतम् ।
केशवार्जुनयोः पुण्यं हृष्यामि च मुहुर्मुहुः ॥76॥
तच्च संस्मृत्य संस्मृत्य रूपमत्यद्भुतं हरेः ।
विस्मयो मे महान्राजन्हृष्यामि च पुनः पुनः ॥77॥
यत्र योगेश्वरः कृष्णो यत्र पार्थो धनुर्धरः ।
तत्र श्रीर्विजयो भूतिर्ध्रुवा नीतिर्मतिर्मम ॥78॥

ॐ तत्सदिति श्रीमद्भगवद्गीतासूपनिषत्सु ब्रह्मविद्यायां
योगशास्त्रे श्रीकृष्णार्जुनसंवादे मोक्षसंन्यासयोगो
नामाष्टादशोऽध्यायः ॥10॥